A COINCIDENCE *of* DESIRES

A COINCIDENCE *of* DESIRES

ANTHROPOLOGY, QUEER STUDIES, INDONESIA

TOM BOELLSTORFF

Duke University Press

DURHAM AND LONDON

2007

© 2007

Duke University Press

All rights reserved

Printed in the United States

of America on acid-free paper ∞

Designed by Katy Clove

Typeset in Sabon

by Keystone Typesetting, Inc.

Library of Congress Cataloging-in-

Publication Data appear on the last

printed page of this book.

for Bill and Dédé, again

each a happy coincidence

CONTENTS

ACKNOWLEDGMENTS

While I cannot thank my Indonesian interlocutors by name due to reasons of confidentiality, I am forever indebted to those who over many years have shared and continue to share the most intimate moments of their lives with me. It is the knowledge that I work to interpret their rich and complex lives, not to provide the definitive truth, that allows me to write at all. I dedicate this book to Bill Maurer, my partner, for all his support and good cheer. I also dedicate it to Dédé Oetomo, who has guided me throughout my work in Indonesia with stunning patience and generosity. This book would not exist without them. I also dedicate this book to the memory of Fran Napier, my aunt, and Ruth Boellstorff, my grandmother, who died within a few weeks of each other in 2005. They were both inspirations to me for their immense wisdom, for all they gave to those around them, and for their ability to enjoy life's moments. My mother, Neva Cozine, has been my anchor of love and comfort in the world. The rest of my family — particularly, my sister, Darcy Boellstorff, my father, John Boellstorff, my stepfather, Daryl Hansen, and my "in-laws," Lisa Maurer, Maureen Kelly, William Maurer, and Cynthia Maurer, have always been there for me and I can never repay all I owe them. My neighbors and friends in Long Beach have provided me with an unmatched sense of home: I thank in particular Michelle Arend-Ekhoff, Christie Chu, Gemma Davison, Tom Douglas, Thamora Fishel, David Hernandez, and Dominic Lakey. Brian Ulaszewski and Gina Wallar have been sources of comfort beyond measure.

Ken Wissoker at Duke University Press showed humbling enthusiasm for this project from the beginning. This book could not have happened without his support, as well as the support of Justin Faerber, Anitra Grisales, and my indexer J. Naomi Linzer.

My colleagues at the University of California, Irvine, have supported me throughout this project; through reading groups and informal discussions they shaped my thinking in key ways. I thank Victoria Bernal, Mike Burton, Teresa Caldeira, Leo Chavez, Susan Coutin, Lara Deeb, Inderpal Grewal, Susan Greenhalgh, Karen Leonard, George Marcus, Michael Montoya, Kavita Philip, Justin Richland, Kaushik Sunder Rajan, Roxanne Varzi, and Mei Zhan.

This book would not have been possible without the stimulation provided by my participation in the Queer Locations group at the University of California Humanities Research Institute from January to June 2004. Alicia Arrizon, Roderick A. Ferguson, Judith Halberstam, Glen Mimura, Chandan Reddy, Jennifer Terry, Karen Tongson, and David Theo Goldberg provided me with an intellectual environment that modeled the promise of true interdisciplinarity.

I thank Elizabeth Freeman, Megan Sinnott, and Robyn Wiegman, who read drafts of the introduction and provided me with many helpful comments and encouragement. Robyn — thank you for everything. Megan Sinnott also provided me with the opportunity to present the introduction and chapter 6 in their final stages as talks at Yale University, and I benefited enormously from those discussions.

Other colleagues whose wise words have inspired me include Anne Allison, Dennis Altman, Ann Anagnost, Leena Avonius, Geremie Barmé, Evelyn Blackwood, Karen Brodkin, Mary Bucholtz, Pheng Cheah, Lawrence Cohen, Katherine Coll, Jane Collier, George Collier, Jean Comaroff, Robert Corber, Tony Crook, Carol Delaney, Paula Ebron, Deborah Elliston, Joseph Errington, Shelly Errington, Judith Farquhar, James Ferguson, Ferdi Thajib, Katherine Gibson, Byron Good, Sharyn Graham, Akhil Gupta, Karl Heider, Stefan Helmreich, Gilbert Herdt, Irwan M. Hidayana, Terrence Hull, Nurul Ilmi Idrus, Miyako Inoue, Peter A. Jackson, Iris Jean-Klein, Margaret Jolly, Carla Jones, Elizabeth Keating, Bruce Knauft, Don Kulick, William Leap, Johan Lindquist, Martin Manalansan, Purnima Mankekar, Liisa Malkki, Hirokazu Miyazaki, David Murray, Diane Nelson, Don Nonini, William O'Barr, Aihwa Ong, James Peacock, Charles Piot, Janice Radway, Adam Reed, Annelise Riles, Kathryn Robinson, Lisa Rofel, Renato Rosaldo, Louisa Schein, James Schultz, Michael Silverstein, Patricia Spyer, Mary Steedly, Anna

Tsing, Ann Waltner, Margaret Weiner, Saskia Wieringa, Yunita T. Winarto, and Sylvia Yanagisako. I thank Dédé Oetomo and Stephen Shirreffs for helping me find many issues of the zines examined in chapter 1. I also thank the anonymous reviewers for the original versions of chapters 1 through 5, as well as two anonymous reviewers for the book as a whole.

Support for my research in Indonesia has been provided by the Social Science Research Council, the National Science Foundation, the Department of Social and Cultural Anthropology at Stanford University, the Morrison Institute for Population and Resource Studies, the Ford Foundation, the Center for Asian Studies and Academic Senate Council on Research, Computing, and Library Resources at the University of California, Irvine, and the Center for the Teaching of Malay and Indonesian.

All non-English terms used in this book are Indonesian unless otherwise noted. Following standard practice, I italicize Indonesian terms at first use only, except for the terms *gay*, *lesbi*, and *normal*, which I italicize throughout due to their similarity to English terms. I follow standard Indonesian orthography except that in using *gay* language terms I write the front unrounded vowel /é/ (spelled "e" in Indonesian, along with the schwa) as "é" for clarity. In Indonesian plurals are usually marked by reduplication (*buku* "book," *buku-buku* "books") or not at all if clear from context (*dua buku* "two books"). For clarity, I use English plural markers on Indonesian terms—for example, warias as the plural for waria. Finally, all translations are my own unless noted otherwise.

✳︎

INTRODUCTION

QUEERING DISCIPLINES IN TIME

It is night in Indonesia when he walks into the park. The park might be in Jakarta, the national capital; it might be in one of the larger cities scattered about the archipelago; or it might even be the central square (*alun-alun*) of a smaller provincial town. The man calls himself "gay." It is a word he sees as part of the Indonesian language, but a word he knows is found outside Indonesia as well. He has come to this park nearly every Thursday night for several years. At the park he finds other men who call themselves "gay," one of whom he terms his partner (*pacar*). He will spend much of the evening chatting with his friends: talking about an attractive man he saw yesterday; or perhaps mentioning the fact that his parents have told him it's time he marry a woman, and he wonders if such a marriage might not make sense. And between every phrase of the conversation — from the most innocuous gossip to the most heartfelt confession — lines of connection link this man to his friends, to other Indonesians, and to "global" forces as real in the muted laughter of the park as in the corridors of a transnational corporation.

Thousands of nights like this have been lost to history: remembered, if at all, only in memories called forth in the stillness of a sleepless night. Within Indonesia itself, a growing corpus of magazines, books, and films address nights like this, though their number is still small. But nights like this have also drawn the interest of scholars within Indonesia and beyond. Their number is also small, but a further limitation involves the question of discipline. Who should study nights like this, undertake the labor of language learning, theoretical training, and travel — all issues even for "local" scholars, though in differing ways? Who should listen to these stories, listen to the words and the silences too, and draw from them the sometimes explicit, sometimes implicit, linkages, patterns, and discourses that give them meaning and social consequence?

In the Western academy, nights like this occupy the interstices of disciplinary authority and interest. Anthropologists have paid relatively little attention to any form of homosexuality or transgenderism in Indonesia, despite the large and insightful body of anthropological scholarship about the archipelago. Queer studies scholars have produced relatively little scholarship outside the contexts of Europe, North America, and Australia, particularly with regard to regions of the globe that do not have substantial immigrant representation in the United States or Europe. How, then, are we to learn about nights like this, so as to debate their significance and their place in a politics of justice?

In this book I argue for an answer to this question in terms of new forms of collaboration between anthropology and queer studies. I begin by setting forth the following hypotheses: anthropology has always been a bit queer, and queer studies has always betrayed an anthropological sensibility. Through their intertwined histories, patterns of interchange with a range of disciplines, and shared analytical agendas, anthropology and queer studies could be said to stand in a relationship of coincidence to each other.

Coincidence raises questions of time. In current academic frameworks, anthropology and queer studies appear out of temporal joint. Betraying its nineteenth-century origins in the "-ology" suffix it shares with disciplines like psychology and sociology, rather than being named "studies" as is the newer fashion for "interdisciplinary identity sites" like Asian studies, women's studies, and international studies (Wiegman 2002:149), it might seem that anthropology can provide little more than a history for queer studies.[1] Yet anthropology is far better recognized than queer studies, a field (unstable and contested like all fields, but a field of inquiry all the same) for which in most venues there is little in the way of independent departments, graduate or even undergraduate programs, professional organizations, flagship journals, and dedicated sources of funding.

However, anthropology has something more timely to contribute than the two answers typically given in rejoinder to the question of what anthropology can offer queer studies. The first of these insufficient answers invokes empiricism. This is the view that anthropology gives queer studies a handle on "the real world." The second answer invokes geography. This is the view that anthropology directs attention to places and peoples outside the usual Euro-American purview of queer studies.

There is some validity to each of these flawed responses (or rather caricatures of responses, since I am careful not to attribute them to actual persons and oversimplify each for rhetorical effect). It is true that anthropology has contributed methodological conversations to queer studies, so that queer studies scholars can note with approval how anthropologists make their own archives (e.g., Halberstam 2000:xiii). It is also true that many queer studies scholars engage in ethnographic research (Halberstam 1998:10). Additionally, anthropology has played a crucial role in the geography of knowledge. Whatever legitimate concerns continue to be raised about power relationships between anthropologists (indeed, all scholars) and those they study, it remains the case that there are wide swaths of the world, including rural and nonliterate societies, as well as societies without significant immigrant communities in the United States, that would receive no attention from the academy in the United States if not for the work of anthropologists.

In this book I argue for anthropological futures of queer studies beyond these two responses. Anthropology's greatest potential contribution to queer studies is not to ethnographize it or transnationalize it, but to anthropologize it. The distinctive contribution of anthropology to queer studies lies not in its traditional focus on non-Western contexts or lived experience. Instead, it lies in the attention that anthropology, "a positive and definite study of the human knowledge of the human" (Wagner 2001:xvii), brings to the foundationally *social* character of human being.[2]

The synergistic potential runs both ways: anthropology can certainly benefit from a closer interchange with queer studies. Contemporary anthropology, for all its attention to complex issues of modernity, neoliberalism, and indexicality, as well as the specificities of class, gender, race, and location, has contributed remarkably little to the canons of queer studies, an absence made possible by the elision of queerness from the history of anthropology itself. A concern with sexuality and kinship runs right through the canonical core of the discipline (Lyons and Lyons 2004). Many of the social thinkers of the late nineteenth century and early twentieth, like Herbert Spencer and Émile Durkheim — thinkers whose works shaped the emergence of anthropology — saw gender as the first social differentiation. They thereby set into place a heteronormative theory of human relations as the foundation of sociality (Durkheim

1984 [1893]:17–18; Spencer 1864:12). Durkheim and Marcel Mauss, in their 1903 classic *Primitive Classification* (1963:23–24), saw heteronormative kinship as the origin point of logic and thus of cognition itself.

Critical perspectives on such narratives extend back at least to Henry Louis Morgan (1818–1881), whose *Systems of Consanguinity and Affinity of the Human Family* (1870) questioned the view that the nuclear heterosexual family was the norm throughout human history. Morgan's evolutionism led him to rank forms of heterosexuality, with "primitive promiscuity" leading to forms of group marriage, culminating in monogamy between an unrelated man and woman. Although he was in the last instance heteronormative, Morgan and other Victorian-era social thinkers denaturalized heterosexuality by raising the possibility that it is a historical product (Collier, Rosaldo, and Yanagisako 1997). Morgan's evolutionism endeared him to Frederick Engels, whose book *The Origin of the Family, Private Property, and the State* was subtitled *In the Light of the Researches of Lewis H. Morgan* (Engels 1884). To briefly mention only one of many other possible examples, in *Sex and Repression in Savage Society* (1927) Bronislaw Malinowski (1884–1942), a central figure in British anthropology, drew upon his fieldwork in the Trobriand Islands (near Papua New Guinea) to question the Freudian framework that had become influential by the third decade of the twentieth century: "If family life is so fateful for human mentality, its character deserves more attention. For the fact is that the family is not the same in all human societies" (1927:3).[3]

Anthropologists throughout the twentieth century worked to further denaturalize gender and kinship: a truncated list of those so involved would surely include Ruth Benedict, E. E. Evans-Pritchard, Margaret Mead, Claude Meillassoux, Michelle Rosaldo, David Schneider, and Sylvia Yanagisako. Prior to the mid-1970s, however, topics like homosexuality were rarely the focus of anthropological work (see Davis and Whitten 1987; Weston 1993). During this period only a few scattered overviews of homosexuality can be located (Ford and Beach 1951); significantly more work, focusing on the United States, took place in sociology and psychology. As Gayle Rubin notes: "It is ironic that so influential a discipline [as anthropology] has also been oddly parochial in resisting the study of sexuality . . . Many scholars who work on gay, lesbian, bisexual, or transgender issues, for example, assume that such research began in the 1990s, is derived almost entirely from French theory and is primarily located in fields such as modern languages and literature, philosophy, and film studies. Many anthropologists, in turn, are unaware of the extensive history of social science attention to sexualities and may think of gay research as something accomplished mainly in the ethereal realms of aesthetic critique" (2002:18–19).

An explicit focus on topics like homosexuality and transgenderism is quite recent within anthropology, extending back to pathbreaking works like Esther Newton's *Mother Camp* (1979) and Evelyn Blackwood's edited volume *Anthropology and Homosexual Behavior* (1986; see also Weston 1993). Since the mid-1980s, anthropological scholarship on topics like homosexuality and transgenderism has greatly increased.[4] The potential now exists for coalitional projects that permit anthropology and queer studies to draw from each other's intellectual and institutional strengths. Rather than view anthropology as a past formation superseded by queer studies, or queer studies as an already outdated formulation eclipsed by anthropology, perhaps queerness itself can temporally mediate anthropology and queer studies through coincidence. I return later to this idea of temporal mediation.

I am uninterested in (and will not name) anthropologists who dismiss work in queer studies with the claim that such work is narrow or unscientific. I am also uninterested in (and will not name) queer studies scholars who dismiss ethnographic work with the claim that such work is empiricist or tainted with colonial inequalities (as if all disciplines, not least literary critique, do not have colonial genealogies [Said 1978]). Such spurious critiques attempt to delegitimate entire approaches to knowledge, and I do not wish to expend intellectual energy on them. Rather than heed the complaints of failed literary critics or bad ethnographers, I see an epistemological and political imperative to forge interdisciplinary networks of theory and practice that draw upon the locatedness of careful, invested scholarship. I thus argue for the virtue of research, of *listening*, in a sharply anti-intellectual modernity where the pundit has displaced the intellectual as figure of reflection and debate.

COMING TO INDONESIA

If "anthropology" and "queer studies" are the primary disciplinary referents of this book, "Indonesia" is its primary substantive referent. Despite having over 220 million citizens spread out over about six thousand inhabited islands and speaking, by some counts, nearly seven hundred local languages alongside the national language of Indonesian, Indonesia is little known to most Americans beyond the association of Java with coffee and Bali with tourism. Indeed, in the United States I am sometimes asked if Bali is near Indonesia. This ignorance is not simply a lack of knowledge but rather its active production by a structure of power. My sustained attention to Indonesian lifeworlds that even in Indonesia receive little consideration is thus a call to broaden the range of voices that inform our theorizing.

The islands now called Indonesia have, for the most part, been integrated into global networks for centuries (Reid 1988; Ricklefs 1981; see figure 1). As key to the great trade networks linking far eastern Asia (including present-day China, Japan, and Korea) with India, the Middle East, Africa, and Europe, these islands have not only served as points of passage but as important destinations in their own right, most famously in the case of the "Spice Islands" (namely the Moluccas, in eastern Indonesia), which long were the world's only source of nutmeg, cloves, and other important spices. Although the Portuguese were the first colonial power to reach the archipelago (in the early sixteenth century), Holland was the dominant force in the region for over three hundred years. By the early twentieth century the "Dutch East Indies" stretched over a region greater in distance than that from California to New York, and included in Sumatra, Java, Borneo, and elsewhere lucrative plantations of tea, coffee, spices, rubber, and many other products.

By the 1920s a nationalist movement was increasing in size, and calls for independence had become an irritant to the colonial power. When the Japanese ousted the Dutch at the dawn of World War II, they were initially greeted as fellow Asians liberating Indonesia from European domination. But soon their brutal rule turned many Indonesians against them. In Jakarta a group of nationalists led by Sukarno, a young engineer trained in Holland and active in the nationalist movement, declared Indonesia's independence on August 17, 1945, but the formal transfer of sovereignty from Holland did not take place until 1949, following a protracted guerrilla war as the Dutch tried to retake their colony.

From 1945 until 1998 Indonesia knew only two presidents. Sukarno became Indonesia's first president and was known for his spirited resistance during the cold war to Western and Soviet domination; the inaugural meeting of the Non-Aligned Movement was held in Bandung

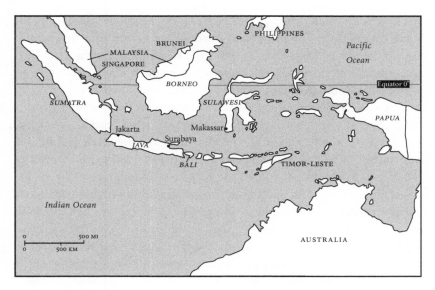

FIGURE I Indonesia.

in 1955. By the 1960s, however, Indonesia was in economic and political crisis, and Sukarno's hold on power was maintained by a precarious balance of military, Muslim, and communist groups. Following a period of enormous violence and strife, Sukarno was ousted and replaced by Suharto, a military figure who unlike Sukarno had little education or knowledge of the world beyond Indonesia's borders. Naming his rule the "New Order" in contrast to what was now termed the "Old Order" of Sukarno's presidency, Suharto stayed in power for three decades. He presided over a period of unprecedented economic growth, including the first real emergence of an Indonesian middle class, during which were created strong linkages with the United States and development bodies. Suharto's rule was also marked by the suppression of ethnic minorities, including Indonesians of Chinese descent, and the invasion of East Timor in the early 1970s (the eastern half of Timor had remained a Portuguese colony and never became part of the Dutch East Indies). It was also characterized by enormous corruption, which by the 1980s and 1990s most spectacularly included members of Suharto's family. Following Suharto's resignation in 1998 in the context of political and economic turmoil, Indonesia has seen a succession of presidents (including one of Sukarno's daughters). Although during this time there has been a notable growth in press freedom, regional autonomy, and democratic reform, there is also growth in ethnic and religious extremism, poverty, and patterns of government corruption that have made it difficult to respond to natural disasters and environmental degradation.

However, despite the frequent Western focus on Indonesia as a country in crisis, the national culture has proven remarkably stable, resilient, and vibrant, in which there is tolerance and pluralism not just hatred and conflict. The national language of Indonesian (formerly known as "Malay," a Sumatran language that became a trade language in the archipelago) is spoken by most Indonesians, millions of whom are functionally monolingual (Sneddon 2003:202–5). There are five officially recognized religions, including Christianity and Hinduism, but nearly 90 percent of Indonesians are Muslim. A wide range of Islamic schools of thought, practice, and community play a powerful role in shaping public culture. Despite the ongoing forms of everyday and state violence, tolerance across lines of difference is a strong feature of the archipelago, as a remarkably cosmopolitan populace continues to forge new visions of what it means to be Indonesian.[5]

This brief summary of Indonesian history and society is intended to provide a basic context for the arguments presented in the remainder of this book, all of which are based upon data I have personally collected concerning Indonesians terming themselves *gay*, *lesbi*, or *waria* (male-to-female transvestite) in at least some contexts of their lives. I italicize the terms *gay* and *lesbi* throughout this book to indicate that they are Indonesian-language terms that are not reducible to the English terms "gay" and "lesbian," despite the clear links between them. For consistency I also italicize the term *normal*, an Indonesian word referring to normative sexuality and gender. Fundamental to my approach is rejecting the view that "Indonesia" is merely a political pretense; I continue to be impressed by the ways in which national discourse shapes everyday life in the archipelago. It is important to distinguish nationalism from patriotism; the fact that one's selfhood is shaped by national discourse (and the national spatial scale associated with that discourse) does not predict one's affective stance toward that national discourse.

I am often asked by colleagues working in the humanities why I have devoted so much time to Indonesia; indeed, I have even been asked if I am of mixed heritage. These questions are certainly legitimate ones, though anthropologists are more likely to understand that while the desire for knowledge is never disinterested, learning about cultures outside of one's own can be personally and intellectually rewarding for those lucky enough to have the opportunity to do so. I came to Indonesia by a circuitous route. Right before graduating from college in 1991 with degrees in music and linguistics, and already active in queer rights and HIV prevention work but with no background in anthropology, I learned that the International Gay and Lesbian Human Rights Commission (IGLHRC; which at that point was a handful of volunteers working out of an apartment in San Francisco's Mission District) had organized a symposium in the Soviet Union. I was able to attend the symposium and — as someone just out of college with no job — I volunteered to stay a few additional months to teach gay groups in Moscow how to use a Macintosh computer donated by IGLHRC so that they could publish their writings without government interference.

A couple of weeks after the symposium, with the other North Americans gone, I awoke in my Moscow flat and walked bleary-eyed into the main room to turn on the television. The first channel showed the image of a brook from a tedious nature documentary. I then turned the channel only to see the same brook appear each time. How odd to have the same show on every channel, I thought. Two Russian gay men living in the flat then came into the room. One of them, a well-known activist, immediately panicked: "Gorbachev is dead." This seemed to me to be a premature conclusion, but we soon learned that his fears were not unfounded. There had been a coup and Gorbachev was under arrest, even shot for all we knew.

Thus began three heady days of fear and hope. Yeltsin was holed up in the parliament building resisting the plotters of the coup, but he had no access to a printing press. However, we managed to get a copy of his pronouncement denouncing the coup and then made a fearful taxi circuit around town, picking up reams of paper from one apartment and a small photocopy machine from another. Back in our apartment, we typed up the pronouncement on the Macintosh, printed it out, then spent a long night blowing on a dangerously overheated transformer no bigger than a fist as the American-made photocopy machine, unused to Russian voltages, spewed out copies one by one. The next day we went to the parliament building and delivered the flyers, walking through an eerily festive scene with quiet tanks on one side and impromptu barricades on the other. The barricades had been formed by cobblestones pulled up into mounds; behind them were tin shacks with babushkas doling out bread to those wandering about, and tugboats were pulled up to the river's edge so that no military ships could dock. In the following days we were thrilled to see posted in the subway stations and on the sides of buildings our flyers calling for resistance — with the logo of the Russian gay group Tema visible on the flyer's edge.[6]

I have never before now written about these experiences in Russia, but in retrospect I realize they played a formative role in my decision to become an anthropologist. I had in those brief months learned the usefulness of sustained engagement in a particular cultural location, even limited by my bumbling skills in the Russian language. And I had learned that activism and intellectual inquiry need not be in opposition. I drew upon my experiences in Russia to travel in 1992 to Malaysia and then to Indonesia as an HIV prevention worker, not yet a graduate student in anthropology. I became fascinated by Indonesia, which like the United States is a multicultural nation of great diversity and crosscutting unities. Through my work as an HIV prevention consultant I came to know *gay* communities in several parts of Indonesia, and as I shared stories with my new friends I realized there were both similarities and differences in our lives.

Because I was interested in these similarities and differences, as well as dimly aware that notions of "same" and "different" were part of the problem, particularly as they relate to questions of social justice and globalization (Brown 1995:153), I dropped out of a Ph.D. program in linguistics at Berkeley to take up graduate training in anthropology at Stanford (though language remains for me a topic of interest; see chapter 3). I have continued to do HIV prevention work and am best known to most of my Indonesian colleagues in this role, but for well over a decade I have been exploring the lives of *gay,* waria, and *lesbi* Indonesians. Like most anthropologists, I have built up a long-term relationship with the place I study, though of course my knowledges are limited. The ability to speak the Indonesian language has been crucial to my ability to carry out ethnographic research.

My fieldwork thus far has been carried out during multiple visits to Indonesia since 1992, and it is supplemented by my ongoing archival, Internet, and activist work.[7] Much of this work is detailed in my book *The Gay Archipelago: Sexuality and Nation in Indonesia* (2005), which can be read as a companion volume to this one. My ethnographic research was carried out in three primary field sites. The first of these is Surabaya. With a population of over three million, Surabaya is Indonesia's second-largest city; the provincial capital of East Java; and a famous site of resistance to colonial occupation (Dick 2002; Frederick 1989). The second site is Makassar, the provincial capital of South Sulawesi. Makassar is an important commercial center dominated by the Bugis and the Makassarese ethnolocalized groups, and it is a city with a long history of trade and of religious piety (Cummings 2002; Gade 2004). The third site is the island of Bali, a province in its own right. It is predominantly Hindu (though it is a form of Hinduism quite different from that found in India), and it is powerfully shaped by its status as tourist hub for Indonesians and foreigners alike, with its own history of conflict (Picard 1996; G. Robinson 1995; Vickers 1989). I chose these sites because they were relatively close to one another yet contrasted in ethnic and religious makeup, degree of contact with non-Indonesians, and position in the Indonesian nation-state. I have also visited eight other urban or rural areas of Indonesia with *gay,* waria, and *lesbi* communities, including sites in Kalimantan, Central Java, and the national capital of Jakarta.

ETHNOGRAPHY

The meaning of "ethnography" is greatly misunderstood in the humanities and in much of the social sciences. Many researchers say they do work in ethnography, but in actuality they employ methods that would not be recognized as ethnographic by most anthropologists (for instance, conducting interviews in isolation from other activity, then transcribing and coding them according to predetermined variables). Ethnography is both an epistemological approach and a linked series of methods, with "participant observation" as the key practice. This oxymoronic term refers to spending extended periods of time with the communities being studied, participating in the flow of daily life as much as possible. In my own case, over the years this has meant activities such as playing volleyball, doing drag in a show, helping write a grant for an activist group, contributing an article to a zine, standing around in a park at night, going to a movie in a shopping mall, visiting relatives in the countryside, and listening to someone's story of falling in love. Participant observation cannot be fully taught in academic settings because of all methods it is the one most shaped by the times and places in which it is carried out: participant observation demands flexibility, humor, and patience through the misunderstandings, missteps, incorrect replies, and accidental offenses.

The fact that participant observation is by definition impossible— How can one participate and observe at the same time?—is its greatest strength. For instance, it would be naive to assume that the Indonesians with whom I have lived were not affected by the presence of a white male Westerner in their midst, even if he has labored to learn Indonesian and to know something of the context of their lives. Even when the researcher is a "halfie" (Abu-Lughod 1991) or a "native" member of the communities under study, her or his presence as researcher shapes the context studied. Anthropologists, however, do not subscribe to a view of science that sees the presence of the researcher as a contaminant. Since cultures are always changing and interacting with others of various kinds, the key is not to pretend that one can avoid shaping the context studied, but to make one's presence and accommodations to that presence part of what is being researched. Although the presence of an anthropologist (or any "outsider") can have negative effects, the orientalist trope that cultures are timeless, fragile, and liable to be compromised forever in their encounter with difference is also naive. The unique power of participant observation lies in its potential for addressing what Marilyn Strathern terms anticipation: a "routine crisis in the pursuit of knowledge, which is how to deal with the unforeseen" (2004:5). Questions of anticipation and the unforeseen are questions of temporality— that is, of coincidence. As Strathern writes:

> What research strategy could possibly collect information on unpredictable outcomes? Social anthropology has one trick up its sleeve: the deliberate attempt to generate more data than the investigator is aware of at the time of collection. Anthropologists deploy open-ended, non-linear methods of data collection which they call ethnography; I refer particularly to the nature of ethnography entailed in anthropology's version of fieldwork. Rather than devising research protocols that will purify the data in advance of analysis, the anthropologist embarks on a participatory exercise which yields materials for which analytical protocols are often devised after the fact. (5–6)

For all the important problematizations of ethnography (e.g., Clifford and Marcus 1986), it remains a useful tool for the temporally conscious investigation of culture because it is an "open-ended mode of study" that permits one to "recover the antecedents of future crises from material not collected for the purpose" (Strathern 2004:7). This is what Strathern terms "anticipation by default" (7). Ethnography is thus a methodology well suited to strategies of coincidence. This is a mode of inquiry that could be characterized in terms of what Charles Pierce termed "abduction." As Stefan Helmreich summarizes it, "While *induction* is reasoning by inference from particulars toward general conclusions, and *deduction* the drawing of conclusions from known principles or theories, *abduction* is reasoning from premises that *may* materialize in the future" (Helmreich 2006).

Ethnography produces what Donna Haraway termed "situated knowledge" (1988: 581) whose strength originates in its self-recognition as limited and provisional. Ethnographic knowledge — based above all on participant observation — collects data on a range of interlinked social groups. As an inherently limited methodology, ethnography always produces more data on some groups than on others. This result stems not only from the researcher's priorities but also from the embodied nature of participant observation itself. For instance, if a researcher is older, it is usually harder to gather data on young people; if Muslim, it is usually harder to gather data on Christians; if male, it is usually harder to gather data on women. Some cultural contexts resist the assumptions of identity politics; even in the United States it can sometimes be that an older person can gather unique and useful data on young people, a woman can gather unique and useful data about men, and so on. These inevitable differences in the amount of data gathered need not be a source of consternation, but they must be addressed, theorized, and where possible compensated for by methods including modifying one's research protocol, drawing upon the work of other researchers, and archival research.

In regard to my research in Indonesia, a concern in theorizing sexuality and gender has been that the greatest amount of my ethnographic data is on *gay* men, with a lesser amount on warias and even less on *lesbi* women. This is a dilemma faced by all researchers on sexuality and gender: since these domains are relational (male/female, heterosexual/homosexual, and so on), the subject of analysis seems to demand a multiple focus at the theoretical level that cannot be sustained at the methodological level. For example, during my various fieldwork experiences, I was able to spend time with *lesbi* women by engaging in activities including a pilgrimage to a mystic shrine in Java, hanging out in a restaurant with a *lesbi* group in north Bali, and holding HIV prevention trainings with *lesbi* women in the city of Makassar. Yet all of these experiences with *lesbi* women total up to about 10 percent of my overall ethnographic work; in Indonesia, men and women often do not socialize together outside circumscribed contexts. It would be misleading to treat my material on *gay* men, warias, and *lesbi* women as equivalent, yet excising my material on warias and *lesbi* women would be more misleading. The various chapters of this book deal with this issue in different ways.[8] I do not try to provide equal representation across gender but instead use my more extensive work on *gay* men to investigate how the ranking of masculine over feminine has consequences not just for gender and sexuality in isolation, but their imbrication with other domains of experience. It is important that any theoretical study of sexuality specifically discuss the different contexts and practices of male and female subjects to the greatest degree possible, not as a qualifier or an afterthought but as a central theme.

No book can be all things to all people. In writing, we always make choices about how to shape the stories we tell: the audiences we assume and invoke; the theoretical and methodological frameworks we draw upon and extend in turn. In this book, I work to enact emergent collaborations between queer studies and anthropology in the spirit of ethnographic critique. I want to show what such linkages might look like through specific case studies rather than on an abstract level. The primary way in which I do this is through four separate in-depth explorations of the lives of men who term themselves *gay* (and one exploration focusing on warias) in Indonesia, the world's fourth most populous nation and home to more Muslims than any other country. These explorations, in chapters 1 through 5, are all revised versions of articles previously published in a range of scholarly journals. Each chapter is free standing, but also each has been revised so as to build upon the arguments of this introductory chapter.

Collectively, the chapters insist on the primacy of empirical (not empiricist) investigation to any queer studies project that wishes to speak to the specificities of lived experience. This is a question of adequation; in other words, a question of the relationship between the claims an individual makes (in this case, a queer studies scholar or activist) and the object toward which those claims are made. If the object of analysis is everyday life with all of its complexities, specificities, and inequalities, then I would argue that participant observation should be central to the analysis of this object. Participant observation refers to the method of spending extended periods of time in daily interaction with those about whom the reasearcher wishes to speak; it is usually the primary method used to create ethnographies — interpretations of cultural lifeworlds. For instance, if we wish to speak about gay male sex tourism in Laos (rather than, say, the representation of such sex tourism in Western gay magazines), it behooves us to take the time and energy to interact with gay male tourists in Laos and also the Laotian men with whom they have relationships of various kinds.

This approach involves investments: for example, learning Laotian if one does not know the language, traveling to Laos if one does not live there, spending time with a variety of people, analyzing popular media and historical archives in Laos and elsewhere, and so on. Such investments ideally produce a sense of humility and generosity toward the object of study regardless of the degree to which one sees oneself (or is seen by those of whom one speaks) as a member of the cultural lifeworld under consideration. This approach also permits analysis not just of political economic contexts (globalization, neoliberalism, etc.) and oppositional forces (transnational activist networks, nongovernmental organizations, etc.), but also the contingent yet foundational ways in which practices of everyday life rework, within a range of limitations, these contexts and forces (de Certeau 1984). Participant observation has a crucial role to play in queer methodology; its ability to decenter personal experience as the source of embodied knowledge can head off the slippage between critiquing and criticizing that threatens to render queer studies into a self-congratulatory exercise where the cast of characters is settled and the conclusion known in advance.

Of course, there is more to anthropology than participant observation, and the next five chapters all set participant observation alongside methods ranging from textual analysis to the examination of linguistic forms. In chapter 1, "Zines and Zones of Desire," I examine the informal magazines or "zines" that *gay* and *lesbi* Indonesians have been publishing since 1982.[9] In this examination I bring together literary and participant observation methods to examine how Indonesian *gay* and *lesbi* subjectivities are linked to national belonging and a sense of global linkages. Drawing upon the notion of merography, or part-whole writing, I explore how questions of context and intentionality shape sexual subjectivities in a postcolonial context. The notion of merography also proves useful at a reflexive level because it can help diagnose the ongoing debate over interdisciplinarity in queer studies — or, indeed, the exhaustion of the paradigm of interdisciplinarity, since the notion participates in the dominant Western logic that presumes objects (disciplines, in this case) are ontologically prior to relationships.

In chapter 2, "*Warias,* National Transvestites," I investigate the place of *warias,* roughly translated as "male-to-female transvestites," in Indonesian society.[10] Drawing upon Derrida and Lacan, among other theorists, I challenge the prevalent notion in queer studies of "third genders," and I turn attention to the relationship between waria subjectivity and nationalism.

Gay Indonesians speak a unique slang, *bahasa gay,* which has specific grammatical rules and norms of use; increasingly, it is being taken up by Indonesian popular culture. In chapter 3, "*Gay* Language, Registering Belonging," I combine a linguistic analysis of bahasa *gay* with an analysis of bahasa *gay*'s use to explore questions of sexuality, nationalism, and globalization.[11] Here I am fundamentally concerned with the relationship between language, subjectivity, and community.

In chapter 4, "Between Religion and Desire," I explore the place of Islam in the lives of *gay* Indonesians.[12] In referencing debates over multiculturalism and faith, I use the concept of "incommensurability" to examine tensions between doctrine and lived exegesis as *gay* Indonesians find ways to reconcile sexuality and religious devotion.

In chapter 5, "The Emergence of Political Homophobia," I extend the analysis of Islam in chapter 4 by examining a series of incidents in which groups of men, identified with Islamic fundamentalism, violently attacked gatherings of *gay* men in Indonesia.[13] Here I argue that this violence cannot be understood solely in religious or psychological terms. Instead, it reflects a broader pattern in which the attempt by *gay* men to gain access to public space is seen as threatening Indonesian society, thereby revealing the heteronormative logic at the heart of Indonesian nationalism, as is the case in so many contexts worldwide (Alexander 1997:84).

In chapter 6, "Comparatively Queer in Southeast Asia," I place the ethnographic and theoretical materials of chapters 1 through 5 in conversation with a series of excellent ethnographic studies conducted elsewhere in Indonesia as well as in Laos, Malaysia, the Philippines, Singapore, and Thailand. Asking how we might think of queerness as comparative and comparison as queer, I set forth questions concerning globalization, sexuality, and the entangled futures of anthropology and queer studies. Taken as a whole, my aim in this book is to hold out the possibility of new "coincidences" between anthropology and queer studies, a topic I discuss further below.[14]

I wish to emphasize here at the outset that my investigations in chapters 1 through 5 are part and parcel of theory and not empirical evidence marshaled in support of theory. Kath Weston, in her review of lesbian and gay anthropology, noted that many an anthropologist "opens with an obligatory nod to Foucault before presenting research findings, but more commonly, the researcher's theoretical perspectives remain embedded in apparently straightforward reports from the field. In effect, the absence of theory becomes the submersion of theory" (1993:344). Paraphrasing this insightful statement, we can add that many a queer theorist opens with an obligatory nod to participant observation before presenting theoretical claims, but more commonly the theorist's empirical perspectives remain embedded in apparently straightforward theorizations. In effect, the absence of data becomes the submersion of data; the theorist's own experiences stand in for the ostensible object of study. This is, once again, a question of adequation, one shaped by an identity politics of knowledge and thus by forms of queer normativity.

I mean my paraphrase of Weston to serve as a reminder to queer studies, so identified with queer theory, that all theorizing takes place against an empirical background (which is not the same thing as an identitarian formation), even if this is the disavowed and unacknowledged background of the theorist's own life experiences. The turn to substantive data is therefore not a turn away from theory but a turn toward the empirical contexts through which all theory is derived and toward which all theory ultimately makes its claims. This is what Theodor Adorno (1903–1969), a major figure in the "Frankfurt school" of critical theory, identified as "immanent criticism." Adorno noted that no work of art, no theory, indeed no aspect of culture "has ever exhausted itself in itself alone, in its being-in-itself. They have always stood in relation to the actual life-process of society from which they distinguished themselves" (1967:23). As against transcendent critique, which "assumes an as it were Archimedean position above culture" (31), immanent critique explores the contradictions between social phenomena and ideology from within culture. It bears noting from the outset that the notion of interdisciplinarity, so often valorized in queer studies scholarship, presumes transcendent critique.

Since its origins, anthropology has served as a form of cultural critique "with the aim of disturbing [its readers'] cultural self-satisfaction," according to George Marcus and Michael Fischer (1986:111). Yet as they further note, anthropology can do more than the "transcendent" move of pointing out variation and difference (the "relativism" for which it is famous); it can work as situated knowledge, thereby resonating with forms of queer critique, such as queer-of-color critique, that typically insist upon the immanence of theory (Ferguson 2003, 2005). This is a question of interdisciplinarity; women's studies scholars in particular have foregrounded the dominance of literary methodologies and epistemologies in the study of sexuality and the importance of interdisciplinarity both within the academy and as a response to globalization (Grewal and Kaplan 2001; Wiegman 2002).

This book examines potential intersections between queer studies, which has profoundly shaped my research and activism, and anthropology, the primary discipline in which I now work. I ask what forms the intersections between anthropology and queer studies might take, rather than make programmatic statements about what is or should be. I am interested not in codification but coincidence, where "coincidence" is taken to refer to temporal intersections that work outside the linear regime of temporality that I term "straight time."

While I do not assume that queer studies is, or should become, a discipline, I speak of intersections because it is through them that questions of adequation can be addressed: as Strathern notes, there is a "need to conserve the division of labor between disciplines, if only because the value of a discipline is precisely in its ability to account for its conditions of existence and thus as to how it arrives at its knowledge practices" (2004:5). Indeed, intersectionality is of particular importance to anthropologists because culture itself is intersectional: "Culture consists in the way analogies are drawn between things, in the way certain thoughts are used to think others" (Strathern 1992a:33).

I approach anthropology and queer studies at their best, from a stance of critical generosity — seeking potentiality, innovation, and coalition. This is important because while anthropology is a more established discipline than queer studies, both exist in a precarious academic universe. With its corporatization, the contemporary university in the United States increasingly mistakes "technology" for "science" and frames the goal of education in terms of skill sets and information acquisition rather than critical thinking, intellectual curiosity, and adaptability, or a vision in which the pursuit of ideas progressively displaces unequal material gain as the human project.[15] This corporatization often manifests itself in the call for interdisciplinarity, which is seen to provide more practical, patentable, and grantable forms of knowledge than the ostensibly limited practices that take place within disciplines. There is great need for a coalitional and unabashedly intellectual interdisciplinarity that values disciplinary knowledge and does not make a poorly defined applicability the procrustean horizon of academic work.

At its best, anthropology works to place different ways of thinking and living into dialogue, but not to claim that there is no such thing as right or wrong. Instead, anthropology asks what possibilities emerge from taking difference seriously, and how notions of sameness and difference are shaped by society, history, and power (where these are taken as perspectives rather than mutually exclusive categories). From its beginnings, alongside the goal of interpretation — rending the "other" legible — anthropology has worked to render "us" illegible by doing what many have called "making strange," by unsettling assumptions and showing that what counts as "common" sense depends on time and place.

At its best, queer studies scholarship, which first emerged and remains predominantly located within the humanities versus the "more reluctant" social sciences (Corber and Valocchi 2003:1), "makes strange" heteronormativity — the idea that heterosexuality and traditional gender roles hold a monopoly on being natural, holy, or proper.[16] It is through the concept of heteronormativity that we can challenge heterosexuality's privilege of naming itself "sexuality." Here there is an important difference between the categories of sexuality and gender. Even the most patriarchal cultures do not image a society made up only of men: the existence of women, along with their oppression, is assumed. However, while homosexuality can act as a "constitutive outside" for some heteronormativities (Bunzl 2004a), others are animated by a fantasy of a world with no homosexuals in it (Sedgwick 1993).

Queer studies examines how heteronormativity shapes the domains of life that might appear distant from domains of gender and sexuality (nationalism, economics, race, aesthetics, and even disciplinarity). It does not essentialize "queer" but allows the concept to "do its outlaw work as a verb," destabilizing those realms of being seen as normal (Freccero 2006:5). Queer studies also destabilizes notions of the normal by speaking of homonormativities, queer normativities, and so on, highlighting how the project of establishing a norm — a project which in the contemporary world is linked to the rise of statistics and modernist governmentality (Foucault 1985, 1991) — is not limited to dominant forces, though these other forms of normativity have less social power and more circumscribed effects.

Queer studies scholars are sometimes warned that the term "queer" is not accepted by everyone in the United States, including many calling themselves lesbian or gay, and it is certainly not accepted by many people outside the West (the term remains virtually unknown in Indonesia, for instance). Such a warning misses the mark because it is almost never accompanied by a similar warning against facile uses of terms like woman, man, person, house, work, and so on. The problem of conceptual translation is not unique to the term "queer"; as I have argued elsewhere (using the notion of "dubbing culture"; see Boellstorff 2005), queer studies may have a unique contribution to make to this problem. Like anthropology, queer studies makes a virtue of the adequational slippage between object of study and theoretical framework.

The classic distinction between emic (insider) and etic (outsider) terms is helpful here. Used etically, "queer" should be no more controversial than "exogamous" (marrying outside one's group), "ergative case," "discursive field," "cross-cousin marriage," or any other term used in an analytical rather than experiential sense. Terms are conceptual tools rather than transparent labels for entities in the world, and we should ontologize them with care. At issue is that queer can be emic; it is sometimes used as a term of identity and community. Many other terms share this double status as emic and etic (everything from "religion" to "gender" to "globalization"). That a term can be used in emic and etic senses is fine so long as we are aware of how it is used; most problems relating to "queer" result from unanalyzed slippages between emic and etic usages, not to mention between descriptive and prescriptive usages. I would therefore argue that the pressing issue with regard to "queer" is not one of adequation because this is a general issue of analysis and critique; instead, the pressing issue is one of timing, the issue to which I now turn.

QUEER TIMING

The *Oxford English Dictionary* notes that the word "queer" is "of doubtful origin."[17] Although the term "queer theory" has no such doubtful origin (it was coined in 1990 by Teresa de Lauretis and first appeared in print in de Lauretis 1991), doubt certainly haunts the idea of queer studies. Queer studies has been termed a "discipline that refuses to be disciplined" (Sullivan 2003:v); it has appeared as a moniker for gay and lesbian studies, lesbian, gay, transgender, bisexual, and intersexed studies, the study of non-normative sexualities and genders, and the study of all normalizing discourse, with an emphasis on resistance and transformation. In this book I will refer to "non-normative sexualities and genders" as the best compromise term for the topic under consideration. This is not meant to imply that things like homosexuality and transgenderism can never be "normal," nor that they do not play a role in defining the normal; the "normal" as a concept that arose with statistics and the notion of the "population" (Foucault 1991) depends on the non-normative outliers to define its Gaussian curve.

In "Paranoid Reading and Reparative Reading" (2003), Eve Kosofsky Sedgwick questions the paranoia that characterizes so much critical inquiry. What Sedgwick means by "paranoid reading" is the assumption that critique must be a suspicious and distrustful enterprise that works by finding fault, forming negative judgments, or pointing out failures and absences. Noting that "queer studies in particular has had a distinctive history of intimacy with the paranoid imperative" (126), Sedgwick maintains that paranoid approaches lead to "an unintentionally stultifying side effect: they may have made it less rather than more possible to unpack the local, contingent relations [that is, the cultural relations] between any given piece of knowledge and its narrative/epistemological entailments for the seeker, knower, or teller" (124). Sedgwick links paranoid readings to temporality, emphasizing the limitations of linear conceptions of time: "To recognize in paranoia a distinctively rigid relation to temporality, *at once anticipatory and retroactive*, averse above all to surprise, is also to glimpse the lineaments of other possibilities. . . . Practices of reparative knowing may lie, barely recognized and little explored, at the heart of many histories of gay, lesbian, and queer inter-textuality (146, 149; emphasis added).

Sedgwick's analysis has turned my attention to temporality, where I have also been stimulated by a range of colleagues who have taken up the question of queer time, usually with three linked referents in mind.[18] The first domain of queer time concerns the individual life course. Judith Halberstam, in *In a Queer Time and Place*, identifies queer time as linked to an "epistemology of youth" that marks "the potentiality of a life unscripted by the conventions of family, inheritance, and child rearing" (2005:2). By questioning "reproductive temporality" (4) — an under-standing of time predicated on the heteronormative family, childbearing, and maturation — queer time opens up new possibilities for selfhood, community, and resistance to relations of domination. Halberstam's cri-tique of reproductive temporality shares some elements with Lee Edel-man's critique of "reproductive futurism" in *No Future: Queer Theory and the Death Drive*. For Edelman, "queerness names the side of those not 'fighting for the children,' the side outside the consensus by which all politics confirms the absolute value of reproductive futurism" (2004:3). The analytical frameworks of Halberstam and Edelman are congruent with the "queer temporality" that Stephen Barber and David Clark iden-tify in Eve Sedgwick's work, which cleaves to the "childhood scene of shame . . . as a near-inexhaustible source of transformational energy" (2002:5). It is also congruent with Carla Freccero's use of "prolepsis" to mark "the spirit of queer analysis in its willful perversion of notions of temporal propriety and the reproductive order of things" (2006:2).

A second domain to which queer time is taken to refer is social time, particularly the temporal logic of capitalism in which production, cir-culation, and consumption feed a general dynamic of "progress." Queer scholars have looked at the possibility that this forward movement could be stopped or even reversed. Halberstam, for instance, in her discus-sion of Brandon Teena, the female-to-male transgender whose murder in rural Nebraska was the subject of several films, notes that queerness can induce a sense of temporal dislocation, so that a figure such as Brandon can represent "anachronism (an earlier model of gay identity as gender inversion)" (2005:16). In her work, Elizabeth Freeman has introduced the notion of "temporal drag, with all of the associations that the word 'drag' has with retrogression, delay, and the pull of the past upon the present" (2000:728; see also Grosz 2004; Roof 1996; Weston 2002:58).

A third usage of queer time concerns queer studies itself. Since the theoretical work of queer studies is often actualized through analyzing other works in queer studies (e.g., Butler 1997), it seems fitting to examine the 2005 special issue of *Social Text* addressing the futures of queer studies.[19] Several aspects of the issue's introductory chapter raise questions of time that reappear in many contributions to the volume. As the special issue's title suggests — "What's Queer about Queer Studies Now?" — the status of queer studies is linked to a linear temporal framework, originating "around 1990" and moving through the journal's publication of other special issues; that is, the foundational question is how queer studies "in the present offers important insights" relative to "queer studies in the past" (Eng, Halberstam, and Muñoz 2005:1, 2, 7). This linear framework is mapped onto the life course of individual queer scholars. A queer reproductive temporality is produced that makes intelligible the claim that the collection of essays is "largely authored by a younger generation of queer scholars" (1); this recalls "the agonized conversations about feminism's generational transmission" (Wiegman 2004a:164). Finally, the forward progression of queer studies is actualized in terms of recognizing that "sexuality is intersectional" (Eng, Halberstam, and Muñoz 2005:1). This might not seem to be a claim about time at all, but a key goal of this chapter is to ask after resonances between anxieties about time and anxieties about disciplinarity. Queer studies seems to be at a juncture where disciplinarity and temporality suggest each other, so that the movement from past to future is also a movement toward greater intersectionality, and intersectionality becomes a model for articulating difference.

These queer takes on the individual life course, the temporal structures of capitalism, and the disciplinary formation of queer studies all enact a "reverse discourse" (Foucault 1978:101). The origin point of their theorization, an origin point that they share with the heteronormative temporality they ostensibly critique, is the belief that time is linear — that time is "straight." They work within — and thus do not entirely reject — the linear paradigm of straight time; their intervention lies in envisioning life courses, social histories, and interdisciplinarities that move differently on straight time's continuum. In these analyses, this takes forms of retrogression, stoppage, and drag that interrupt straight time's smooth flow but still operate in terms of its conceptual purview.

Straight time has methodological and disciplinary ramifications; this temporality is shaped by a telos of the single orgasm co-occurring with ejaculation, a time whose tempo climaxes in production and reproduction. This logic equates male sexuality with penetration, female sexuality with lack, and transgender sexuality with unintelligibility. I argue that straight time, capable of portraying temporal relationships only in terms of anticipation or drag, limits the range not just of queer critique but of anthropological critique as well. Johannes Fabian, in *Time and the Other: How Anthropology Makes Its Object*, suggests as much with reference to classic modes of anthropological knowledge production. In summarizing Fabian's argument, Matti Bunzl notes that there is "a contradiction inherent to the anthropological discipline: on the one hand, anthropological knowledge is produced in the course of fieldwork through the intersubjective communication between anthropologists and interlocutors; on the other hand, traditional forms of ethnographic representation require the constitutive suppression of the dialogical realities generating anthropological insights in the first place. In the objectifying discourses of a scientistic anthropology, "Others" thus never appear as immediate partners in a cultural exchange but as spatially and, more importantly, temporally distanced groups" (Bunzl 2002:x). Fabian thus notes how a particular understanding of time in anthropology is used to "give meaning to the distribution of humanity in space" (1983:25). This makes what he terms "coevalness," and what I term "coincidence," anthropology's key problem with time. In other words, anthropology tends to frame "natives" as belonging to an earlier phase of human history and often finds it difficult to regard them as existing in the same time as the researcher (Fabian 1983:38).

Here I would like to raise the possibility of radical temporalities for both queer studies and anthropology that displace (rather than just slow or reverse) straight time; in so doing they suggest new forms of interdisciplinarity. A queer anthropological critique of straight time could forge possibilities for deploying time in ways other than reproducing hierarchy along the trajectory of straight time—a trajectory that climaxes in an implicit modernist vision of progress. In other words, anthropology can *anthropologize* rather than simply ethnographize queer time and the work of queer studies more generally. When queer studies scholars wish to anthropologize time — which has long been a subject of interest to anthropologists and other social theorists (see Munn 1992) — they typically turn to studies such as Carol Greenhouse's *A Moment's Notice* (1996). Although this excellent work and others like it inform my argument in this chapter, I also turn to classic but lesser-known essays on time by two of twentieth-century anthropology's canonical figures, Edmund Leach and Clifford Geertz, with an important aside taken from the literary theorist Mikhail Bakhtin. These anthropological digressions on time provide tools for rethinking the forms that queer temporality might take, thereby opening a conceptual and political space from which to think of such temporality not in terms of "queer time," but in terms of "queer timing."

QUEER CHRONOLOGIES, QUEER CHRONOTOPES

Edmund Leach (1910–1989) first published "Cronus and Chronos" in 1952; a revised version (which I employ here) appeared as the first of "Two Essays Concerning the Symbolic Representation of Time" (Leach 1961). Leach begins his essay with the obvious but crucial point that English "time" conflates a range of phenomena that people in various cultural contexts may not see as a single phenomenon. Drawing upon material from Burma, Leach notes the distinctiveness of Kachin phrases like "a long *time*," "spring*time*," "at any *time* of life" (*na*, *ta*, and *asak*, respectively), and he emphasizes the point that these concepts would not be seen as synonymous (124). The culturally contingent bundling of conceptual entities under the English-language term "time" (see also Evans-Pritchard 1940:103; Hoskins 1993:58) is almost never mentioned in discussions of queer time; at best, it surfaces implicitly in punning titles (of which this chapter is an example).

Leach's next denaturalizing move is to note that "our modern English notion of time embraces at least two different kinds of experience which are logically distinct and even contradictory" (125). On one hand there is the notion of repetition or iteration: "It may be the ticking of a clock or a pulse beat or the recurrence of days or moons or annual seasons, but always there is something which repeats" (125). On the other hand there is the notion of nonrepetition: that "all living things are born, grow old and die, and that this is an irreversible process" (125). In Leach's view, it is due to religion that these two aspects of time are equated: "The idea of Time, like the idea of God, is one of those categories which we find necessary because we are social animals rather than because of anything empirical in our objective experience of the world" (125). Leach emphasizes that opposing ostensibly Western linear time to ostensibly non-Western cyclical time does not escape dominant conceptions because both perspectives assume a geometric experience of time. If one examines everyday notions of time around the world, then "the metaphors of repetition are likely to be of a much more homely nature: vomiting, for example, or the oscillations of a weaver's shuttle, or the sequence of agricultural activities, or even the ritual exchanges of a series of interlinked marriages. When we describe such sequences as 'cyclic' we innocently introduce a geometrical notation which may well be entirely absent in the thinking of the people concerned" (126).

Like the yearly movement of the sun from the highest point in the sky to the lowest point and then back again, these conceptions of time are framed in terms of "a sequence of oscillations between polar opposites: night and day, winter and summer, drought and flood, age and youth, life and death. In such a scheme the past has no 'depth' to it, all past is equally past; it is simply the opposite of now" (126). Such an understanding of time "implies the existence of a third entity — the 'thing' that oscillates" (126). To further investigate such temporalities Leach turns not to some "remote" indigenous group but to ancient Greek thought. For the Greeks this oscillation was above all between male and female (Uranus and Gaia, parents of Cronus, king of the Titans). As a result, "it is the sexual act itself which provides the primary image of time" (127), so that "not only must male be distinguished from female but one must postulate a third element, mobile and vital, which oscillates between the two. It seems clear that the Greeks thought of this third element in explicit concrete form as male semen" (129–30). Leach notes that if time is thus understood as an alternation between male and female, then "castration stories linked up with the notion of a phallus trickster who switches from side to side of the dichotomy 'make sense.' . . . *If time be thought of as alternation, then myths about sex reversals are representations of time*" (130; emphasis added).

Leach here articulates not just a notion of time in terms of alternation, but a notion of time in which the moment of intercourse between regimes of time is queer — a transgendered transition, a sexualized coincidence. Leach's notion of the phallus trickster who represents time itself recalls the appearance of the temporal trickster in the writings of Mikhail Bakhtin (1895–1975). In his essay "Forms of Time and of the Chronotope in the Novel" (1981 [1975]) Bakhtin sets forth the idea of the chronotope as "the intrinsic connectedness of temporal and spatial relationships that are artistically expressed in literature" (84). In other words, Bakhtin was interested in examining how assumptions about time become embedded in forms of literature, and by extension in forms of culture. The chivalric romance, which contributed to the rise of the "biographical time" that is now the dominant Western chronotope, is marked by the figures of the rogue, clown, and fool: "Essential to these three figures is a distinctive feature that is as well a privilege — the right to be 'other' in this world, the right not to make common cause with any single one of the existing categories that life makes available; none of these categories quite suits them, they see the underside and the falseness of every situation . . . They re-establish the public nature of the human figure . . . Their entire function consists in externalizing things" (159–60). Standing outside social norms, these trickster figures provide "new forms for making public all unofficial and forbidden spheres of human life, in particular the sphere of the sexual and of vital body functions" (165–66). These queer figures act in that space of productive contradiction that anthropologists term participant observation: "At last a form was found to portray the mode of existence of a man who is in life, but not of it, life's perpetual spy and reflector" (161).

From the anthropological approach of Leach, I draw insights in order to develop a queer critique of straight time. Leach notes a masculinist bias underlying at least one prominent historical conception of straight time, in which male essence is the "third element" making time happen. In this framework maleness — associated with movement and regeneration — is, so to speak, more timely than the feminine. This may be one reason for "the gravitational pull that 'lesbian' sometimes seems to exert upon 'queer'" (Freeman 2000:728), so that maleness appears as the force moving history forward. Further, Leach identifies the heteronormativity underlying straight time: copulation is presumed to be copulation between men and women. However, Leach also hints at a queer temporality, the "phallus trickster" who moves between male and female — and in so doing is, in a profound sense, temporality itself. This is not a queer time that engages in drag, stasis, or regression within the paradigm of straight time. While reverse discourses that work within a prevailing discourse are certainly legitimate and in some circumstances may be quite theoretically and politically effective, Leach raises the possibility of a profoundly alternative queer timing that shifts between depthless pasts and generative presents.

Leach's contention that "myths about sex reversals are representations of time" recalls Bakhtin's analysis of the rogue figure whose chronotope is concerned with being "in life, but not of it, life's perpetual spy and reflector." By standing outside social norms, this figure can act as a "third entity" oscillating between temporal regimes. This is a chronotope of coincidence—in life, but not of it. Coincidence is somewhat difficult to operationalize within straight time because it implies two events occupying the same moment. This is why anthropology historically placed its object in the past.

However, we can follow Leach in recognizing that in many times and places, temporality has been conceptualized in terms of alternation between two poles. In this way of thinking about time, the "future" is a place we've already been, so coincidence makes sense: it is the future's presence in the here and now. In terms of queer studies, it seems provocative to think about the alternative—the queer—as, in the words of Bill Maurer, "oscillating in time, like alternating current in an electric wire" (2005:50). Surely we can find forms of what Maurer terms lateral reason, which enable theorizing oscillations of coincidence without conceptualizing male essence as the thing that alternates between pasts and presents. I am thinking in particular of the ultimate male essence in the Western tradition: Christ. It is hard to prevent the assumptions of straight time from drawing us into the orbit of a Christian metaphysics, of a divine figure who lived, died, and lives again. A queer critique could interrupt what Walter Benjamin terms this "messianic" time, this straight time organized around a climactic end so that "every second of time was the strait gate through which the Messiah might enter" (1955:264; see also Derrida 1994:181).

To push further toward a notion of queer timing, I turn from Leach to Clifford Geertz (1926–2006), arguably the most significant anthropologist of the last half century, whose work has served to move an interpretive approach to the center of the discipline. In his essay "Person, Time, and Conduct in Bali," first published in 1966, Geertz set forth a conception of "permutational" time (I cite the 1973 version of the essay here; see also Bourdieu 1977:105; Evans-Pritchard 1940:95–102). Like Leach, Geertz wished to problematize dominant Western conceptions of time, which Leach termed "geometric" and Geertz termed "durational" (the straight time within which drags, lags, leaps, and even cycles are thinkable). Geertz's analysis of permutational Balinese calendars is worth quoting here at length:

> The permutational calendar . . . consists of ten different cycles of day-names. These cycles [or "weeks"] are of varying lengths. The longest contains ten day-names, following one another in a fixed order, after which the first day-name reappears and the cycle starts over. Similarly, there are nine, eight, seven, six, five, four, three, two, and even — the ultimate of a "contemporized" view of time — one day-name cycles. . . . Any given day has, at least in theory, ten different names simultaneously applied to it, one from each of the ten cycles. Of the ten cycles only those containing five, six, and seven day-names are of major cultural significance . . .
>
> The outcome of all this wheels-within-wheels computation is a view of time as consisting of ordered sets of thirty, thirty-five, forty-two, or two hundred and ten quantum units ("days"), each of which units has a particular qualitative significance of some sort indexed by its trinomial or binomial name: rather like our notion of the unluckiness of Friday-the-Thirteenth . . .
>
> The nature of time-reckoning this sort of calendar facilitates is clearly not durational but punctual. That is, it is not used (and could only with much awkwardness and the addition of some ancillary devices be used) to measure the rate at which time passes, the amount which has passed since the occurrence of some event, or the amount which remains within which to complete some project: it is adapted to and used for distinguishing and classifying discrete, self-subsistent particles of time — "days." The cycles . . . do not accumulate, they do not build, and they are not consumed. *They don't tell you what time it is; they tell you what kind of time it is.* (392–93; emphasis added)

Jeff Dreyfuss adds that this regime of temporality (found in Java and other parts of Indonesia in addition to Bali) produces "coincidences" of time, so that, for instance, "when a child is born on Java, no name is chosen for a *selapan hari,* or the thirty-five days until the coincidence of days on which the child was born recurs" (1985:762). In this temporality, every day — not just Friday the thirteenth — is understood in terms of the co-occurrence of multiple cycles of time (the seven-day week, the five-day week, and so on). These cycles do not count the duration of time so much as classify time into genres of conjunctural meaning; in the West, we do not say "this is the thirty-sixth Friday the thirteenth I have experienced" in the way that, since the rise of the modern era, we now enumerate things like birthdays and anniversaries within the regime of straight time (Frykman and Löfgren 1987:32).

How might coincidental time shift the notions of interdisciplinarity and intersectionality produced within straight time? Dreyfuss identifies a key entailment of coincidental time: "*Kebenaran* (the word in Indonesian and Javanese that may be translated as 'coincidence') may also be translated as 'truth' . . . [In coincidental time] there is no 'mere coincidence'" (1985:762). Here is a temporality that produces truth through coincidence, through intersectionality. We may even say that it is a temporality that produces truth through interdisciplinarity, through matters of timing. Not through a hypostatized straight time along which one drags, lags, or foreshadows, but a queer timing made possible through intersecting cycles of coincidence. This queer timing is profoundly performative: if we don't miss our cues, if our timing is correct, then we produce truth; and missteps produce their own takes on truth as well. Can we imagine queer time in terms of unique regimes of temporality that "coincide" with — and thereby transfigure — straight time, while remaining distinct from it?

TEMPORALITY AND DISCIPLINARITY

What relevance do these discussions of temporality hold for notions of queer time, and for questions of the relationship between anthropology and queer studies? Both Leach and Geertz make the classic anthropological move of destabilizing "common sense" by showing other cultural frameworks that have existed as viable forms of human being. The conceptions of time they identify are radically different from those familiar to most queer studies scholars. Thinking about queer time in terms of coincidence might give us ways to think about the futures of queer studies in terms other than generational reproduction or interdisciplinarity narrowly defined. These conceptions of time might provide new perspectives on everything from the "future" of the academy to the "timeliness" of same-sex marriage.[20] It might seem incorrect to even term coincidental temporality as "time," but it bears emphasizing that those who use this temporality do term it "time" — five-day or seven-day "weeks" that reference things like a naming ceremony or the day that a village market is open. To refuse to see this as a form of time would be logically circular; it would be to assume that only durational forms of time like straight time are "time," and would also assume that "time" is always durational.

Setting aside such ethnocentrism in favor of taking coincidental time seriously raises the possibility of a queer timing that, recalling Sedgwick, is more than anticipatory or retroactive; one that does more than drag, speed up, or stop along the linear path of straight time. The contribution of Leach's and Geertz's analyses, then, lies not in ethnographizing but anthropologizing time. Geertz draws a contrast between Bali and the West but does not oppose them in binary terms. Leach is primarily concerned with bringing an anthropological sensibility to ancient Greece, which has held a canonical place in queer studies (Bravmann 1997; Foucault 1985, 1986). This recalls how the best anthropological work draws from the destabilizing experiences of ethnography (whether of "one's own culture," "another culture," or somewhere in between) to rethink the naturalized conceptual horizons that sometimes underlie even the most vanguardist critiques.

My conclusion is not that we can do without time altogether: it is too experientially significant for too many people for such a move to be tenable. Rather than deconstruct time, we can disontologize it. One of the most significant interventions of anthropology in the nineteenth century and early twentieth was the transition from a notion of "Culture" — basically a synonym for "civilization," marking a single trajectory along which all humanity could in theory be placed — to a notion of "cultures." However, the linear notion of time that undergirded Culture was not discarded at the same time as Culture itself. It therefore seems appropriate to move from Time to timing; that is, to disontologize temporality by locating it within contexts of culture, place, and power.

In addition to its potential for destabilizing and reformulating the queer subject, rethinking temporality holds promise for rethinking the disciplinary boundaries between anthropology and queer studies. If in acting as time itself queerness can oscillate between two entities, could it oscillate between disciplines as well? Can disciplines exist in a coincidental relationship where they regularly intersect while remaining distinct, without orienting themselves toward a messianic endpoint? Questions of temporality and disciplinarity are not unique to queer studies and anthropology. Indeed, they have been debated with particular insightfulness in feminism, which informs both queer studies and anthropology (e.g., Halley 2004; Strathern 1987; Visweswaran 1997; Weed and Schor 1997). In "On Being in Time with Feminism," Robyn Wiegman examines "the difficulty of being in time with feminism, by which I mean the difficulty of sustaining a relationship to a political and intellectual project that is itself historically transforming and transformative, and whose transformations are neither produced by nor wholly disengaged from the historical and psychic temporalities of the subjects who act in feminism's name" (2004a:163).

Linking together notions of straight time that inform notions of the individual life course and of history (what Halberstam terms "generational time" or the "time of inheritance" [2005:5]), Wiegman notes that the language of generations "wrestles feminism's constitutive otherness into a systemic historical form wed to progressive understandings of time and indebted to reproduction as its implicit epistemology" (2004a:165). Wiegman's call for nomadic over disciplinary thinking (165, 167) provides a nonphallic model for Leach's trickster who, in moving between past and present, represents time itself — and whose position "in life, but not of it" speaks to the possibilities of a queer anthropology. Wiegman's nomadism also resonates with a notion of coincidental time in which temporalities intersect without standing in an ontological relationship to each other. Such reconfigured conceptions of temporality and disciplinarity might prove helpful, for instance, in theorizing how straight time undergirds the linear notions of "post-ness" presupposed by notions of postcoloniality, postmodernity, poststructuralism, and even the problematic figures of the postfeminist and postqueer.

I am interested in the potential of a temporal model of coincidence for nonhierarchical interdisciplinary relationships between queer studies and anthropology, a complement to the corporeal model of the cyborg that Strathern draws from Haraway (1991) to rethink relationships between feminism and anthropology: "The cyborg supposes what it could be like to make connections without assumptions of comparability. Thus might one suppose a relation between anthropology and feminism: were each a realization or extension of the capacity of the other, the relation would be of neither equality nor encompassment. It would be prosthetic, as between a person and a tool" (1991:38).

I opened this discussion with Sedgwick's critique of paranoid reading practices (see also Halley 2004:62–63). One way to define paranoia is as a negative relationship to coincidence: Why are these two things happening at once? What conspiracy brings them together? By drawing upon critiques of temporality such as those of Leach and Geertz, I aim to craft a positive relationship to coincidence. It is these kinds of potential analytic synergies that instill in me an optimistic rather than paranoid stance toward a "new queer studies" (Manalansan 2003:6). While it is inevitable that writings in defense of paranoid reading will appear, I want to insist on the potential of a reparative stance. I frame this optimism in terms of coincidence because my goal is not to insert anthropology into queer studies or vice versa: I do not want to think of disciplinarity in terms of fortifying a canon. As Strathern noted earlier, disciplinarity is best understood in terms of situating knowledge practices, not in terms of a fantasy — based upon straight time — that situatedness could be eliminated in the future. This is precisely the point Roderick Ferguson makes with regard to the exclusion of African American sociologists: "While seemingly a progressive and democratic move, including African American sociologists within the definition of canonical sociology actually denies the regulatory and exclusionary practices of canonical formations and suggests the perfection of the discipline. This sort of move is really liberal ideology applied to epistemology" (2003:23).

In light of such critiques of canonicity in both anthropology and queer studies, I would not argue that disciplines are outmoded. The fantasy of an interdisciplinarity that does away with disciplines altogether makes as little sense to me as the idea that humans can speak "language" without speaking German, Indonesian, Swahili, or any other historically and culturally produced set of linguistic norms. It is a deeply Western fantasy of the autonomous subject, ontologically prior to social context, that remains a figure of cathexis for identitarian traditions of scholarship whose "inaugural value form" is "a confederacy between subject and object, knower and the object to be known" (Wiegman 2004b:104). This includes, despite itself, queer studies. Disciplines are best framed not as outmoded regimes of knowledge production, but as coincidental communities of truth.

One way to frame my optimistic rather than paranoid stance would be in terms of queer hope. In *The Method of Hope*, Hirokazu Miyazaki aims to "approach hope as a methodological problem for knowledge and, ultimately, as a *method* of knowledge deployed across a wide spectrum of knowledge practices, as well as of political persuasions" (2004:2). This is a fundamentally interdisciplinary understanding of hope that has something important to offer queer anthropology and anthropological queer studies, given the pivotal place of desire in queer theory: "Unlike the subject of desire, which inherently invites one to analyze it with its infinitely deferrable quality, I argue, the conceptualization of hope as a method invites one to hope" (5). That is, the conceptualization of hope as a method—an "optimism of the intellect" (Harvey 2000:17)—invites a reflexive and collaborative stance toward knowledge, not unlike the paradox of participant observation or the productive instability of "queer."

Notions of hope are often grounded in straight time: hope for a heteronormatively generative future. Hope, however, might be queered; we might avoid conceding hope to heteronormativity, such that only paranoia or a relation of abjection to futurity remains. Rethinking temporality is a methodological move as much as a theoretical one: How can anthropology and queer studies investigate social life through lenses of coincidence, or matters of timing? Coincidence as I provisionally define it is thus a kind of queer hope, a hope whose method appears at the intersection of disciplines but without erasing disciplinarity.

The chapters that follow, then, are not meant to bring us closer to an anthropological queer studies or a queer anthropology. They do not "move" us anywhere. I want to conceptualize them as oscillating between anthropology and queer studies, sometimes within a single paragraph or sentence. I want to conceptualize them as a productive form of "discordant temporality" (Wiegman 2004b:94); as points of coincidence where queer studies and anthropology exchange insights without forcing themselves into a linear trajectory—into straightness pure and simple. This is a provisional conceptualization that asks after the feasibility of a queer shift from one chronotope to another without occupying any space between. Not anticipatory or retroactive, not drag or delay, not progression or development, but oscillation from one mode of inquiry to another, permutations of coincidence. In such reparative attempts to reconfigure established approaches, it may be possible to queer disciplines in time.

ONE

ZINES AND ZONES OF DESIRE

Desire might seem the most personal of emotions; something that originates in the deepest recesses of the soul and then reaches out in search of connection. However, work in queer studies and anthropology, among other disciplines, has long established how desire is not sui generis. Desire may feel like a product of the individual self, but it is shaped by the fields of culture, history, and power that Foucault referred to as discourses. This state of affairs can be hard to accept when discussing "nonnormative" sexualities — for instance, homosexuality — because often there does not appear to be any discourse corresponding to them. In most contemporary societies, great labor is expended on maintaining heterosexuality — for example, in areas such as norms of dating, gender roles, marriage laws, even architecture. Just as we can identify a dominant medical discourse that has shaped modern Western understandings of health and disease (Foucault 1973), we can identify discourses that have shaped modern notions of heterosexuality. But nowhere in the world has there existed a "homosexual lobby" with the power to shape notions of homosexuality in such a broad and sustained manner.

Theorists since Freud have offered two primary answers to this problem of homosexual desire. The first is that homosexual desire is a kind of "reverse discourse" — in other words, a discourse that reverses the polarity of an oppressive discourse without transcending it altogether: "The appearance in [the] nineteenth century . . . of a whole series of discourses on the species and subspecies of homosexuality . . . also made possible the formation of a 'reverse' discourse: homosexuality began to speak on its own behalf, to demand that its legitimacy or 'naturality' be acknowledged, often in the same vocabulary, using the same categories by which it was medically disqualified" (1978:101). This recalls notions of queer time that frame it in terms of a temporal reversal or slowing down yet still work within straight time.

The second answer involves questioning the idea that there is a one-to-one relationship between discourses and fields of social relations: "People think and act at the intersections of discourses" (Yanagisako and Delaney 1995:18). This is a vision of culture as coincidental, foreshadowed by many visions of interdisciplinarity. It is central, for instance, to queer-of-color critique and women of color feminisms, which typically understand sexuality "as a constitutive component of racial and class formations" (Ferguson 2005:85). It raises the possibility that, for instance, forms of homosexual desire can arise even when they are neither positively called into being through a discourse of "gay rights" nor negatively called into being though a "reverse discourse." It raises the possibility of coincidental mergings of discourses, wherein homosexual desire may appear as an unexpected effect — one that may have great staying power while bearing the traces of the particular historical conjuncture through which it came into being.

This chapter and the four that follow are concerned with specific cases of this process. They trace how national discourse shapes the subject positions *gay*, *lesbi*, and *waria* (male transvestite) in Indonesia. This coincidence of discourses of nation and sexuality has consequences for understandings of belonging, modernity, and a range of other issues. By "subject position" I mean basically what is meant by the everyday term "identity": a socially recognized category of selfhood; one with a particular history and typically inhabitable in multiple ways. Subject positions include roles like "woman," "doctor," "youth," and "heterosexual." "Subjectivities" are the senses of selfhood persons have as they inhabit a subject position (and we all take up many such subject positions throughout our lives), but in ways that always exceed and transform the subject position's logic even while being powerfully shaped by that logic. The term "identity" is in many cases an acceptable substitute for "subject position," but given its connotations of self-aware identification, and also its inability to distinguish between categories of selfhood versus senses of selfhood, I find the heuristic binarism of subject position and subjectivity to be helpful in my work.

In this chapter I focus on what I term "zines" — namely, informal magazines that *gay* Indonesians have been producing since 1982. By following the introduction with a study of these texts — a relatively unknown genre of Indonesian print media — I hope to demonstrate that anthropology and queer studies can build interdisciplinary connections through shared methodologies as well as shared topics of investigation and theoretical frameworks. I aim to demonstrate coincidences between the systems of meaning deployed by the producers and consumers of these zines, on the one hand, and Indonesian national discourse on the other. As privately circulated, small-scale publications, *gay* zines challenge definitions of "mass" media by providing unique insights into the relationship among print technologies, sexual subjectivities, and narratives of belonging. In particular, the producers and readers of *gay* zines do not see them as countercultural or as a "reverse discourse." Instead, they see the zines as part and parcel of the national character of *gay* sexuality, embodying and demonstrating the worthiness of *gay* Indonesians for social inclusion.

My goal is to show how zines could hold such meaning. These zines are permeated with two zones, or discourses, of desire — homosexual desire and a desire for national belonging. Zines relate these two zones in the idea that love [*cinta*] can be the ultimate *prestasi* (a word meaning both "good deed" and "performance"), indicating to society that *gay* people are worthy of national inclusion. In these zines, *gay* Indonesians assume that prestasi must be visible to society to have these effects of inclusion. Since speaking positively of same-gender love in Indonesia is difficult, love fails as a prestasi. Belonging is deferred, and tropes of separation permeate *gay* zines as a result. Thus, although same-gender desire is clearly sexual, I argue that the second zone of desire — national belonging — is sexualized in a manner not exclusive to *gay* Indonesians. My ultimate goal in this chapter, therefore, is to show how *gay* zines reveal a wide-ranging logic of heteronormative citizenship at the heart of the very real "national culture" of postcolonial Indonesia.[1] In the final paragraph of this chapter, I attempt to simulate this regime of affect — the imaginable but unattainable, indeed incommensurable moment when love, for so long linked to the idea of national belonging (Laffan 2003:157), takes on a homosexual cast.[2]

LESBI ZINES

In this chapter I base my conclusions on an analysis of over seven thousand pages of *gay* zine text, informed by my fieldwork among *gay* men.

Lesbi women have also published zines; however, I face a certain quandary in addressing these texts. Only a few have been published (the total corpus numbers around two hundred pages); this imbalance appears to be due not to any lack of desire to publish but instead to the difficulty that *lesbi* women face in securing the time, space, and resources to produce the zines. In the two cases in which *lesbi* women have published outside the capital of Jakarta, their zines have appeared as inserts within *gay* zines; as such, it is a situation of *gay* men sharing with *lesbi* women their relatively greater (but still meager) resources. Given this imbalance, along with the fact that my ethnographic work with *lesbi* women is less extensive than with *gay* men, I focus on *gay* zines in this chapter. I wish to keep in mind the feminist insight that "male" and "female" are not homologous (even in Southeast Asia, where conceptions of gender complementarity are widely distributed [Errington 1990; Hoskins 1998]), without erasing what data I do have on *lesbi* zines.

My heuristic compromise in this chapter is to focus my discussion on how *gay* zines illuminate masculine conceptions of national belonging but bring in *lesbi* material in a comparative vein where such data exist. In this way, I underscore some of the differences between *lesbi* and *gay* zines. For instance, *lesbi* zines are more likely to view Indonesia as a better place to live compared to countries in Euro-America; they are more likely to debate the implications of visibility; and they are more likely to express frustration with the difficulty of meeting other women given the limitations on women's mobility and privacy in most parts of the archipelago. Additionally, Indonesian women are affected by the state's family principle [*azas kekeluargaan*] that sets forth the unattainable goal of simultaneous domesticity and career within a heterosexual couple (see, for example, C. Jones 2004; Sen 1998; Suryakusuma 1996). Although men are affected by this state discourse, it is easier for them to fulfill the requirement of proper sexual citizenship and still sustain a *gay* life.[3] In addition to identifying differences between *gay* and *lesbi* zines, I also note some parallels between them in regard to the relationship between homosexual desire and national belonging.

PRODUCTION AND CONSUMPTION

In the United States, zines originated with sci-fi fanzines in the 1930s and 1940s, reappeared in the 1980s with punk counterculture, and then became a full-fledged genre in the 1990s (Duncombe 1997:6–8; Friedman 1997:9–13). One writer's definition of zines describes them as "noncommercial, nonprofessional, small-circulation magazines which their creators produce, publish, and distribute by themselves" (Duncombe 1997:6). In many respects this is an apt characterization of the print media created by *gay* Indonesians, and for this reason I use "zine" as the best English equivalent for these texts.

My primary data source is a textual analysis of the complete run of nine separate zines, for a total of 7,385 pages of text. This represents, to my knowledge and the knowledge of these zines' producers, 100 percent of all *gay* and *lesbi* zines ever produced from the appearance of the first such zine in 1982 up to November 2001. These zines were published in Surabaya, Yogyakarta, Jakarta, Makassar, and Semarang, with reader contributions literally from across the nation. Three of the texts are *lesbi* zines and the rest are *gay* zines, some of which have occasional *lesbi* content (see table 1). I hone in on two elements of these zines: the communication between producers and readers (editorials, letters to the zine, and personal ads), and the short stories [*cerita pendek* or *cerpen*] sent in by readers. In this category I also include the genre of true-experience narratives [*pengalaman sejati*], also sent in by readers, which do not differ greatly from the short stories.[4] I present images included in *gay* and *lesbi* zines to reinforce my analysis of the textual materials. A secondary source of data stems from my fieldwork, which includes interacting with *gay* and *lesbi* Indonesians as they create, read, discuss, and exchange zines. With the exceptions of *K-79* and *New Jaka-Jaka* (*NJJ*), I am personally acquainted with the producer of each *gay* and *lesbi* zine published up to November 2001.[5]

One should not be surprised to find some general distinctions in this wide spectrum of zines, based on the differing political and cultural sympathies of their editors. For instance, the zines published in Yogyakarta, a center of intellectual life and student activism, have tended to address issues of politics more directly than other zines, particularly following a change of editorship in 1999. The editors of *K-79* (published in Semarang) treated homosexuality as a disease in need of curing more than the editors of any other zine. Such distinctions, however, are quite minor and are further mitigated by the relatively high amount of content sent in by readers.

The fairly even tenor among zines extends chronologically as well as

TABLE 1 Background data on *gay* and *lesbi* zines.

Zine title	Abbreviation used in this chapter for this zine	Years published	Published in	Notes
G: *Gaya Hidup Ceria*	G	1982–84	Semarang	first *gay* zine
Jaka	–	1985–88	Yogyakarta	second *gay* zine
GAYa Nusantara	GN	1987–present	Surabaya	some former staff from G; *gay* zine (with some *lesbi* content)
GAYa Lestari	GL	1994	Jakarta	first *lesbi* zine; published inside GN
MitraS	–	1997–98	Jakarta	*lesbi* zine
Suvara Srikandi	*Suvara*	2000	Jakarta	*lesbi* zine; some former staff from *MitraS*
Jaka-Jaka	JJ	1992–94?	Yogyakarta	some former staff from *Jaka*; *gay* zine
New Jaka-Jaka	NJJ	1997–99?	Yogyakarta	some former staff from *Jaka-Jaka*; *gay* zine
Gaya Betawi (*Buku Seri IPOOS*)	GB	1994–98	Jakarta	*gay* zine
K-79/*GAYa Pandanaran*	–	1993	Semarang	*gay* zine
Gaya Celebes	–	1994–2002	Makassar	known as *Paraikatte* for first three issues; *gay* zine (with some *lesbi* content)

geographically. Indeed, the continuity in zine thematics is notable, given that the time period under discussion, 1982 to the early 2000s, was a time of great change in Indonesia. I can offer several hypotheses to explain this continuity. First, the sixteen-year period between 1982 and 1998 was actually a time of remarkable stability — enforced by an authoritarian government — compared with sixteen-year periods before it, for instance, 1965–81, 1948–64, or 1931–47. Second, 1982–98 was the period during which the *gay* subjectivity came into its own as a conceivable way of life, if one largely hidden from Indonesian society and rarely claimed as an identity. The *gay* subject position appears to have emerged in the 1970s, becoming in the 1980s and 1990s a socially self-conscious national network of primarily (but not solely) urban friendship networks and occasionally organizations. It originated through transforming conceptions of homosexuality from outside of Indonesia, with little input from "traditional" homosexualities and transgenderisms.

A distinct question of continuity arises in regard to the post-Soeharto period — that is, since 1998. Given the hypothesis I develop in this chapter concerning the relationship between nationalism and sexuality, one might reason that this major shift in the nation-state form would affect *gay* zines (and *gay* sexuality in general). A few of the examples of post-1998 zine materials cited in this chapter could be construed as indicating this kind of shift; however, for two reasons — one methodological, one theoretical — I want to caution against an interpretation based on the view that everything has changed. Methodologically, a confounding variable exists in that all *lesbi* zines and every *gay* zine except *GAYa Nusantara* ceased publication by 2003. From my conversations with zine producers and others during my visits to Indonesia since 1998, there seems to be a variety of reasons for this, including a fear of militant Islam in Yogyakarta, funding problems in Makassar and elsewhere, and group infighting or lack of subscribers (even during the 1982–1998 period, most zines were published for only a few years). Given that *GAYa Nusantara* continues to publish, and new *gay* and *lesbi* zines have come into existence since 2002, some novel linkages and delinkages between nationalism and sexuality may yet appear. For instance, one could hypothesize that current movements toward regional autonomy [*otonomi daerah*] could lead to efforts to reinterpret *gay* subjectivity in terms of locality and tradition. This seems unlikely, however, since these movements have tended to cast themselves in terms of revitalizing tradition, while the *gay* and *lesbi* subject positions are, if nothing else, clearly understood by those who inhabit them as novel (not originating in local tradition) and linked to national and transnational conceptions of sexuality.

My theoretical caution against assuming that the end of Soeharto's New Order rule in 1998 might have had a clear, consistent impact upon zines written since that time concerns the relationship between subject positions and social forces. Researchers have long known that social phenomena bear traces of their period of origin and do not shift in lockstep with broader cultural changes. As Émile Durkheim noted, "There is a close relation between what [a practice or an institution] is now and what it was in the past. Doubtless . . . it has been transformed . . . but these transformations in turn depend on what the point of departure was" (1963:180). An instance of this from the domain of sexuality can be seen in the case of the Euro-American gay and lesbian subject positions: many aspects of their dominant contemporary character (the notion of coming out, experiences of sexual drive and romance, conceptions of liberation, intersections with notions of race, and so on) remain shaped by the late-nineteenth-century sexological and psychoanalytic thinking in which they took form (Ferguson 2005; Foucault 1978; Stoler 1995, 2002). Since *gay* zines and subjectivities are shaped by New Order discourse, it is surely significant that these zines (and the contemporary concept of *gay* selfhood) took their current form in the 1980s and 1990s at the height of the New Order's hegemony.

Although I heuristically term these texts "zines," all rough equivalents are imperfect and *gay* zines diverge from the typical interpretations of Euro-American zines in two primary ways. First, analyses of Euro-American zines often claim that by and large they "are the expression and the product of an individual" (Duncombe 1997:12). Some analyses of Euro-American queer zines posit a voluntaristic self who discovers (even while destabilizing) identity through zines (Barnard 1996; Sutton 1999). Although individuals shape the tone and content of *gay* (and *lesbi*) zines, in Indonesia these zines not only are the work of a collective but often also constitute that collective as a group. Second, Indonesian *gay* zines diverge from dominant interpretations of Euro-American zines in that the Indonesian texts rarely present themselves as alternative in the sense of rejecting accepted understandings of propriety and citizenship. Even though producers of *gay* zines occasionally term them *media alter-*

natif, media semi-formal, or even amateur publications [*terbitan ama-tir*], for the most part their producers and readers simply call them magazines [*majalah*], bulletins [*buletin*], or periodicals [*buku seri*]. Although the producers of *gay* zines are aware of the marginality of *gay* sexualities in modern Indonesia, their rhetoric is not one of alterity but inclusion — a claim that *gay* men are just as Indonesian as members of general society [*masyarakat umum*]. *Gay* zines rarely leave Indonesia (i.e., they do not globalize as such), and they do not evince a strong disjuncture between producer and consumer. This is not only due to their informal circulation but also because readers contribute much of the copy by sending in short stories, poetry, letters, and images. Other readers appear in the personals section found in all *gay* zines — marketing themselves alongside others in search of sex, friendship, and romance.

The *gay* zines examined in this chapter generally measure 8.5 inches by 6.5 inches. They are typically twenty to sixty pages long (occasionally only two pages or as many as eighty), and most often they were produced by groups of two to five *gay* men using Windows-compatible desktop publishing software. In the early 1980s (and sometimes later), the copy was produced on typewriters, followed by manual cut-and-paste layout. The producers of these *gay* zines were usually in their twenties or early thirties. One reason for this age limitation is that heterosexual marriage made it more difficult to have the free time necessary to produce a zine; another is that because Indonesians did not start calling themselves *gay* in large numbers before the 1990s, relatively fewer older men considered themselves *gay* during the time period under consideration. The zines were reproduced at family-run photocopy shops or print houses and distributed by hand and through the mail. They rarely carried advertising (a marked contrast to most Indonesian print media since the eighteenth century [Adam 1995:3–4]).[6] *Gay* zines were published without government approval, and as a result they were almost never sold publicly (no zine examined in this chapter ever had a print run over eight hundred).[7] They were often given away for free or sold for about the same price as a regular magazine (four hundred rupiah for the first zine in 1982; six thousand rupiah, or about seventy-five cents, for *GAYa Nusantara* in the early 2000s). Although reports of zine subscribers as well as my own fieldwork clearly indicate that copies of zines are circulated among friends (*Jaka* [1983, 11:3; 1987, 13:3]; *GN* [1988, 3:6; 1988, 5/6:2]),[8] even if (following the estimate of some *gay* zine publishers) one assumes that each zine is read by ten persons, this translates to a total readership of at most seven thousand for any one zine and a generous estimate of eight thousand readers for all *gay* and *lesbi* zines at any point in time thus far.[9] To date, all *gay* and *lesbi* zines have been published in cities, but the heavy interchange among rural, semi-rural, and urban Indonesians means that the zines have a rural readership as well.

Most Indonesians who produce and read *gay* zines already see themselves as *gay* through encounters with the terms in regular mass media. Since zines are published and circulated outside of official channels, their consumption is rarely solitary. Most people who read zines were apparently first given the zine by someone else and often continue to exchange zines with friends, even if they become subscribers. The consumption of these zines sustains *gay* networks rather than alienating the reader from preexisting kinship or community ties. In other words, if and when *gay* Indonesians begin to read zines, this tends not to isolate them but can lead to the creation of new networks through the trading of the zines.[10]

That these zines do not appear to introduce Indonesians to *gay* subjectivities does not mean, however, that they have no influence on the character of these subjectivities. For instance, the longest-running and most widely distributed zine, *GAYa Nusantara*, combines in its name *gaya* (which means "style" but can also mean "gay," with the first three letters capitalized) with *Nusantara* which means both "archipelago" and, colloquially, Indonesia itself). This is meant to recall the archipelago concept [*wawasan nusantara*], a key trope of national ideology that is analogous to (if more formalized than) the "melting pot" in the United States.[11] Since this zine began publishing in 1987, about half of *gay* groups (and several *lesbi* groups) have named themselves with reference to *GAYa Nusantara* by pairing *GAYa* with a "local" term, even if the group does not publish a zine. Groups named in this manner that have published a zine include *GAYa Celebes* in Sulawesi and *GAYa Betawi* in Jakarta; zines named in this manner include *GAYa LEStari* (*GL*), a *lesbi* zine from Jakarta; groups without zines include *GAYa Siak* in Sumatra, *GAYa Tepian Samarinda* in Kalimantan (Indonesian Borneo), *GAYa Semarang* in Java, *GAYa Dewata* in Bali, *GAYa Batam* on Batam island, and *GAYa Intim* in Ambon (which ceased operation in the early 1990s). In 1993 the zine *K-79* changed its name to *GAYa Pandanaran* (*GP*) (after the hero of a local myth) with the following explanation:

Di tahun ini nampaknya banyak sekali	This year we see the emergence of very
muncul organisasi GAY, semoga dengan	many GAY organizations; we hope that
munculnya wajah baru dengan beraneka	with the emergence of these new faces
GAYA kita akan menambah persatuan	with diverse STYLES we will add to the
dan kesatuan antara sesama. . . .	unity and integrity between us. . . .
	(1993, 3:8)

The tropes apparent in this excerpt are common in zines from the early 1980s to the present. As indicated by the use of set nationalist phrases like "unity and integrity" [persatuan dan kesatuan] and "diversity" [aneka], as well as the metonymic chain that links gay to gaya to nusantara, the use of GAYa is part of a larger pattern of migration, letter writing, and imagining through which gay and lesbi Indonesians see themselves as national. Even this brief example illustrates how, in Indonesia, forms of mass media not only play an important role in "mediating" understandings of the nation in the context of globalization (Jurriëns 2004), but also help constitute notions of national selfhood through the "dubbing" of ostensibly globalized and ethnolocalized images, texts, and meanings (Boellstorff 2002, 2003). This shows how the ultimate impact of gay and lesbi zines will certainly be greater than the level of readership alone might imply; as is true for mass media generally, their effects on social relations and cultural logics are multilayered and contingent.

REPRESENTATION AND THE CRISIS OF CONTEXT

As noted earlier, this chapter focuses on the interaction of two of the most pervasive discourses or zones in gay zines — homosexual desire and a desire for national belonging. Although occasionally the topic of explicit commentary, these discourses (and their intersections) are often implicit. The analytic that I bring to this material parallels that commonly found in ethnography: the goal is not simply to report what people say they do but also to interpret the often tacit assumptions by which their invested actions make sense to them.

A growing debate in media studies, sometimes called the crisis of context, asks whether mass media can be understood in isolation from the everyday milieu in which they are produced and consumed (Schlecker and Hirsch 2001). Although fieldwork informs my analysis, in this chapter I do not attempt to show that the cultural logics I find in *gay* zines are present in other contexts. This is partly due to limitations of space (it should be quite easy to see evidence of these cultural logics in the other chapters of this book). Additionally, I am uneasy with the idea that there is nothing to learn from texts themselves as documents that crystallize and comment upon culture. The demand that every textual analysis comes paired with fieldwork is indicative of a particular theory of knowledge, which Marilyn Strathern terms "merography":

> Merography (literally *mero* = part, *graphy* = writing) is about the way in which Euro-Americans make sense of things by describing them as part of something else. . . . However, as Euro-American knowledge conventions posit the a priori uniqueness of all given entities (individuals, objects, actions, events, etc.), "nothing is in fact ever simply part of a whole because another view, another perspective or domain, may redescribe [write] it as 'part of something else' " (Strathern 1992b:73). A priori uniqueness entails that while, for instance, two individuals may be described as part of the same contexts of occupation, religion and age, there will always be another context that will exclude one of them. Every analogy is thus bound to be a partial one. (Schlecker and Hirsch 2001:71)

It thus follows that *"the turn to ethnography in media and science studies indicates the ambition of researchers to combine multiple contexts, hoping to garner ever more knowledge"* (Schlecker and Hirsch 2001:75, emphasis in original). The notion of merography is helpful for reconsidering notions of interdisciplinarity: if interdisciplinarity is construed as adding contexts in the service of knowledge, this merographic assumption not only reifies disciplines but creates an unending demand for more contexts. Queer studies itself is highly merographic; the predominant way in which queer analysis proceeds is by showing how, for instance, understandings of race shape understandings of sexuality.

In two respects, my analysis remains merographic: it aims to shed light on *gay* Indonesians more generally, and I bring together two zones of desire into an interzone in which greater understanding can take place. However, I frame this intersection of discourses not as a whole comprised of parts but as an unstable conjunction — a coincidence (see the introduction). Taking a cue from *gay* Indonesians, I employ the archipelago metaphor as one mitigating strategy, which is why I find that the spatial metaphor of zones usefully complements the auditory metaphor of discourse (Boellstorff 2005). An archipelago is whole and part: it does not have a clear external boundary marking it off as part of something else, yet it incorporates what appear to be internal wholes in the shape of bounded islands. As Indonesians are keenly aware, archipelagos are not described but delimited; their boundaries are not given. An archipelagic methodology is antimerographic in that it participates in the constitution of the subject of study. It gestures toward an alternate ethnography that can "acknowledge that description and what it describes are not separable . . . With this re-envisioned ethnography, each description is understood to contain within itself that which it describes. Here, part and whole collapse into one" (Schlecker and Hirsch 2001:80). Here too, interdisciplinarity might be framed in archipelagic terms. It could be that exchanges between disciplines do not blur boundaries but make their borders more porous, so that truth is produced through coincidence.

I also attempt to resist a merographic framework by questioning the distinction between text and context. Such a division takes for granted what should be the target of analysis: the entextualizing processes by which things or ideas come to be seen as set apart from any particular context (Silverstein and Urban 1996:10; see also Silverstein 1992). For many *gay* Indonesians, zines are not just texts but also a primary context through which they understand their desires for homosex and membership in a national *gay* reading public: "where else are we free to be open [*terbuka*] if not in GN?" (*GN* 1991, 15:8).[12] I thus treat these zines not as artifacts but as socially situated processes that concretize, comment upon, and communicate key aspects of the *gay* subject position. I do not imply that all *gay* Indonesians think exactly in line with the cultural logics found in zines, but rather that they find such logics intelligible even if they disagree with them. Zines provide a window onto broader systems of meaning. Many Indonesianist anthropologists have had great success in examining texts from an ethnographic perspective (Rodgers 1995; Siegel 1997; Watson 2000). Although such work often has a historical emphasis, here Akhil Gupta's admonition regarding the use of newspapers is pertinent to zines: "Obviously, perceiving them as having a privileged relation to the truth of social life is naive; they have much to offer us, however, when seen as a major discursive form through which daily life is narrativized and collectivities imagined . . . Treated with benign neglect by students of contemporary life, they mysteriously meta-morphose into invaluable 'field data' once they have yellowed around the edges and fallen apart at the creases. And yet it is not entirely clear by what alchemy time turns the 'secondary' data of the anthropologist into the 'primary' data of the historian" (1995:385).

Of course, although *gay* zines present many dimensions of the *gay* world and affect its character, the zines are not isomorphic with that world and their producers are not necessarily representative. Even though lower-class groups have created zines, in general the producers of zines — like the producers of mass media in general — are better educated (though not necessarily wealthier) than the readers of zines.[13] One founding member of *Jaka* cited among others Friedrich Nietzsche, Albert Camus, and Jean-Paul Sartre in his editorials (1985, 4:2, 5:2, and 1986, 6:2, respectively). This issue of social status is a point of commonality between *gay* and *lesbi* zines: the form for entering oneself into the personal ads section of *MitraS* provides three options (in English) for "last education completed": high school, academy, and university. In 1997 the editors of *New Jaka-Jaka* (a more recent *gay* zine published in Yogya-karta) apologized for the lateness of the July edition by noting that "a large number of our members have been busy with their end-of-semester exams" (1997, 2:3).

Perhaps the most salient consequence of this disjuncture is that relative to the readers, the zine producers tend to be better informed about gay and lesbian communities and movements outside Indonesia. *Lesbi* producers of zines, in comparison with the predominantly working-class *lesbi* women whom I have met through my fieldwork, are better linked to Indonesian and transnational feminist movements (including the Indonesian Women's Coalition and the Asian Lesbian Network) (*Swara* 2000, 1:6). Similarly, *gay* producers of zines are better linked to Indonesian and transnational HIV/AIDS prevention and treatment networks than is the average *gay* man.[14] A second disjuncture, linked to the first, is that the producers of zines tend to be more politicized than other *gay* or *lesbi* Indonesians. Nowhere is this better illustrated than in the 1993 imaginary interview [*wawancara imaginer*] in *Jaka-Jaka* (*JJ*) between a "member of the editorial staff" and "an imaginary *gay* character" (1993, 4:15–17). When asked why the number of *gay* men seems to be increasing, the imaginary character replied that, "in my opinion, what's increasing isn't the total number of *gay* people, but that more *gay* people are brave enough to open themselves" (15). When the interviewers pointed out that *gay* Indonesians are not well accepted by society, the imaginary character countered that "there will always be colonialism [*penjajahan*] of all forms. The remaining problem is if those who are colonized will accept that or not . . . If our freedom fighters had thought ahead of time if they had the military strength to expel the Dutch, we certainly would not yet be free" (16–17). In Indonesia, such imaginary interviews can be used to caricature public figures (see Sulistyo 2002). This presents a difficulty in the case of *gay* men, however, since very few *gay* Indonesians think of their sexualities in such explicitly politicized and public terms (only a literal handful have been willing to be identified as *gay* by the general mass media). Perhaps for this reason, the producers of *Jaka-Jaka* were compelled to fabricate an interviewee, a circumstance that makes the ties between the *gay* subject position and national discourse all the more intriguing.

In this imagined interview, the producers of *Jaka-Jaka* forge a corollary to the imagined national community — the imagined *gay* national subject. Although the politicized dimension of this imagined subject diverges from many *gay* Indonesians' self-understandings, it shares with them a desire for national belonging. This idealized political *gay* subject speaks of opening oneself [*membuka diri*] to the world in general — a rough analogue to the notion of coming out in many Euro-American queer communities. In the Indonesian context, this is an unusual use of the "opening oneself" metaphor; the metaphor usually refers only to participation in the *gay* world [*dunia gay*] to the extent that heterosexual marriage is not seen as incompatible with *gay* subjectivity (see Boellstorff 1999). For instance, a *gay* man will refer to a city as *terbuka*, implying not that *gay* men in that city are open to the public but that they are open to each other and meet in parks, discos, and other locales in large numbers.

The hegemony of national discourse appears in the linkage of nationalism to this unusual notion of coming out to society in general. For instance, the relatively small number of *gay* Indonesians who know of the English term "coming out" often translate the phrase not as *membuka diri* but instead as *memproklamirkan diri* (to proclaim oneself — a reference to Sukarno's 1945 *proklamasi* of an independent Indonesian state); *17 Augustan alias proklamasi* (referring to Indonesia's Independence Day); or *merdeka* (freedom, a key term of the anticolonial struggle) (*GAYa Betawi* 1993, 6:14, 7:17, and 1994, 12:16, respectively; see also the discussion of the English term "coming out" in *GAYa Nusantara* 2001, 86:17). There are even phrases such as "freedom or death" [*merdeka atau mati*] also from the anticolonial struggle (*GAYa Betawi* 1994, 13:3). *Gay* zines often oscillate between this notion of opening oneself to the whole world and the more common sense that the *gay* world need not intersect with the regular world. A *gay* man once wrote to an advice column in *New Jaka-Jaka* with the problem that he also wanted to marry a woman and thus was not sure which world he should choose. The publishers recommended that he "just take up both of them, live in two worlds," but they also emphasized that in the *gay* world he should "struggle against the injustice and colonialism against yourself as a *gay* person" and "free [*memerdekakan*] yourself" (*NJJ* 1997, 4:13–14). This exchange, where contrasting views of heterosexual marriage are juxtaposed without comment, illustrates a broader point: the disjuncture between producers and readers is less complete than might first appear. This is mainly due to the extensive use by *gay* zines of materials mailed in by readers (often 75 percent of an issue's contents originate in this way). Subscriber surveys conducted by *GAYa Nusantara* have indicated that while some readers are certainly well educated, others are of average schooling—often from small villages outside the political, economic, and cultural hegemony of Java.

LOVE AND THE NATION IN INDONESIAN PRINT MEDIA

Gay zines link personal narrative, love, and national consciousness in a manner consistent with tropes of Indonesian literature. As Susan Rogers notes, "Personal narratives have deep public resonance in twentieth-century Indonesia, where the process of growing to adulthood and traversing a life is often recalled in terms similar to those used to think about society and the past in a more general sense. . . . In other words, Indonesian historical memory and personal memory are both animated by certain closely related key scenarios and social images, and societal histories and personal narratives interpenetrate" (1995:3). Although being love sick [*sakit cinta*] is, as James Siegel notes, a powerful theme in Indonesian nationalist literature, "sick person" [*orang sakit*] is ironically now a term that some *gay* Indonesians use to refer to themselves

(1997:145). How can a sick love complete its circuit of recognition? This is the crucial question addressed implicitly and explicitly in *gay* zines, the question for which prestasis will be the answer. Love for *gay* Indonesians is also a desire for sexual citizenship.

A key point in this regard, one I return to in chapter 6, is that while gender and sexuality obviously intersect and are mutually constitutive, they are also analytically distinct; as such, it is important not to conflate them. Although in *gay* zines *gay* Indonesians address a sense of failure (to belong), they do not experience this in terms of gender per se. They do not feel that they are failures as men; they do not feel, for instance, that they are warias (see chapter 2). Although warias, who are acknowledged if often ridiculed members of Indonesian society, have never published zines despite having the educational skills to do so, zines have proven to be an important and enduring means by which *gay* men reflect upon and make claims for a national belonging that feels beyond their grasp.

The importance of love is linked to the fact that in Indonesia, as in much of the world, marriage has become construed as a matter of choice rather than arrangement (Chauncey 2004; Coontz 2005). When marriages are arranged, as was the norm in Indonesia until the 1960s, sexual orientation is quite irrelevant; one could argue it does not exist as a conceptual category. The prevalence of potions and spells used to get husbands and wives to find each other attractive and have sex, as well as a history in much of the archipelago of high rates of divorce after the first marriage or of not marrying at all, indicates that such attraction was not assumed to happen "naturally" (Chabot 1996:195–99, 206, 227–29; Jones 1994). Writing of the late 1960s, Barbara Hatley notes this shift in her discussion of *ludruk* theater in Java: "Most Ludruk plots focus on marriage, often depicting the conflicts involved in an arranged match . . . Ludruk teaches that marriages arranged according to class considerations and family connections can often lead to unhappiness and that marriage based on romantic love is the modern ideal" (1971:96). Arrangement is certainly not gone from the marriage scene in Indonesia, and there are ways that parents and others can exert subtle and not-so-subtle pressure on the unmarried, but the norm is now that marriage should be based on love and choice.

This shift to chosen or love marriage has enormous consequences. For instance, it links marriage to a whole field of modernity structured by "choice" — just as you vote to choose a leader and choose products in the free market, so you now are to choose your spouse in a marriage market. But perhaps the most far-reaching consequence of the shift to chosen or love marriage is that this form of marriage brings sexual orientation into being as a new kind of problem. Since arranged marriages are often construed as unions between two entire families, not just two individuals, the failure of an arranged marriage lies primarily on the family's failure to select a proper spouse. But marriage based on choice and love implies a choosing self whose choice must be a heterosexual one: men choosing women and women choosing men.[15] In such a regime *gay* Indonesians fail as sexual citizens, even if they marry heterosexually in addition to their lives in the "*gay* world"; their homosexual love lies outside the heteronormativity of the family principle, where the nation is seen to be made up of heterosexual nuclear families. Against Foucault's (1991) claim that the importance of the family fades in modern societies, to be replaced by statistical conceptions of "the population," powerful links between heteronormative family and nation are being redeployed in new ways in the West (particularly in the United States) and in a range of postcolonial contexts as well. An examination of the two zones of desire described below, as well as the interzone of their imbrication, can thus shed light on the way that heteronormativity can be sutured to national belonging in the contemporary world.

THE FIRST ZONE: HOMOSEX AND HOMOLOVE

One zone of desire in *gay* zines is homosex: the representation, discussion, and celebration of sexuality between men (or between women in the case of *lesbi* zines). Positive discussion of homosexuality appears in virtually no other Indonesian mass media beyond these zines, in which such discussions are a constant theme of personals, editorials, dictionaries of *gay* language, guides to outdoor meeting areas [*tempat ngeber*], and images (see figures 2–5).[16] Moreover, homosexuality is a guiding force in the narratives that make up the bulk of *gay* zines.

Rarely do the zines' images and narratives of homosexuality present explicit sex (see figures 4–5 for exceptions). Obviously this is not because *gay* Indonesians lack interest in eroticism; neither is it simply to avoid censorship, since zines are not published through legal channels. When publishers of *gay* zines politely reject requests for sexually explicit stories or images, they cite not a fear of censorship but the possible

FIGURE 2
The object of male
homosexual desire in an
image from *Jaka* (1985, 5:1).
Here the erotics involved
concern desire for bodies.

FIGURE 3
The object of female
homosexual desire in an
image from *GL* (1994,
3:16 [inside *GN* 31]).
Here the erotics involved
concern desire for sexual
acts.

FIGURE 4
Image from *K-79*
(1993:16) featuring
explicit homosex.

foreclosing of recognition: the failure to be accepted by society [*diterima oleh masyarakat*]. The zine should be proper [*sopan*]; a wish expressed not only by publishers but by readers who send in letters complaining of explicit representations of sex. A striking example of this took place in 1993, when *GAYa Betawi* (*GB*) published two versions of its fifth issue. The first contained explicit representations of sex between men (both line drawings and reproductions of Euro-American gay pornography). The editorial in the second version of the issue noted that the first had been found invalid [*tidak sah*] by *GAYa Betawi*'s own editors because it had "gone against the ethical codes of journalism and society" (*GB* 1993, 5:3). This is the only case of any *gay* zine republishing an issue. The second issue noted that the general magazine *Jakarta-Jakarta* had for the first time written about the zine (and the organization that produced it), but had unfortunately focused on the sexually explicit issue. This coverage thus gave the impression that *gay* men are only interested in sex, when in fact the goal of the zine and organization was to create unity [*persatuan*, a nationalist term] among *gay* men and to motivate them to do positive things for society (*GB* 1993, 6:24–25).

Despite this deemphasis on sex, erotics remain present in zines by appearing in stories that speak of sexual acts (often in veiled terms) as well as in imagery that emphasizes the face (and often the partially clothed body). One difference between *gay* and *lesbi* zines is that there

FIGURE 5
Image from *GN*
(1988, 4:31) featuring sex
between a Euro-American and
an Indonesian.

have been very few images of *lesbi* women (and none in any state of undress). Images of *lesbi* women are typically in the form of drawings, while images of *gay* men are fairly evenly divided between photographs and drawings. This does not seem linked to the admonitions against showing the female body in Islam, since eroticized images of Indonesian women are common in contemporary Indonesian advertising and entertainment. The absence of photographs of *lesbi* women seems instead to flag questions of visibility (see figures 6–7). Although few *gay* men wish to appear in electronic or print media, even with a false name, a surprising number are eager to appear in zines as cover boys—for which they provide photographs and even home addresses. The number of *gay* men willing to be photographed is still small in absolute terms, but even fewer *lesbi* women are willing to be photographed. The greater tendency of women to be dependent on either a husband or family members for financial support—or if in a higher class to be in a career where female propriety is emphasized—makes such visibility an even greater risk.

What *gay* and *lesbi* zines emphasize is not sex but love. In reading over seven thousand pages of zine text I did not find a single issue of any *gay* zine in which the topic of love did not appear; indeed, often two or three

GAYA LESTARI

edisi 05 April 1994

Halaman Lesbian Indonesia, atas kerja sama dengan Gaya Nusantara dan di bawah koordinasi KKGLN (Kelompok Kerja Lesbian dan Gay Nusantara) serta Chandra Kirana (Jaringan Kerja Lesbian di Indonesia).

Gaya Lestari adalah halaman lesbian dalam buku seri Gaya Nusantara. Terbit dua bulanan. UNTUK KALANGAN SENDIRI. Diterbitkan oleh "CHANDRA KIRANA", jaringan kerja lesbian di Indonesia. Jaringan kerja ini bekerjasama dengan GAYA NUSANTARA dalam koordinasi KKLGN (Kelompok Kerja Lesbian dan Gay Nusantara). Terbuka bagi setiap lesbian dan seks alternatif yang lain tanpa memandang SARA. Chandra Kirana anggota jaringan ALN dan ILGA [International Lesbian and Gay Association]. Edisi ini diracik dan dikerjakan oleh Djuna, Gayatri dan Kenia. Penulis Tetap: Meylankolis Queen Terima kasih kepada rekanita Rion atas kiriman karyanya. Alamat Pos: Gaya Lestari, P.O. Box 6525 JKSDW Jakarta 12065

FIGURE 6   Women as flowers: a symbol of *lesbi* community and social invisibility (*GL* 1994, 5:1 [inside *GN* 28]). The text identifies the zine as part of the "Archipelago Lesbian and Gay Network" and as open to all ethnicities.

Kembangkanlah dirimu.

FIGURE 7
The back cover of *GL*
(1994, 5:1 [inside *GN* 28]):
a flower with the caption
"Develop yourself."

articles will have "love" in their titles. A first clue to this discourse of love is a particular semiotic chain: sexual acts (kissing, anal penetration, rubbing genitals together, and so on) are distinguished from generalized sexual lust [*nafsu* or *birahi*], which in turn is distinguished from love. An early reader of *GAYa Nusantara* complained of sexually suggestive images by invoking this chain: "I don't want to be a hypocrite because even I have a million sexual desires. But what is more valuable than all that, friends, is Love. Love is what's given me the strength to live this long. . . . What will happen if we continue to allow lust to hold the reins of this life, which is already set apart?" (*GN*, 1988, 3:6–7). In a short story from 1991, Andre confronts his *gay* friend Yuzo, who seems interested only in sex. Andre confesses his love to Yuzo, who asks, "Why have you been avoiding me?" Andre replies: "Because you just think of me as a sexual object! I can't live like you, switching partners and forgetting them. I desire a proper and *normal* life like *hetero* people, to meet someone and fall in love with them so as to live together. I can't live prioritizing sex over love" (*GN* 1991, 15:29–30). In one installment of a comic strip that ran in *Jaka* from August 1985 to December 1986, the protagonist (named *Jaka* [bachelor]) becomes promiscuous after his lover, Tomo, marries a woman. Tomo learns of Jaka's behavior, and in the final two panels (see figure 8, lower right-hand corner) he confronts Jaka at the gym: "This is the image of '*gay*' that you present to me! Apparently it's true that you're just chasing satisfaction of your lusts!" In the following issue Jaka runs away to Europe and with the help of a white boyfriend—whom he does not love—sets up a salon business. Sitting alone at night he confesses to himself: "Now I can buy anything I want

FIGURE 8   The valorization of love over desire
(*Jaka* 1985, 5:12).

with my money, but what I need now is 'love!' Where I can share good and bad times, serve his needs. That has no price. . . . Oh, how beautiful it would be!" (1986, 6:14). When a man who saw himself as *normal* had sex with another man and wanted to know whether he might be *gay*, the editors of *GAYa Betawi* responded: "To become *gay* is not just proven with same-gender sex but other factors like the feeling of love. . . . If after that event you continue to have same-sex relations with the addition of feelings of love, . . . it could then be said that you are *gay*" (1997, 16:24). Employing nationalist language, an article sent to *K-79* in 1993 noted that "love unites [*mempersatukan*] us. . . . Without love we are nothing, creatures without connection. . . . When will it be that we can find a pure love that is not based on lust and selfishness?" (4:7–8).

The pattern is clear: sex is displaced onto desire and then onto love, with each term more valorized than its predecessor.[17] Desire is presented as unidirectional, while love is framed as inherently relational and thus social; proper to a citizen-subject who gives and receives. In Foucauldian terms, this is not repression but an incitement that beckons sex and desire into the service of love. This incitement takes the form of discovery that the desired Other reciprocates love; that is, the desired Other recognizes one as *gay*. Even when self-knowledge is the theme, recognition usually figures prominently — and this also occurs in *lesbi* zines, as in the autobiographical narrative of Leonie, a *lesbi* woman: "When I was in my second year of high school, I was invited by a girl-friend to watch a porno film and by chance that film had a *lesbi* scene. There I got to know the life of *lesbi* in bed. Then with another girlfriend, for the first time I acted out such a scene and lost my virginity" (*GN* 1989, 10:37). In the *gay* short story "I Reach for My Love," the protagonist, Koko, is in high school and attracted to Yogi, a young man one class ahead of him. Yogi has been following Koko around, but Yogi's motivations remain obscure to Koko while he is "still stupid" [*masih bodoh*, a phrase often used in nationalist literature to refer to premodern ways of thinking]. One day, however, Koko states: "As we were walking home, Yogi explained the contents of his heart to me. Before he had spoken very long, it was clear that the path of his life was almost identical to my own autobiography [*otobiografi*]. My feelings at that point were like a fish splashing into the water, or a bowl meeting its lid" (*Jaka* 1985, 1:11–14).

There is joy in discovery, and discovery in these narratives is the dis-

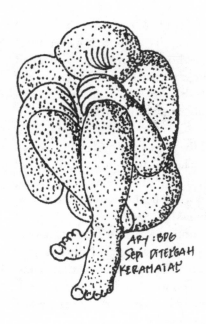

FIGURE 9
"Lonely in the midst of the
bustle" (*GN* 1994, 27:7).

covery of recognition; it is a climactic, almost orgasmic, moment, like
when a fish meets water or a bowl meets its lid. For some *gay* men, but
especially for *lesbi* women, the period prior to discovery is marked by
isolation, a sense of being an island alone in a sea of heteronormativity
(see figure 9). Since it is self-evident to *gay* Indonesians (and other Indonesians) that the concept *gay* originates neither in locality nor tradition,
the moment of discovery—when one is recognized, when the desired
Other becomes a desiring Other—replaces feelings of isolation with a
sense of belonging to a national homosexual community. This founding
in the nation shapes the sense of an imagined archipelagic communion
with gay and lesbian persons across the national archipelago and outside
of Indonesia as well (Boellstorff 2005). These implicit cultural linkages among zines, isolation, and an archipelagic imaginary occasionally
become the topic of commentary. In one cartoon, an archipelagic twist
on the trope of the deserted island, a man dreaming of food finds a
zine parachuted to him as a source of sustenance (see figure 10). Behind
the image (meant for an Indonesian readership where everyone lives
on an island) is an archipelagic zone of homosexual desire, with zines
connecting "islands" of individuals and communities. The image shows

FIGURE 10   A zine as a link for individuals beyond their "islands" (*GB* 1993, 6:30).

the climactic moment right before the *gay* man makes contact with the zine.

SEPARATION

In the short story "A Thought," the protagonist, Iwan, falls in love with a *normal* friend, Soni. He decides that he must be honest about his self [*jati dirinya*] and asks Soni, "If you had a friend who turned out to be *gay*, what would be your reaction?" Soni replies he would feel "just as usual," and a surprised Iwan tells Soni that he is *gay* and loves him. Soni then admits that he has a "secret" of his own: he is *gay* and reciprocates Iwan's love. Iwan is shocked by the dual discovery: "Soni, who's always being chased by women, who's handsome, who's smart, who has so many achievements [*prestasi*], is *gay* too!" Iwan is full of happiness, but the following week he learns that Soni has moved to Australia without leaving word (*GN* 1997, 51:35). Iwan, and the zine reader, are left in the dark.

If discovery involves recognition by the now-desiring Other, in *gay* zines this circuit usually leads to separation. "Happily ever after" stories in which two *gay* men share a household or sustain an ongoing relationship are rare. *Gay* zines portray separation as the inevitable complement to discovery: one recounting of a *gay* man's life in Yogyakarta concluded that, "like the classic *gay* story, he had to be separated from his boyfriend" when the boyfriend left town to continue his schooling (*NJJ* 1997, 3:26). Sometimes a general sense of social rejection leads to separation. In the "true experiences" story "Separation" [*Perpisahan*], the *gay* protagonist tells his lover that they must separate after two years because the protagonist's mother has discovered the relationship: "You forget that we live in society, we cannot live apart from it, and we can't just do anything we want. Sometimes society can be more cruel than we suspect" (*GN* 1994, 30:20).

Gay and *lesbi* zines often portray some force as causing separation by coming "between" love. In the true-experiences story "Between Love and Greed," Rion, a *lesbi* woman, falls in love with Mira — who is glamorous, beautiful, and married to Franz. Franz thinks that Rion is just Mira's friend and allows them to spend time together. Rion and Mira discover love for each other, and Mira leaves Franz. However, because Rion cannot keep Mira in the glamorous lifestyle to which she is accustomed, "Mira decided to return to Franz's embraces" (*GL* 1994, 5:8–9 [in *GN* 28]). In another true-experiences story, "Between Duty and Love," the *gay* protagonist falls in love with a civil servant temporarily filling a position in a small Central Sulawesi town. Once his two-week shift is completed, the civil servant's duty is to return to Manado (the provincial capital of North Sulawesi). On their final night together, the civil servant begs for forgiveness in national terms: "We both serve the needs of our country and people" (*GN* 1993, 22:20). In a third such story, "Between Love, Parents, and Studies," Edo, a *gay* man from Biak, a small island near the island of New Guinea, encounters problems when his boyfriend's former lover calls Edo's parents to tell them that Edo is having sex with a man. Edo's fanatically Christian parents beat him and forbid him to see his lover. Here, the boyfriend's former lover commits a kind of anti-prestasi that separates Edo from both *gay* community and family (*GN* 1997, 48:23–25).[18]

The overall dynamic of *gay* zine narratives, then, is one of discovery followed by separation from a beloved Other. *Gay* Indonesians discover recognition, but the person who makes this recognition possible — the *gay* lover — is placed beyond reach. This narrative structure predominates despite the fact that it is not a simple reflection of *gay* experience. Although their lives can be hard, many *gay* men do continue same-sex romances after heterosexual marriage. The attraction of these narratives lies in how they narrativize and concretize a belief that to be *gay* involves a profound sense of separation. What is it that gives this separation its special sting in *gay* zines — a sense not just of desire thwarted but also of selfhood called into question? The answer lies in the nexus between love and nation.

SECOND ZONE: NATIONAL SEXUALITIES

Although the first zone of desire is concerned with homosex and homo-love, the second relates to the sense that the *gay* subject position has a national scale. Three factors sustain this linkage to national culture: language, a deemphasis of the local and ethnic, and a deemphasis of Euro-America. All *gay* (and *lesbi*) zines ever published have used Indonesian, never an ethnolocalized language like Javanese, Balinese, or Batak (except for occasional terms suggesting local color).[19] Since zines are published informally, this use of Indonesian is not simply a matter of kowtowing to state policy. My fieldwork indicates that publishing a zine in any other language has simply never occurred to these Indonesians. Why make it inaccessible to so many potential readers — that is, the "we" referenced so often in zine writing?

In line with foregrounding the national tongue, *gay* zines invoke an Indonesian personhood. Although those calling themselves *gay* may think of themselves in ethnolocalized terms — as Bugis, Javanese, and so on — in some aspects of their lives, in regard to their sexualities, they think of themselves as Indonesians. One motivation for this is that the term *gay* appears to be understood universally not to be an indigenous concept — I know of no cases in which one learns the meaning of *gay* from one's family or tradition. Such distancing from ethnolocality is encapsulated in names like *GAYa Betawi*, where terms indexing ethnolocality are subsumed in the pattern *GAYa X*. Since adjectives follow nouns in Indonesian, this pattern ontologizes the national; the "local" term appears as modifier and *GAYa* (based on *GAYa Nusantara*) as the subject.[20] To my knowledge, almost every appearance of ethnolocality in *gay* zines has occurred when Dédé Oetomo has published occasional articles on what some term traditional homosexualities and transgenderisms (collected in

Oetomo 2001; see Boellstorff 2005). These articles appear under the rubric "customs of the archipelago" [*adat Nusantara*]. The articles also frame the persons involved as outside the imagined readership of *gay* zines. Their customs are presented as interesting, but never to my knowledge are they set forth as providing an autochthonous pedigree for *gay* subjectivities (and never for *lesbi* subjectivities, since such traditional homosexualities and transgenderisms are almost exclusively associated with men).[21]

The world beyond Indonesia plays a relatively minor role in *gay* zines. Although occasionally news clips or lengthier articles on gay or lesbian life in the non-Euro-American world (for instance, the Philippines or Brazil) are reprinted, such reportage appears only sporadically in short stories, poetry, or letters sent in by readers. Euro-America itself (which for most Indonesians includes Australia and New Zealand) does appear in these zines but is not emphasized. Although *gay* Indonesians clearly understand the term *gay* to be derived in part from the Euro-American concept "gay," it is portrayed in national terms. This does not mean that linkages to Euro-American homosexualities are erased or denied: an archipelagic relationship pertains in which *gay* Indonesians are one island in an openly acknowledged, even celebrated, global archipelago of homosexuality. Such a sense of global belonging with regard to sexuality in no way precludes anti-American or antiglobalization views with regard to political and economic issues. *Gay* zines sustain this archipelagic relationship by referencing Euro-America, but these references are intermittent, in keeping with the fact that most *gay* Indonesians do not speak English or any Euro-American language, have never traveled outside Indonesia, and only rarely if at all have met gay or lesbian Euro-Americans. *Gay* zines have incorporated Euro-Americans since the early 1980s in the form of drawings (see figure 5) or characters in short stories; recall the white boyfriend of *Jaka* (see figure 8). Euro-Americans also appear in stories as tourists falling in love with Indonesian men, and Euro-American gay men have sent in personals to *gay* zines since their beginnings. In 1998 *GAYa Nusantara* even ran what was jokingly termed the "white-guy edition" [*edisi bule*] (no. 54), which included tips on how to respond to personals from white men.

Stories on lesbian and gay life in Australia, Europe, or the United States occasionally appear in both *gay* and *lesbi* zines. The *lesbi* zine

MitraS has run articles on violence against lesbians in the United States (1997, 1:8) and even reprinted Euro-American erotic lesbian short stories (1998; 2:15–17, 3:15–18). One of the starkest differences between *gay* and *lesbi* zines is that when *lesbi* zines report on Euro-America they are more likely to emphasize homophobia and violence against homosexuals, concluding that while things are difficult in Indonesia, *lesbi* women are better off than their Euro-American sisters (a perspective I have also encountered in my fieldwork). In contrast, *gay* men usually assume Euro-America is a gay paradise, with "free sex" delinked from bonds of relationship, and at the same time, legal same-sex marriage. Despite these varied ways in which Euro-America figures in *gay* and *lesbi* zines, however, its footprint is quite small. Like the concept of the nation, which originated outside Indonesia but is now seen as authentically Indonesian, in fundamental ways *gay* and *lesbi* Indonesians consider their sexualities to be founded in the archipelago.

INVOKING THE NATION

Beyond these implicit references, the nation figures as a zone of desire explicitly, as the background against which *gay* selfhood and community play themselves out. This appears most succinctly in terms like "*Indo*G*sian* people" (*bangsa Indo*G*sia*) (GN 1994, 25:40), in which *G* (a common written shorthand for *gay*) is literally implanted into the core of "Indonesia." More extended references to the nation are common in editorials. In the first issue of *GAYa Nusantara*, the publishers justified the incorporation of *nusantara* in the zine's name as a reminder of "the special national/archipelagic [*khas Nusantara*] lives of *lesbi* and *gay* people, which we hope will be reflected and supported by this bulletin" (1987, 1:6). When a reader complained that early *GAYa Nusantara* zine covers had too many images of shadow-puppet theater, the publishers replied, "There has been an effort to give *GAYa Nusantara*'s covers themes of the archipelago's culture" (GN 1988, 3:6). Six years later, the zine commemorated Independence Day (August 17) with a cover featuring two men standing side by side; one held the red-and-white Indonesian flag and the other held the gay rainbow flag that originated in San Francisco, modified with two vertical red-and-white stripes recalling the national flag. As the issue's editorial explained:

This August we remember an important event, the Proclamation of Indonesian Independence 49 years ago. This event could take place . . . because of a surge of new thinking from the beginning of the twentieth century that resulted in nationalism. . . . The *lesbi* and *gay* movement can be compared with this national movement. . . . It's clear that in the communities of the archipelago there have always been homosexual relations, . . . and with the coming of modern civilization there have appeared comprehensive homosexual identities. But only in the 1980s did homosexual identities become a foundation for a struggle for emancipation and self-empowerment among us. Particularly in the 1990s, we see clearly the development of *gay* groups in our network that gain attention of observers within and outside the country. (*GN* 1994, 32:3–4)

Such framing of homosexuality in activist terms by *GN*'s editors is one of the clearest discrepancies between these zines and the everyday lives of *gay* men, for whom such understandings are rare. What is shared by even the most blatantly political zine writing and everyday *gay* life, however, is a sense of desiring recognition by the nation. This dynamic can be found in other *gay* and *lesbi* zines. As the premiere issue of the *lesbi* zine *MitraS* noted: "There is definitely no place for *gay* and *lesbi* to act as freely as those who live on the Western half of the globe, . . . but that doesn't mean that *gay* and *lesbi* in the Western countries are always more lucky than we who live quietly in Indonesia" (1997, 1:8). Invoking the nationalist trope of land and water, the editor of *K-79* noted that through the zine "we can meet with friends of the same fate throughout our lands and waters [*tanah air*] without any barriers" (1993, 2:6). The editors of *GAYa Betawi* noted from early on that their zine was for *gay* men from the "whole archipelago" [*diseluruh nusantara*] (1992, 2:1). The editors of *Jaka-Jaka* once noted that the goal of the zine (and the organization connected to it) was to "build" *gay* people full of skills and self-esteem, so that they could give their best to the "people and nation" [*bangsa dan negara*] (1993, 5:15).

Readers also draw on national imagery in *gay* zines. The cover boy interviewed in the issue of *K-79* noted above implored readers to "support the unity and integrity [*persatuan dan kesatuan*] between us" (1993, 2:7). Such phrases are common in letters to zines: one reader sent "greetings to the brotherhood of the Indonesian lands and waters" [*persaudaraan setanah air Indonesia*] (*GB* 1997, 15:4); another exclaimed "how beautiful it is to have *gay* friends from the whole archipelago. . . .

We must be united in line with the third of the Pancasila [national princi-
ples], 'the unity of Indonesia' " (*GN* 1995, 37:15). Often the appeals
found in personals are for "friendship with people like me from across the
archipelago." Further, they sometimes have an explicitly nationalist referent, as in the case of a Sumatran man who wrote that "with a foundation
in democracy we struggle for freedom for *gay* people, like other normal
human beings" (*G* 1982, 1:13). The emphasis is on a national community; to my knowledge, never has a personal ad requested someone from a
particular ethnicity or region, a fact that is in contrast to heterosexual personals in Indonesian magazines, which usually specify a desired ethnicity.[22] The desire, instead, is for persons from the whole archipelago [*se-
Nusantara, setanah air,* or *se-Indonesia*]. As one individual put it, "After I
appeared in the personal ads, I got many letters from friends of the same
fate as myself from every corner of the Archipelago. My perspective [*wawasan*] broadened concerning the *gay* world so full of joys and sorrows"
(*GN* 1993, 24:11; for a *lesbi* example, see *GL* 1994, 3:6 [in *GN* 31]).

PRESTASI

These invocations of the nation as place occur simultaneously with the
invocation of a complementary practice; *gay* zines construe citizenship
as an active process, not as a static category of membership. Such practices are called *prestasis* in *gay* zines. This term bears colonial traces; it
derives from the Dutch *prestatie*, a noun meaning "achievement" or
"feat"; the verb form of which can mean "achieve" and "perform." In
standard Indonesian, prestasi also means both to achieve and to perform. Like any performance, prestasis require observers: "hidden prestasi" is an oxymoron. As a result, when *gay* Indonesians refer to prestasis, it is always with an audience in mind, and, with one exception
noted below, the national or general society [*masyarakat umum*] is that
audience, not the *gay* community. Prestasis can be helping directly, such
as adopting a child or caring for a sick relative, or they can be personal
achievements that reflect favorably on one's community, such as going
on the hajj to Mecca if one is Muslim or succeeding in one's career. The
distinguishing characteristic is that prestasis are positive and foster social connectivity, in contrast to selfish actions with destructive or cen-
tripetal consequences. Prestasis are often described as leading to success
[*sukses*], a key New Order state term for the exercise of proper citizen-

ship (Pemberton 1994:9). The editor of *K-79* once set forth a *Gay* Seven Charm Program [*Sapta Pesona Gay*], including closeness [*keakraban*] and social solidarity [*kesatyakawanan sosial*]. This concept transforms the Seven Charms devised by the New Order government in the early 1990s as principles for encouraging tourism (such as safety and cleanliness), but these *gay* prestasis are conceptualized with reference to national society.

The idea that *gay* persons can do prestasis as well as other Indonesians is a frequent theme in zine editorials. As the publishers of *Jaka-Jaka* once wrote: "We all know and perhaps already feel the attitudes and behaviors of most hetero people towards *gay* people. . . . Is it right that we be 'goat-class' citizens, that only have sex? Of course not! There are many *gay* people who have reached the heights of status. . . . *Gay* people have quality and abilities equal to anyone else. . . . To have meaning and respect, one must have a high level of self-worth and self-respect. For that one must have prestasis" (1993, 4:11). Another Yogyakarta zine mused that "prestasis . . . will become a fortress strong enough to repel those minor tones [of social disapproval]" (*NJJ* 1997, 4:6). In 1998, during the worst period of Indonesia's currency crisis, an editor of *GAYa Nusantara* congratulated *gay* Indonesians for continuing their activities, noting that these activities "have an extra value for Indonesian *gay* people in the eyes of hetero society, [showing] that we continue to exist and carry out positive activities" (1998, 55:5). Zine readers also care about prestasis, as illustrated by an article titled "What Can *Homos* Do?" written by a reader of *GAYa Nusantara* from Malang in East Java: "We are becoming aware that although we are fated to be *gay* there are still many things that we can do for ourselves, our families, society, our beloved country and people, the Indonesian people. . . . We must 'go public' with our activities . . . and mix with regular society, for instance with social activities that serve society, like rehabilitation centers for handicapped children, the insane, beggars, the homeless, and so on. . . . What's most important is that these efforts have a humanistic character (beyond the goal of helping our own people, but rather aiding humanity in general)" (1995, 39:33–35).

As a reader of *GAYa Nusantara* from the town of Kisaran explained in an essay to the zine: "Our *gay* friends who are elites and celebrities with influence must have the courage to open themselves, to show the Indonesian government that *gay* people have prestasis and sukses in all matters and compare to hetero people. In this way, it's hoped that the opinion of society and the Indonesian government will change of its own accord" (2000, 65:33). A cover boy from the town of Mojokerto, when asked his opinion about Indonesian society's view of *gay* men as only interested in sex, replied that "the reality is indeed that *gay* people are always equated with sex. It's up to how we as *gay* people change that judgment. We can do it with showing our positive attitudes. We can show our prestasis, so that maybe that judgment will eventually go away, and society can accept our existence to the fullest" (*GN* 1999, 59:13–14). The short story appearing in the final issue of *Jaka* closes with a scene in which the protagonist, a young man, reveals himself to his parents. With tears in his eyes, his father says, "You are still our only son, and you make us proud. No matter what choices you make in your life, what's important is that you become a person who takes care of himself and is useful to society" (1988, 18:15). Nine years later, a *gay* man's confessions in a successor zine to *Jaka* echo this theme: "My mother would be sad if I engaged in *free sex* [English in the original] or other frivolous things without reigning myself in. Even if my *gay*-ness [*kegayan*] is seen as a shortcoming, I just keep working to be a good child who's devoted to his parents, a good Muslim who prays regularly, a good student with good prestasis. In short, I want my mother to be proud of me. Even though I'm *gay*, I prove that I'm much better than those who are hetero" (*NJJ* 1997, 4:12). Such statements consistently emphasize that sex does not qualify as a prestasi.

Given this performative model of citizenship, the act of publishing zines could itself be framed as a prestasi, the only prestasi not directly oriented toward the general public (as noted earlier, non-*gay* Indonesians rarely read these zines; they are intended for consumption within their "own circle" [*kalangan sendiri*]). The editorial in the premiere issue of *GAYa Nusantara*, reflecting on the activities that the zine was to undertake, declared that "all of it has one goal, the acceptance of *gay* and *lesbi* people as a group with the same rights and responsibilities in Indonesian society" (1987, 1:2). This sensibility is shared by *lesbi* zines. As one editorial in a *lesbi* zine proclaimed, "*Swara* will become our pages that give voice to us" (*Swara* 2000, 1:7). In the premiere issue of the *lesbi* zine *MitraS*, the editors expressed frustration that "there isn't a bit of media that can become a forum for information and communication for us in Indonesia, like what's been carried out by *gay* men with their '*GAYa*

Nusantara,' . . . so we found the courage to try publishing this 'special' bulletin after consulting with brother Dédé Oetomo" (1997, 1:3). Thus, "beginning from a feeling of concern about the fate of *lesbi* media that are always appearing and then disappearing to unknown places, four *lesbi* women in Jakarta met to discuss the possibility of publishing a newsletter. From this discussion came a serious agreement. 'There must be *lesbi* media!' " (*Swara* 2000, 1:6). In 1985 a zine reader from Medan (North Sumatra) wrote: "As a *gay* who could be called a veteran [because of his age], I am very proud and touched by your efforts and creativity. In the life of *gay* people, whom almost all people think of as just interested in satisfaction and not to be taken seriously, you emerge bringing a mission that is fundamental for the whole *gay* society [*masyarakat gay*]. Through this media, we can open our eyes clearly" (*Jaka* 1985, 5:3).

I have encountered this sense of zines as prestasis in my fieldwork. One afternoon in Surabaya, I received a phone call from a *gay* man who said he was part of a group that had been involved in entertainment but now wanted to engage in more "serious activities," in particular in developing a new zine (which he termed a *buletin*). The group knew of my work and wanted to know if I would be willing to provide an exclusive interview. I agreed and met them at a boardinghouse where several *gay* men and a *lesbi* woman rented rooms. The interview was one of many occasions of reverse ethnography in my fieldwork, where my thoughts, beliefs, and behaviors became the fodder for *gay* or *lesbi* theorizing about homosexuality in Euro-America. Once finished with a series of questions — beginning with my height, weight, favorite foods, and hobbies and then ranging from my life in the United States to my impressions of Indonesia — I was asked not to tell any other zine-publishing groups of the interview. The explanation for this request was that "we don't want people to hear about the zine before it is published, in case it isn't a success [*sukses*]" — in other words, if it failed to be a prestasi. On another occasion in a different city, I remember speaking with a *gay* man who was one of only two people with editorial responsibility for a zine that had once had a much larger volunteer staff. When I asked why he persisted in publishing the zine, he replied, "I feel a responsibility to make sure the zine doesn't die, because many mass media in this country [*negara*], especially *gay* media, do die out." For *gay* Indonesians, then, a prestasi is a good deed that sets in motion a cycle of moral exchange whereby society, in repayment for the prestasis of *gay* Indonesians, will accept and receive [*terima*] them. Through prestasis, *gay* Indonesians express a desire to overcome separation and be reunited with the nation.

THE INTERZONE: CINTA AND SEXUAL CITIZENSHIP

In the first zone of desire, zines portray *gay* sexuality as moving on a continuum away from sex; its endpoint is a relational self formed through the discovery of, but separation from, love. In the second zone of desire, zines portray *gay* Indonesians as desiring national belonging — a trope of overcoming separation, a trope of recognition depending on prestasis. A crucial cultural logic animating *gay* zines — and, I would argue, *gay* subjectivities — thus emerges in the intersection of these two zones of desire,[23] as illustrated by the lyrics to a song published in the zine *Jaka* in 1987:

PGY Yogyakarta	The Yogyakarta *Gay* Brotherhood
Datang dengan cinta,	Comes with love,
Berjuang dan berupaya	Struggles and labors
Demi hak sesama.	For the sake of equal rights.
Dengan semboyannya,	With our slogan,
Gaya hidup ceria,	The style of a happy life,
Giat berkarya	Working energetically
Demi negara dan nusa bangsa.	For the state and island nation.
Ayo kawan semua,	Come all friends,
Gulung lengan baju,	Roll up your sleeves,
Mari bahu membahu,	Let us stand shoulder to shoulder,
Jangan ragu-ragu,	Don't hesitate,
Tunjukkan pada dunia	Show the world
Bahwa kita sedia.	That we are ready.
Baktikan jiwa	Devote your soul
Membangun bangsa Indonesia.	To building the Indonesian people
	(*Jaka* 1987, 14:3)

In this interzone, love itself emerges as the implicit prestasi qualifying *gay* Indonesians for sexual citizenship (see table 2). The paradox, and the source of the particular sting of exclusion and separation found in *gay* zines, is that *gay* love remains almost completely hidden from society. *Gay* love fails as a prestasi because the postcolonial nation rejects homo-

TABLE 2 Zines and zones of desire.

	Desire for	Justified through	Unfulfilled desire construed as
First Zone	*gay* partner	*gay* love	separation from *gay* partner
Second Zone	national belonging	prestasi	nation withholds recognition
Interzone	*gay* national belonging	*gay* love as a prestasi	nation withholds love from the *gay* person

sexuality; it will not act as an audience authorizing it. *Gay* Indonesians presume that heterosexual Indonesians are citizens by default; they may choose a spouse, but their relation to the nation is "arranged." *Gay* Indonesians, however, lack this relationship to the nation: the implication of the cultural logics of *gay* zines is that *gay* Indonesians must secure national belonging through active choice. Choosing the nation as the object of *gay* love stands as the prestasi that could in theory lead the nation to end its disavowal. *Gay* desire for national belonging fails to overcome separation: it is a sick love.

Zines thus present love as the ultimate prestasi, proving that *gay* Indonesians are equivalent to *normal* Indonesians. As the publishers of *Jaka* once noted, "Our differences with hetero people don't need to be blown out of proportion. In fact, if we respect each other, we can stand shoulder to shoulder and build this beloved nation and people. . . . As a minority that's 'put down,' we have to show that our patriotism and nationalism doesn't fail to compare!" (1988, 17:2). An article sent to *GAYa Nusantara*, "Between Love and Lust," uses the trope of between-ness to set forth love as a prestasi:

> The lives of *gay* people are scrutinized and marginalized by hetero people, above all in regards to love. They accuse *gay* people of not having feelings of love, but only lust and desire. As one of many *gay* people in this country, I feel very apprehensive about this accusation. . . . [If *gay* men love each other,] we *gay* people will still be scrutinized, but the comments will change: "Wow, look

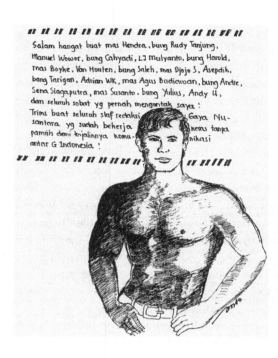

Salam hangat buat mas Hendra, bung Rudy Tanjung, Manuel Wowor, bung Cahyadi, LJ Mulyanto, bung Harold, mas Boyke, Van Houten, bung Saleh, mas Djojo S, Asepdik, bang Tarigan, Adrian WK, mas Agus Budiawan, bung Andre, Sena Siagaputra, mas Susanto, bung Yulius, Andy U, dan seluruh sobat yg pernah mengontak saya:
Trims buat seluruh staf redaksi Gaya Nusantara yg sudah beherja keras tanpa pamrih demi terjalinnya komunikasi antar G Indonesia!

FIGURE 11
The interzone: male beauty juxtaposed with greetings to penpals from across the nation and with thanks to the publishers of *GAYa Nusantara* for their prestasi of "working so hard without reward for communication among 'G' Indonesians!"
(*GN* 1995, 36:7).

at the example that *gay* couple is setting!" In that way, hetero people will slowly become impressed with the model of *gay* love. I have a friend who is a *lesbi* woman and who lives in peace, having built a household with her lover. They sail their prosperous ship of life and have even adopted a child. It's the same with a *gay* couple that work as lowly trash collectors. . . . Although they live in a simple home, their strong love shocks hetero people. . . . If *gay* people form lasting relationships, society itself will be taken aback and not reject us. . . . Let us hope that *gay* people are aware that we do not live only to fulfill our lusts, but that love is the ultimate thing. (1989, 11:31–32)

Despite this optimism, separation haunts the interzone: *gay* zines voice a clear awareness that *gay* love for the nation is not reciprocated. This dynamic is illustrated by fantastical short stories, two examples of which are given below. In these parables, *gay* love magically produces the prestasis that should make it worthy of recognition, but the prestasis lead to separation — dooming the love to a nonsexual plane and exiling the beloved from the nation.

In one such story by a *GAYa Nusantara* reader from Jakarta, the married protagonist works as a geologist at a remote oil field in Sumatra. Soon after his unhappy wife leaves for Java, he meets a handsome young man, Nana, along the road near a forest. Nana follows the geologist to the oil-field camp, where he sits next to the geologist as the geologist ponders a map. "Nana, watching over my shoulder, with a smile said that from this place to this place there would certainly be oil. When I asked him how he knew he only smiled." They become lovers and Nana's test wells are rich in oil. The boss is elated with this prestasi, for which the geologist takes credit. Nana continues to find oil on behalf of his beloved geologist and even heals the boss's fever. Eventually the boss gives the geologist a promotion to Jakarta, but Nana is silent. "When I asked if it was because I had a wife in Java, he said no. . . . Finally he just said that he wanted to return to the area where I first found him." Nana disappears into the forest; suddenly, an old gray civet cat approaches the geologist. The cat kisses his feet, "strangely, appears to be crying," then leaves. The geologist then sees an old man who says the forest is inhabited only by a 230-year-old civet cat that can take human form. "Now I live alone, my wife left me because I didn't pay attention to her. . . . Oh Nana, I love you so much" (1996, 44:17–21).

In another story, by a reader from the city of Solo, the protagonist, Calvin, falls in love with a fellow college student, Harold. One day in Harold's room Calvin sees a brilliantly written thesis with the same title as his own. There is a note: "I will leave after I find what I'm looking for." Harold explains he has been expelled for having sex with a professor and Calvin can use his thesis. That night they have sex; the next morning, Harold is gone. When Calvin finds Harold's grandmother and asks where Harold might be, the shocked woman replies that Harold died a year previously, "before he could graduate. He was disappointed with his schooling and killed himself. He left a message that he would leave if he found what he was looking for, but I didn't understand. Maybe you are what he was looking for. I beg of you, stay here with me, so that Harold can be at peace" (GN 2000, 74:35–36).

In these stories, fantastical gay men perform prestasis for their beloved, bringing them success in national society, but the love-recognition that should ensue does not come to pass. Both stories end in separation. Even short stories without fantastic elements often present this same dynamic, as in "A Red Orchid for Kresna," which was sent to GAYa Nusantara by a gay man from Purworejo. In this story, Kresna is the

FIGURE 12
A figure in *GAYa Nusantara*,
holding the zine in one hand
and a sign reading "*gay* love"
in the other (1993, 21:30).

childhood friend of Har, the protagonist, but as they get older Har's
feelings get stronger: "What is this feeling? Is it love? . . . Does that
mean . . . I'm a *gay* person?" (2001, 82:32). Eventually Kresna tells Har
that he reciprocates his love, but in fear Har runs away and marries a
woman. This separation is set to end when Har, realizing he is *gay*,
divorces his wife and returns to Yogyakarta to find Kresna.[24] He arrives
at Kresna's house to find the family in an uproar: Kresna, whose parents
rejected him after learning Kresna was *gay*, went to work at an orphanage and recently donated a kidney to a young orphan — the orphan
was saved but Kresna died from complications. Har, filled with the pain
of separation, writes to Kresna in his diary: "I have found the true meaning of love. . . . Today, you are no longer a *gay* person who dies without
honor, but a knight who has fallen in shining armor" (34).

If *gay* zines bring together homosexual desire and a desire for national
belonging under the sign of love-as-prestasi, it is only logical that *gay*
zines could be construed not only as prestasis but also as something
loved (see figure 12). Professions of love to zines have been frequent since

the zines' beginnings, and sometimes they are mixed with fears of separation: "I've fallen in love with *Jaka;* what's more, if I can get to know other lovers [*pencinta*] of *Jaka*, the feelings will be a million times greater" (*Jaka* 1986, 7:3); "It's like *Jaka* has become the heart of our people [*jantungnya kaum kita*]"; "I fell in love with *Jaka* at first sight, and it grows deeper and deeper. I feel fearful and sad when I imagine *Jaka* disappearing" (*Jaka* 1986, 8:2; see also *GN* 2001, 81:47).

Zines sometimes even appear as agents of love. Toward the end of the story "A Million Lamps of the Heart," the author-protagonist, Ar, is in his last year of high school and has met another student, Budi. One day Budi invites Ar to his house while Budi's parents are still at work:

> In the bedroom, Budi straightaway took off his shirt and pants. Wearing nothing but his underwear, he opened a bookcase, took out a magazine [*majalah*] and gave it to me. I started to read the magazine; its black-and-white cover just had a big "G" surrounded by "*gaya hidup ceria*" and the edition's number. Seeing me read the magazine, Budi smiled shyly and approached me.
>
> "What about it, Ar? . . ."
>
> "Sure, Budi," I replied. "Now?"
>
> "Yes, now." Immediately I took off my clothes. . . . Suddenly we were kissing. . . .
>
> "If I'd just known before, Ar — " he said.
>
> "What would you have done?" I interrupted.
>
> "I would have done like this!"
>
> And right away he moved on top of me. . . . Now I feel that I'm not alone anymore. Now I have a friend of the same world as me, in other words who also likes those of the same sex. Not just that. There is still something else. What? That magazine! Yes, that "G" bulletin. Now I feel that with the publication of that magazine I can get many friends who have the same feelings and joys as myself. Before I found that "G," I felt my world was dark. Now that I've found that "G" I feel it's not so dark anymore. Now my world is bright and clear because a million lamps of the heart shine together. (*G* 1983, 5:7–9)

This zine-within-a-zine flags the interzone where homosexual desire and a desire for national belonging come together: the "million lamps of the heart" is the *gay* archipelago itself, the national network of *gay* men whose sexual desires find form through the prism of national discourse.[25]

In the interzone, then, homosexuality and national belonging come together under the sign of love. As zines are produced in the interstices of everyday life and read in stolen moments on a bed or in a friend's room, *gay* men imagine a new Indonesia. Through this national romance, they desire recognition from a nation-lover where now there is only separation. This is the story behind the story, so to speak, of *gay* zines. What fantastical story of my own might leave the reader with an appreciation for the raw emotional sensibility of this implicit, unattainable interzone? It would be to construe Indonesia, the nation itself, as returning the gaze coming from the faces of *gay* men on zine covers. A nation that at long last turns to the *gay* Indonesian and looks you right in the eye, that accepts your prestasis and closes distance. An Indonesia that beckons you and in that impossible moment is consumed by homosexual desire. An Indonesia that gathers you, finally, into the warmest of embraces and whispers in your ear — "you are loved." And you are home.

TWO

WARIAS, *NATIONAL TRANSVESTITES*

In this chapter I continue my investigation of the unexpected consequences of national discourse by turning to Indonesia's *warias*, or "male
transvestites." In so doing, my emphasis shifts from sexuality to gender.
In the Indnonesian context (and elsewhere) it seems quite clear that
sexuality and gender are distinct but interlinked domains. For instance,
nowhere does "homosexual," which technically means a "desire for the
same," refer to the mutual desire of two youths (or two Christians)
whether they are two men, two women, or a man and woman. Similarly,
nowhere does "heterosexual," which technically means a "desire for
difference," refer to the mutual desire of a youth and an old person (or
the mutual desire of a Christian and a Hindu) whether they are two men,
two women, or a man and woman. The referent of "homo," "hetero,"
and even "bi" is assumed to be gender, not age, religion, ethnicity, or
any other conceivable category. Since discussions of gender are almost
always discussions of gender difference, collapsing sexuality into gender makes it difficult to understand forms of "desire for the same" like
homosexuality. This chapter illuminates the complementary problem:
discussions of sexuality may be insufficient for theorizing forms of desire
where gender is deployed within categories of "male" and "female."[1]

One element shared by discourses of gender and sexuality is that many
cultures worldwide tend to "naturalize" them by eliding their historical
variability and the systems of power that sustain them (Yanagisako and
Delaney 1995). In order to counter this tendency toward "essentialism,"
the notion of "social constructionism" has been developed in a range of
disciplines. Debates in the 1980s and 1990s that set these terms against
each other have now been recognized as ineffective (e.g., Vance 1989)

relative to theoretical frameworks that avoid posting the binarism together. This is one reason for the great popularity of the rubric of "performativity" (Butler 1990), which is often used to suggest a kind of constantly enacted subjectivity that is neither an essence nor a construction. In this chapter I develop an ethnographically contexualized concept of performativity by drawing upon the Indonesian term *playback*, which warias use in reference to lip-synching. Since waria gendering is linked to broader cultural understandings of gender, the concept of playback as developed in this chapter is relevant to understanding the formation and maintenance of gender norms for all Indonesians.

How might one encounter warias in Indonesia? Taman Remaja Surabaya (Surabaya Youth Park) is located on a downtown thoroughfare next to the Surabaya Mall. It is nighttime and the mall is closed — as I pass a sea of motorcycles, pedicabs [*becak*], and buses pulling up at the curbside it looms as a hulking, padlocked mass. Along with several thousand Surabayans, I plunk down 1,300 rupiah to pass under the glittering neon and white light bulbs at the gates of Taman Remaja.[2] With its assortment of carnival rides — a Ferris wheel, bumper cars, a shooting gallery — it appears to my Midwestern eyes as a county fair that never left town. The sea of voices in the background is constant; occasionally a single voice emerges from the cacophony — a generous laugh, a child's wail, a shouted retort — then disappears into the noise. Every few minutes a low electric drone announces the approaching monorail, a cramped affair four feet wide and no longer than a car. It grinds uncomfortably along a red steel track only five feet above the ground. Those leaning absentmindedly against its pillars receive a good-natured tap from a neighbor and then duck as the bright yellow beast crawls overhead. Beyond the monorail's track, encircling the carnival rides, is a wide stage fitted out with colored lights and glittering disco balls, looking out over a seating area with rows of wooden benches. Behind the benches is a group of public toilets. To the right of the stage is a six-foot-high permanent sign declaring: "Waria Night with Live Band, Thursday Nights."

The band is warming up before the promised performance, and by 8:30 the seating area is jammed. Perhaps 80 percent of the audience is made up of men between fifteen and thirty years old; flip-flop plastic sandals and well-worn clothes mark their blue-collar, low-income status. Cleared of benches, the twenty-yard area in front of the stage is occupied by these men, who are smoking and conversing with each other. The benches behind the front area are filled by a more diverse audience, including better-dressed husbands and wives, and young children perched on laps or chasing each other down the aisles. There are about thirty warias in the audience; some sit at the benches in small groups, but most gather next to the stage. *Waria*, a combination of the terms *wanita* [woman] and *pria* [man], can be roughly translated as "male transvestite."

Now the first singer, a woman, appears before the audience. Many of the single men in front of the stage begin to dance with each other, both feet on the ground, swaying slowly and sensually to the music, laughing and comparing moves, or swinging their hips and rubbing arms to chests with closed eyes, hypnotically, as if alone in a small room. A few warias dance in a corner by themselves or in pairs with a man. The female singer is followed by a male emcee, who announces that three door prizes will be given out before the main part of the show. "This first prize is especially for women [*cewek*]. I'm looking for a woman who's from outside Surabaya." Two or three women rush the stage; the first to make it up the stairs proudly presents her identity card (KTP or *Kartu Tanda Pendukuk*) to the emcee, who scans it with a flourish before handing her a prize. The woman descends the stage with a brightly wrapped box as the emcee shouts "the next question is especially for men [*cowok*]. I'm looking for a man whose name begins with R." Several men dash up the stairs; the first to reach the emcee presents his KTP and, identity confirmed, receives the requisite gift. Then the emcee says: "This last question is especially for warias. I'm looking for a waria whose hair is braided." An elegantly dressed waria with braided hair is first to reach the emcee — no identity card requested in this case — and accepts the prize. Now the emcee retires and the band starts up again, this time with a waria singer resplendent in red sequins and high heels, and the audience begins an evening of dancing and relaxing to waria voices.

Although the Thursday night waria show at Taman Remaja is a well-known showcase for warias in eastern Java (e.g., Plummer and Porter 1997:43–45), warias are salient members of contemporary Indonesian society more generally. Better known as *bancis* or *béncongs* (both derogatory terms), these male transvestites are visible in daily life — above all in salon work, which includes bridal makeup — to a vastly greater degree than Indonesians who identify as *gay* or *lesbi*. Warias are also far more visible than female-to-male transgendered Indonesians, or "tomboys." However, despite this visibility and the general visibility of male transgenderism in Southeast Asia (a topic that I discuss, along with tomboys, in chapter 6), warias have received little attention in the scholarly literature. This chapter represents one step toward a more sustained exploration of waria life. In using ethnographic material on warias to reflect on Western theoretical debates, this chapter (like the others in this book) aims to produce coincidences between anthropology and queer studies. The bringing together of theory and ethnography is of particular importance given that the study of transgenderism, in the words of Kath Weston, "has not been immune to the documentary impulse that brushes aside theory in the rush for 'facts,' or to a tendency to reify and idealize 'traditional' forms of homosexuality in nonindustrial societies" (1993:340). This "ethnocartographic" impulse—which, extending Weston, also includes a tendency to reify and idealize transgenderism (see Towle and Morgan 2002)—hides how the division between theory and ethnography is illusory. As discussed in the introduction, throughout this book I insist that effective intersections between queer studies and anthropology will be forms of immanent critique and of situated knowledge, since description always takes place within the horizon of some set of theoretical assumptions and theorization always takes place within the horizon of some set of phenomenon construed as data.

In the following pages, I provide material concerning the history of the waria subject position and contemporary waria subjectivities. Within the scope of a single chapter I cannot present a comprehensive portrait of warias or delve into every dimension of their rich and diverse lives. Instead, I provide vignettes exemplifying certain aspects of waria life so that I might center my analysis on two key areas in which the "tendency to reify and idealize 'traditional' forms of transgenderism" has been particularly strong. First, although warias live in a postcolonial nation-state, analyses often frame them in terms of locality, tradition, and ritual (e.g., Andaya 2000; Plummer and Porter 1997:43). My analysis will instead illustrate how warias emphasize a sense of belonging to (and exclusion from) national society and popular culture, which provides an important point of continuity with my discussion of *gay* zines in chapter 1. This issue was foreshadowed in what might have appeared to be an insignificant event: Why was the waria who climbed the stage at Taman Remaja not asked to show an identity card?

The second area is the tendency to construe warias as belonging to a "third gender" (e.g., Andaya 2000). Although there are people in various parts of the world who could arguably be seen as inhabiting third genders, the third-gender concept is often overemployed and poorly defined. I argue that warias are not a "third gender" but rather a male femininity. This interpretation is suggested by, of all things, the case of Taman Remaja's toilets. There are two toilets, not three, and since at least 1992 the sign on one of these toilets reads *wanita* (women), whereas the sign on the other reads *pria/waria* (men/warias). Why are warias grouped with men rather than women, or not given a third toilet, since it would not be expensive to build? My analysis will show how the concept of "waria" operates within the orbit of male gendering. Furthermore, I argue that the position of warias as feminine males is informed by, and in turn shapes, their sense of partial belonging to national society. I will call this the playback of authenticity and argue that it is a question of recognition.

DEFINITIONS AND HISTORIES

Although any English gloss for warias falls short, I prefer "male transvestites" to "male transgenders" for the theoretical reasons I explore throughout this chapter and in chapter 6. No English-language term perfectly describes these individuals. I use the phrase "male transvestites" as an overall term because "transvestite" captures how warias usually see themselves as originating from the category "man" and as remaining men in some fashion.[3] A drawback to the term "transvestite" is that in the West it often describes heterosexual men who dress as women for sexual pleasure. However, other terms also have drawbacks. For instance, "transgender" usually implies a kind of moving beyond gender, which poorly represents the complex reworkings (not transcendings) of gender in which warias engage, and "transsexual" usually implies genital change surgery, which the majority of warias do not undergo and many do not wish to undergo. As is always the case with any act of interpretation, terms are always to be taken as contingent analytical devices. The goal is not to find a perfect or permanent term but to craft a working vocabulary — the modification and clarification of which is part of cultural critique itself.

My use of the phrase "male transvestites" also poses a problem regarding pronouns, since Indonesian (like most Austronesian languages) uses a single term (*dia*) for third-person singular reference ("she," "he," and "it"). One perfectly legitimate way to address this problem (and one I have used myself in the past) is by coined pronouns like "hir" and "s/he" (Blackwood 1998; Graham 2001; Johnson 1997). A significant short-coming of such neologisms, however, is that they exoticize the individuals so described. For instance, in Indonesia warias (and tomboys) are referred to with the term *dia*. No coined pronoun is used for them; they receive the same pronominal treatment as any other Indonesian. Employing a coined pronoun in an English-language discussion of them thus makes their gendering appear culturally out of joint in a manner that speaks more to Euro-American fascinations with gender nonconformity than to the Indonesian context. As a result, in this chapter — and in this book in general — I will use "she" for warias and "he" for tomboys, with the knowledge that social gender is productively imprecise (see Boellstorff 2005:9).

Three sources of possible confusion about non-warias (including both anthropological analysts and "normal" Indonesians) stem from the rich terminological and sexual landscape in which warias live. The first possible source of confusion concerns the relationship between the term *waria* and the most common day-to-day term for these persons, *banci*; its *gay* language variant *béncong* has entered vernacular Indonesian as well.[4] But since *banci* can also mean "effeminate male," it can sometimes distinguish men from warias; that is, one can say "I saw a man who was very effeminate, a banci not a waria."[5] For this reason, and due to the derisive tone with which it is typically deployed, many warias find the term *banci* offensive. The preferred term *waria* originates not in tradition but in government dictate and dates from 1978.[6] A second source of misunderstanding originates in the many terms for warias linked to "ethno-locality," the presumed conjunction of place and ethnicity (Boellstorff 2002). These terms include *kedi* (Javanese and Balinese, but also found in Sulawesi), *kawe-kawe* (Makassarese, but also used by many Buginese), *wandu* (Javanese, but also found in Sulawesi), and *calabai'* (Buginese, but also found in Kalimantan, possibly due to Bugis migration).[7] I have never been able to establish any consistent differences between individuals who identify themselves through these various terms (and who all appear to use the terms *waria* and *banci* in some contexts). For instance, in Sulawesi not only warias but others (including *gay* men) say that kawe-kawe and calabai' are local terms for warias in the same way that *pete-pete* is the local term for *bemo* ("minibus"). As one Bugis waria explained to me: "I'm called calabai' with family . . . usually we say calabai' based on ethnicity but it means the same thing as banci. For instance, I'm a Bugis; I might say 'that's a calabai.' If I were Makassarese, I might say kawe-kawe." When I asked her if kawe-kawe is the same thing as calabai', she replied, "The same! Calabai,' kawe-kawe, béncong, waria, banci, they're all the same. . . . They're only terms [*cuma sekedar istilah*]." Here Bronislaw Malinowski's observation concerning the Trobriand lexicon remains relevant more generally: "Though important as a clue to native ideas, the knowledge of terminology is not a miraculous short-cut into the native's mind. As a matter of fact, there exist many salient and important features of Trobriand sociology and social psychology, which are not covered by any term, whereas their language distinguishes sub-divisions and subtleties which are quite irrelevant with regard to actual conditions" (1922:176–77).

A third source of misunderstanding is that in many parts of Indonesia there have been (and still are) what I term "ethnolocalized professional homosexual and transvestite subject positions" or ETPs (Boellstorff 2005, chapter 2). I use this terminology to avoid referring to these as "traditional" or "indigenous" homosexualities or transgenderisms because I do not want to assume which kinds of sexualities are authentic in contemporary Indonesia. In the case of ETPs, homosexuality or transgenderism is secondary to a specialized ritual or artistic activity; they are first and foremost professions, not sexual or gendered subject positions. One is not born into them nor does one "become" them in a developmental sense, rather they are learned through apprenticeship. In many cases the ETP has fallen out of use or has been resexualized. For instance, *waroks* in eastern Java were historically male actors who took on younger men (known as *gemblak*) as understudies and sex partners. There are still men who become waroks, but since the 1980s their understudies have been women and they have distanced themselves from homosexuality. This is linked not only to the political upheavals of the 1960s but also to the fact that "being gemblak is now seen as incompatible with the 'national personality,' or not in line with 'Indonesian culture'" (Fauzannafi 2005:135). The waria subject position is not an ETP, although warias can occupy some ETPs with proper training. In the popular imagination they are sometimes linked to notions of tradition such as Javanese shadow-puppet theater [*wayang*], though as noted below this association is anachronistic and confuses the waria subject position with that of ETPs (e.g., Riantiarno 2004:66).

The history of the waria subject position is a topic unto itself, and since this chapter focuses on contemporary waria subjectivities I provide only a summary here. I know of no records of warias being associated with ritual practices, and to my knowledge they do not appear in ritual texts. Nor is there much colonial documentation on any form of trans-genderism or homosexuality during the 350-year Dutch period. Thus, while ETPs appear in travelers' accounts and local histories as early as the fourteenth century, the waria subject position has a recognizable con-tinuity going back only to the early 1800s, as is the case for male trans-vestite subject positions across Southeast Asia (see chapter 6). Around this time there begin to appear scattered references to effeminate men in coastal trading centers and in some rural contexts; these references are linked not to ritual but to petty commodity trading, lowbrow entertain-ment, and sex work. Employment along the lines of contemporary salon work (women's makeup, especially for brides, but also cutting men's hair) does not appear to have been significant at the time. Accounts of individuals occupying this subject position (the earliest name for which appears to be *banci*) agree that they were male-bodied but dressed in an effeminate manner — not necessarily all of the time but frequently enough that casual visitors would notice them.[8]

From the beginning warias do not appear to have been seen as limited to any one ethnic group or locality. By the 1830s, the dances of the "Bantji Batavia" (literally, Batavian Transvestite) could in the words of Pauline Milone be interpreted as "a typical manifestation of Batavian [Jakartan] popular culture. It was exclusively Batavian (though similar to the Surabaja *ludrug* [Surabaya *ludruk*]) and was thought to be of Balinese origin. It was performed by young men clothed as women, sometimes wearing Western dresses, with long white hose and an ankle ring" (1967:472). In 1855, the Dutch lexicographer Rooda van Eysinga listed *banci* with *pâpaq* and *roebia* as "local, Malaysian terms alongside the Arabic *chontza* for 'hermaphrodite'" (quoted in Bleys 1995:179). Newspaper accounts from Batavia (now Jakarta) indicate that some districts were known "as the haunts of banci (transvestites), whose ori-gin in Batavia seems to go back to the late nineteenth century" (Abeyase-kere 1987:92, 127). In 1937 Miguel Covarrubias, the Mexican intellec-tual and cartoonist whose book *Island of Bali* helped popularize Bali as a tourist destination, stated: "There are in Bali curious individuals called *bentji*, interpreted by the Balinese as 'hermaphrodites' — a condition which is characteristic of gods, but bad and ridiculous among humans. The bentji are men who are abnormally asexual from birth (impotent, according to the Balinese), who act and dress like women and perform the work of women. In Den Pasar there was one of these pitiable creatures, a man who dressed like a girl and talked in falsetto, selling goods at a public stand in the main street" (1937:144). The fact that *banci* appears as a "local" Batavian term in 1830, a "local" Malay term in 1855, and a "local" Balinese term in 1937 (see also Mead 1949:107) suggests that despite the tendency of observers to ethnolocalize warias (note Covarrubias's language of "gods" with reference to predominantly Hindu Bali), the subject position had a broader scope from its beginnings (see Murray 1997).[9]

By the 1960s warias had become well known for their presence in markets and as sex workers, as well as for their roles in lowbrow performing arts. The best-known example of this is the Javanese dramatic genre known as *ludruk*, the first recorded performance of which dates from 1822 and included "transvestite performers" (Peacock 1968:29).[10] One seventy-year-old waria from rural southern Sulawesi noted that when she was young, "warias almost never went out during the day. Those who did would be called names by the kids; men would hit us and scream blasphemies at us. Warias just slept at home [during the day] under cold cream."[11] Several warias in Surabaya confirm the following observation by an older *gay* man, Eddy, who recalled that in earlier times "there were no bancis wearing dresses. None at all. They weren't brave enough to do that back then . . . That began around 1980. Before that there were bancis, but only in the ludruk dramas.[12] During the day they'd be *normal*; then at night they'd work as a woman. But it was certain those people were bancis. They weren't wearing women's clothes 24 hours a day, but they were effeminate all the time in the way they walked and carried themselves."

The lives of warias in James Peacock's 1960s Surabaya do not appear markedly different from those of Covarrubias's Bali or Hirschfeld's Batavia of the 1930s, or those of the earliest known accounts of warias in the 1830s. However, this characterization changed between the late 1950s and late 1960s. Strains within the new nation, particularly around Islam, led to a new marginalization of warias. Some warias associate this period of intolerance with places where Muhummadiyah (a modernist Muslim organization) had a strong following. This was exacerbated by the mass violence around the birth of Soeharto's New Order, which does not appear to have been directed at warias (see Wieringa 1999a), but did lead to a virtual abandonment of the public and market spaces where warias found community and employment. As Eddy's narrative indicates, it appears that one of the biggest shifts in the waria subject position was in the mid-1960s to early 1980s (depending on locale, with the key period of 1965–1970). It appears to be at this point that the majority of warias shifted from wearing women's clothes only in certain contexts like performances or nighttime sex work to wearing women's clothing all of the time.[13] It also appears to be at this point that salon work became the prototypical waria employment. The new visibility of the waria subject position seems to have coincided with the coming to power of Soeharto's New Order government in the late 1960s, which coupled authoritarian rule and developmentalist economics.

CHILDHOOD DREAMS AND ADULT TRANSFORMATIONS

For those visiting Indonesia since the 1980s, the social salience of warias seems utterly different from the Western situation. Although rosy fantasies of tolerance are overstated, *waria* is now an important cultural category. Even educated, urban Indonesians are not always familiar with the terms *gay* or *lesbi*, but everyone knows what *banci* means.[14] Indonesians expect to find warias in salons, and could easily assume that their daughters' wedding makeup will be applied by a waria. Some of the tailors and shopkeepers in any given neighborhood are likely to be warias, and at night in many locales warias can be seen looking for men near the town square. Warias seem to fall into three economic classes: those who own salons or some other business (and who can be quite wealthy), those who work in salons, and those who neither own nor work in salons but sometimes engage in sex work to support themselves. Warias occasionally "pass" as women to coworkers in a salon, or even to sex-work clients (hiding their penis between their legs if the client wishes to penetrate them anally). Warias themselves, however, see such cases as exceptional: typically the social others with whom a waria interacts at home, in the neighborhood, on the street, and at work know she is waria and not wanita (a woman), yet accept her as a member of the community. Representations of warias appear on television sitcoms and in advertisements, as well as in news reports in the print media. In 2000, a commercial for Bayer aspirin on national television featured an apparent waria.[15]

Since the waria subject position is both widely known and visibly embodied, the process of occupying it involves from the outset the reactions and commentary of others. Unlike *gay* men, warias rarely speak of "opening themselves" [*membuka diri*] in terms of revealing who they are; indeed they often discover who they are because others point it out to them. Although there are occasional cases of Indonesians becoming warias later in life, most warias think of themselves as such by their early teens, and in some cases as young as five years old. In this they differ from *gay* men, who according to my research typically begin to identify as *gay* in their late teens to early twenties. A desire for men is not the genesis of waria subjectivity (as it is for *gay* subjectivity); almost all warias come to see themselves as waria during childhood and do not necessarily recall an attraction to men as key to this early development.[16]

The first and most absolute condition of the waria subject position is that only males, it is assumed, can occupy it. One cannot become waria if one is seen to be born with a vagina, and despite misconceptions on the part of the Indonesian public, few warias are intersexed. All narratives of waria selfhood are driven by a movement away from normative masculinity. As children, most warias engaged in play atypical for boys. As one waria recalled, "The signs [*tanda*] of my waria-ness [*kewariaan*] have been visible since I was a child. Usually, boys who are going to become *normal* ride bicycles, play tag. I was different [*beda*]; I hung out with the girls and played jump rope, played with dolls." Some warias see these activities as formative and speculate that they would not have become waria had their parents forbidden them. Others believe gender play only reveals that they had "the soul of a woman since birth," as one waria put it. Such an interpretation is common among warias who grew up in environments where gender play was actively discouraged.[17] Although warias are generally known to contemporary Indonesian society, this does not mean that families welcome a waria member. As Ita, who was from the island of Lombok but had lived in Makassar for fourteen years when interviewed, recalled: "In my village there aren't warias; they don't understand about warias. There, even though our movements may be effeminate, we cannot dress up like women. We can become banci,[18] but we cannot use makeup, wear women's clothes, or have long hair. . . . I think so much about my family and the fact that they don't accept me. It's a great load upon my thinking. . . . My name is not spoken there."

Ita's tale is by no means unique. Many warias are not accepted by their families, at least not initially. Young warias have been beaten until they bled, have been held under water by their fathers until they have almost drowned, or have had an older brother force them to stick their finger into a light socket. Estrangement from the family sometimes continues through adulthood, as in Ita's case. Others are accepted to some extent. Many warias are acknowledged as such while small children. Others reach an understanding with their families when they are in their teens: "I explained that if I die and am reborn, I will still be a banci." Warias sometimes bring waria friends home, "so my parents would know that it's not just me who's like this," or else bring home a male partner (the acceptance of whom is usually seen as a definitive acknowledgment of their waria status). Belonging and recognition are important: the goal of these efforts is to be accepted [diterima] by the family, just as warias also hope to be accepted by society.

Although many warias struggle with a sense of sin, by adulthood most have made some kind of peace with their religious beliefs (compare with the discussion of gay Muslims in chapter 4). In caring for family members or even saving for years to send a parent on the pilgrimage to Mecca, warias say they hope to wipe away the sins they have caused their family [menghapus dosa]. Good deeds can compensate for their being waria, even as many warias say that being waria is a divine decree [takdir]. As one waria recalled, "When I was small I got very sick. My mother prayed: 'what does my child have to become in order to live?' I survived and this was the result, and for that reason she accepts me." When my waria interlocutors speak of sin they tend to speak of things warias do (particularly promiscuity and sex work) rather than the state of being waria itself, which is often seen as God's wish [kemauan atas]. Warias have formed Christian prayer organizations and Muslim prayer rooms [musala] where they wear women's garments [mukenah] while at prayer.[19] Some Muslim warias have made the hajj pilgrimage to Mecca as men; others have done so as women (some as many as nine times) without the knowledge of their fellow pilgrims.[20] Speaking to one such waria, I asked: "Does God think of you as man, woman, or waria?"

She answered: "God thinks of me as a waria, not a woman or a man. To be waria is my fate [*pasrah*]." In the context of the all-powerful nature of God, many warias take their inability to change as evidence that God wishes them to be waria. Although the quotation above seems to imply an understanding of the waria subject position as a third gender, when warias wrestle with the question of sin they typically conclude not that God created three genders, but that they were created with a feminine soul.[21]

Indeed, to only be interested in women's clothes or activities is not usually seen as sufficient to make one waria; at some point, usually during childhood but sometimes in the teenage years, warias come to know that they have the soul [*jiwa*] of a woman, or at least a soul that is more woman than man. Warias also speak of having the temperament [*sifat*] or feelings [*perasaan*] of a woman. To bring the body into alignment with the soul by wearing women's clothes, makeup, and so on is a source of pleasure for warias. Although warias do sometimes fool people into thinking they are women, the goal is not to "pass" but to look like a waria. This is one sense in which waria could arguably be spoken of as a "third-gender" subject position. Despite usually dressing as a woman and feeling that they have the soul of a woman, most warias think of themselves as warias (not women) all of their lives, even in the rather rare cases where they obtain sex change operations (see below). One reason that third-gender language seems inappropriate is that warias see themselves as originating from the category "man" and, in some sense, as always men: "I am an authentic [*asli*] man," one waria noted. "If I were to go on the pilgrimage to Mecca, I would dress as a man because I was born a man. If I pray, I wipe off my makeup." To emphasize the point she pantomimed wiping off makeup, as if waria-ness were contained therein. Even warias who go to the pilgrimage in female clothing see themselves as created male. Another waria summed up by saying, "I was born a man, and when I die I will be buried as a man, because that's what I am."

When I began learning of these two understandings of what makes someone waria — soul and clothing — I suspected that the sense of having a woman's soul was more central. This reflects the dominant Western conceit that both gender and sexuality originate as internal essences that must be confessed to ever greater spheres of life to be authentic and valid (Foucault 1978; Sedgwick 1991). This ontology of the closet draws heavily from a Christian metaphysics construing the transient body as secondary to the everlasting soul. It is not, however, the ontology of waria subjectivity, and there appear to be both diachronic and synchronic reasons for this. Diachronically, looking like a woman may for warias be becoming more important, and having a woman's soul may be becoming less important, compared to prior decades. Should this prove to be the case—that is, should the waria subject position place increasingly less emphasis on "confessing" an interior state—this would run counter to the stereotype that globalizing processes create greater sameness. Synchronically, warias do not always assume that the soul makes one wear women's clothes; the causality can be seen to work in the other direction or to be mutually constituting, thereby reflecting the widespread assumption in Southeast Asia that internal state and external presentation naturally align with each other (Errington 1989:76–77; Garcia 1996:65; see chapters 5 and 6).

This assumption might explain why it is that among warias there is no consensus as to whether looking like a woman or having a woman's soul is causally prior. Probably most warias see external practices as manifestations of an internal state: as one explained to me, "It is the soul that pushes us to wear women's clothes"; while another stated, "To dress in women's clothes is just to perfect our appearance: our soul is 90 percent of the matter." Yet many see the soul as shaped by external practices: warias sometimes claim they were infected [*ketularan*] because of wearing women's clothes for entertainment or because they played with warias when they were children.

To occupy the waria subject position is seen to encompass sexuality as well as gender: warias have sex with men, according to warias and to other Indonesians. What is significant is that the waria subject position is not founded in a sexual orientation: warias usually assume that their desire for men flows causally from a prior mismatching of soul and body.[22] Although *gay* male desire is usually understood in terms of "desiring the same" and could thus be roughly translated as "homosexuality," warias often understand their desire for men as the desire of femininity for masculinity—that is, as heterosexual desire. As a language of *homoseks* and *heteroseks* becomes better known in Indonesia, many warias regard themselves as heterosexual, not homosexual, even though HIV prevention discourse often groups them with *gay* men under the rubric of men who have sex with men (MSM). Their feminine souls and bodily presentations mean that while male-waria sex is understood abstractly as a form of homosexuality, it is clearly distinguishable from sex "between two men."

By adulthood most warias have a clear sense that they are unalterably warias for the rest of their lives. They have usually identified as waria for many years, and in contrast to *gay* men, their social interlocutors have also identified them as warias. Women's clothing, makeup, and hair-styling are the important external markers of contemporary adult waria subjectivity, although a few warias dress as men during the day or while on public transport to avoid being teased, and some mix articles of women's and men's clothing. This clothing is usually in a modern style (for instance, jeans and a Western women's shirt) but can also be "tradi-tional" women's clothing, especially on formal occasions. In terms of bodily comportment, warias stress moving "like women" when walking, gesturing, lifting objects, sitting down, or dancing. The goal is a refined, coy, slow grace — that is, to be *halus* (cf. Geertz 1983:61). In terms of speech, the ideal is a high, melodious tone and rhythm at a soft volume. Non-waria Indonesians interviewing warias for news stories typically comment on how the waria in question "is as beautiful as a woman" or "speaks exactly like a woman." This is a performative sense of gender as something that must be achieved and reachieved; that is, iterated (Butler 1990). It is this association of warias with ongoing transformation that makes them seen as ideally suited to work in salons, where they can transform others (cf. Cannell 1999; Johnson 1997).

However, warias do not equate being feminine with being female — they distinguish *wanita* [female] from how they usually refer to them-selves, namely *gaya wanita* or *kewanitaan* (roughly, "in the style of a woman"). Indeed, waria subjectivity is marked not so much by the whole-sale adoption of feminine forms as by the mixing of men's and women's styles, just as warias amalgamate a woman's soul to a man's body, or the term *waria* amalgamates "male" and "female." Warias can incorporate typically masculine forms of bodily comportment and speech when the occasion demands — a joke, a perceived slight, a sex-work client who refuses to pay, a threatening situation in public, or a jealous confronta-tion. Warias are often said to be stronger than men and capable of ex-tremely rude speech and obscene gestures. *Gay* men frequently observe that warias can be more "man" than themselves. As one *gay* man put it in a conversation with some street youth asking about warias, "You can't push them around too much. If you get them mad, their maleness comes out [*keluar*], and they'll beat up the person who's threatening them."

Activities known as "putting on makeup," which includes things like shaving one's legs or styling one's hair, are categorized with clothing as an temporary body modification that a waria undergoes on a daily basis. The term for all this is *dandan*, which is often referred to as *déndong* through the same transformation (associated with *gay* language; see chapter 3) that turns *banci* into *béncong*. As an example, one evening I visited a waria who operated a salon from the front room of her small house. Vera, who worked and lived at the salon, was beginning to déndong with Sita, another waria, who like many warias had grown her hair and fingernails long. Vera led me to the living room where we joined Sita, along with a young boy and an older married man who lived nearby. We engaged in small talk while Vera, sitting on the floor, shaved her legs and then plucked her eyebrows and chin with tweezers and a small hand-held mirror. After bathing, she continued her preparations with Sita in a little bedroom in the back of the house. Vera's makeup began with lotion over her arms, legs, and face, followed by a liquid foundation, then a regular foundation, then rouge, lipstick, eyebrow pencil, and eye shadow. Sita began by smearing small amounts of lipstick all over her face to give it a pink look, followed by foundation. Then Vera put on a stuffed bra, a pink long skirt, and a matching pink sweater. Sita put on an orange pastel dress with shoulder straps. During this process people walked in and out of the room, exchanging comments with Vera and Sita. At one point, I asked the older man, "Have you ever dressed up as a woman?" "No," he replied, "I'm a man." "Then what is Vera?" I asked. Vera, back to shaving her legs, deadpanned without even looking up: "I'm a *cewok*." We laughed at the clever turn of phrase, combining *cewek* (woman) and *cowok* (man), paralleling the combination of *wanita* and *pria* in *waria*.

Warias and non-warias alike expect that a man who identifies as waria will déndong, and conversely that a man who déndongs on a daily basis is waria. *Gay* men, it is true, will occasionally déndong for entertainment, but not for sex, since their subjectivity is framed in terms of "desiring the same" (Boellstorff 2005). Those few *gay* men who déndong to obtain male partners talk about themselves as crossing the boundary from *gay* to waria; it is possible to cross this boundary because both *gay* and waria are forms of maleness. I have never heard of a waria becoming a tomboy, or a tomboy becoming a *gay* man, or a *lesbi* woman becoming a waria.

Gay déndong includes the kinds of transformations undergone by Vera. For most warias, however, bodily modification also includes more permanent alterations such as silicone injection and (much more rarely) sex-change operations. Significantly, I have never heard modifications like these called déndong. They are, in fact, more optional than déndong: you can be a waria without injections, but if you never wear women's clothes you will not be viewed as a waria. From oral history data it appears that before the 1970s warias would modify their bodies in two primary ways: drinking "traditional" medicines [*jamu*] said to make the body more feminine, and inserting objects (balloons filled with salt water, a rubber ball cut in half) under a blouse to create breasts. Inserting objects under clothing is rare nowadays; in its place are three main types of more permanent body modification. Although I know of no survey research that could provide a definitive distribution of these procedures, the most common of these seems to be consuming massive doses of female hormones by swallowing birth control pills or by injection. Rita has large breasts of which she is very proud: "When I was around 14 years old and decided I wanted to change [*merubah*], I took three birth control pills at once, four times a day. Now I just take two a day."[23] For warias the goal of hormone therapy is to grow breasts and achieve an overall bodily softness [*lembut*], in contrast to the rigidity [*kaku*] associated with masculine bodies. The second kind of body modification is injecting silicone.[24] The injections are often performed by untrained "experts," often warias themselves, who in 1998, for example, charged as little as 30,000 rupiah (about four dollars at the time). A number of health problems have arisen from injections that move under the skin or become infected, and silicone has as a result become increasingly controversial. It is theoretically possible to have regular plastic surgery to obtain results similar to those sought through silicone, but due to the higher cost this is more rare.

The final kind of body modification is undergone by warias who have sex-change operations. However, while these operations have been available for almost thirty years, few warias have them.[25] Although the operations are beyond the financial resources of many warias, the relative lack of warias who undergo them cannot be explained in financial terms.[26]

The pilgrimage to Mecca, for instance, costs about four times as much as a sex-change operation, yet some warias perform the pilgrimage or pay for a family member to participate. A second reason is the fear of a loss of sensation or that the operation "can have mental effects." A third reason is because warias see themselves, on some level, as men. As a waria in Makassar put it, "that thing has a function for me." Sometimes this is phrased in terms of religious belief, as in the case of a Muslim waria who said: "We just have to thank God for what we already have." I have heard warias speak of a waria who has undergone a sex-change operation as "becoming a woman" [jadi perempuan], and in the media, postoperative warias are described as considering themselves women.[27] But from my ethnographic work and that of others, it seems clear that such persons are still considered warias socially, even if they can become women in a legal sense (Oetomo 1996). Unlike some transgender subjectivities (e.g., see Cohen 1995; Nanda 1990; Reddy 2005 for hijras in India), genital alteration is not central to being waria. How, then, does male femininity operate in warias' understanding of themselves and their place in Indonesian society?

PLAYBACK

I think the answer to this question began to dawn on me the day that the low-slung wooden ferry from Makassar, belching fumes, pulled up to the dock at the Isle of Heaven [Pulau Kayangan]. "Heaven" is a small place: no more than one hundred yards on each side, this tiny islet is one of many off Makassar's waterfront. Covered entirely in cement, it sits in a tin-roofed shadow as a getaway for city dwellers interested in picnics, fishing, and swimming. Walking off the pier, I passed a sign reading "Today's Event: Waria Playback Contest [Lomba Waria Playback]." After passing several small restaurants and tiny hotels, at the center of the island I came to a stage that was open to the sea on three sides. The benches were packed with several hundred city dwellers, mostly young couples with infants, toddlers, and young children, as well as a few gay men who were there to support waria friends. Inside the dressing rooms to one side of the stage at least thirty warias were frantically applying makeup, rearranging miniskirts, or practicing dance steps. Exiting one dressing room was Siska, a Bugis waria who ran a small salon in Makassar in the house she shared with her family. She wore a white Indian sari with jewelry to match. Her braided wig, entwined with flowers, fell to the small of her back.

A middle-aged professionally attired woman took center stage as the emcee; behind her was a large poster that read "Isle of Heaven Waria Playback Singing Contest." After introducing the three-member jury composed of local entertainment personalities, the emcee explained that each of the twenty waria contestants would perform *playback* (lip-synching to prerecorded cassette music). An eruption of hooting and hollering greeted the first waria as she took the stage in a black top and flowing red dress, performing "My Heart Will Go On" from the *Titanic* soundtrack. The second waria also performed to "My Heart Will Go On"; indeed, about half the performers used Western music (including Miami Sound Machine, Debbie Gibson, and Toni Braxton) and the others used popular Indonesian songs. Near the end of the competition, Siska took the stage to perform a well-known Bombay show tune, and suddenly the island was filled with the echoes of Indian tabla drums. No one knew the words, but Siska's playback was enthusiastic, complete with twirling head movements and tinkling ankle bells. Finally, it was time to announce the winners, and first place went to Siska. "She won because she was unique [*unik*]," said one of the *gay* men to nods of agreement, "and because her movements were so good."

Here, in a nutshell, is a central distinction between waria and *gay* subjectivity. Warias have performed Indian dances for many years; for instance, they performed Indian dances at Taman Remaja in the late 1970s (Moerthiko 1980:86). But such performers do not imagine themselves performing as Indian male-to-female transgenders [hijras]. A few warias have encountered Australian, European, or Southeast Asian transgenders during travels outside Indonesia, or they have friends or relatives who have done so, and some mass-mediated images of transgenders outside of Indonesia make their way into the archipelago. For the most part, however, warias do not see themselves as linked to a global network. This is in contrast to *gay* Indonesians, whose subject positions presuppose the existence of gay Westerners with whom they share a "desire for the same." How do warias understand their place in Indonesia, as symbolized by Siska's victory as well as by the toilets of Taman Remaja with which I began this chapter?

The answer to this question perhaps lies in the Indonesian term *playback*, often used to designate waria performances. Playback (lip-synching) is when someone performs a song to a recorded soundtrack. It is akin to yet distinct from dubbing, which is when someone overlays their own voice to recorded images (Boellstorff 2005). In dubbing, mouth and speech do not match up. In playback they do; instead, it is person and persona that do not match up. The waria singing playback is not actually "singing," but neither were Celine Dion or Diana Ross in the videos from which warias get inspiration for costumes and poses.

Playback is a kind of performative déndong, a "making up" that lies between authentic and inauthentic, natural and artificial. Note that I am speaking of performativity here as a general process, ritualized in contexts of performance like that described above but not limited to them. It is important to keep performance and performativity distinct. As Don Kulick notes, "The difference is this: performance is something a subject does. Performativity, on the other hand, is the process through which the subject emerges. This is a crucial distinction that was completely missed by many critics of [Judith] Butler's work" (2003:140).

With this distinction in mind, playback is a productive theoretical concept because of the central position that authenticity [*asli*] holds in Indonesian understandings of both ethnolocalized tradition and modern nation. The opposition between authentic and false is key to Indonesia's encounter with modernity (Siegel 1998:52–65): colonial rule is deemed false; the postcolonial state is deemed authentic. *Asli* is a complex term; it is a loanword in its own right (from Sanskrit) and is difficult to translate into English. Echols and Shadily's dictionary *Kamus Indonesia Inggris* gives its meaning as "original, genuine, authentic, indigenous, native, autochthonous, aboriginal, primitive, innate, inborn." Someone who is from a place, rather than an immigrant, is *asli Bali, asli Indonesia,* or *asli Amerika.* Someone will speak of a lake or well as asli water in comparison to piped water, or complain in a shopping mall that the coldness from air conditioning can make one's arthritis hurt, while the asli cold found in a mountain village is pleasant. An adopted child can sometimes be distinguished from an asli child. For warias and other Indonesians as well, asli is a cultural keyword through which gender is cognized and negotiated. For instance, one night at Taman Ramaja, a *gay* man pointed to a tall waria in black standing nearby and whispered, "she's never had an operation — she's asli."

Successful playback involves not authenticity but haunting (for instance, playing back Celine Dion through an appropriately made-up, glamorous body moving lips in imitation). Playback does not aim for authenticity, nor is it deceptively false. Playback is spectral in a contemporary Indonesian context where the boundary between the original and inauthentic is so fractured that "there is a neologism, *aspal*, stemming from an acronym, to designate it" (Siegel 1998:54). *Aspal* means "asphalt" in standard Indonesian, but it also brings together *asli* and *palsu*, authentic and false, just like *waria* brings together female and male, *wanita* and *pria*. Aspal permits successful performativity like asphalt enables movement: what distinguishes the aspal diploma from the simply palsu diploma is that the former can get you a job. Warias are, in a certain sense, aspal, "real-but-false" (Siegel 1998:54); they playback femininity in a manner that genders them and also stakes a claim to national belonging. This is how the waria Chenny Han could say that any waria who had a sex-change operation would be "an aspal woman, authentic but false [*perempuan aspal, asli tapi palsu*]" (quoted in Soentoro 1996:207), yet Cindy, one of my inerlocutors during fieldwork, could proudly say on one occasion "I'm authentically waria [*saya asli waria*]."

SEX AND ROMANCE WITH MEN

A dichotomy prevails in the Indonesian public's perception of waria sexuality. On one hand is the belief that warias "are sexually impotent and/or have abnormally small or even shriveled genitals" (Oetomo 1996:261). Other Indonesians (including warias themselves) believe warias normally have sex with men rather than women or other warias.[28] Waria sexuality has long been linked to money, and indeed many (but by no means all) warias engage in some form of sex work.[29] The most common practice during sex work is receptive oral sex. Anal receptive sex is also common and sometimes carried out in public locations (usually behind a bush or tarp). However, some men ask to suck the waria's penis or to be penetrated anally by the waria (see Oetomo 1996:263).

During my 1998 fieldwork there was an undeveloped field, the size of a city block, located near the governor's office in the Balinese provincial capital of Denpasar. This space, called "Renon," was swampy and overgrown with weeds, except for a few dirt paths traversing its expanse. Warias would find their clients among the men passing by on motorcycle or foot, and sex would take place right there in the grass. In the afternoons before heading off to Renon, many warias visited the house of a waria named Donna. Her home was popular because of its location, which was only a few hundred yards from the field. With cement walls, two small rooms, and a color television set, it was a step above what most warias could afford on their own. One afternoon I was talking to a few warias at Donna's house, and I asked Tina, a sex worker at Renon, if her clients ever ask to be anally penetrated. Tina replied, "Oh yes, the majority of them want that. It usually just happens right there in the field, behind a bush or something." Since she was one of the few warias at Renon to have had a sex-change operation, Tina carried a dildo to service men who asked to be penetrated: "I bought the dildo when I was in Jakarta once." Donna had been listening to our conversation, "Oh yes, lots of men want me to screw them up the ass, even the schoolkids. So I have to do it. Because they're real men, not *gay*, and if you don't do their bidding and penetrate them they'll be shamed" (*malu*; see chapter 5).

What interests me here is that I have never heard a waria question a man's masculinity because of a desire to be anally penetrated. Indeed, many warias enjoy penetrating men. A waria in Makassar emphasized how she likes to penetrate because "after all, I have the body of a man!" Should a man consistently wish for warias to penetrate him, gossip about his masculinity might ensue; the relevant point is that soul and bodily presentation, not just sex, secure gender in Indonesia. This contrasts with many parts of the world (even other parts of Southeast Asia) where, under what is often termed an active/passive logic, to be anally penetrated is the "moment of truth" that immediately and fundamentally compromises masculinity (see Kulick 1998). In Indonesia, the waria subject position is a male femininity marked not by lacking a penis or receptive sexual practices, but by having a woman's soul in a man's body; being a man (or rarely, an intersexed person) with a feminine social presentation; or both. In other words, another reason warias rarely have sex-change operations is that *normal* men expect them to possess penises.

Normal men who have sex with warias either do not know the term *gay* or do not find it applicable to them: instead, "they form a nameless category" (Oetomo 1996:263) that can be a source of confusion to other Indonesians (Emka 2003:183). However, as noted by Malinowski, cultural concepts (including subject positions) are not always lexicalized: it is not the case that these men stand outside culture. "Surya" is a small, half-abandoned plaza next to Taman Remaja, and during my fieldwork it was completely dark at night. On Thursday nights after the waria show, warias and lower-class men would make their way there to meet for sex. One night at Surya I sat down beside a group of young men as scores of other men and warias milled around the plaza. In the course of our conversation, I had, when asked, revealed that I was gay. "Oh!" one young man replied. Pointing to a man sitting next to him, he said: "This guy likes guys too. He probably likes you." The man in question looked up calmly but was silent. I asked the men if they liked warias. A third man replied amid the shrugs of the others: "No, but they do this," and stuck a finger into his mouth as a gesture for oral sex.

Neither warias nor the mostly blue-collar unmarried men who spend time at Surya would term themselves *gay*. Yet these are not simply "men who have sex with men"; this is not sex without sexuality. An interpretation that explains these men's practices in terms of obtaining a substitute for women — an interpretation expressed by my interlocutor at Surya — could not address why some men who know of Surya do not go there; nor could it explain why men who do go to Surya do not go to inexpensive female sex workers, why some ask to be anally penetrated, or why some enter into long-term romantic relationships with warias. It is not that these men have a "situational" homosexuality opposed to the "innate" sexuality of warias. There is a colonial history of bifurcating homosexuality into innate and situational variants and then claiming that situational homosexualities are ephemeral, unlinked to subjectivity, and inauthentic (Bleys 1995). Subject positions like waria and *gay* are situational as well as innate in that they are linked to specific places and times.

Although most *gay* men marry women, this situation is usually incompatible with waria subjectivity. As one waria in Makassar put it, "Everyone agrees that if someone doesn't want to get married, that means they're 100 percent banci." Occasionally a waria's family will suggest (or insist) that they marry a woman. Most families, however, release warias from the marriage imperative. Warias are perhaps the only class of persons in contemporary Indonesian society other than the disabled who are typically not expected to marry. Therefore, instead of heterosexual marriage most warias seek romance in the form of a long-term boyfriend [*pacar*] or "husband" [*suami*], who typically identify as *normal* and are accepted by their waria partners as such. Although these relationships are not formalized, they are in all likelihood as old as the subject position itself.[30] As is the case for female-to-male transgenders in other parts of the world (Kulick 1998), one way that warias hold onto male partners is by supporting them financially. Many warias share the feelings of one of my waria interlocutors who complained that "men always want money. If that's all they want, then eventually we let them go. But if they give us care and affection [*kasih sayang*], we'll take care of them. . . . My husband is brave [*berani*] enough to hug and kiss me in the open, to take me to a movie when I'm dressed as a woman and ignore what people say. And that's what we bancis really want—a man who will give us care and affection. But in the end it all comes down to money." This statement reveals a key dynamic of waria subjectivity. For Brazilian travesti, the goal is to have a "man in the house" who secures their transgender subjectivity by penetrating them (Kulick 1998). Indonesian warias, however, emphasize having a man who will take them out of the house and into the public sphere—who will act as the conduit to secure their recognition by *normal* society (see, e.g., Soentoro 1996:217).

For warias with an unmarried boyfriend, a major concern is retaining the boyfriend after they are married to a woman. Since most warias assume that all men eventually marry (and often feel that this is best for them), the goal is to sustain the relationship after marriage, with or without the wife's knowledge. Wives are often unaware that their husbands are continuing a previous relationship with a waria or beginning one after marriage—in the same way that, given the pattern for separate socializing between husbands and wives in much of Indonesia, it is possible for husbands to carry on sexual relationships with other women or with men (and also possible, albeit trickier, for wives to carry on illicit sexual relationships with other men or with women).

While I was not able to interview in any depth the wives of men partnered with warias, it appears that wives who know of their husband's relationship with a waria accept the matter because warias are more likely to give the husband money than the other way around; there is no chance of the waria being taken on as a second wife and no fear of illegitimate children; and this arrangement is relatively easy to hide from one's neighbors. These are the same reasons wives give for accepting their husbands' affairs with *gay* men (see Brenner 1998).

Sometimes a waria and her partner live together as a conjugal couple, and the man rejects heterosexual marriage altogether. Even though warias are rarely confused with women, their gender presentation is such that male partners are sometimes supported by their families in their decision not to marry. Such couples are often accepted by neighbors, and in some cases they may also raise children who may be adopted or from either party's previous marriage to a woman. The relationships between warias and their boyfriends illustrate not only important moments of romance, affection, and sex, but also a linkage between the waria subject position and what *gay* men and warias term general society [*masyarakat umum*] or the *normal* world [*dunia normal*].

WARIAS IN NATIONAL SOCIETY

One evening in Makassar, we headed to the Family Planning Foundation office for an event to celebrate a new program sponsored by the United Nations Development Fund to help waria sex workers learn salon work. Cindy, a well-known waria, was the guest of honor at the event. The audience included members of the program's first class; owners of the salons where the apprenticeships would take place; staff members from the HIV prevention organization that was administering the program; and well wishers like myself. Cindy and the director of the HIV prevention organization spoke before the crowd about the need for discipline and cleanliness; the director added that "warias are needed by society because they have skills." At the end of the ceremony, Cindy motioned to a waria apprentice who then rose and moved to the front of the room. As cameras flashed, Cindy handed over with great solemnity a bag containing scissors, shampoo, hairspray, and other items as the event came to an end.

Warias and their social interlocutors do not see them as exclusive to Balinese culture or Javanese culture or Ambonese culture: warias are seen to be, and see themselves as, elements of national culture. Since warias can be found in rural areas, this is not simply due to an association with an "emerging metropolitan superculture" (Geertz 1963); its national spatial scale draws from the same colonial boundaries and social dynamics to which the postcolonial nation-state is heir. Despite these links to the national, the waria subject position — unlike the *gay* and *lesbi* subject positions — has hitherto not been linked to globalizing discourses of gender and sexuality. This does not mean that warias imagine there are only men and women in the rest of the world. Most assume the existence of "transvestites" elsewhere. However, warias imagine these transvestite Others in the most general terms, in the same way an Indonesian imagines there are "trees," or "men," or "lunchtime" in other places; that is, a roughly equivalent semantic category but not a subject position linked to their own across space.

To date, the waria subject position does not evoke transnational community. Some warias have seen images of non-Indonesian transgenders (for instance, by renting the movie *The Crying Game*), but these images are still difficult to obtain. Waria subjectivity, unlike *gay* and *lesbi* subjectivity, is at present poorly linked to transnational print and electronic media. Rarely to date has transgenderism outside Indonesia been covered by Indonesian media, as in a *Tempo* article that compared the sex change operation of a waria in 1998 to a similar operation that year in Egypt.[31] Only a very small number of warias have traveled to other countries and met transgenders there (mostly Singapore), and only a few have learned of such transgenders indirectly through "Westerners" visiting Indonesia.[32]

It appears that from the time of the first formalized waria groups in the 1970s, such groups were understood to be in conversation with national culture, not tradition [*adat*]. In 1972, the Jakarta mayor Ali Sadikin "supported the creation of the waria association Himpunan Wadam [later Waria] Jakarta" (Abeyasekere 1987:231). Its name recalls Perhimpunan Indonesia (*perhimpunan* is a variant of *himpunan*), the first anticolonial organization to use "Indonesia" in its name; its "stress on the Indonesian nation and its promotion of a national, as opposed to a regional, identity, were of lasting importance" (Ingleson 1975:71). In justifying his support, Sadikin spoke in terms of national belonging rather than preserving tradition: "I feel responsible for everything that happens to my citizens . . . I saw that this group was not regarded as having a right to exist. They were ostracized by society . . . we must see them as humans, as citizens of this city, as citizens of this country" (Atmojo 1986:18). Sadikin's phrasing reflects how my waria interlocutors in the 1990s and in the first decade of the twenty-first century have spoken of wishing to be "accepted by general society" (the phrase often used is *diterima oleh masyarakat umum*), and I suspect Sadikin was voicing a viewpoint shared by the warias of Himpunan Wadam Jakarta themselves. Warias are now familiar figures in the political sphere: they perform at party rallies, express preferences for candidates, and occasionally run for office themselves.[33] Warias in Makassar recall how in 1999 a waria beauty contest was sponsored by a local district official [*bupati*], during which the official told those gathered that "society must accept warias, because ninety percent of all salon people are warias" — and the audience clapped in response.[34] The acknowledgment of warias even extends to official circles. For instance, some warias in East Java have successfully lobbied the provincial government for a special "male (waria)" designation on their identity cards (Oetomo 1996:266), a formulation recalling the toilets at Taman Remaja.

Warias' understanding of their history often reflects a national imaginary. One of the clearest statements of this in my fieldwork came from Tri, a Bugis waria living in Makassar. When I asked Tri how warias in different parts of Indonesia were similar or different, she explained that they were "branches off a single tree" rooted in Bugis culture, then scattered across Indonesia because of a war.[35] This tree metaphor seems to reflect widespread Austronesian conceptions of relationality, but like the use of the banyan tree image by Golkar, the political party of former President Soeharto, it receives a national twist. When I asked if any warias scattered to Malaysia or the Philippines, Tri hesitated: "I don't know, because I have never been to those places." But although Tri had never been to parts of Indonesia beyond Sulawesi, Kalimantan, and Bali, her imagined community extended confidently to the limits of the nation.

The waria subject position has long been linked to performance, though as noted above the processes of performativity by which persons inhabit the waria subject position are by no means limited to performance narrowly construed. In the postcolonial period, waria performances have often been understood in terms of national belonging. For instance, although warias have been performing in ludruk theater since at least the 1920s, after independence in 1945 they became increasingly linked to the nation so that by the early 1960s "the transvestite singer is the only ludruk performer who regularly and directly exhorts an audience to be *madju* [progress-oriented] and loyal to the nation . . . he beseeches 'all ethnic groups' to be united . . . the transvestite addresses a system, the Nation" (Peacock 1968:208–9). Similarly, Barbara Hatley notes that by the 1960s the waria singing in ludruk performances was "an outspoken proponent of new ways and ideas . . . the singers exhort people to work together to build their nation and make a success of the five-year development plan" (1971:100–101).

Warias will spontaneously ruminate on their place in society (rather than solely in the family or their immediate social environs) and interpret daily events such as catcalls from a neighbor or the organizing of a successful beauty pageant as indicators of a shifting state of being accepted by society. At such pageants, earnest waria contestants call for societal acceptance in much the same way that Miss America contestants are parodied as calling for peace on earth. Warias in all three of my major field sites and throughout Indonesia emphasize recognition; it is a desire joining everyday belonging to national belonging through the performance of good deeds or accomplishments (sometimes called *prestasis*; see chapter 1). Like *gay* men, warias almost never say they should be respected just because of who they are (as the status-based language of Western human rights discourse might lead one to expect) but rather in terms of good deeds: "We've got good deeds too [*kita punya prestasi juga*]." Sometimes good deeds lead to greater acceptance from the family: "When I was young my brother hit me, but I followed my heart until one day when I won a beauty contest, and then they not only accepted me but supported me!" But the good deeds that really matter to warias are performed not on behalf of other warias or one's family, but on behalf of society [*masyarakat*]. Frequent turns of phrase are that the acceptance of warias is up to each waria [*tergantung dari waria sendiri*] or that warias must become high quality [*jadi waria yang berkualitas*], with "high quality" referring both to beauty and good deeds. In this line of thinking, warias who are not accepted have brought this upon themselves by not being smart at presenting themselves [*tidak pintar menetapkan diri*]. Good deeds include self-presentation: Cindy once lectured some young warias at her salon about how "it depends on how we treat others. We must dress cleanly and be polite so that we can be valued [*dihargai*]." Her comments suggest a performative theory of recognition.

The most significant prestasi performed by warias is their work in salons. The ultimate expression of this salon work is wedding makeup and hairstyling, where the bride, and also the groom, are "made up" as prototypes of the true Indonesian, the idealized citizen-subject. In line with the national motto of "unity in diversity," the bride and groom are usually made up twice, once in modern garb (a white dress for the bride, a suit for the groom) and once in "traditional" ethnolocal garb. Warias create and manage heteronormative ethnicity; a poor woman in rural Java or southern Sulawesi becomes a Javanese or Buginese princess.

FIGURE 13
The author and his
partner made up as a
"traditional" Buginese
heterosexual couple by a
waria in Makassar.

Even the ethnographer and his partner can be made up in such an ethno-localized fashion, as when I became a Buginese maiden in 2000 for an entertainment event in Makassar (see figure 13).[36]

One can thus playback not just gender but also ethnicity and national belonging. Salon work can encapsulate a national imaginary akin to the "theme park-ization" of national culture (Pemberton 1994), where local culture, which is by definition nonmodern, takes form and meaning through the prism of the national. The waria Chenny Han notes as one of her greatest *prestasi* that she memorized how to do hair buns [*sang-gul*] both in the modern style and in the traditional style of each of Indonesia's then twenty-seven provinces (Soentoro 1996:34, 112). Another waria, in discussing the good things that warias do, noted proudly that during the 1997–1998 economic crisis "salons beat the banks" [*salon mengalahkan bank*] because they stayed open and continued to serve society. "The banks lost society's money [*merugikan masyarakat*] but not the salons."

Good deeds can also be produced at smaller events. I recall arriving one night at the salon of Marina, a leader in Makassar's waria community. Later that evening we were to attend the wedding celebration of the brother of one of Marina's waria staff, and the salon was a buzz of activity as warias put finishing touches on their outfits. Marina was splendid in a traditional-looking outfit with batik skirt [*kebaya*], lacy blouse, and cloth thrown over her shoulders; she explained that the outfit was not Makassarese but mixed [*campuran*]. We headed to the north side of town where the wedding celebration was underway—a typical affair in which a tarp on tall bamboo posts forms an impromptu roof over a neighborhood street cordoned off and filled with hundreds of guests. After the obligatory greeting of the bride and groom, we made our way toward the stage at the far end of the street where a band played. The area was filled with warias and *gay* men while family members, neighbors, and well wishers sat on the periphery. The *gay* men along with the other guests were spectators as the warias (who came from across Makassar and also many regions of southern Sulawesi: Pangerang, Sidrang, even distant Pare-Pare) checked the makeup and dresses of their friends (and themselves) with intense care. By about eleven o'clock the bride and groom had departed, and it was time for the presentation of waria awards based on voting earlier in the evening. The award for "most unique [*unik*] waria" went to a waria with a glittering silver outfit and short blond hair. There were awards for most beautiful waria, older waria [*waria nostalgia*], and many others. Endi was one of the two warias making the presentations, and she wanted to be sure the audience understood the good deeds of warias. "Long Live Waria!" she cried. "Warias are now being accepted by society because of all of their good works, especially in the fields of beauty and fashion. This shows that our heroes [*pahlawan*] are not just men and women, but warias. In this era of reform [*era reformasi*], there should be a place for warias, because warias have organizations and do good things in society."

WARIAS, AUTHENTICITY, AND PLAYBACK

In moments such as these, warias talk explicitly about belonging to national—not local—society. In this concluding section, I explore the underlying cultural logics that shape both the gendering of warias and their included-but-marginalized place in the nation.

At the toilets of Taman Remaja, as I have shown, warias are grouped with men. I have indicated at several points in this chapter that while some might argue that the waria subject position is a third gender,[37] the designation seems inappropriate overall, and it is not clear what "gender" would mean in such an expression. Framing "waria" as a third gender positions it as equidistant from "male" and "female," eliding the fact that warias begin life as men and tend to see themselves as feminine men throughout their lives. Likewise, a growing number of scholars have difficulty with Marjorie Garber's claim that the "third-gender" concept "questions binary thinking and introduces a crisis" (1992:9–13). Such scholars disagree with Garber's assertion that, in Rosalind Morris's summation, the concept "function[s] in an inherently critical manner" (Morris 1997:62), noting how it actually "tends to stabilize" conceptions of male and female (Halberstam 1998:261). "Third gender" suggests that individuals so identified who "do not fit the male-female binary fall outside it and transcend it, rather than disturb it, blur it, or reconfigure it . . . third-gender language leaves the traditional male-female binary intact" (Kulick 1998:230; see also Garcia 1996:84–87; Towle and Morgan 2002; Weston 2002). It also has romanticizing effects: for instance, while often used when speaking of Native American transgenders (e.g., *berdache*) or transgenders outside the West, sissies, tomboys, and drag queens in the United States are rarely cast as third genders. Although third-gender language might appear to disrupt the isomorphism between gender and sex (three or more genders cannot be slotted into what are assumed to be two sexes), it can only do so by treating "gender" as the signifier of "sex" in the same way that Ferdinand de Saussure's famous illustration (see figure 14) of the semiotic function pairs an image of a tree with the word "tree" (1959:67; this version of the image is taken from Lacan 1977:151).

Saussure stressed that signs gain meaning in relationship to other signs. Lacan (1971:151) illustrated this point through what he termed "urinary segregation," contrasting Saussure's tree image with a pair of toilets (see figure 15). Here male and female gain meaning not through reference to physicality (toilet doors need not use images of genitalia), but in relation to each other, sign to sign. Lacan saw this not only as an illustration of semiosis but as a foundational moment in human subjectivity: "These are the only possible [two] definitions of the share called man, or else woman, for anyone who finds themselves in the position of inhabiting language" (Lacan 1985:150).

Lacan's illustration recalls a very concrete "bathroom problem" for persons who deviate from gender norms, one that "illustrates in remarkably clear ways the flourishing existence of gender binarism despite rumors of its demise" (Halberstam 1998:22). It illustrates that to date even the most radical conceptions of transgenderism, whether MTF (male-to-female) or FTM (female-to-male), do retain F and M in some fashion. This is one factor making "third-gender" language so unfocused and proscriptive (calling for transcending binarisms), rather than reflecting any actual system of gendered meaning. It is, therefore, ultimately rehabilitative of gender binarism. There is no a priori reason that a third, fourth, or *n*th gender could not exist, but I find theoretically limiting the assumption in much of the literature on sexuality that this binarism is — by definition and independent of any real-world context — limiting and oppressive. It might be more productive to ask under what circumstances the male-female binarism is oppressive, the various ways such oppressions operate, and under what circumstances it is not oppressive at all. Consider, for instance, how the toilets at Taman Remaja differ from Lacan's image (see figure 16). As before, ladies (wanita) are on one side and gentlemen (pria) on the other. But below pria is that government-invented but now everyday term *waria* — combining "ladies" and "gentlemen" but categorized under only one of them. Waria appears not as a third term but part of a secondary binarism within maleness, as also exemplified by the "male (waria)" identity cards that were issued for a time in East Java.[38]

On the subject of identity cards, why was the waria who climbed the stage at Taman Remaja not asked to show one? It cannot simply be that warias can be identified by sight alone, because this is typically true for Indonesian men and women as well. Most warias carry identity cards marking them as male, and even a "male (waria)" identity card makes warias a subtype of male. If both the identity card and the toilet signs are signifiers, then what exactly do they signify? The answer is simple: they signify "waria." But more importantly, what is the ontology of this "waria" that is signified? What is its status of existence? This is the issue that unites the two key questions under discussion: the gendering of warias and their place in national society. At the Taman Remaja toilets, "waria" does not have an independent ontological status but rather appears subsumed within "male." Warias' narratives of personal history are also animated by a relation of abjection to the male, a movement toward a male femininity that is, in the eyes of dominant gender norms, a

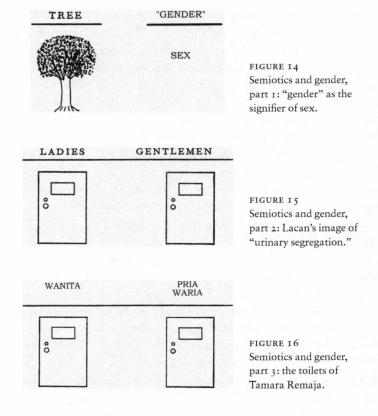

FIGURE 14
Semiotics and gender,
part 1: "gender" as the
signifier of sex.

FIGURE 15
Semiotics and gender,
part 2: Lacan's image of
"urinary segregation."

FIGURE 16
Semiotics and gender,
part 3: the toilets of
Tamara Remaja.

movement toward failure. It seems the waria subject position exists as a kind of ghost in the machine of the male. Traditional ontology cannot explain this kind of presence that literally, through makeup (déndong), "makes itself up" as it goes along. Makeup is key here: while warias often take female hormones or inject silicone, no waria would do such things without also making themselves up. This is a case of what Jacques Derrida terms "hauntology": the waria subject position haunts maleness. Derrida develops this concept in the context of thinking through how performativity — a concept that has played a powerful role in gender theory — plays out in the context of politics and recognition: "The act that consists in swearing, taking an oath, therefore promising, deciding, taking a *responsibility*, in short, committing oneself in a performative fashion . . . [is] the limit that would permit one to identify the political" (1994:50–51).

What, then, is the key to the performativity of waria-gendered subjectivity? It is not the waria show at Taman Remaja; not all warias "perform" in this manner, and those who do are still warias when not performing. The true waria performance is déndong; their subjectivity is "produced by the regulation of attributes along culturally established lines of coherence" (Butler 1990:24). "Making oneself up" (Hacking 1992) is the performance that makes a waria, that makes up the very thing it makes up. And the exact same activity, déndong, is the prototypical prestasi or "good deed" that — in the eyes of warias and in the eyes of Indonesians more generally — makes warias worthy of belonging to society. Déndong "makes up" warias as a haunting presence as it also "makes up" (i.e., compensates) for their failure as masculine men. Warias are unique in Indonesia in that the gendered thing that they do to themselves is the same thing they prototypically do to others, but with radically different consequences. Warias signify their gender by making themselves up, but when they make up Indonesian women or cut the hair of Indonesian men they "make them up" as better representatives of proper modern Indonesian womanhood and manhood, without which what the state terms its family principle of heteronormative governance [*azas kekeluargaan*] would not be intelligible.[39]

But no matter how good the makeup, warias cannot make themselves up as women, nor would they want to do so in most cases. Nor are they representatives of a third gender. "Waria" is a gendered subject position haunting maleness. In subjectivity as in sex, the prototypical waria has a penis. Both the gendering of warias and their marginal place in Indonesian society are effects of this haunted condition of existence; this is where these two issues come together. I am not making a structuralist argument here: were warias a true third gender they might still be marginalized. Instead I am claiming that the haunting form their marginalization takes is of a piece with the dynamics of their gendering.

And if there is one thing that the hauntological cannot be, it is authentic [asli]. We find an assumption that to be crafted through human action (i.e., through prestasis) renders things false [palsu]; un-asli, inauthentic, colonially contaminated. The status of the authentic, the asli, is self-evident; it does not have to be performed. Consider once again how warias base claims for belonging *and* establish gendered subjectivity through déndong, the good deed of making up, rather than status-based claims to "tradition." *Gay* men also talk about good deeds and authenticity. But for *gay* men the good deeds that could lead society to accept them (working in an orphanage, publishing a zine, or even behaving politely) are not the same things that establish their gendered and sexual subjectivities (see chapter 1).

Warias themselves, as well as Indonesian society more generally, view waria gender in terms of performance, not status: this is why it was unnecessary at Taman Remaja to ask the waria contestant for her identity card. It is probably also not coincidental that the man and woman were called — or hailed, in Althusserian parlance (see chapter 3) — on the basis of status (place of residence), whereas the waria was hailed on the basis of braided hair: déndong. How can we understand a claim to belonging that is framed not in terms of the status-based rights discourse familiar to Western sexual rights movements but in terms of the performance of good deeds? And how can we understand the special tension between a claim to belonging based on performance in a context where belonging is understood in terms of uncrafted authenticity? How do warias hope to gain national belonging through performing prestasis when authenticity lies beyond prestasi's limit, evaporates at prestasi's very touch? How can one playback cultural citizenship?

This claim to belonging remains unanswered. As compared with transgendered persons in many parts of the world, warias are accepted, but their acceptance is incomplete. As Indonesia moves further into the uncharted waters of its era of reform, the visibility of warias appears to be increasing, but true social acceptance remains an open question. I end, then, with words of hope, spoken in 2000 by a young waria in Makassar, transforming the "year of living dangerously" phrase famously uttered by Indonesia's first president and thereby locating warias once more on the stage of national belonging: "This is the Year of the Awakening of Warias [*Tahun Kebangkitan Waria*]!"

꙳

THREE

GAY *LANGUAGE, REGISTERING BELONGING*

> Imagine, then, a linguistics that decentered community,
> that placed at its center the operation of language *across*
> lines of social differentiation, a linguistics that focused
> on modes and zones of contact between dominant and
> dominated groups . . . that focused on how such speakers
> constitute each other relationally and in difference, how
> they enact differences in language. — Mary Louise Pratt,
> "Linguistic Utopias."

Many *gay* men speak what they call *gay* language [*bahasa gay*], a linguistic phenomenon based upon Indonesian [*bahasa Indonesia*], Indonesia's national language. Throughout this chapter I mark Indonesian terms in italic. *Bahasa gay* involves derivational processes, including unique suffixes and word substitutions, and a pragmatics oriented around community rather than secrecy. Although mainstream knowledge of the existence of *gay* men is limited compared to the visibility of warias, *bahasa gay* is increasingly being appropriated by Indonesian popular culture. By examining *bahasa gay* in terms of state power and register, I ask how this form of speaking might contribute to better understanding how *gay* subjectivity is bound up with conceptions of national belonging that, as indicated in chapters 1 and 2, are so important to both *gay* men and *warias*.

Bahasa gay, terms from which I mark with bold italics throughout this chapter, is also known by *gay* men and other Indonesians as *bahasa banci*, a closely related language variety. As discussed in chapter 2, *banci* is a nationwide (and somewhat derogatory) term for male transvestites;

two well-known *bahasa gay/banci* variants of the term are **binan** and **béncong** (thus this language is also called *bahasa **binan*** or *bahasa **béncong***). In contemporary Indonesia, male transvestites prefer the term *waria*, and I use *waria* to refer to these persons for the remainder of this chapter. I do this not only out of respect but also for analytical precision, because *banci* can also be a joking term between *gay* men or a general term of opprobrium, somewhat like "faggot" in English. *Bahasa banci* therefore also has the connotation *"waria* and *gay* language," even "queer language" or "faggot language." It appears that *bahasa gay* originated as a variant of *bahasa waria*. Although I have encountered both *gay* men and *warias* who insist that their languages differ, the two varieties retain many similarities, are spoken in overlapping everyday social worlds, and borrow from each other to the extent that they are sometimes treated as the same entity.[1]

I, too, view *bahasa gay* and *bahasa waria* as essentially the same thing despite minor differences. Thus, although this chapter seeks to highlight the particular features and implications of *bahasa gay* as spoken by *gay* men, my conclusions regarding the impact of the nation-state on *gay* language may be relevant to *waria* language as well, since *warias* are also found nationally (and are not seen as limited to any particular set of ethnicities), and concern themselves with their place in national society.

REGISTERING BELONGING

Throughout my fieldwork, I have looked for regional or local distinctions in *bahasa gay*. To date I have found only minor and temporary variations. Given the well-documented and extensive variation in local cultures across the Indonesian archipelago, such similarity is striking. This chapter provides linguistic evidence for the hypothesis that *gay* subjectivity is bound up with a fractured but real national culture (for further discussion of *bahasa gay*, see Boellstorff 2004).

My analysis does not hinge on examples of *gay* men using *bahasa gay* to speak about their sense of belonging to a national community. People cannot and do not always comment explicitly on the cultural beliefs they hold; this is one strength of ethnography over methodologies based on elicitation. To say that language is shaped by x is not the same thing as saying that x is the topic of conversation: gender norms can shape language use even when gender is not under discussion, and ethnic dialects are not used only for talking about ethnicity. After all, "language ideology . . . is only partly captured in what people say about language. People's talk about language is likely to be less nuanced than their practical but tacit understandings that are embedded in how they actually *use* language" (Keane 1997:98).

In this chapter I approach *bahasa gay* as a register. This concept is notoriously ill defined, even "pretheoretic," in scholarly analysis (Iwasaki and Horie 2000:519; see also Hervey 1992:189 and Biber and Finegan 1994:4). Most early definitions framed register as variation according to use (social context) rather than variation according to user, which was often termed dialectal variation (Asher 1994:3509; Bussmann 1996:402; Leckie-Tarry 1995:6). More recent scholarship on register has revealed how "inference choices drawn from stylistic choice reflect back on information about the language-user" (Hervey 1992:192); the pendulum has swung from use to user such that registers can now be seen as "independent of . . . parameters" of use (Paolillo 2000:217).

The most productive analysis of this oscillation between use and user is Asif Agha's claim that "diversity of metalinguistic opinion on the part of linguists is motivated, to an extent, by differences of metapragmatic opinion on the part of language users" (Agha 1998:154). Agha's point is that the relationship between social identities and social context — between user and use — is "leaky"; that is, ways of speaking are "stereotypes" about kinds of people and vice versa. In other words, the issue is not to resolve whether registers are about kinds of speakers or contexts of speaking; registers linguistically perform and sustain both this conceptual dichotomy and its inevitable "leakage" in actual practice. This formulation recalls not only work in the anthropology of sexuality that exposes the contradictions of the identity/behavior binarism (Elliston 1995), but also work on language ideology that reveals how beliefs about language reflect beliefs about society (Irvine and Gal 2000; Kroskrity 2000; Silverstein 1979, 1998). My analysis draws upon these literatures to suggest that *bahasa gay* indicates how the lifeworlds of *gay* men are "leaking" into Indonesian national culture even as most Indonesians remain at best ignorant of, and at worst openly hostile to, their existence. It is the productive tension between context and subjectivity that, as I discuss later, makes *bahasa gay* so amenable to appropriation by Indonesian popular culture. *Bahasa gay* suggests that as *gay* men become better known in Indonesia, their social stereotyping (Agha 1998:168; Hervey

1992:195) is increasingly as members of national culture, not "local" or "traditional" cultures.

Most theories of how power systems shape subjectivities frame this influence in one of two ways. The first is in terms of "interpellation" through a dominant ideology. As articulated by Louis Althusser, interpellation is the process by which an ideology "hails" persons into understanding their selfhood within that ideology's terms. In Althusser's analysis, this is necessary in capitalism (or any economic system) because "the reproduction of labour power requires . . . a reproduction of its submission to the rules of the established order" (1971:132). The second common way of understanding how power systems shape subjectivities makes the opposite assumption: it is the view that in rejecting a dominant system of power, persons form senses of selfhood that are at odds with that dominant system, though of course still influenced by it. Examples of this kind of framework include notions of "reverse discourse" (Foucault 1978), "oppositional consciousness" (Sandoval 1991), or "disidentification" (Muñoz 1999; see also the introduction).

Could there be a third possibility, where the influence of power systems is neither direct nor oppositional, but more contingent and contextual? *Bahasa gay* raises the possibility that systems of power can create structuring conditions for subject positions that they neither call into being nor repress. In such cases, the subject position in question would not be in alignment with or antagonistic toward the ideology to which it would nonetheless be beholden for cultural coherence. In Indonesia, for example, the imbrication of the *gay* subject position with national discourse can persist regardless of particular *gay* Indonesians' views on the nation. *Bahasa gay* may therefore help us see how a system of power can result in subject positions that speak neither with nor against that system, yet articulate their unexpected logics in terms of that system's grammar — literally and figuratively.

ELEMENTS OF *BAHASA GAY*

The Setting Many *gay* men emphasize that they have a way of speaking in the *gay* world [*dunia gay*] that differs from speech in typical Indonesian society — what they (and Indonesians more generally) often term the *normal* world [*dunia normal*]. During my fieldwork I quickly learned about *bahasa gay* from my *gay* interlocutors. They were happy to teach it to me informally, as they had taught each other (such teaching was almost always limited to lexicon). *Gay* Indonesian men knew me as a self-identified gay U.S. citizen, and they enjoyed showing me what they saw as an interesting and important part of their world—which they were often happy to show to *normal* persons as well. These men believed *gay* men and gay men to be similar in some respects, yet they saw the Indonesian *gay* world as distinct.

Then as now the *gay* world refers not to a fixed topography but to an imagined geography where *gay* men can be open [*terbuka*]. It comes into being any time *gay* men gather at the slightest remove from the *normal* world. This imagined *gay* world is not contiguous but rather composed of an archipelago of physical locales ranging from parks and salons to shopping malls and individual apartments; it also includes intangible romantic, sexual, and friendly networks of affiliation (Boellstorff 2005). Physical locales typically become part of the *gay* world only when occupied by *gay* men. Some of these places are given names, the motivation for which tends to be idiosyncratic. In the city of Surabaya in eastern Java, where places in the *gay* world are most commonly given names originating outside Indonesia, such names are learned from the mass media (and associated with the West) but often have an additional local motivation: *Texas* sounds like a contraction of Indonesian *terminal bis* [bus terminal]; *Kalifor* (from "California"), which is located next to a river, begins with *kali* [river]. In the city of Yogyakarta in central Java, the town square is known by many as *L.A.*, which recalls the Indonesian word for town square, *alun-alun*, while the town square in the city of Solo in central Java is often termed *Manhattan*. The town square in the city of Makassar on the island of Sulawesi is simply called *kampus* [campus], reflecting its status as a place where men gather away from home, and the term *kampus* is used in many other cities as well.

Bahasa gay has arisen in a context rich in secret languages and specialized argots, the best known of which is *prokem*, an urban street language based on Indonesian (Chambert-Loir 1984; Dreyfuss 1983; Rahardja and Chambert-Loir 1990; Saleh 1988). *Prokem* appears to have originated in the criminal underworld of Medan and Jakarta in the early 1960s, spreading to street youth by the late 1960s and to university-educated youth by the mid-1970s (Chambert-Loir 1984:115). *Bahasa gay* probably began in the 1970s, and a few items of bahasa gay (such as *se'* [homosexual man]) probably date back to the 1960s (Oetomo 2001) and were part of the earlier male homosexual worlds that are one important source shaping the contemporary *gay* subject position. The earliest record of *bahasa gay* of which I am aware is a word list of twenty-five items gathered in the mid-1970s in Yogyakarta by Amen Budiman (1979:106–7); many items from this list are still in widespread use.

Given the size of Indonesia's population and its considerable linguistic diversity, I had every reason to expect that as I moved from island to island and between different regions within islands, I would encounter differing *gay* languages based on, say, Makassarese or Balinese. What I discovered was something *gay* men already knew: namely that local variations in *bahasa gay* vocabulary exist but all are part of a national *bahasa gay*.

Of course, lexical items of *bahasa gay* that are limited to certain areas can be found in many locales; *bahasa gay* changes quickly, although some terms and phonological patterns persist for decades. However, based on my fieldwork there appears to be a widespread understanding among *gay* men that such variations are just that; local variations on a *bahasa gay* that is at its core the same [*sama*] across Indonesia and grammatically based on the Indonesian language. *Sama* is also the term that *gay* men use to describe their homosexual desires — that is, a "desire for the same." The common belief that *bahasa gay* is the same across Indonesia is reinforced by the fact that, to date, all of the derivational patterns used to produce *bahasa gay* lexemes originate in one region of Indonesia but became nationally distributed through *gay* social networks.[2] As one *gay* man put it, "In the end [due to this borrowing] the language of our people is almost the same. In Indonesia" [*Akhirnya, biasanya bahasa kaum kita hampir sama. Di Indonesia*].

One variation on this pattern is that terms that are claimed to be Javanese (though often of unclear origin) have become elements of *bahasa gay* in Makassar (see table 3). This is not simply an instance of the broader incursion of Javanese into the national vernacular (Anderson 1990a) because these terms are not used by *gay* men on Java itself; their use is distinctive to *gay* Makassar, thus reflecting a sense of translocal connection. One *gay* man in Makassar spoke of this process as *gay* men in Makassar "socializing" [*memasyarakatkan*] terms learned on visits to Java. This man also noted that one result of this process is that as these terms become transformed in the "local" context, many *gay* men in Makassar (and those who spend time with them) mistakenly believe that

TABLE 3
Lexemes found in the *bahasa gay* of Makassar claimed to be from Javanese.

Term (origin)	Meaning	Replaces Indonesian Term
aluk (unknown)	penis	*kontol*
mendolo (Javanese)	pop-eyed	*lihat* (to see)
kula (Javanese)	I, me, my	*saya*
longka (probably Javanese *langka* [exceedingly big])	big	*besar*
muttu (unknown)	have sex	*main seks*
neka (unknown; possibly Javanese *eka* [one])	he, she, it	*dia*
ora (Javanese)	no, not	*tidak*
sampeyan (Javanese)	you	*kamu*
sibollo' (unknown)	friend	*sahabat*
ta'belo (possibly from Javanese *tabel* [puffy, swollen])	bad	*jelek*
tabu (unknown)	eat	*makan*

they are speaking Javanese when they are really speaking *gay* language: "They think, 'Oh, maybe this is Javanese, but they are really speaking *gay* language" [*mereka pikir "oh mungkin, ini bahasa Jawa," tapi sebenarnya dia bicara dalam bahasa gay*].

   To readers coming from a queer studies background, the fact that *gay* language is based upon Indonesian may not seem noteworthy. It is crucial to emphasize that anthropological approaches to the region almost never take the nation-state as an ethnographic unit: for example, one studies "Javanese" or "Balinese" not "Indonesian." This framing of culture in terms of ethnolocality (Boellstorff 2002) has been crucial to the dominant conceptions of anthropological fieldwork that assume that "anthropology's distinctive trademark" is to be found in "its commitment to 'the local'" rather than "its attentiveness to epistemological and political issues of location" (Gupta and Ferguson 1997:39). It is the legacy of this tradition that makes so urgent the need for what I have termed an anthropology of similitude (Boellstorff 2005) — an anthropology that could offer "a conception of fieldwork that frames the ethnographic encounter beyond the Self/Other dichotomy" (Bunzl 2004b:436).

The tradition of framing culture in terms of ethnolocality also has a genealogy in the long period of Dutch colonialism, and it has long been connected both to Dutch anthropology's historical linkages to an "applied anthropology" in the service of colonialism (Malinowski 1945:4) and to the politics of language. "Indonesian," originally a Sumatran language, had since before the colonial period been used as a trade language in much of Southeast Asia, often under the name "Malay" or "Melayu" (Siegel 1997). Unlike many colonial powers, the Dutch did not wish their "natives" to learn Dutch itself: "Explicitly rejecting a language and education policy such as pursued by the English in British India . . . a conscious decision had been made . . . not to introduce Dutch as the general medium of communication in the archipelago" (Groeneboer 1998:1). Instead, the Dutch turned to Malay, already widely spoken but not seen as the property of any one ethnic group, as the language of communication with and between the bewildering variety of the more than six hundred languages spoken in the colony.

A gamble the Dutch took (and lost), however, is that their "natives" might eventually think that Malay could index an archipelago-wide community uniting the ethnolocal groups over which the colonial system exercised its power. The colonial bureaucracy thus inadvertently prepared the way for nationalism by inculcating a conceptual shift "from heteroglossia to polyglossia" (Maier 1993) wherein other languages (now termed *bahasa daerah* [regional languages]) were assumed to transparently index distinct groups (Javanese implies Java implies Javanese people; Balinese implies Bali implies Balinese people; Torajan implies Torajaland implies Torajan people). It was only logical to extend this line of thinking to infer from Malay's ubiquity that the colony could be construed as a unified entity. By the twentieth century, a reverse discourse had formed in the sense that the prevalence of Malay, albeit an instrument of colonial power, began to fuel a belief that the disparate ethnic groups of the archipelago could be part of a transethnic and translocal imagined community opposing colonialism. In the hands of nationalists and later the postcolonial state, Malay was renamed Indonesian and was made "perhaps the most important single ingredient in the shaping of the modern culture" (Liddle 1988:1, cited in Errington 1998:4; see also Anderson 1966, Errington 2000:208, Laffan 2002:98–101; Siegel 1997).

For my interlocutors in Java, Bali, and Sulawesi, most of whom were born in the 1960s or later and for whom Soeharto's New Order was all they knew until the era of reform [era reformasi] beginning in 1998, Indonesian was a feature of everyday life (Errington 2000:209). All of my interlocutors spoke Indonesian, as does almost 90 percent of the nation's population, approximately 15 percent of whom now speak it as their first language. This percentage is increasing, and the use of Indonesian as a first language is increasingly linked to middle-class identity (Oetomo 1996b; Sneddon 2003).³ The near-total absence of monolingual Indonesian speakers from the ethnographic record speaks to the enduring power of ideologies of primitivism, indigenity, and ethnolocality in anthropology, and it indicates ways in which a queer studies approach that "queers" not just sexuality and gender but race, place, and class might make possible new forms of coincidental critique (see the introduction).

Bahasa gay, founded in Indonesian, partakes of Indonesian's nationalistic tenor; bahasa gay is also a language "that lacks a primordial ethnic community of native speakers" and is "less nonnative than unnative" (Errington 2000:206). I later return to bahasa gay's founding in Indonesian as part of a discussion of ideology and hegemony. One point I make among others is that bahasa gay does not act as what Michael Halliday termed an antilanguage—that is, "the acting out of a distinct social structure . . . the bearer of an alternative social reality" (1976:572). This is because bahasa gay's fundamental logic is not one of alterity but the creative transformation of a dominant discourse—namely, state discourse—thus remaining within its horizon. Similarly, it does not fit Marcyliena Morgan's definition of a "counterlanguage" as "a conscious attempt . . . to represent an alternative reality through a communication system based on ambiguity, irony, and satire" (1993:423). This is because although bahasa gay is a conscious (and often humorous) language game, it represents not an alternative reality but the queering of a dominant reality.

Derivation Although competence in *bahasa gay* includes intonation, pragmatics, and ideology about *bahasa gay* itself, what *gay* men (and those who appropriate *bahasa gay*) find most salient is its lexicon; indeed, scholarly and everyday commentaries on *bahasa gay* frequently refer only to this facet. The *bahasa gay* lexicon is, however, more than just a collection of words; it is a set of patterned derivational processes that together constitute a language game. In its emphasis on derivational processes, *bahasa gay* resembles not only *prokem* but gay languages elsewhere in Southeast Asia and beyond, including Filipino "swardspeak" and British "Polari" (Baker 2002; Garcia 1996; Lucas 1997). However, unlike "swardspeak," in which one process, "ipis talk," is said by some to make the face look "queenie" due to the frequent [i] and [v] sounds that purse the lips (Manalansan 1995:203), the derivational processes of *bahasa gay* are not considered inherently effeminizing. It is the existence of these productive derivational processes that typifies *bahasa gay;* true fluency is signaled not just by knowing vocabulary but by knowing the processes and being able to coin neologisms oneself.

There are several ways to create *gay* terms, most of which involve retaining the first syllable of a standard Indonesian word and then modifying the ending. Thus most terms in *bahasa gay* form a kind of commentary on standard language and in this sense resist dominant norms, although such resistance is not always overt (see Oetomo 2001:67–71).[4] Particularly since the mid-1990s the most popular process is *syllabic substitution*, where a word replaces a standard Indonesian word with which it shares a syllable (typically the first syllable). For instance, *tidak* [no, not] is replaced by *tinta* [tint; see table 4]. This process may have begun in the city of Medan in Sumatra (Oetomo 2001:65). In some cases the substituting word comes from a local language, but most come from Indonesian. To my knowledge *bahasa gay* terms are never formed from Sanskrit loanwords; nor are they formed from Arabic loanwords, despite the frequency of the latter in contemporary Indonesian. This situation suggests that *gay* subjectivities take form less through organized religion or the historical links between Indonesia and India than through national and transnational mass media.

There is usually no semantic link between the substituted word and the original, and this semantic dissonance is part of the humor of *bahasa gay*, although weak semantic motivations are sometimes discernible. Examples are **kelinci** [rabbit] replacing *kecil* [small] (but **jelita** [lovely]

TABLE 4   Syllabic substitution in *bahasa gay*.

Bahasa gay term	Original meaning in Indonesian	Replaces Indonesian term	Meaning
amplop	envelope	*ampun*	in set phrase *ya ampun* (oh my God!)
Balikpapan	city in Kalimantan	*kembali*	you're welcome
BBC	British Broadcasting Corporation	*becak*	pedicab
bodrex	cough medicine	*bodoh*	stupid
ciptadent	brand of toothpaste	*cium*	to kiss
émbér	pail, bucket	*émang*	indeed
jelita	lovely	*jelek*	bad
lapangan	open field	*lapar*	hungry
Makassar	city in Sulawesi	*makan*	to eat
mawar	rose	*mau*	to want
Polonia	airport in the city of Medan (in Sumatra)	*pulang*	to go home
Samarinda	city in Kalimantan	*sama-sama*	you're welcome
semangka	watermelon	*semak*	to like
sutra	silk	*sudah*	already
tinta	tint	*tidak*	no

TABLE 5 Neologisms in *bahasa gay*.

Bahasa gay term	Replaces Indonesian term	Meaning
akika	*aku*	I (familiar)
cuco	*cakep*	handsome
jahara	*jahat*	evil

replacing *jelek* [bad]), and the standard Indonesian phrase *ya ampun* [Oh my God!; *ampun* literally means "forgiveness"] being replaced with *ya amplop* [*amplop* means "envelope"]. Sometimes the substituting word comes from a product name, as in *bodrex* [a cold medicine] replacing *bodoh* [stupid], or from a place name, such as *Makassar* for *makan* [to eat]. This use of place names, seen also in the naming of some hangout places with geographic terms, such as *Texas, Kalifor*, and *Manhattan*, appears to reflect a connection between *bahasa gay* and the idea of the *gay* world as a distributed network of locales.

Two other derivational processes are related to syllabic substitution. The first is *neologism* (table 5), in which the Indonesian term is replaced by a form that shares with it the same first syllable or sound but does not have a prior meaning of its own. Only a handful of *bahasa gay* terms originate in this manner; *bahasa gay* is overwhelmingly a language of transformation. The second process is *semantic shift*, whereby an Indonesian term is given a new meaning (table 6). Semantic shifting is a feature of non-*gay* urban language as well, where it is termed *plesetan* (Chambert-Loir 1984; Oetomo 2001).

Another important derivational process in *bahasa gay* is *suffixation and vowel shift* (table 7), which is usually used to transform a standard Indonesian term but occasionally involves a *bahasa gay* item, a local language term, or an English loanword. The most common suffixes are *-ong* and *-es; -i* is a less productive variant that arose in the 1990s (Oetomo 2001). In the case of *-ong* suffixation, the vowel of the immediately preceding syllable of the lexeme to be transformed shifts to *é*. Oetomo notes that the same process takes place with the *-es* suffix, but at least in Makassar I have found that a shift to the schwa, rather than *é*,

TABLE 6   Semantic shift in *bahasa gay*.

Bahasa gay term	Original meaning	Meaning in *bahasa gay*
brondong	*fusillade*	young man
goreng	*fry*	anal sex
kucing	*cat*	male sex worker

can sometimes accompany this suffix. Oetomo suggests that suffixation and vowel shift first appeared in Jakarta and in areas most directly influenced by the Jakartan dialect of Indonesian and may be derived from *prokem*, although the suffixes differ; he also notes that a few terms of *-ong* shifting, namely **béncong** (from *banci* [male transvestite]) and **népsong** (from *napsu* [desire]) appear to have come into existence before *bahasa gay* took form (2001:62). In 1984, Henri Chambert-Loir noted that "transvestites are generally known to use words with the suffix *-ong*, such as **polesong** (> *polis* [police]), **keménong** (> *ke mana* [where to?])" (1984:110); in a footnote he added, "Apparently homosexuals use similar words, for example, **lékong** (> *lelaki* [man, male]); **gedong** (> *gede* [big]); **mesrong** (> *mesra* [intimate]); and so forth" (1984:110). At least some of these (e.g., **polésong, lékong, gédong**) remain current in *bahasa gay*. As in the case of all other derivational processes for *bahasa gay*, the most common kinds of transformed words are nouns and adjectives, but verbal lexemes can be transformed as well, as in the case of **keménong**, or **terjédong** for *terjadi* [to have happened].

Beyond syllabic substitution (including neologism and semantic shift) and suffixation with vowel shift, there are several minor processes for creating *bahasa gay* vocabulary through affixation and acronyms. *Si-prefixing* is primarily found in Javanese-speaking areas (Oetomo 1999, 2001), but like all elements of *bahasa gay* it has spread elsewhere. In this process the first syllable of a term is prefixed with *si-*, other syllables are deleted, and a consonant is added at the end of the word if the syllable ends in a vowel. *Si* is a Javanese and Indonesian particle indicating categories of persons; in *bahasa gay* it usually retains this meaning. Examples

TABLE 7   Suffixation and vowel shift in *bahasa gay*.

Indonesian or *bahasa gay* term	Meaning	New *bahasa gay* term
banci	*waria*	*béncong* or *bences*
berapa	how much?	*brépong*
dandan	put on makeup	*déndong* or *dendes*
homo	homosexual	*hémong*
lelaki	man	*lékong* or *lekes*
loco	masturbate (Javanese)	*lécong, leces,* or *léci*
pura-pura	pretend	*péres*
sakit	sick ("attracted to the same sex" in *bahasa gay*)	*sékong, sékes,* or *sekes*
terjadi	to have happened	*térjedong*

include *silan* (from Javanese *lanang* [man]), *sihom* (from *homo*), *siban* (from *banci*), *siG* for *gay*, and *siL* for *lesbi* (the letter *G* is pronounced [gei] in Indonesian; *L* is pronounced [el]). The town square in Yogyakarta, known in *bahasa gay* as *L.A.*, is sometimes called *Si-A.L.*; the *L* and *A* are switched in this case to create a pun (*sial* is Indonesian for "bad luck").

With *-in- infixing*, the infix *-in-* is "inserted between the consonant and vowel of every syllable, usually with a shortening of the product so that it becomes two syllables long" (Oetomo 1999:28). Thus *banci* becomes *binancini*, which becomes *binan*. *Linak*, a *bahasa gay* term for "man," is another example of this process [*laki* > *linakini* > *linak*], as is *lines* for "lesbian" [*lesbi* > *linesbini* > *lines*]. Oetomo (2001) notes that this process appears to have begun in Jakarta and Bandung and then spread across Indonesia (it is known in Makassar, for instance). Infixing is not unusual in Indonesian wordplay: Chambert-Loir considers the *-ok-* infix to be "the only *bahasa prokem* element, the uniqueness of which cannot be disputed" (1984:111–12); the infixes *-in-* and *-ark-/-arg-* appear in Javanese urban languages, and in the case of *-ark-/-arg-* in Indonesian ones as well (Chambert-Loir 1984:109).[5]

An additional process is *-se' suffixing*, in which all but the first syllable of a word is deleted (plus the first consonant of the following syllable, if the first syllable ends in a vowel) and the remaining syllable is suffixed with *-se'*: *homo* > *hom* > *homse'*; *Cina* "Chinese" > *Cin* > **Cinse'**.

Yet another means of forming *bahasa gay* terms involves the reinterpretation of standard Indonesian terms as acronyms: For instance, **kopi susu** (coffee with milk) can mean *(ko)ntol (p)anjang (i)tu (s)angatk(u) (su)ka* "I really like that big cock" (Boy and Yasiano 1999:41–43). This process is best documented in the city of Bandung in West Java. In *prokem* such reinterpretations are a long-standing form of wordplay (Chambert-Loir 1984:107), and I have often heard examples in everyday vernacular Indonesian.

Intonation   Though far less emphasized than patterned lexicon, speaking in what is considered to be an effeminate manner is also sometimes asserted by *gay* men to be indicative of *bahasa gay*. By "effeminate" (in standard Indonesian *kewanitaan* or *feminin*; *bahasa gay* terms include **ngondhek, mégol, kriting** [curly]), these men refer to the high-pitched tone and rising utterance-final intonation that Indonesians associate with images of demure femininity and softness [*lembut*].[6] For example, one night at **Texas**, Karno, a gay man, told me he was preparing for a vacation in Bali with the aim of meeting Western men. (One reason Bali is a popular internal tourist destination is that it provides an opportunity to observe Westerners.) Karno asked, "How can you tell which white people are 'like this' [*begini*] and which ones aren't?" We discussed some Western gay symbols, and then I turned the question around, asking if he could tell which Indonesian men might be *gay*. Karno and the other men present agreed that one usually could tell, and Karno emphasized speech as an indicator. About half an hour later I was speaking with another man in the group when Karno interrupted me: "That's it! You're talking how *gay* men talk right now! Instead of saying 'like that' [*begitu*] normally, you just said it this way," and he imitated my use of rising utterance-final intonation.

SECRET LANGUAGE OR COMMUNITY LANGUAGE?

As I gained some competency in *bahasa gay*, I discovered that I needed to learn not only words but the pragmatics of their use in everyday inter-action. To my knowledge, people are never directly instructed in these pragmatics as they are for matters relating to lexicon. Indeed, one of the two consciously articulated ideologies concerning *bahasa gay* proves to be an unintentional red herring: if asked, "Why does *bahasa gay* exist?" many gay Indonesians respond that it is a secret language [*bahasa ra-hasia*]; or what Michael Aceto (1995) calls a "cryptolect." I am far from alone in encountering this response: for instance, Budiman (1979) refers to *bahasa gay* as *bahasa rahasia*, and Richard Howard's study of *gay* men in Jakarta notes that "individuals explained to me that they use gay slang because they could speak freely about their homosexual desires and experiences without worrying that other people could understand what they were saying" (1996:9). He adds, however, that "the use of gay slang also functions to foster a sense of belonging to a community" (9; see also Oetomo 2001:67). Similarly, Philippine gay men explicitly jus-tify their "gayspeak" or "swardspeak" as "communicating with each other in a way in which the outside . . . world is unable to make sense of it" (Manalansan 1995:202).

I once heard this understanding of *bahasa gay* articulated by Linda, a *tomboy* (see chapter 6) who had learned *bahasa gay* from *gay* friends. One day Linda decided she needed to visit a mystical shrine on the slopes of a volcano several hours outside Surabaya; she had lost her job and didn't have a girlfriend and was hoping for some insight on both fronts. I accompanied her, and on reaching the mountainside village where the shrine was located, we checked into an inn owned by a man named Sunardi, who knew neither that Linda was a tomboy nor that I was gay. The next morning Linda and I saw an effeminate man on the neighbor's porch cutting someone's hair. "That's my younger brother," Sunardi said. "He moved to the city a few months ago and works in a salon there." My suspicions that the younger brother might be *gay* were heightened about half an hour later when Linda made a joke and Sunardi added *"péres,"* a *bahasa gay* particle meaning "gotcha!," derived from *pura-pura* [pretend]. Sunardi explained that his younger brother had "learned a new language at the salon in town" and had taught some of it to him. On the ride back to Surabaya that afternoon, Linda was incensed. "Sunardi's younger brother isn't very professional [*kurang profesional*] to tell everyone about *bahasa gay*. That's for our group alone, so we can talk without other people understanding."

I call this widespread view that *bahasa gay* is a secret language a red herring not because Linda and others are dissembling, but because while "the theme of secrecy is a familiar one in what we might call 'folk anti-linguistics' . . . it is unlikely to be the major cause of [its] existence" (Halliday 1976:572; see Bolton and Hutton 1995 and Goyvaerts 1996). *Bahasa gay* can act as a secret language in some cases, but its actual pragmatics appear to reflect more closely the second consciously articulated ideology about it, which is provided by both *gay* men and outside commentators: *bahasa gay* is a "slang" in the sense of a language of association and community [*bahasa gaul*]. My argument is that it is the goal of association that makes a particular utterance a valid "move" in the game of *bahasa gay* and that what is at issue in this association is a sexual community understood in national, not ethnolocalized, terms.

AGAINST THE "SECRET LANGUAGE" HYPOTHESIS

A number of factors make it clear that *bahasa gay* is not a secret language. First, not all *gay* men know about this ostensible "secret." It is neither a necessary nor sufficient condition for *gay* subjectivity: persons who do not know a word of *bahasa gay* can identify as *gay*, and non-*gay* Indonesians who spend time in *gay* places (e.g., *warias*, *tomboys* like Linda, female sex workers, pedicab drivers, salon workers) can become proficient in it. *Bahasa gay* could thus be at best the secret language of a subset of *gay* men, and it cannot serve to keep secrets from precisely those non-*gay* Indonesians who spend time in and around *gay* communities.

Second, in contrast to language games such as pig latin, it is not typical to find an entire phrase or sentence in *bahasa gay*. As noted below, when so often only a single word in an utterance is changed to *bahasa gay*, and that word shares a first syllable with the standard Indonesian term it replaces, the resulting utterance is not very secret. Occasionally every word in an utterance will be in *bahasa gay*, as in the following examples:

(1) Standard Indonesian: *Aku tidak mau*
                                    I don't want

     Bahasa gay: **Akika tinta mawar**
                                      [neologism] tint rose

(2) Standard Indonesian: *Lelaki cakep, [kamu] mau ngésong?*
                                    boy cute, [you] want fellate?

     Bahasa gay: **Lekes cekes, meses ngeses?**
                                    boy cute, [you] want fellate?

In example 1, the standard Indonesian phrase *Aku tidak mau* "I don't want" is replaced with **Akika tinta mawar** [I (neologism) tint rose]. The effect is roughly like what an English speaker would hear if "I don't want" were replaced with "Eyesore donut wonton," or if "That boy is cute" were replaced with "That Boeing is Q-Tip." In example 2, each lexical item is replaced by a suffixed *bahasa gay* variant, so that *Lelaki cakep, mau ngésong?* becomes **Lekes cekes, meses ngeses?** [boy cute, (you) want fellate?]. Here, the effect is somewhat like an English-speaker substituting for "Cute boy, you'd like to suck him?" the pig-latinesque phrase "Cutong boyong, wantong sukong" [cute boy, want suck?]. Such linguistic strings, however, are atypical: the language game of *bahasa gay* is usually played by altering only a single foregrounded word in the utterance, as in "hungry" in example 3.

(3) Standard Indonesian: *Saya mau makan nanti malam*
                                    I want eat later tonight

     Bahasa gay: *Saya mau* **Makassar** *nanti malam*
                                    I want eat later tonight

Here, *makan* is replaced with **Makassar.** This ends up sounding like the English sentence "I want to eagle later tonight." But just as one can imagine a naive English speaker soon learning the meaning of "eagle" as "eat," so the meaning of *saya mau* **Makassar** *nanti malam* would not stay secret for long.

But if *bahasa gay* so rarely serves the cause of secrecy, why should it exist at all? It seems that *bahasa gay* typically works to create a sense of *gay* community in a social world in which *gay* men often spend a great deal of time together in public environments (parks, shopping malls, and so on), but rarely have access to localities identified specifically as *gay*. In such a context, language can help forge a sense of belonging, of space "tactically" transformed by a marginalized community: "The weak must continually turn to their own ends forces alien to them" (de Certeau 1984:xix). Many languages in Indonesia, though not in Indonesian itself, have honorific registers. The best-known example is Javanese, which is commonly described as having an overall distinction between High and Low variants (Errington 1985). The relationship between Indonesian and *bahasa gay* is somewhat parallel to the relationship between High and Low Javanese. For instance, given that High Javanese has a vocabulary of only about one thousand words (Anderson 1990b), entire utterances in High Javanese are infrequent. Many common terms have no High Javanese equivalent: "The word for table is *meja* no matter to whom one is speaking" (Geertz 1960:249; see also Agha 1998:162). However, substituting a single High Javanese lexeme in an otherwise Low Javanese utterance marks the entire utterance as High Javanese. Similarly, one or two *bahasa gay* lexemes move an Indonesian utterance into the register of *bahasa gay*. The key difference is that whereas honorific registers invoke difference, *bahasa gay* invokes sameness and belonging.

I encountered one of many instances of this pattern in Makassar. On August 25, 2000, I recorded a discussion at a meeting held by a group of about twenty *gay* men at the house of Amir, a well-known community leader who, supported by a local nongovernmental organization, opened up his small house for meetings about the trials and tribulations of the *gay* world. Such meetings often began stiffly; even though they took place in part of the *gay* world, their designation as "focus groups" with nongovernmental sponsorship gave them an air of formality. It should not be surprising, then, that although the meeting grew steadily more relaxed and informal, only six widely scattered tokens of *bahasa gay* appear in the first thirty minutes of the recording. Eventually the conversation moved to the question of interactions at the town square or *kampus* between *gay* men, *warias*, and the *normal* men who come to *kampus* in search of sex with one or the other (and who many suspect may secretly be *gay* men or *warias* themselves). The conversation grew more and more animated until finally one of Amir's friends told everyone to stop talking and said the following (example 4):

(4) *kita perlu ramah sama waria* [. . .]	WE NEED FRIENDLY WITH WARIA [. . .]
*soal **lékong-lékong** juga ini, mungkin*	PROBLEM MAN [*lékong* = *lelaki* + *-ong*] + PLURAL ALSO THIS MAYBE
karena sikap-sikapnya	BECAUSE ATTITUDE-PLURAL-3RD POSSESSIVE
***bences** mungkin, bukan*	WARIA [*bences* = *banci* (waria) + *-es*] PERHAPS NOT
*sikap-sikap **lekes**.*	ATTITUDE-PLURAL MAN [*lekes* = *lelaki* + *-es*]

"We need to be friendly with *warias* . . . [because with regard to the] problem of these **men** maybe they really have the attitudes of ***warias***, not the attitudes of **men**."

In this utterance, suffixation with vowel shift is established as a *bahasa gay* game in this conversation. It is here that the conversation takes on a more relaxed and intimate tone and the topic shifts to more personal questions of desire and belonging. Ninety seconds later into the recording, another man commented (example 5):

(5) *masalahnya kita memang*	PROBLEM-3RD POSSESSIVE WE-INCLUSIVE INDEED
***sémong** begitu suka*	GAY [*sémong* = *sama* (same) + *-ong*] INDEED LIKE
menggoda orang	TRANSITIVE-SEDUCE PEOPLE

"The problem is we who are *gay* like to seduce people."

Shortly thereafter, the pattern was extended when someone else asked (example 6):

(6) ***sépong?*** "Who?" [*sépong* = *siapa* (who) + *-ong*]

Although this conversation took place on the island of Sulawesi in 2000, several of these terms (including *bences* and *lékong*) are in Amen Budiman's word list of *bahasa gay* from 1979, and all of them would be recognizable to those conversant in *bahasa gay*, *gay* or otherwise, anywhere in Indonesia where *bahasa gay* has become a presence. To utter only a few words of *bahasa gay*, then, shapes a larger cultural context. Like High Javanese, *bahasa gay* marks and structures social relationships. One motivation for the choice of Indonesian as a national language was its lack of registers. However, at least one register occurs in Indonesian—in the form of *bahasa gay*. This register does not serve the cause of secrecy but rather reveals and sustains the interlocutor's inclusion in the *gay* world.

The examples from the Makassar conversation illustrate a third reason why the "secret language" ideology seems insufficient: *bahasa gay* is typically not used in the presence of people who do not know it. Instead, it appears most often in contexts like a section of a park where only *gay* men are present, or even inside the apartment of a *gay* man. Relevant in this regard is that Linda's anger over the disclosure of the "secret" was not semantic but pragmatic, regarding not revealed content but inappropriate use. A similar pattern of use can be found in *bahasa prokem;* though it is sometimes used as a secret language by criminals and street children, "university students . . . do *not* use it in public or at home with the intention of not being understood by others . . . they use *bahasa prokem* . . . among themselves" (Chambert-Loir 1984:116).

This characteristic of *bahasa gay* can be illustrated by examples from fiction in *gay* zines (see chapter 1). Many stories in zines concern life in ostensibly public sites such as parks and town squares that double as locales in the *gay* world. In this context, determining whether a newcomer is *gay* can be a significant concern. In fictionalized narratives of encounters in zines, initial contact with other men usually takes place without the use of *bahasa gay*, and *bahasa gay* usage indicates that the position of both interlocutors in the *gay* world has already been established. The following excerpts illustrate two deviations from this pattern. In the first, from *GAYa Betawi* 1998:22, Jim is trying to determine if Dario, a man to whom he is attracted, is *gay*. The two men are at Dario's home, not in a public place. Dario has just mentioned that he has an MBA, and Jim asks what the acronym stands for:[7]

*"Mau Bisnis Aja," canda Dario. "Oh saya kira **Meong Brondong Aja"** sambut Jim mencoba terka apakah Dario mengerti bahasa yang sering dipakai di kalangan gay. "Lho itu apalagi artinya?" tanya Dario. . . "Masa abang enggak tahu sih . . . ?" kata Jim penasaran "Betul, saya tidak tahu kok" jawab Dario. . . "Udahlah bang . . . nanti juga akan tahu . . . itu bahasa preman" kata Jim dengan lebih mendekatkan badannya ke Dario.*

"Just Want Business," Dario joked. "Oh, I thought **Just Sex with Young Guys**," answered Jim, trying to guess if Dario understood the language often used in *gay* circles. "My, what does that mean?" Dario asked. . . "Surely you know . . ." said Jim anxiously. "Really, I don't know," answered Dario. "Okay . . . later you'll know . . . it's the language of street youth," said Jim while bringing his body closer to Dario.

The use of *bahasa gay* by one man to another before it is known that both are *gay* is usually considered shocking in these zines, particularly in a more public space such as a park or town square, as in the following story from the city of Yogyakarta (Al Marshal 2001:43–44). A new man has arrived with a friend but is now alone; he approaches the *gay* protagonist:

*"Eh, anterin aku yuk!" kalimatnya yang pertama langsung meluncur begitu saja. Wah, ini orang sok akrab banget, pikirku. Padahal aku tidak mengenalnya. "Tadi sama temanku, tapi dia dapat **méongan**, terus aku ditinggal." Akhirya singkat cerita, aku mengantar orang itu pulang. Kalau kupikir lucu juga, karena kami belum belum saling kenal.*

"Hey, take me [home]!" was the first sentence he just threw out at me. Wow, this guy sure pretends to be chummy, I thought. Even though I didn't know him. "I was with my friend, but he got a **screw** (**méongan** [screw] = *méong* [meow] + *-an* [nominalizer]), so I got left behind." So to make a long story short, I took that guy home. I thought it was funny, because we didn't know each other yet.

In this excerpt, the stranger uses the *bahasa gay* item *méong* [screw], a word that means "meow" in standard Indonesian. The term is doubly motivated because it also appears to have an *-ong* suffix (although in fact it is a single morpheme). That the use of *bahasa gay* primarily marks the conversation as too quickly intimate is indicated by the fact that **méongan** is italicized in the zine itself, as if it were a non-Indonesian term, in the same way that English or Arabic terms are italicized. This is a common technique for the representation of *bahasa gay* in zines, and it gives the sense that it is a language in its own right. Once again it appears that *bahasa gay* works to create a sense of community, even a community brought out into the open too quickly, rather than to keep *gay* community or subjectivity secret.

THE APPROPRIATION OF BAHASA GAY

Finally, the most important indication that *bahasa gay* does not act as a secret language is that it is becoming a feature of the *normal* world. Most *gay* men do not speak *bahasa gay* in the presence of their family or non-*gay* acquaintances (or tell them they are *gay* at all). However, *gay* men can sometimes be openly *gay* when interacting with *normal* Indonesians in contexts like salons. Social encounters like these create the potential for *bahasa gay* terms and even derivational patterns to enter vernacular Indonesian. In this way, elements of *bahasa gay* slowly but surely become part of a national vernacular or *bahasa gaul*. In the *normal* world, the register that results from changing a word or two in an utterance to *bahasa gay/gaul* seems to invoke an Indonesian public culture of freedom from official stricture. The spread of *bahasa gay* has been furthered beyond the salon environment by the appearance of *bahasa gay* in the mass media. By the mid-1990s, during the twilight years of Soeharto's New Order, *gay* men commented on how talk-show hosts and celebrity guests on television shows such as *Abad 21* [21st Century] or *Portret* [Portrait] on the Indosiar and SCTV stations, respectively, would sprinkle their audience patter with *bahasa gay* terms such as *ember* (see table 4) and *péres* (see table 7).

Following the loosening of controls on the mass media after Soeharto's fall in May 1998, there has been a dramatic rise in the appropriation of *bahasa gay*. In 1999, the *gay* zine *GAYa Nusantara* (see chapter 1) ran an article titled *"Bahasa Gay Menjadi Bahasa Gaul"* (*"Bahasa Gay Becomes Bahasa Gaul"*). The article noted the rapid increase in the presence of *bahasa gay* in the mass media in the late 1990s. Here *bahasa gay* is treated as merely a lexicon: "Words of the national homo people [*kebangsaan* (national) *kaum* (people) *hémong*] . . . frequently slide with ease from the lips of Indra Safera or Eko Patrio [stars of the television program *KISS*] . . . Their guests like Anjasmara, Inneke Koesherawati,

Hedy Yunus, Cut Tari and others don't fail to speak similar words . . . It could be said that the program *Lenong Rumpi* [Wicked Folk Theater] on station RCTI was the one to begin introducing *hémong* language . . . It's even said that Jakarta youth that cannot use this language are said to be socially inept and behind the times" (Ibhoed 1999:29–30).

Bahasa gay took an even greater leap into the Indonesian public eye with the publication of *Kamus Bahasa Gaul* [Dictionary of *Bahasa Gaul*] by television personality Debby Sahertian (1999). The dictionary focuses on terms, not derivational patterns, itself a common pattern in how *bahasa gay* is understood primarily as a vocabulary. An instant hit when first published in 1999 and in its eleventh edition by 2003, the text openly acknowledges that much of *bahasa gaul* comes from *bahasa gay*. In fact, I have heard *gay* and *lesbi* Indonesians express frustration over Sahertian for "revealing our secrets," and it is said that Sahertian once apologized for popularizing *bahasa gay*. Such discussions of *bahasa gay* in popular books continue to proliferate (e.g., Emka 2003:186–97). Mass media coverage of *bahasa gay* is also increasing. For example, when a *gay* man appeared on a local talk show in September 2000 in Surabaya, a newspaper covering the event noted that "when answering questions, he often used terms that are frequently used by the *gay* community in Surabaya; for instance, '*Texas*' for a meeting place and '*endang*' for the word '*enak*' [good]" (*Jawa Pos* 2000). More recently, news of *bahasa gay*'s appropriation by Indonesian national culture has reached the international media. In January 2002, the *Australian Financial Review* ran an article on *bahasa gay*, which it called *bahasa gaul* (Dodd 2002).[8]

CONCLUSION

An ethnographic examination of *bahasa gay*'s use in contemporary Indonesian culture reveals a constant theme of connection and belonging. *Bahasa gay* seems to build a sense of *gay* community, and through its public appropriation it also seems to build a sense of *gay* Indonesians as part of the nation. When "normal" Indonesians use *bahasa gay*, it marks them not as *gay* but as part of Indonesian popular culture. It may be that the national connotations of *bahasa gay* can so easily be separated from its denotation of homosexuality because being *gay* is so powerfully imbricated with national discourse. Thus while *gay* Indonesians might appear as inauthentic members of Indonesian society — not belonging to any local culture or "tradition," perhaps even the product of foreign contamination — they are in fact powerfully shaped by national discourse, revealing the workings of the heteronormativity upon which that discourse is based.

The appropriation of *bahasa gay* by Indonesian popular culture indicates that it is transitioning from a "genre register," dependent upon context, to a "social register" indexing "stereotyped personality types" (Hervey 1992). But the stereotyped personality type it indexes is not just "*gay*" but also "Indonesian." Thus in this chapter, as in chapters 1 and 2, what we can provisionally term queer Indonesian subjectivities are fundamentally shaped by national discourse, a clear ethnographic warning to those who would treat globalization as a universal process resisted, if at all, only by a romanticized image of the local (e.g., Massad 2002). *Bahasa gay* registers not alterity but rather belonging — belonging in a world where the nation-state remains the default imagined community, where the "transnational" is the primary form "the global" takes.

FOUR

BETWEEN RELIGION AND DESIRE

The anthropology of religion has long concerned itself with the relationship between orthodoxy and practice, as well as with the problem of making intelligible widely divergent religious beliefs (Tambiah 1990). Such problems of "cultural translation" (Asad 1986) within and across religious traditions have been important to anthropology from its beginnings (Frazer 1915; Tylor 1958) and through many key moments of consolidation and innovation—for instance, in the work of Clifford Geertz, to whom I return at the end of this chapter. As we adjust to a world powerfully redefined—like it or not—in terms of a "war on terror," anthropologists confront a range of official and popular ideologies that portray religion, particularly Islam, as a source of unbridgeable difference. How can fundamentally conflicting understandings of religion and ultimate order regarding issues from jihad to same-sex marriage be understood and lived side by side in a diverse world?

Elizabeth Povinelli has diagnosed the problem posed by such fundamental conflicts of worldview as one of "incommensurability," which refers to a state of affairs where "an undistorted translation cannot be produced" between two systems of thought, language, or culture (2001:320). Noting an increasing ethnographic emphasis on incommensurability, from the contradiction of "other modernities" in China (Rofel 1999) to the paradox of spirit possession in a globalizing Thailand (Morris 2000), Povinelli draws on philosophers of language to link incommensurability to the question of translation and its failures. In this chapter, I explore *gay* Muslims in Indonesia—a case where cultural translation appears to meet its incommensurable limit.

With this concept of "cultural translation" I continue an interest in language theory that marks not only the previous chapter on *gay* language, but notions of playback (chapter 2) and dubbing (Boellstorff 2005) that resurface throughout my work. This use of language theory reflects my own training in linguistics and also the interest in language that has marked anthropology's history (e.g., Malinowski 1935; Sapir 1921). That language theory has been important in queer studies as well, as in Foucault's reworking of the metaphor of "discourse" and Judith Butler's reworking of J. L. Austin's notion of performativity (Austin 1980; Butler 1990), suggests that language could play a pivotal role in shaping what I term "coincidences" between queer studies and anthropology (see the introduction).

In examining *gay* Muslims' sense of inhabiting incommensurability, I do not imply that other religions are more tolerant than Islam, as the enthusiasm for banning same-sex marriage among certain Christian groups in the United States clearly indicates. My interest lies rather in responses to circumstances in which public norms render *gay* and Muslim "ungrammatical" with each other. From the voices amplified from mosques five times a day to fasting during the month of Ramadan to living openly as a husband and wife, Islam in Indonesia (as in many other parts of the world) is not just a matter of personal belief and prayer but constitutes a public sphere that includes the nation itself. Indeed, it is clear that the very notion of Indonesian nationalism was powerfully shaped by pan-ethnic notions of Muslim brotherhood; influences from the Arab world may have been as significant as those emanating from Holland in forming the Indonesian imagined community (Laffan 2003). It is clear from Michael Laffan's work that it was almost exclusively men who participated in the networks of pilgrimage and scholarship in question; Laffan does not discuss how Islam thus served to further inculcate a sense that the national citizen-subject was normatively heterosexual and male. This is a topic that I take up in this chapter and continue in chapter 5. The incommensurability that I discuss in this chapter is not reducible to the experiences of gay Muslims outside Indonesia; Islam, like all "world religions," takes on historically specific forms, and in the case at hand the imbrication of religion, sexuality, and nation is pivotal to discourses of belonging and exclusion.

Heterosexually identified Indonesian men find a long-standing, voluminous, and public Islamic discourse addressed to their transgressions and concerns. Sex between men, in contrast, is unintelligible: *gay* Indonesians find above all the silence of incommensurability.[1] On the relatively rare occasions when Islamic figures speak of male homosexuality, it is typically in terms of absolute rejection. As noted in the periodical *Republika*, "Homosexuality is clearly a social illness, a morally evil trend that must be eliminated, not a human right to be protected as [Western] gays now claim."[2] Male homosexuality does not bifurcate into the meritorious and sinful: it is incomprehensible as a form of sexual selfhood, and this incommensurability is a fundamental difference between how *gay* Muslim Indonesians and heterosexually identified Muslim Indonesian men experience their sexualities.[3] This incommensurability is further strengthened by the fact that although both homosexuality and heterosexuality in contemporary Indonesia operate on global and national spatial scales, no local tradition (*adat*) sanctions contemporary *gay* subjectivities, which are distinct from ritual transvestite practices (Boellstorff 2005, chapter 3). Yet *gay* Muslims exist: How do these Indonesians resolve the apparently incommensurate statuses of being *gay* and being Muslim?[4]

The special challenge of incommensurability in regard to male homosexuality (rather than those proscribed forms of male heterosexuality, like adultery, glossed as *zina*) becomes evident in relation to the public character of Islam in Indonesia, as in other Muslim-majority countries. In his book *Sexuality in Islam*, the influential Tunisian scholar Abdelwahab Bouhdiba notes that "anything that violates the order of the world is a grave 'disorder,' a source of evil and anarchy. That is why zina (adultery) arouses such strong, unanimous condemnation. However, in a sense, zina still remains within the framework of order. It is a disorder in order: it does not strictly speaking violate the fundamental order of the world; it violates only its modalities. It is, in its own way, a form of harmony between the sexes. It is a false *nikah* (marriage), it is not an anti-nikah. It recognizes the harmonious complementarity of the sexes and its error lies in wishing to realize it outside the limits laid down by God" (1998:30–31). Bouhdiba emphasizes that "Islam remains violently hostile to all other ways of realizing sexual desire, which are regarded as unnatural purely and simply because they run counter to the antithetical harmony of the sexes . . . in Islam, male homosexuality stands for all the perversions and constitutes in a sense the depravity of depravities" (31). Not all Muslims agree with Bouhdiba, but it is important to acknowledge the dominance of such views in Indonesia and elsewhere. For Bouhdiba, forms of proscribed heterosexuality, as forms of "false marriage," remain comprehensible within an Islamic framework: to use a linguistic metaphor, they are false utterances on the order of "the earth is square." Male homosexuality, however, is not just false but ungrammatical, like "earth happy twelve the": for Bouhdiba and most Indonesian Muslims, sex between men is incommensurable with Islam.

This fundamental difference is starkly evident in the scholarship on Indonesian Islam, which correctly emphasizes Islam's public character (Gade 2004; Hefner 2000). For instance, in one of the most comprehensive studies of Indonesian Islamic thought in recent years, John Bowen notes that his "primary objects of study are socially embedded forms of public reasoning" (2003:5). Yet while he emphasizes that "the constant element in the narrative concerns gender, the equality of rights and relationships among men and women" (5), the topic of homosexuality is entirely absent from his study. Similarly, M. B. Hooker's study of Islamic judgments makes only a single brief reference to a 1998 judgment forbidding male and female homosexuality (2003:185). Robert Hefner's important *Civil Islam: Muslims and Democratization in Indonesia* (2000) also ignores homosexuality. That these three (and many others; see Laffan 2003) recent and comprehensive studies of Islam in Indonesia make so little mention of homosexuality accurately reflects how, to date, homosexuality has been incommensurable with Islam as a public discourse.

If, as Bowen and many others have noted, Islam in Indonesia is not a unified dogma but a set of debates, what is significant is that with rare exceptions homosexuality is not even debated in Indonesian Islam (compare this with the predominant place of homosexuality as the Christian Right's "perfect enemy" [Gallagher and Bull 2001]). It is not that there are not *gay* Muslims; as discussed below, most *gay* men follow Islam. Nor is it that being *gay* is never public. While for the most part the "*gay* world" exists as a kind of distributed network — a largely invisible archipelago — amidst the "normal world" of Indonesian national culture, there are cases where male homosexuality appears in the mass media or other public venues. However, there has been virtually no context where Islam and male homosexuality have come together in the public realm. Indonesians find ubiquitous public display of proper heterosexuality and frequent debate over improper heterosexuality (for instance, concerning adultery and female prostitution) but there are no *gay* Muslim publics. Herein lies the incommensurability of being *gay* and being Muslim.

SPATIAL SCALES AND NATIONAL BELONGING

The incommensurability between Islam and male homosexuality in Indonesia is shaped by local and national spatial scales. Recall that Indonesia is home to more Muslims than any other country. Islam has spread through the archipelago since at least the thirteenth century, primarily through the trade networks that linked many coastal communities to each other and, via the Straits of Malacca, to the great commercial system linking the Far East with South Asia, Africa, the Arab world, and Europe (de Graaf 1970). The Dutch were the dominant colonial power in the region for the 350 years preceding World War II; during this time, colonial officials like Snouck Hurgronje called for working against Islam as a potential political movement and for strengthening understandings of it as a set of localized religious beliefs (Steenbrink 1993). This meant, above all, identifying Islam with discrete local customs, or adat. To this day, "ethnolocality" is consistently framed as a starting point, as the origin — however contested and reconfigured — of authenticity that is subsequently placed into dialogue with national and global spatial scales (Boellstorff 2002). This grounding in ethnolocality often leads to a shared frame of reference for modern-day Indonesians and modern-day Indonesianists alike: "I start from the level of village disputes and work upwards" (Bowen 2003:6, chapter 3).

Gay Muslims face a particular challenge because being *gay* is incommensurable with ethnolocality — the "level of the village" that is so important to notions of Islamic selfhood and community in the contemporary archipelago. It is self-evident to *gay* Indonesians (and other Indonesians) that the concept *gay* is not learned from one's elders or from traditional beliefs, and to date there have not been individuals terming themselves "*gay* Javanese" or "*gay* Buginese" or organizing communities based on such identifications; as I discussed in chapters 1, 3, and 4, being "*gay*" is a foundationally national concept linked to globalizing notions of homosexual subjectivity. *Gay* Muslims cannot retreat to "the level of the village" and must find other spatial scales in which to inhabit the incommensurable space of being *gay* and Muslim.

Islam is one of several official religions in Indonesia (the others are Protestantism, Catholicism, Buddhism, and Hinduism — all globally recognized religions rather than localized or "animist" traditions). Despite this concession to national unity, since nearly ninety percent of Indonesians are Muslim, an Islamic ethos predominates in national popular culture and in many regions of the archipelago; indeed, every president has been Muslim and it is widely understood that it could not be otherwise. The vast majority of my *gay* interlocutors have been Muslim. From the existence of a department of religion to the requirement that all Indonesians have an approved religion on their identity cards and marry within their faith, the state links publicly recognized religion to national belonging, a linkage with a history stretching back to the preindependence period (Bowen 2003:178–85, 246–52; Laffan 2003).[5] In postcolonial Indonesia, every citizen is to have a religion just as they are to have a gender — it is an essential attribute of being modern. Having a sexuality is also modern: worldwide, sexuality typically plays an important role in notions of proper citizenship (Mosse 1985). Leslie Dwyer notes in her study of Indonesian family planning that "sexuality and gender may be reified as essential, non-negotiable attributes of national identity" (2000:27). Although family planning discourse focuses on women's sexuality, it also shapes notions of "proper masculinity" so that " 'to make sense as a man in Indonesia' one must get married and function effectively as a dutiful husband and provider . . . the importance of adequately performing one's familial duties and obligations is now linked to notions of progressiveness and good citizenship" (Howard 1996:13,172). Religion, nation, and gender/sexuality thus represent the three points of a triangle that posits the heteronormative nuclear family household as the foundational unit of nation, piety, and proper citizen selfhood.

Because *gay* Muslims almost never find themselves in environments where they can be openly *gay* and Muslim at once, in what ways do they find not the resolution of incommensurability, but its habitation? I have never encountered a *gay* Muslim who had not thought carefully about the relationship between his faith and his homosexual desires, and *gay* Muslims often discuss questions of religion among themselves, though such conversations do not typically take place in official sites like mosques. Most *gay* Indonesians understand Islam to emphasize heterosexual marriage (and having children in that marriage) as the only acceptable basis for a pious life. Yet although *gay* Muslims find the domain of religion conflated with what they term the *normal* world [*dunia normal*], as they move through what they term the *gay* world [*dunia gay*] these Indonesians do not leave their faith behind. Inhabiting apparently incommensurate spaces of religion and *gay* subjectivity becomes largely a matter of individual exegesis—albeit exegesis often shared with *gay* friends. It is for this reason that I focus on individual narratives in this chapter; such narratives accurately portray how most *gay* Indonesians link homosexuality and Islam.

If the question of religion is not surprising to *gay* Muslims, neither is it surprising to Western audiences. Some of the most common questions I am asked are "How do *gay* Indonesians deal with being Muslim?" and "Does Islam in Indonesia accept homosexuality?" These are not just the questions of a layperson. In texts ranging from the earliest sustained Western scholarship on Islam in the archipelago by colonial officials like Snouck Hurgronje, to mid-twentieth-century writing (e.g., Siegel 1969), to more recent work (e.g., Beatty 1999; Bowen 1993, 2003; Hefner 1985, 2000; Laffan 2003; Siapno 2002) there has been great interest in how Islam shapes social relations, law, and governance—even if, as noted earlier, homosexuality is virtually absent in this scholarship.

Another common question I am asked is "How is it that there are Indonesians calling themselves *gay* at all?" Indeed, it is only in the last thirty years that some Indonesians have started calling themselves *gay*, and only in particular and limited circumstances—a significant difference from the much longer history of gay identification in much of the West, including the United States (Chauncey 1994). Many Indonesians still do not know of the term *gay*, or if they do they sometimes think it is an English version of the much better-known terms *banci* and *béncong* (male transvestites, for whom the more respectful term is *waria;* see chapter 2). Among those Indonesians who do know of their *gay* fellow citizens, many portray them as selfish and exclusive. In reality, most *gay* Indonesians are working class and learn of the concept *gay* through mass media or friends, rather than travel outside Indonesia or meeting gay Westerners. Given this situation, it is not surprising that anthropological work on Islam in Indonesia has paid virtually no attention to homosexuality. However, this chapter offers more than an improved understanding of *gay* lives, worthy as such a goal may be. My hope here is that the example of *gay* Muslims can contribute to anthropological and queer studies conversations concerning cultural responses to incommensurability, a topic of increasing importance as globalization becomes experienced less as an impending process and more as a de facto state of affairs. If a resolution to incommensurability exists, I suggest it is likely to be found in a time of coincidence rather than the linear framework of straight time (see the introduction).

DOCTRINE

Most *gay* Muslims understand Islamic orthodoxy to be incommensurate with sex between men, but no orthodoxy provides a complete roadmap for faith; each represents "a structure of ideas and practices that penetrates but does not encompass the lives of its practitioners" (Barth 1993:177). Although some *gay* Muslims recall hearing from religious authorities that homosexuality is sinful, the overarching concern with sexuality that they encounter is the proper channeling of heterosexuality into marriage. Islam is often referred to as a "sex-positive religion" in the sense that sexuality is regarded as a gift from God and the right of every person: "In the quranic view of the world, physical love impinges directly on the social order" (Bouhdiba 1998:9–10). In Islamic thought in Indonesia, as elsewhere, the central concept organizing sexuality is that of marriage, which has historically been seen as a contract between families, not just two individuals.[6] The sins against marriage in Islamic doctrine are typically adultery, premarital sex, and prostitution; male homosexuality is not included because sex between men is assumed not to lead to children. If male homosexuality is mentioned, it usually takes the form of incidental references rather than sustained commentaries, as reflected in the scholarly literature on Islam in Indonesia.

This emphasis on heterosexual marriage and the de-emphasis of male homosexuality is shared by the Indonesian nation-state, whose "family principle" [*azas kekeluargaan*], promulgated through a range of polices including a pervasive family planning regime, stresses that the nation is made up of heterosexual nuclear families, not individual citizens (Suryakusuma 1996). A theme I stress throughout this book is that in Indonesia (and many other national contexts) national belonging and heteronormativity are mutually defining and supporting, such that those who fall outside official sexual norms are failed citizens. Marriage in Muslim communities throughout Indonesia is usually seen as the very foundation of sociality — thereby determining boundaries of kinship and ethnicity, ensuring social reproduction (since children are presumed to be the result of heterosexual couples), and literalizing one's relationship to the divine (Idrus 2004). Marriage is typically a key element of Muslim orthopraxy. It is not simply an expression of sexual desire or a sign of being pious, but a practice that makes one a more pious Muslim (see Mahmood 2004). Given the dual emphasis of Islam and the nation on heterosexual marriage, it is not surprising that so many *gay* Indonesians marry (Boellstorff 1999). It is not inaccurate to speak of a "religious–familial complex" where kinship and faith are part of a single cultural domain. Richard Howard, in his study of mostly Muslim *gay* men in Jakarta, found that they "recognized that they carried within themselves a divinely inspired nature [*kodrat*] as men, which could only be fulfilled through marriage and the continuance of the life cycle" (1996:3).

As heterosexual marriage tends to be the positive concept organizing sexuality, so adultery tends to be the negative one. In the Qur'an and in most Islamic writings, zina is defined primarily in terms of illicit sex between a man and woman. Anal sex between men [*liwath*] is viewed as a sin in the Qur'an, but in a rather oblique manner: Lot [*Luth*] is mentioned, but the cities of Sodom and Gomorrah are not, and in contrast to the detailed attention given to adultery, male homosexuality is not one of the abominations for which specific punishments are listed (Murray and Roscoe 1997:307).

Many scholars see in the Islam of the Mediterranean and Arab worlds a generalized "will not to know," where sex between men, while officially frowned upon, is tolerated so long as its practitioners do not make their acts or desires publicly visible. Such interpretations seem generally valid in the Indonesian case. If asked directly, most Indonesian Muslims will say that Islam disapproves of sex between men, and even liberal writers conclude it has been strongly forbidden in Islam (e.g., Fadhilah 2004). In recent years, there have been scattered incidents of "political homophobia" where Muslim groups attack *gay* men attempting to claim public space (see chapter 5).

In practice, however, male homosexuality has not represented a major concern in Indonesian Islamic thought: the typical perceived opposite of normative heterosexual marriage is the failure to marry, or heterosexual sex outside the marriage bond. In Indonesia it is sometimes unclear as to whether sex between men counts as zina. For instance, the popular

Indonesian Islamic sex manual *Bimbingan Seks Islami* [Islamic Sexual Guidance] states that "some experts in Islamic jurisprudence are of the opinion that male homosexuality is the same as zina, with the result that its penalty is the same as for zina" (Asrori and Zamroni 1997:192). However, the chapter on adultery [*pezinaan*] flatly states that "zina is sexual relations between a man and a woman outside of marriage" (197). The authors posit that zina is damaging because it makes the lineage of children born from the zina uncertain and poses the threat of adverse effects to the fetus from sexually transmitted diseases (203), neither of which is relevant to sex between men. Significantly, the authors claim that zina is on the rise in Indonesia, and they attribute this to the influence of Western media, globalization, urbanization, and modernity (198–200). They do not mention male homosexuality as increasing, nor do they link it to globalization. Its sinfulness lies simply in the fact that it can lead people away from marriage. Because *gay* Muslims find little information on sex between men beyond silence or denunciation, it is primarily through interpretation that they inhabit these incommensurate spaces of religion and desire.

INTERPRETATION

Seeing Being Gay as Sinful   *Gay* Muslims find themselves in a doctrinal environment that speaks little of sex between men, but it is also an environment where notions of interpretation [*ijtihad*] are debated and enacted on a variety of levels, from judicial decisions to personal notions of "virtue" and "sin" (Bowen 2003). Acts of interpretation are also held to be central to being a modern citizen: one votes, one consumes, and in contemporary Indonesia one now typically chooses one's heterosexual marriage partner through love rather than "arrangement," which is increasingly deemed backward and undemocratic (see chapter 1). It is through acts of interpretation, not reference to established conventions in Islamic thought, that the majority of my *gay* interlocutors have arrived at the conclusion that being *gay* either is not sinful or is a comparatively minor sin, so long as they marry women and have children.

Before turning to the apparently predominant view among *gay* men that sex between men is not necessarily sinful, I wish to examine the interpretive practices of those *gay* Muslims who do feel that they are sinning; even in these cases, we find struggles with incommensurability.

At one extreme are those who see their sexuality as a serious sin. One *gay* Muslim in Bali, citing the story of Lot, felt that "being *gay* is a big sin in Islam, one of the sins that cannot be forgiven."[7] A young Muslim man in Surabaya underscored this view by stating that "you know, being *gay* is a sin — a big sin." Reflecting the relative de-emphasis of male homosexuality in Indonesian Islamic thought, many of these *gay* Muslims who feel they are sinning cannot recall where sex between men is prohibited in the Qur'an, or in another approach they combine narratives, as in one *gay* man's rendition of the story of Lot [*Nabi Luth*]: "The people of Lot in Sodom were *gay*, *lesbi*, and waria. One day an angel came to Sodom disguised as a very handsome man. The people of Sodom wanted to have sex with the angel. Lot tried to offer his daughters instead, but the people of Sodom were not interested. So God told Lot to build a big boat and fill it with all the animals of the earth, because he was going to flood the earth. And he flooded the earth, and the people of Sodom were drowned."

My *gay* Muslim interlocutors who felt they were sinning cited the story of Lot and Sodom more than any other as they struggled to interpret their homosexual desires. Another frequently cited story concerned King David as a prophet who fell in love with a man (some say he married the man as well) and was then cursed by God. In Surabaya, one *gay* man combined the stories of Lot and David: "Once there was a city called Sodom. There, men had sex with other men and women had sex with women. Now the prophet David was instructed by God to bring them back, so they would become normal again. So at that time, God sent two angels to Sodom in the guise of two very handsome men. They went to the room of prophet David in Sodom. And once they were there, everyone started saying 'there are these two very handsome men in the house of David.' So they all rushed to the house of David and wanted to force themselves in. The angels went out, and they helped David escape from Sodom. But because they didn't want to change back, that city of Sodom was cursed by God. And all of the *gay* people there were turned into ash and the city was destroyed."

Syncretic narratives like these reflect how many *gay* Muslims perceive prohibitions against sex between men in a rather diffuse manner. A few *gay* Muslims who thought being *gay* was sinful saw their desires for men as having a divine origin, with the injunction being to control desires at odds with God's plan for the world. One such Javanese *gay* Muslim believed *gay* people were created as "a test from God, to see if we can overcome it and still marry and have children." A Sumatran *gay* Muslim believed that "in Islam all people are created with feelings of love towards women and towards men. How large those feelings of love are is dependent on the person." Many *gay* Muslims who saw being *gay* as sinful subscribed to environmental etiologies, as in the case of the following man living in Bali but originally from rural East Java.[8] He felt he became *gay* after being seduced by a boy five years older than him: "I remember being happy about the way it felt. I think that's when I started having feelings for men; I don't think it was something that started from birth, and for that reason I don't agree with your Muslim friends who say that *gay* people were created that way by God. Back then I didn't know the word *gay*, but I had heard the word *homoseks*, and I knew that it was a big sin under Islam. I still feel that way; I feel that it is a big sin. But I also feel that I have to enjoy my life. I can't help it that I like being with men, and don't like being with women. What can I do about it? So I just go on sinning."

Many of these *gay* Muslims located sinfulness in practices, as in the following example: "The sin is from the *gay* activities. In my opinion, all religions are against being *gay*. But whether it's a sin or not depends on what you do. For instance, if you have lots of sex partners, that's a sin, not the *gay*ness itself . . . For instance, say you become *gay*. There are people who become *gay* only here [points to his heart]. They don't actually have sex. They're just happy when they see people of the same sex. And I think that's not a sin . . . Especially in Islam, marriage must come first. It's not supposed to be sex first. But the times demand that style . . . And there are other people who are worse than me, who commit rape or murder."

Muhammad, from a rural part of South Sulawesi, shared this view of sin as arising from acts. Married to a woman, Muhammad nonetheless frequented places in the city of Makassar where *gay* men congregated. He reconciled marriage and what he saw as innate homosexual desires through behavior management: "Well, yes, it is a sin. But I don't do it too much. I have tried to stop; I'm always praying to God and fasting, asking that I won't be like this anymore. But the feelings are still there in my heart, and eventually they just can't be held in anymore; after one to three months they get too strong [points to his chest]. So I have to let it out."

This view that the sinfulness of being *gay* lies in actions rather than status is why some *gay* Muslims avoided certain sexual practices, particularly penile-anal sex. One *gay* man from Makassar, Iwan, noted that "Even up to today, one thing I won't do is penetrate someone or be penetrated anally by them. Because I think that's even more of a sin. There are some people who say you're not an official *gay* [*gay resmi*] if you don't do that, but I don't care." In this understanding, sexual acts, being the responsibility of the self, have greater import than homosexual desire, created by God. Hadi, a *gay* man from Surabaya, was from a devout family; both of his parents had already gone on the pilgrimage to Mecca, and he felt they would disown him should they ever learn he was *gay*. Hadi, like Iwan, worked to "reduce [his] sin as a *gay* person" [*mengurangi dosa saya sebagai gay*]. Unlike Iwan, however, he did this not through avoiding certain sexual practices, but by being a *gay* person who is "successful in his career" [*berhasil dengan karir*]. For Iwan and many other *gay* men, success in society could affect the domain of religion, mitigating the sinfulness of male homosexuality.

Seeing Being Gay as Not Sinful   The range of narratives presented above illustrates how many *gay* Muslims interpret their homosexual desires as being sinful. However, what I found most striking during fieldwork was that such views were not predominant among my *gay* Muslim interlocutors. Instead, most either did not see being *gay* as sinful or understood it to be a minor sin easily forgiven by God. Incommensurability was inhabited and understood as part of God's plan. It was meant to be that one is *gay*, yet also meant to be that being *gay* and being Muslim can never be made commensurate. The starting point for these *gay* Muslims was a belief in God's omnipotence and omniscience. Given that God is all knowing, all wise, and all merciful, many *gay* Muslims concluded that they were created *gay* by God and thus that they were not sinning.

In these views, all forms of desire [*nafsu*] are planted in each individual by God and represent irresistible forces that cannot be denied—a common view among Indonesian Muslims (Brenner 1998:149–57; Siegel 1969). This point was brought home to me when I visited Ketut and Suhadi, a *gay* couple who shared a home with an elderly woman and a little male dog, Tika. Ketut, who was Balinese Hindu, had bought the dog several months earlier and lavished it with affection. His partner Suhadi, a Javanese Muslim, had grown to love the dog as well despite the fact that Indonesian Muslims rarely keep dogs as pets because they are seen as polluting [*najis*]. Tika was several months old and just coming into sexual maturity, playfully mounting the legs of anyone who stopped to pet him. Shaking his head, Ketut said, "Well, it's about time we get him castrated." Suhadi looked at Ketut with a mixture of revulsion and alarm. "It would be so sad that he wouldn't have nafsu. If we do that, would he still want to guard the house?" In this view, nafsu is a vibrant, essential aspect of being that can be temporarily controlled but not forever denied. For *gay* Muslims who do not see their subjectivities as sinful, homosexual desire, planted in one's soul at birth by God, represents a fate [*nasib*] that must be accepted, since "nasib is the ultimate explanation for events in this life: that it was written as the will of God, that so should be" (Barth 1993:184). In the following excerpts, four *gay* Muslims, two Javanese and two Buginese, engage in this line of reasoning:

> In fact, it's a sin, right? But what can we do about it? God created me as *gay* . . . He created me to desire men, not women. God already knows all this, right? So we could also say that it's not a sin. Unless we do it wrong . . . if we have sex with an authentic man [*laki-laki asli*], that's a sin [for both of us]. That man should think, "Gosh, I'm an authentic man; why am I having sex with another man?" That's a sin. But if we are made by God as homo . . . if we have sex with each other — *gay* with *gay* — why is that a sin? He was the one who made us this way! . . . It's fate [nasib], right?

> I know that I was created the same as hetero. It's only that I desire men. I know that God knows my feelings, knows that I like men. So I think it's something that's ordinary and natural [*lumrah dan wajar*] . . . I now realize that God has created everything, including *gay* people, so in fact it's not a sin. I didn't choose to be *gay*. Did you choose to be *gay*? Of course not.

> After I read many books, I came to the belief that God has a different plan for me to have made me a *gay* person. And there is a kind of poetry that is good for me, that is good for you and for all *gay* people. "God has given me the ability to accept the things that I cannot change about myself, and has given me the ability to change the things that can be changed." Because *gayness* [*kegayan*] is inside of me. If it was just a thing like this [pointing to a chair],

maybe I would have already thrown it away by now. But it's everywhere inside of my body. Inside of my nerves, inside of my blood.

Why do I think it's not a sin? Because it is God who creates us as *gay* . . . if for instance we have a *gay* soul [*jiwa gay*], and we try to be like a hetero man, it's transgressing God's will for us [*justru keluar dari kodratnya kita*].

Sometimes a sense of being *gay* as not sinful can even emerge from interactions with religious figures. Ardi, a *gay* man from near Medan in north Sumatra, was known for his skills in magic [*ilmu*], which he had learned at a syncretically minded Islamic boarding school [*pesantren*]: "My religious teacher would speak in an indirect way. For instance, he knew that I was *gay*. I never told him directly, but he knew. And he never said anything about it to me directly, he never said that being *gay* was a sin or anything like that. But he did advise me not to take semen into my mouth or up my butt, because if I did it would weaken my ilmu."

That the incommensurability of being *gay* and Muslim is inhabited rather than superceded is indicated not only by Ardi's religious teacher's indirectness, but by the fact that Ardi planned on marrying a woman and living a "normal" life alongside, not in place of, his *gay* life. Indeed, the greatest concern of most of my *gay* Muslim interlocutors was typically not the sinfulness of homosexuality, but their desire to marry heterosexually. This desire was powerfully shaped by religious and familial pressures but was not just an external imposition; for many it was another form of authentic desire. In the following narrative from Surya, a *gay* Muslim man living in East Java, both Islam and *gay* selfhood repeatedly surface around the issue of marriage. As Surya entered his early twenties, his parents and also his *gay* lover, Hendy, told him that it was his duty to marry and have descendents. Surya also wished to marry: "I felt that I wanted to be normal [*rasa ingin normal*],"

So eventually I married a woman who was a villager and a religious fanatic [*fanatik agama*]. But I couldn't get an erection with her. I tried fantasizing about Hendy while having sex with her, but in order to put my penis into her I had to open my eyes, right? And as soon as I'd do that I'd go flat. So I tried and tried for a whole year . . . Eventually I told her about Hendy. She said it was against Islam, a sin [*dosa*], and I had to stop, but I told her I couldn't. She didn't understand that it's not a physical matter, it's a matter of the soul [jiwa] . . . She cried, "If you're like this, why did you marry me?" She was right because usually one marries for choice [*pada umumnya orang kawin pilihan*] . . . Once I got her pregnant I was so proud! I felt like I'd fulfilled my duty as a man. Now that I'm married, no matter what I have to take care of her and the child because according to Islam that's my responsibility. And fulfilling the sexual function is one of these responsibilities . . . When she found out I was still seeing Hendy, she said I had two choices: get a divorce or stop seeing him. I told her that under Islam she couldn't initiate a divorce and I didn't want a divorce but I was still going to see Hendy. And he and I are still together to this day.

Note how for Surya choice is a defining feature of marriage, *gay* love, and faith — albeit one in which male privilege under his understanding of Islam makes his choice more consequential than his wife's attempt to force a different kind of choice. The shift from marriage based on arrangement to marriage based on choice and love is a key marker of being modern and properly national in Indonesia (Siegel 1997; see chapter 1). Choice is how one consumes in a shopping mall, how one votes in a democracy, and how one implements "family planning," so important to state-sponsored ideologies of sexuality (Dwyer 2000). The importance of choice and love in the context of God's omnipotence even appears in many of the narratives from the minority of my *gay* Muslim interlocutors who claimed they would never marry, as in the following example: "If a man chooses a man and lives together with him, and that is what makes happiness, does that not count as a partner? God created day and night. Sun and moon. God also created man and woman. So why cannot a man with a man be understood as partners? I think that what's clear is that if they love each other, I think that's okay."

Those *gay* Muslims who say they will never marry usually come to that conclusion through acts of interpretation as careful as those of *gay* Muslims who do marry. Islamic law places all human actions within five categories: obligatory acts like daily prayer and fasting [Arabic and Indonesian *wajib*]; commendable but not required acts like performing extra prayers [Arabic, *mandub*; Indonesian, *sunatrasul*]; acts toward which Islam is indifferent, like eating foods that are not forbidden [Arabic, *mubah*]; reprehensible but not forbidden acts like divorce [Arabic, *makruh*]; and forbidden acts like adultery and theft [Arabic and Indonesian, *haram*].[9] Islamic jurists tend to regard marriage as required [*wajib*], but some claim that there are justifiable reasons why some people need not marry: "Marriage in Islam is a sacred contract which every Muslim must enter into, unless there are special reasons why he should not" (Ali 1990:445–46; see also Hallaq 1997:175). These "special reasons" can include not only financial and physical ability but also mental and spiritual ability. Some of my *gay* Muslim interlocutors reasoned both that marriage is commendable but not required [*sunatrasul*], and that their homosexual desires make them physically and spiritually unfit for marriage. As one man noted: "In my opinion I've been this way ever since I was born; I was created this way. So I'm meant to be this way and I have to walk this path. None of us ask to be born this way, right? So it's definitely something that's meant to be. In my view, marriage is a duty [*kewajiban*] for Muslims only if they are capable [*mampu*]. And by mampu I don't just mean financially but spiritually, mentally, and physically as well. So by those criteria I'm not meant to get married and so it's not a sin that I don't marry."

What all of these *gay* Muslims share is a sense that interpretation is necessary in the face of incommensurability between religion and desire. In the void created by the relative lack of Islamic discourse concerning male homosexuality, they feel they must use interpretation to forge answers, however imperfect and uncertain, to the question of how they should live. Even if engaging in these acts of interpretation in isolation from other *gay* men, all of my *gay* interlocutors understood *gay* as a national category of selfhood that is linked to notions of gay selfhood found across the world. I recall a conversation in 2000 with Ali, a *gay* man living in Makassar, a few weeks after Anwar Ibrahim, the deputy prime minister of Malaysia, had been accused of sodomy and sentenced to nine years in prison. I asked Ali if he or his friends were concerned that a similar event could happen in Indonesia. "There's been no influence here," Ali replied. "Malaysia is an officially Muslim country [*negara Islam*]. Indonesia is not a Muslim country, but a country founded on Pancasila [the Five Principles of the nation, including 'Belief in One God,' but not specifying Islam]." For Ali, the fact that Islam was not Indonesia's official religion opened the door to inhabit the apparently incommensurate domains of religion and homosexuality that made the prosecution of the latter comprehensible in the Malaysian context. Yet, even in a nation founded on Pancasila, most Indonesian Muslims understand Islam as a religion of calls to prayer, mosques, and collective rituals like the communal feast [*slametan*] — a religion that participates in a moral public sphere it construes in heterosexual terms. *Gay* Muslims also confront incommensurability with regard to community.

COMMUNITY

My discussion thus far has intentionally presented the intersection of *gay* subjectivity with Islam in privatized terms. This is an accurate impression of the fundamental divide between religion and homosexuality that these Indonesians experience. In Indonesia there is currently no way to be publicly *gay* and seen as a pious Muslim, and thus it remains "ungrammatical." It is clearly not the case that *gay* Muslims do not think about the relationship between Islam and their sexualities; it is precisely that thinking is, to a great degree, the only way they can experience this relationship at all. *Gay* Muslims do not necessarily feel excluded from their religion — I have never heard a *gay* Muslim say they no longer felt they were Muslims due to their sexuality — but they imagine a life course of incommensurability where they are *gay* in the *gay* world, marry heterosexually in the *normal* world, and find religious community in that *normal* world alone. Even many of those *gay* Muslims who do not feel that being *gay* is sinful, and who additionally do not plan on marrying heterosexually, expect to find religious community solely in the *normal* world. I know of no cases to date where *gay* Muslims pray collectively and openly in a mosque or other formal venue.

It is not simply social disapproval that leads to a lack of *gay* Muslim community. Indeed, a handful of *gay* Christian groups have existed in urban centers. Examining a meeting of one such group in a northern district of Surabaya in 1997 will help to highlight the situation of *gay* Muslims. The evening of the meeting I arrived at a storefront closed with a heavy metal gate. In front of the gate were fifteen people, a mix of *gay* men, *warias*, and a few *lesbi* women. After waiting almost half an hour for the person with the keys to show up, we entered the building, a beauty college. We walked through a large room filled with desks: on each one a mannequin head awaited a student's careful powder brush. At the far end of the room was a circular iron staircase; climbing it, we came to a room the same size as the one below, also filled with desks and heads. One wall was completely mirrored and the others sported posters detailing the latest makeup designs, happy customers with facial masks, and giant eyes displaying various eye shadow combinations. Everyone got to work clearing the tables from the room and setting out chairs in five long rows, facing a podium with a placard bearing the salon's address and the words "Prayer Alliance." Three *warias* along with a man and a woman—the leaders of the group—moved to the front of the room holding hands and praying audibly with bowed heads. Meanwhile more men and *warias* entered; soon there were thirty people in the room gossiping, laughing, or praying with heads bowed and eyes closed.

The prayer circle ended and the leaders took their seats at the front of the room. A waria came up from the back of the room to operate an overhead projector; another moved to the podium to begin the service by singing to lyrics shown on the projector. I was told that usually a man accompanied the group with a guitar, but he was absent because he was marrying a woman the following day. Nevertheless, everyone sung with gusto, clapping their hands. The waria leading the singing shouted, "We have no music but still have the spirit to sing and praise God." The singing ended after twenty minutes and the waria asked if there was anyone who wanted to come forward and give testimony. One man told how he had feared he would be late because he worked in the factory on the outskirts of town, but that God had provided transportation in the form of an unexpected ride. The testimony was followed by a sermon, focusing on the importance of following in God's footsteps. The meeting ended with songs, a closing prayer, and invitations to the next meeting in two weeks' time.

This Christian prayer group—significantly, it did not call itself a "church"—was sponsored by a local church but was not allowed to meet on its premises. In a nonpublic context, the group rendered Christianity and *gay* subjectivity commensurate, even though many participants wished to be "cured" and homosexuality was rarely openly discussed. Since the early 2000s, a few Muslim intellectuals have taken tolerant stances with regard to *gay* Muslims, calling for Indonesian Islam to publicly recognize homosexuality and even same-sex marriage (Al Qurthuby et al. 2004). Yet to my knowledge and the knowledge of my interlocutors, no Islamic analogues to the "Prayer Alliance" have existed in Indonesia to date, despite the common existence of informal Muslim study and prayer groups. One explanation for this state of affairs would be that Islam is more disapproving than Christianity of homosexuality.

However, given the range of views in both religions this seems an overly hasty conclusion; at issue is, rather, how for Indonesian Muslims, unlike Indonesian Christians, proper religious practice should be public, not limited to the upper floor of a beauty college. This reflects both Islamic understandings of community [*umma*] and Islam's dominant position in contemporary Indonesia.

A *GAY* SLAMETAN

The ethnographic materials presented in this chapter suggest that whether *gay* Muslims uphold heteronormativity (for instance, by seeing their homosexual desires as sinful, marrying heterosexually, or stating that they plan to marry), or destabilize it on some level (for instance, by seeing their homosexual desires as God given or saying that they will not marry heterosexually), to date no point of commensurability between the "languages" of Islam and *gay* subjectivity has been reached. Yet *gay* lives exist and are lived every day; what we find is a habitation, not a resolution, of incommensurability. This habitation of incommensurability recalls not translation but a process I have elsewhere described as "dubbing culture" (Boellstorff 2005). In dubbing, a topic of recent interest to the Indonesian state, the moving lips of persons speaking one language on a film or television show are set alongside a soundtrack in a different language. The incommensurability of the two languages is not translated in the usual sense; there is no resolution from one language into the other. Instead, the two languages are placed together like rails on a train track that unify only at some ever-receding horizon (see the introduction). It is impossible, say, for a Japanese-language film dubbed into English to have actors whose moving lips exactly match the soundtrack — but this "failure" is presupposed by viewers. Similarly, the simultaneous habitation of the categories *gay* and Muslim is self-consciously incomplete. It might prove interesting to frame this habitation of incommensurability in terms of coincidental time, particularly since such temporalities are found in many parts of Indonesia. The "dubbing" of being *gay* and Muslim might thus be seen as an emic analogue to the coincidental time I set forth in this book as one way to conceptualize new collaborations between queer studies and anthropology.

Such processes might thus hold important lessons for an anthropology of incommensurability by helping to explain "the emergence of radical worlds in the shadow of the liberal diaspora" (Povinelli 2001:320). There may be things—concepts, poems, sublime ideas—that are untranslatable, but nothing is undubbable: "dubbing" is a useful metaphor for inhabiting incommensurability. The narratives discussed above demonstrate how *gay* Muslims do not typically feel that being *gay* will ever be "utterable" in terms of religion and nation. Yet *gay* Muslims exist, inhabiting spaces of incommensurability between *gay*, Muslim, and Indonesian. The religious beliefs and practices of *gay* Muslims are "complementary, overlapping accounts" (Brodwin 2003:86) of faith—that is, habitations of incommensurability involving questions of cultural timing between individual and community.

In *The Religion of Java*, Clifford Geertz identified the communal feast or *slametan* as central to Javanese experiences of Islam. Geertz noted that a slametan resolves incommensurability by acting as a "kind of social universal joint, fitting the various aspects of social life and individual experience together" (1960:11). He further notes that "a slametan can be given in response to almost any occurrence one wishes to celebrate, ameliorate, or sanctify . . . There is always the special food . . . the Islamic chant, and the extra-formal high-Javanese speech of the host . . . Most slametans are held in the evening . . . Upon arrival each guest takes a place on the floor mats . . . When the host has completed the [formal introductory speech], he asks someone present to give the Arabic chant-prayer . . . The preliminaries completed . . . the serving of the food begins" (11–13).

Arno's birthday slametan was held on November 28, 1997, in the little town where he lived, which is located about twenty miles outside Surabaya and, "coincidentally," Geertz's field site for *The Religion of Java*. Arno's friends came in from all over Surabaya (and his boyfriend all the way from Bali) to meet not at Arno's home but at the rented home of another *gay* man, tucked away on a small street on the far side of town. Its small front room had a low ceiling, lit by a single long fluorescent lightbulb and decorated with a quotation from the Qur'an (the *ayat kursi*) alongside photos of the president and vice president. Here Arno could hold his paradoxical gathering—a private slametan—safe from the eyes of family and neighbors, away from the public yet under the indifferent gaze of religion and nation.

Twenty-four men sat in a circle inside the crowded room, their backs pressed to walls. Some of Arno's *gay* friends had been cooking all afternoon. From the kitchen, they emerged to place food in the center of the circle: rice, fried chicken, fried mashed potatoes, peanut sauce, shrimp crackers. The room fell silent as one of Arno's friends began to speak, clearly but informally, in Indonesian rather than in Javanese: "Well, we are here to celebrate Arno's birthday. He won't tell us exactly how old he is, but in any case we're here on his behalf." The assembled guests laughed gently. "So let's take a few moments to pray, each following our own beliefs and praying in our own way. Let's pray for the good fortune and health of Arno. Begin now." A few moments passed in silence with heads bowed. "Okay, that's enough. Now everyone please eat a lot!" Arno moved to the center of the circle and, taking a large pastry server in hand, cut off the tip of the "rice mountain" [*nasi gunung*], putting it on a plate with other food items. Everyone sat quietly: Arno was free to give this first serving to the person of his choice. Turning around on his knees, he approached his boyfriend and gave him the plate as they kissed each other on the cheeks. Approving murmurs reverberated around the circle. Plates were passed around and everyone moved in to eat.

Most slametans involve neighbors, but Arno's slametan grouped together men meeting on the basis of *gay* subjectivity. In place of Javanese narrative coupled with an Arabic chant, obligatory even in the Hindu slametans held by Tengger Javanese (Hefner 1985), these *gay* participants spoke Indonesian and prayed silently, "each in their own way." Inhabiting—not resolving—incommensurability, Arno's slametan was a space of coincidental timing that brought *gay* men together at the social margins. It made no appeal for social inclusion and did not invoke the potential of a *gay* Muslim public. Yet it drew from mainstream religious practice and also national discourses of individuality, national language, and religious egalitarianism. On another night, Arno would hold other events to celebrate his birthday with family members, coworkers, and neighbors. On this evening, however, a *gay* world of faith came into being in a little room around a mound of rice.

FIVE

THE EMERGENCE OF POLITICAL HOMOPHOBIA

On November 11, 2000, about 350 *gay* and male-to-female transvestite Indonesians (*warias*, see chapter 2) gathered in the resort town of Kaliurang in Central Java for an evening of artistic performances and comedy skits.[1] This event, which was held in observance of National Health Day, was sponsored by several health organizations as well as the local France-Indonesia Institute. In addition to the participation of *gay* men and warias, many heterosexual or *normal* Indonesians also attended. Events like this had been held across Indonesia since the early 1990s, and those present had no reason to suspect that this night would be any different from the others.

However, at around 9:30 PM approximately 150 men who later claimed to be members of the *Gerakan Pemuda Ka'bah* (Ka'bah Youth Movement) burst into the Wisma Hastorenggo hall where the celebration was underway.[2] Arriving in a mass of motorcycles and jeeps, many wore the white hats or robes associated with political Islam. Shouting "God is great" and "Look at these men done up like women. Get out, *banci!*"[3] the men assaulted those present with knives, machetes, and clubs. Sounds of shattering glass filled the air as the attackers smashed windows and destroyed chairs, tables, and equipment. No one was killed but at least twenty-five were injured, and witnesses spoke of persons "bathed in blood" from severe wounds. At least three individuals were hospitalized, including the local director of the France-Indonesia Institute, who among other injuries was struck in the head by a sword. Another victim suffered injuries near his right eye after being hit with clubs and a chair; yet another was struck over the head with a bottle until the bottle broke.[4] Others were hurt while fleeing; one *gay* man was injured when leaping from a window to escape. The attackers also robbed and verbally abused their victims, and they vandalized the vehicles used to transport participants to the site. These male attackers displayed a high state of emotion throughout the incident; one *gay* witness described them as filled with cruel anger [*bengis*], possessed by anger [*kalap*], acting hot-tempered and wild [*beringas*], and shouting sadistically [*bentakan-bentakan sadis*].[5] Fifty-seven men were arrested following the event, but all were soon released without charges being filed.

This incident was foreshadowed by a similar situation one year earlier. For two decades in Indonesia a series of groups — ranging from formally structured entities to small groups in rural areas or even individuals — have worked to link together *gay* men and *lesbi* women in a national network.[6] Dédé Oetomo, an anthropologist and linguist based in Surabaya (East Java), has been a major figure in this movement. In the mid-1990s he became involved with the education and propaganda division of the People's Democratic Party (Partai Rakyat Demokratik, or PRD), which includes a call for *gay* and *lesbi* rights in its platform. In 1998 Oetomo even stood as a candidate for national parliament under the PRD banner.

Through the efforts of Oetomo and many others, plans were hatched in the early 1990s to hold a meeting that could strengthen the national network. In December 1993, the First National Gay and Lesbian Congress was held without any negative consequences at Kaliurang, the very location where the violence described above would take place seven years later. From this meeting was born the Indonesian *Lesbi* and *Gay* Network (*Jaringan Lesbi dan Gay Indonesia* or JLGI). The JLGI successfully staged a Second National Congress in Bandung (West Java) in 1995 and a third in Denpasar (Bali) in 1997. Like the first National Congress, these events attracted between fifty and one hundred participants from Java, Bali, and Sulawesi (individuals from other islands rarely attended because there was no money for scholarships). At no time did these events draw unfavorable public attention. The 1997 Denpasar Congress, which I attended, was covered extensively by the local newspaper, *Nusa*, in a five-day series of feature articles (November 24–28, 1997; see figure 17). Much of the coverage repeated stereotypes of *gay* men and *lesbi* women as obsessed with sex, but it also included statements by public figures calling for Indonesian society to "embrace" *lesbi* women and *gay* men.

FIGURE 17　Cartoon from *Gatra* magazine, September 18, 1999, commenting on the Solo incident. Note the angry men in the background, as well as the two men, arms linked in flight, who hold magazines that state "*Rakernas* [*RApat KERja NASional* or "national working meeting"]" and "Lesbian & Gay Solo." The shirt of the man on the left reads "JLGI [Indonesian *Lesbi* and *Gay* Network, or *Jaringan Lesbi dan Gay Indonesia*]"

In the wake of these successes, plans were soon underway for a fourth meeting in 1999 — the first to follow Soeharto's fall from power.[7] That September, members of twenty-one organizations and groups came from Java and Bali to the city of Solo in Central Java to participate in the meeting, which was to take place at the Dana Hotel on September 9–10, with a press conference to follow. Such a press conference had never taken place before, and it represented a substantial move to claim public recognition in post-Soeharto civil society. By at least September 7, however, several Muslim organizations in Solo had learned of the meeting and, in sharp contrast to the indifference that greeted the previous Congresses, they declared that it should not take place. Moreover, this rejection took the form of threatened violence — specifically, to burn down the Dana Hotel and kill anyone found there.[8] The secretary of the local Indonesian Muslim Cleric's Council, Muhammad Amir, stated that the meeting would be "very embarrassing [*sangat memalukan*]. As if we are legalizing the practice of such sexual deviations." The meeting was canceled once these threats became known, but the Muslim organizations soon learned of a backup plan to hold a press conference at the local PRD office. On September 10, a group of youths from these organizations surrounded the office and threatened to burn it down. Death threats were made against Oetomo and a mobilization took place across the city based on rumors that the meeting would be moved to an undisclosed location. As H. Sadili, a member of the governing board for the Solo Muslim Youth Front, stated: "If they become known, they'll definitely become the target of masses running amok."

MASCULINITY AND THE NATION

From one perspective, these incidents appear as cases of the dreary efflorescence of violence following the 1998 fall of Soeharto's "New Order"; that is, violence whose genealogy stretches back through the New Order (1967–1998) to the colonial state. From another perspective, however, the events are bluntly novel: historically, violence against non-normative men in Indonesia has been rare to a degree unimaginable in many Euro-American societies, where assaults on homosexual and transgendered men are familiar elements of the social world.[9] What is in particular need of explanation here is the cultural logic that makes this new genre of violence comprehensible to Indonesians (*gay* or not, Muslim or not) so that these two events could have a continuing, generalized impact.

In a review of the anthropological writing on violence in Southeast Asia, Mary Steedly cautions against either essentializing violence (as an inevitable dimension of human sociality) or culturalizing it (as a necessary element of a particular social system). The third alternative Steedly proposes is to "localize" violence: "By this I mean exploring the full particularity of its multifarious occasions: how it is produced in certain circumstances; how it is deployed, represented, limited, imagined, ignored, or instigated; how it is identified, disciplined, interrogated, and, of course, punished" (1999:445–46). My only quibble with this alternative is that when violence is framed in terms of localization, a presumption that culture is local in the first instance grounds the analysis in the last instance — no matter how emphatically the constitutive role of the state, the legacy of the colonial encounter, or other translocal forces such as "world religions" enter the interpretive frame. In the cases described above, both the "deviant" masculinities and the cultural logics of the attackers drew their structuring assumptions from national and global discourses. Understanding these incidents can illuminate how the full particularity of violence's occasion can involve an imagined Indonesian community (Anderson 1983) rather than the ethnolocal categories (Javanese, Madurese, Buginese, etc.) that, however historicized and problematized, continue to dominate anthropological investigations of the archipelago (Boellstorff 2002). In this chapter I incorporate a view of what was unique about these incidents (that they targeted nonnormative men) with a view of national topographies of culture in order to investigate intersections of emotion and violence. In so doing I complement the important work showing how, historically and at present, violence against women has worked to shape understandings of national belonging (e.g., Dwyer 2004; Idrus 2001; Wieringa 2002) as well as work showing the broader place of violence in Indonesian political culture.[10]

In this chapter I also wish to ask how emotion figures in violence understood as political. In the historical moment in which I write, emotion and political violence come together most starkly in the figure of the terrorist. The "terror-ist" is the limit function of the emotion/violence nexus, and the terrorist's terror is by definition political, otherwise the person is solely a mass murderer. Against claims that emotion is a precultural or even acultural psychological response function, it is clear that the terror produced by political violence is a cultural phenomenon. This means its form is always historically and geographically specific. *Political homophobia* is the name I give to an emergent cultural logic linking emotion, sexuality, and political violence. It brings together the direct object of nonnormative Indonesian men with the indirect object of contemporary Indonesian public culture, making enraged violence against *gay* men intelligible and socially efficacious.

Through highlighting the role of national belonging in this violence, I suggest that norms for Indonesian national identity may be gaining a new masculinist cast. I also hope to foreclose reductive explanations in terms of Islam (see chapter 4). While at present Islam may represent a necessary condition for these new forms of violence, it cannot explain their relationship to masculinity, emotion, and the public sphere; historical linkages between Islam, masculinity, and conceptions of the nation certainly exist (Laffan 2003), but they do not determine these new forms of violence. In reconfiguring official Islam's heteronormative rejection of male homosexuality and transgenderism into political homophobia, the perpetrators of this violence are not just expressing religious belief but reacting to feelings of *malu*, a complex term that can be provisionally rendered as "shame." While informed by Islamic sexual norms, the context and timing of the Kaliurang and Solo incidents reveals a new problematic evoking these feelings. This is the sense that the potential for the nation to be represented by nonnormative men challenges a nationalized masculinity, enabling what has long been understood to be a normative male response to malu — namely, the masculine and often collective enraged violence known in Indonesian as *amok*, a term that has passed into the English language in the phrase "running amok." By definition, amok is always a public act. The attackers in Kaliurang and Solo, who claimed to represent a post-Soeharto vision of the national, may have sought to shore up a perceived shameful threat to the nation through public violence directed at the events themselves. That it is these events that are considered shameful, and that violence is seen as their proper counter, indicates that these attackers' vision of the nation is normatively male. Emotion here can be used to divine politics.[11]

Political homophobia highlights how postcolonial heteronormative sexuality is shaped by the state, but is done so in ways specific to particular colonial legacies and national visions that therefore vary over time as well as space. Political homophobia can thus be placed along the analyses of chapters 1 through 4 as yet another piece of evidence that it is through heteronormativity that gendered self and nation articulate. In the new Indonesia, men who publicly appear to make improper choices threaten this gendered and sexualized logic of national belonging. A substantial literature now documents the massive effort undertaken by the Indonesian state to inculcate gendered ideologies of the ideal citizen, a national masculinity and femininity. Against the wide range of kinship forms found throughout the archipelago, the family principle (*azas kekeluargaan*), with its associated ideologies of "State Momism" (Suryakusuma 1996) and "State Fatherism," sets forth narrow visions of masculinity and femininity as the foundations of society.[12] Implicit is the heteronormative ideology linking these ideally gendered men and women into the citizen-family. As documented in nationalist literature going back to the 1920s, the idea of becoming a modern Indonesian is often framed in terms of a shift from arranged to "chosen" marriage (Alisjahbana 1966,

Siegel 1997, Rodgers 1995). As I discussed in chapter 1, arranged marriages still occur and many marriages in Indonesia as elsewhere lie somewhere between arrangement and choice, but the vision of a marriage that originates in choice is now the ideal, one linked to modernity and national belonging (cf. Collier 1997). When marriage is arranged sexual orientation is secondary, but when marriages are based on love and choice, sexuality becomes a new kind of problem. To be national, in contemporary Indonesia choice must be heterosexual choice, and while both man and woman choose, the dominant ideology is that men pursue while the "choice" of the woman is secondarily that of refusal.[13] Heterosexuality acts as the pivot point linking gendered self and the nation. In the new Indonesia, men who publicly appear to make improper choices threaten this heteronormative logic of national belonging.

It bears noting that so-called traditional homosexual or transgender roles, primarily limited to ritual and performance contexts, can still be found in many parts of Indonesia (Boellstorff 2005, chapter 2). *Gay* Indonesians occasionally draw upon these "traditional" sexualities to claim legitimacy (they are almost exclusively for men). In reality, however, few *gay* Indonesians identify with or even know of these "traditions": they see themselves as *modern* (to employ the Indonesian term), as part of a national community. These Indonesians are found across the archipelago, even in rural areas, and are more likely to be from a lower class than to be members of the jet-setting elite who stand so frequently as a trope of the "third world" homosexual. It is in this sense that *gay* Indonesians, as persons whose sexualities are irreducible to locality or tradition, could be seen as a major, if unintended, success story of Soeharto's New Order — inhabiting truly national subject positions. *Gay* Indonesians are not marginal to the body politic but rather are a kind of distillation of national discourse. This is not an Indonesian version of "Queer Nation"; as I note in the introduction, nationalism is not the same thing as patriotism, and the impact of state ideology on *gay* Indonesians is not primarily at the level of politicization. Few *gay* Indonesians are involved in the kinds of political work exemplified by the failed Solo national meeting. For a dominant ideology to impact subjectivities it is not necessary for that ideology to be loved or even clearly understood, as we see in Euro-American homosexualities shaped by sexological legacies of which many lesbian and gay Euro-Americans are unaware.

Like much of Southeast Asia, Indonesia is often characterized as tolerant of homosexuality, bisexuality, and transgenderism. Like most myths this is a false belief that contains a grain of truth, and to identify this grain of truth I develop a distinction between "homophobia" and "heterosexism." Most behavioral sciences use "homophobia" as if it transparently reflects a set of real-world conditions. Psychological correlational studies employ measurements like the "Lesbian Internalized Homophobia Scale" that assume, for instance, that a lack of desire to affiliate with other lesbians and gay men, or a pleasure at being perceived by others as heterosexual, are a priori indicators of "internalized homophobia" (Szymanski et al. 2001:34; see also Floyd 2000; Wright et al. 1999). In fact, the concept originated in the early 1970s. As Daniel Wickberg notes in his cultural history of the term, "unpacking the idea of homophobia reveals liberal norms and assumptions about personhood and social order rather than just liberal attitudes toward homosexuality itself" (2000:43). Homophobia links Western conceptions of shamed self and threatened society (later I discuss how malu and amok are linked in a similar fashion).

The distinction between homophobia and heterosexism can provide a powerful conceptual rubric to address questions of violence — particularly if we employ the binarism not as a gloss on precultural reality but as embodying heteronormative assumptions about politics and the self. If homophobia employs a Freudian problematic to locate antipathy in the individuated psyche, heterosexism employs a Gramscian problematic to locate antipathy in hegemony. Heterosexism refers to the belief that heterosexuality is the only natural or moral sexuality. It does not imply the gut level response that homophobia does; for instance, a bureaucratic structure may be heterosexist but it cannot be homophobic. It operates at the level of generalized belief and social sanction, rather than on an emotive plane. In the Euro-American context, this gives heterosexism a cultural currency that homophobia lacks. While few Euro-Americans would admit to being homophobic, many — for instance, much of the Religious Right in the United States — would openly affirm that they are heterosexist, often through terms like "pro-family" that presume a heteronormative family form. Homophobia and heterosexism form a binarism, building on distinctions between emotion/thought, personal/public, and ideational/material. While the binarism does not isomorphically diagnose a real-world division between two forms of oppression, it proves heuristically productive for understanding the imbrication of violence and emotion.

In many cases homophobia and heterosexism feed off each other; heterosexism creates a climate where fear and hatred of nonnormative sexualities and genders can take root, and homophobia creates a climate where heterosexuality is assumed to be superior. However, this is not necessarily the case in all times and places. Delinking homophobia and heterosexism gives us new perspectives on sexual inequality, not only in Indonesia but in other parts of Southeast Asia where there is a need for "a more refined model of cultural antipathy" toward homosexuality (Jackson 1999a:229). It is possible to have homophobia with little or no heterosexism (such as in some Latin American contexts where many forms of sexuality are recognized as natural, yet emotional violence against homosexual persons exists) and heterosexism with little or no homophobia, where heterosexuality is presumed superior to other sexualities, yet this does not lead to violence against homosexual persons.

This latter state of affairs, heterosexism over homophobia, has predominated in Indonesia until recently. Euro-American visitors often misrecognize a "tolerant" culture in the archipelago because violence against *gay* men qua *gay* men is almost unknown, and because the Indonesian Civil Code (based on the Dutch Civil Code, which in turn is based on the Napoleonic Code) has little to say about homosexuality and transgenderism (and to my knowledge there have never been arrests for homosexuality in postcolonial Indonesia).[14] This is because for Euro-Americans the constant threat of violence is the disciplinary pedagogy marginalizing nonnormative sexualities and genders. In the absence of homophobia, heterosexism is assumed to be absent as well. However, despite the fact that there is little homophobia in contemporary Indonesia, heterosexism is pervasive. The expectation that everyone will marry heterosexually is voiced in many belief systems across the archipelago, but it gains added contemporary force from the state's portraying it as essential for becoming a modern citizen. The "tolerance" of homosexuality exists only because Indonesians keep these practices secret and do not publicly proclaim homosexual identities.

HOMOPHOBIA AS THUGGERY?

The potential sea change in Indonesia is the masculinist drawing of a connection between homophobia and heterosexism, such that the former can stand as a condition of possibility for the latter — in a context where heterosexism has historically held a dominant cultural position without homophobia's aid. By exploring how changing masculine representations of the nation shape this shift from everyday heterosexism to political homophobia, I hope to avoid reducing political homophobia to either thuggery or Islam. While to date there is no concrete data, it is plausible that the attackers involved in the Kaliurang and Solo incidents were paid, as has been the case with many of those involved in political violence in Indonesia since 1998. That persons were paid, however, does not mean that emotions were not involved (it appears that many men involved in the rape of ethnic Chinese women in Jakarta in 1998 were paid; yet their erections were no less real). I am particularly keen to avoid treating Islam as a source of political homophobia. The pivotal question of this chapter is not whether official Islam disapproves of homosexuality (as a heterosexist cosmology, it obviously does), but how and why Islamic (male) youth groups have, at a certain point in time and within the nation-state of Indonesia, transformed this heterosexism into homophobia. The homophobic reaction of these Islamic youth groups appears not as a specifically religious response (those attacked were not in mosques or demanding religious recognition) but rather as a reaction to feelings of malu associated with representations of the nation.

It is true that in the Kaliurang and Solo incidents the perpetrators represented themselves as belonging to fundamentalist Muslim groups, and that for these groups Central Java is a hotbed. These groups have also attacked other social groups as well as places they associate with immorality such as brothels and discos — though it bears noting that these are not particularly public venues.[15] On one level, then, political homophobia is linked to a wider cultural dynamic where Islam represents an avenue for political struggle that includes conceptions of an Islamic polity (Hefner 2000). However, while Islam may to date be a necessary condition for political homophobia, it is not a sufficient condition and these incidents cannot be "read off" political Islam. Such an analysis could not explain why antipathy toward *gay* men should be expressed in an emotional and violent manner, rather than, say, the passing of an Islamic legal judgment (*fatwa*) or some form of nonviolent social sanction. This linkage of Islam with violence is both an orientalist stereotype (Lawrence 1998:4) and a self-orientalizing stereotype taken up by some "fundamentalist" Islamic groups: Muslim intellectuals in Indonesia have cautioned against taking this representation at face value (Wahid 1999). There are a wide range of Muslim groups and belief systems in contemporary Indonesia, many of which tolerate nonnormative sexualities and genders. Crucially, most *gay* Indonesians are themselves Muslim, and we lose sight of the rich cultural contexts in which they reconcile sexuality and faith if we treat Islam as a direct source of political homophobia rather than as a contributing, but not determining, factor (see chapter 4). Indeed, it is unclear to what degree Islam is a confounding variable, since it is also the normative, majority religion. In contexts where other religions dominate, it is typically the fundamentalist variants of that religion (Hinduism in India, Christianity in the United States) that have the cultural capital to employ violence, and in these cases it is also linked to masculinity (Hansen 1996).

ENGENDERING VIOLENCE

In the rich body of anthropological work on emotion in Southeast Asia, a central conceptual category has been the Malay/Indonesian term *malu* and its analogues (e.g., Javanese *isin*; Balinese *lek*; Bugis *siri'*; Tagalog *hiya*). Malu typically is translated as "shame" or "embarrassment," but the anthropological literature is unanimous in concluding that these words fail to represent the complexity of malu and its centrality to Southeast Asian conceptions of sociality. Long before Clifford Geertz construed Balinese polities as "theatre states" (Geertz 1980), he inaugurated the dramaturgical metaphor in an analysis of lek (the Balinese near-equivalent to malu). Phrasing lek as "stage fright," Geertz concluded: "What is feared—mildly in most cases, intensely in a few—is that the public performance that is etiquette will be botched, that the social distance etiquette maintains will consequently collapse, and that the personality of the individual will break through to dissolve his standardized public identity" (1973:402).

It was from precisely this passage that Ward Keeler launched his critique of Geertz, which is based on his own study of isin (the Javanese near-equivalent to malu). For Keeler, the weakness of Geertz's metaphor was that it "implies a distance between actor and role, and so between self and social persona, which is misleading" (1983:161). In a manner foreshadowing Butler's performative theory of the constitution of the Euro-American gendered subject (1990), Keeler argued that in effect the actor comes into being as a social persona only when on stage. He concluded that isin is neither shame nor stage fright but rather *an awareness of vulnerability in interaction* (158). In my reading of the literature, and based upon my own ethnographic work, Keeler's analysis of Javanese inis is valid not only for Balinese lek but for Indonesian malu and its other analogues. Indeed, there is general agreement that malu is nothing less than a key site at which Southeast Asians become social persons. In their review of the literature on malu, Elizabeth Collins and Ernaldi Bahar conclude that it is "a highly productive concept that has effects in a wide array of personal and social realms," including the political domain (Collins and Bahar 2000:35). They also emphasize the linkages between malu and sexuality: "As with the English concept of shame, malu is closely associated with sexuality. The Indonesian word for genitals (*kemaluan* [*malu* with a *ke-an* circumfix]) echoes the English expression "private parts." Furthermore, sexually provocative behavior by self or others should elicit malu . . . Gender-inappropriate behavior causes both men and women to feel malu. A boy would feel malu if he behaved like a girl, for example by displaying tears in public" (42).

But while sexuality can elicit malu in both men and women, "the most obvious gender difference in the construct of malu is in the appropriate response to being made malu. While women made malu are expected to become withdrawn, crying out of the sight of others, men are expected to react aggressively" (Collins and Bahar 2000:48). In the cases of political homophobia at issue here, we find not only a masculinist expression of malu but a masculinist and politicized trigger of malu. While rarely openly discussed, many Indonesian men have had experiences of being seduced by other men — at religious boarding schools (*pesantren*), at a friend's home, in a park, or elsewhere. While men who think of themselves as *normal* rarely discuss such incidents, *gay* men have described them to me during my fieldwork, as illustrated by the excerpt below, from an informant recalling events near Kediri in East Java:

Shall I tell the story? I used to live in the pesantren, from the last year of junior high school through until the end of high school. About four years . . . it was at that time that I started to understand same-sex relations [*awali mengerti hubungan sejenis*] because I was seduced by my Koranic recitation teacher . . . I was 18 or 19 years old at the time and he was 25 years old. The first time we were together I didn't have any emotions [*belum rasa*] . . . When we were sleeping together he liked to hold me and he'd ejaculate . . . at the beginning I felt very uncomfortable [*risih*]. I didn't like feeling the sperm in his sarung . . . but he started asking me to hold his penis . . . eventually I started to like it . . . He had his own room, so we could do it easily. He was always very helpful to me in my studies; perhaps at the beginning he was only sympathetic [*simpatik*] and eventually there arose desire [*timbul suka-suka*].

Here, my informant uses a language of emotion to describe a landscape of desire in which a *normal* man desires another man sexually. At the point when these sexual relations occurred, my informant did not yet think of himself as *gay;* it was one *normal* man seducing another. What is typical here is that the emotional response is one of discomfort, not rage; when *gay* men talk about *normal* men who spurn their advances the reaction is described as one of refusal, not violence. It appears that what is interpreted as sexually provocative or gender-inappropriate male behavior leads to violence when it involves staking a claim to civil society.

That the sense of malu is masculinized can be seen not only in that the perpetrators of the attacks were male, but also that the response took the form of violent group attacks — that is, of amok. This cultural logic that links malu to amok is of particular interest because if malu is a site of subject-formation, amok is typically understood to be its opposite: namely, a gut reaction where the masculine self disappears into raw action (and, often, into a crowd). The contrast is not interior versus exterior, since malu involves the public self, and amok is an intentional state, not just mindless physical action (it has been evoked, for instance, by resistance to colonialism). The distinction pivots not on interior versus exterior but self versus society. Amok is a gendered response to malu; it counters a sense of vulnerability in interaction with a sense of *invulnerability in action*. The question, then, is why at this point in time would acts by *gay* men to access civil society be perceived as initiating a chain of emotions beginning in malu and ending in amok? In these cases, the entry of male homosexuality into public discourse is framed as motivating a gut-level reaction of malu, as if one's own (male) social self is threatened. I am interested in this dynamic — in how political homophobia bridges malu and amok when a particular kind of nationalized masculinity is at stake. This may be because the nation is perceived to be in immanent danger of being represented by nonnormative men.

EMOTION AND MASCULINE SEXUALITY

While there is a male-specific typical reaction to malu, and while gender-inappropriate behavior can elicit malu, the range of acceptable masculinities has been quite wide in many Indonesian contexts. For instance, in Java, where the Kaliurang and Solo incidents occurred, " 'Pure' Javanese tradition does not condemn homosexuality and regards a very wide range of behavior, from he-man to rather (in [Euro-American] terms) 'effeminate,' as properly masculine" (Peacock 1968:204). This has even included the political realm: the most notable recent example of this was the 1995 incident when Joop Ave, then minister for tourism, post, and communication under Soeharto, fled New Zealand after being accused of accosting a male staff member of the Carlton Hotel in Auckland. Despite widespread rumors that Ave was *gay*, he not only kept his post but the mass media dismissed the "homo rumors" even while openly pondering why Ave had never married.[16] This was not simply due to the journalists' fear of state reprisal but rather reflected a general belief that so long as Ave did not publicly proclaim *gay* status, his possible sexual activities with men, while perhaps leading to gossip, did not threaten his public position.

Until recently the fact that men engage in public male-male sexuality (e.g., at a park, disco, or performance event) has not resulted in malu. For Indonesian men male-male sexuality has either been ignored, used contrastively to underscore an individual's own social propriety, greeted with curiosity and even titillation, or casually looked down upon. But it has not led to a personal feeling of malu that could justify violence. Historically, successful Indonesian masculinity has not hinged on a sole sexual attraction to women, so long as one eventually marries. Prior to marriage, same-sex encounters remain common (but almost never publicly acknowledged) in a wide range of contexts, from religious boardingschools to markets and shopping malls. Often these activities are construed not as sex but as playing around (*main-main*), particularly if anal penetration does not take place. After marrying it is by no means unknown for men to continue to engage in homosex (or to discover it for the first time); a lack of cultural salience for homosexuality and gender segregation make it possible to hide such activities.

In this context where it is assumed that all men will marry women, but also that they may have sex with other men and/or with warias, violence is almost never linked to homosexual erotics. Warias, while hardly celebrated, are an accepted part of the contemporary Indonesian social mosaic and can be found in a wide range of contexts ranging from salons to music videos (see chapter 2). Acts of violence against *gay* men have been rare. When, for instance, an Indonesian man encounters another man expressing sexual interest in him — even in public — the man will typically either politely refuse or agree to the sexual encounter and keep quiet about it afterward.

I recall here another incident from the Kediri region, during which I was in the company of a group of *gay* men from the area and two *gay* men from Surabaya. We were spending the evening in a part of the town plaza (*alun-alun*) where *gay* men meet for conversation and to find sexual partners. As often happens in such a place, other Indonesians could be found nearby — *normal* couples with children in strollers, groups of older men and women running late-night errands. Closest to us, however, was a group of young men sitting on a low wall under a tree. As we walked by, Amir — one of the *gay* men from Surabaya — struck up a conversation. The men were aged from sixteen to twenty-one and had come to this part of the town square without realizing its significance. When they asked what we were doing in town, Amir explained that we had attended a meeting of the local *gay* group. In response to their blank stares, Amir calmly clarified what *gay* meant — and that he was *gay* himself and liked to have sex with men. The youths giggled but did not take offense; indeed, they remained all evening. One of them eventually pulled Amir aside to say that he was interested in having sex with men but did not want his friends to know about it. This story is not atypical; across Indonesia, street youths are a common feature of the public areas used by *gay* men. Yet these young men typically do not accost the *gay* men; instead they either leave them alone, asking for cigarettes or pocket money at most, or sometimes have sexual relations with them (or even become long-term partners).

The pattern seems similar across the archipelago and across religious or ethnolocal difference. On another occasion I was out on Saturday night with three *gay* men in the city of Singaraja in north Bali. We made our way to the park where *gay* men and warias often spend their evenings. I rode on the back of a motorcycle driven by one of the *gay* men; another motorcycle carried two Balinese *gay* men, Made and Danny, who were very much in love. It was late but the park was still busy, with a mix of *gay* men, warias, and *normal* men, many sitting along the benches of a bus stop. I sat down on one bench with several warias and three *normal* men; at another bench six feet to my right, under a streetlight, Made sat with Danny in his lap, their caresses visible to all who drove or walked by.

After a few moments one of the *normal* men, with long hair and a stocky, athletic body, sat down beside me and introduced himself as Gus. A few pleasantries passed our lips, then silence. After a few moments Gus gestured toward a waria standing nearby and said "That one is pretty, like a normal woman" [*perempuan biasa*]. I asked, "Do you like to have sex with warias?" Gus replied, "Yeah, sure, it's *normal*, because there is passion [*gairah*]." Then I pointed to Made, who was embracing Danny at the other bench, and asked "Would you like a man like that, who isn't made up?" Gus shrugged and said "No, no thank you! I couldn't do that, because there is no passion to have sex with someone like that. If he's not in drag [*dandan*], there's no desire." Gus's reaction, like that of the youth in Kediri, was not homophobic. His desire for warias was not paired with an emotional repugnance toward *gay* men; he was not offended by Made and Danny, and he did not find my question insulting. Examples like these are infinitely more representative of contemporary Indonesian society than the Kaliurang incident: for an Indonesian man to attack another man because that other man expresses sexual interest in him, or because effeminate men appear in public, is a rare event.

The emergence of political homophobia indicates how the public presentation of male homosexuality and transgenderism can now occasion malu even if one does not participate oneself, because in the post-Soeharto era, masculinity is nationalized in a new way. With the nation under perceived threats of disintegration, attempts by nonnormative men to access civil society can appear to threaten the nation itself. While both *gay* homosexuality and waria transvestitism figure in this calculus, recall that "waria" is a publicly recognized social category. As Peter

Jackson notes in the case of Thailand, under such a discursive regime male homosexuality can represent more of a danger than transvestitism, since it is more difficult to fit within a heterosexist logic where those who desire men must be effeminate (1999:238). Male homosexuality is also more threatening than transvestitism due to the widespread Southeast Asian assumption that inner states should match exterior bodily presentations (Errington 1989:76). Warias, who identify themselves as men with women's souls, properly display this inner mismatch in their cross-dressing. In contrast, *gay* men have a different kind of desire than do normative men (they "desire the same"), but this inner deviation is not exteriorized; some are effeminate, but most are indistinguishable from *normal* men. The assumption that interior and exterior self should line up has been politicized in the past. For many years following the rise of Soeharto's "New Order" regime in the late 1960s, the government made dire pronouncements concerning the possibility of an underground communist movement that was an "organization without shape" [*organisasi tanpa bentuk*]. This referred to a group whose exterior did not match its interior, in the same way that individual communists were presumably failing to exteriorize their politics. *Gay* men, with their desire for the masculine but lack of a corresponding presentation as feminine, can be seen as a kind of masculinity tanpa bentuk — not when they make sexual propositions to other men in private but when they appear to stake a public claim to civil society; that is, when they appear political. It may be for this reason that *gay* men have been the primary target of political homophobia.

CONCLUSION: THE EMERGENCE OF POLITICAL HOMOPHOBIA

It is in the Indonesian context where heterosexism has predominated over homophobia that the recent attacks gain such significance. For the Muslim youths involved in these attacks, the public presence of non-normative genders and sexualities became interpreted in phobic terms as a psychic threat to proper masculinity. This made violence not only thinkable but sensible as an emotional "gut reaction" to what was now interpreted as an assault on the nation's manhood. We see a shift from an intellectual assumption, rarely voiced because taken for granted, that all Indonesians should marry heterosexually, to an emotional assumption, carried out with knives and clubs, that nonnormative men threaten the nation's future. I term this a shift from everyday heterosexism to political homophobia, and the character of this emotional rage shows us that the nation envisioned by these attackers is normatively male. While all homophobia has political effects, the notion of political homophobia is useful for highlighting the violence deployed as a means of controlling who can make claims to belonging. The violence of the Kaliurang and Solo incidents was directed at the demands for inclusion in a new public sphere and not at the mundane romances and seductions of everyday life.[17]

Alarmism is not my goal in this analysis, and I do not mean to suggest that political homophobia will become an everyday occurrence in Indonesia. There has been an increasing presence of *gay* men in Indonesian public culture, as illustrated by the 2004 hit movie *Arisan!*, which included a subplot concerning a *gay* man and featured two scenes of *gay* men kissing each other. However, the linkage between emotion and violence that these events have set in motion does not hinge on repetition. A single incident can have sustained emotional consequences, as exemplified in the World Trade Center attacks and in the 1992 destruction of the Babri Mosque in India. Indeed, the Kaliurang and Solo incidents continue to affect *gay* Indonesians. We see this most clearly in Yogyakarta (near Kaliurang), an important center of *gay* community and publishing since the early 1980s; following the Kaliurang incident, *gay* organizations in that city ceased meeting and *gay* publications ceased production and did not resume again until around mid-2003. A book launch held by Dédé Oetomo at a Muslim university in Yogyakarta in early November 2001 for a volume of his writings on homosexuality and Indonesian society took place without incident, but a second event to be held at a local bookstore was interrupted by the police, who prevented the event from taking place on the pretext that it would disturb public security.[18] More broadly, intermittent attacks on warias and *gay* men, including assaults on *gay* men in public places and incidents where warias are assaulted and their hair forcibly cut, have occurred in several parts of Indonesia, including Aceh, Bali, and Java.[19] In 2004 near the city of Solo a group of Muslim-identified youths arrived at the end of an event held by the publishers of the racy tabloid *X-Pos* to thank their *gay* readers; upon arriving the youths burned all of the copies of the tabloid they could find as the *gay* men present hid in their hotel rooms or fled the scene. Thus while on the whole there is little evidence that everyday

FIGURE 18   Image from *Rakyat Merdeka*, October 7, 2001:
George W. Bush as emotional transvestite.

homophobia is on the rise, it remains an open question as to whether or
not the increasing visibility of *gay* men will co-occur with greater violence (Oetomo 2001).

Perhaps the most urgent question is how political homophobia will
shape the struggles over Indonesia's emerging post-Soeharto civil society.
Historically *gay* men and warias have appeared — either as topic of discussion or trope — only rarely in the political sphere. When the latter has
occurred, it has usually been to speak metaphorically of persons who
change their opinions (like warias change their gender presentation). For
instance, in a 1999 volume of essays concerned with demonstrating that
Islam is incompatible with political violence (*kekerasan politik*), Abdurrahman Wahid — the noted Muslim intellectual and former president of
Indonesia — spoke metaphorically of intellectuals changing their opinions as changing their sex, jokingly admonishing them not to become
warias (Wahid 1999:182).

Compare Wahid's remarks with the situation two years later, when the
populist and often anti-American newspaper *Rakyat Merdeka* (published from Jakarta) ran a front-page headline concerning the U.S.-led

attacks on the Taliban with the title "*Amerika Bencong!*"[20] The headline was accompanied by a photograph of President George W. Bush doctored to include lipstick, earrings, and a leather jacket (figure 18). Here nonnormative men stand not for shifting intellectual views but for a compromised nation. The article claimed that the United States was a béncong (waria) because rather than challenging Osama bin Laden to a one-on-one duel, Bush had the audacity (*berani*) to invite its allies to attack Afghanistan en masse in search for him. In other words, the United States had no malu, no sense of vulnerability in interaction, and thus felt a rage — a sense of invulnerability in action — that compelled it to enroll others to join in amok violence. The United States is presented as operating under a nationalized intersection of manhood and emotion; and as such the dynamic of the Kaliurang and Solo incidents is displaced onto the figure of the nonnormative male. Under a cultural logic of political homophobia, Bush in drag — representing a nation's failed masculinity — appears both violent and a proper target for violence.

My hypothesis is that it may be political homophobia that makes this image intelligible to the Indonesian public, regardless of religion. In place of national masculinity as benevolent and paternal (however violent in actual practice), we find it embattled and in danger of losing its very manhood. It is thus called upon to deflect this shame in a properly masculine manner by violently striking down any representation of itself by homosexual, effeminate, or transvestite men. As Indonesia continues to struggle through a period of uncertainty, anthropological attention to the public face of emotion and the heterosexist gendering of national belonging can contribute to a better understanding of how violence is not the "primordialist" suspension of culture but the working out of cultural logics of inequality and exclusion to their horrific but comprehensible conclusion.

SIX

COMPARATIVELY QUEER IN SOUTHEAST ASIA

In chapters 1 through 5 I focused upon what could be termed "queer" Indonesians; each essay addressed the questions of disciplinarity and temporality that I discussed in the introduction, but in a largely implicit manner. This approach is intentional. We cannot predict the forms that coincidences between anthropology and queer studies might take. The question of a queer anthropology or anthropological queer studies is more than a widening of the network of authors one cites; instead, it speaks to fundamental issues of discipline, method, and critique — issues that this book can gesture toward but not encompass. In this book I have worked instead to explore some of the topics, methods, and even affects that might characterize emergent collaborations between queer studies and anthropology. Certainly, another aim in this book has been to shed some partial, perspectival light on the lives of "queer Indonesians"; this is not subsidiary to my other goals, but rather one aspect of a trans-disciplinary vision that refuses misleading choices between theoretical work and substantive work, pure research and applied research, criticism and activism.

There is no proper way to conclude a book built around the trope of coincidence, since closure is precisely what the trope resists. This final chapter, then, does not wrap up loose ends or synthesize disparate arguments into what appears to be a seamless whole. Rather than move toward closure, it moves in the opposite direction. It does not "localize" my discussion of Indonesians but moves further outward, comparing "queer" sexualities and genders across Southeast Asia. These are subjects about which additional books could easily be written; my discussion here will be provisional — oriented around questions rather than answers, mysteries rather than solutions. My ultimate goal in this chapter, then, is to open a conceptual space for rethinking comparison in terms of coincidence.

At what point does analysis cross the boundary between "ethnographic" and "comparative"; between "a single case" and "multiple cases?" The five chapters preceding this one demonstrate that this threshold cannot be defined in terms of locality, for I have taken the nation as an ethnographic unit rather than a comparative one, as do disciplines ranging from political science to comparative literature (Wiegman 2002:148). Neither can "critique" define the boundary of the comparative; critique can take the form of noncomparative modes of analysis like ethnography, and comparison is not always informed by a critical sensibility. Questions of the positionality of the researcher such as those I raised in the introduction are as relevant for comparative work as for ethnographic work (Jackson 2001).

Instead, the boundary between the ethnographic and the comparative is better approached as one of immanence versus transcendence (see Adorno 1967 and the introduction to this book). An ethnographic approach takes the material under consideration as part of the same epistemological entity; it assumes, for instance, that two individuals under consideration are part of the "same culture." Depending on the spatial analytic in play, this can be the case whether the two individuals reside in different homes in the same neighborhood, different neighborhoods in the same city, different cities in the same nation, or different nations in the same region. In other words, it takes the socioeconomic fields of representation in question as immanent to each other. This is the approach I have used in this book thus far, and it is the approach typically used in anthropological inquiry more generally.

A comparative approach typically implies that the material under consideration comes from multiple epistemological entities; it assumes, for instance, that two individuals under consideration are part of "different cultures," regardless of the spatial analytic in play (see Garcia 1996:xvi). In other words, it takes the socioeconomic fields of representation in question as transcendent to each other. For instance, a comparative analysis of Muslims and Christians, men and women, or young and old will, on some level, treat the groups in question as distinct (otherwise there would be no "groups" to compare), even though such groups are analytical heuristics. Comparison can take place across time (this was the meaning of comparison in the nineteenth-century environments that gave birth to anthropology) and across space. It is the spatial mode of comparison that I employ in this chapter, as I compare nonnormative sexualities and genders in Southeast Asia.

Of course, even the dualisms of immanent/transcendent and ethno-graphic/comparative are analytic conveniences rather than fixed essences. That immanence shades into transcendence (and ethnography into comparison) is illustrated by the phenomenological philosopher Maurice Merleau-Ponty, who described how, when a person sees a road, they experience that road as having a width that decreases to zero as it nears the horizon. Merleau-Ponty emphasized that neither the experience of the road as wide or as narrow is "more true," but that "the close, the far-off, the horizon in their indescribable contrast form a system, and it is their relationship with the total field that is the perceptual truth" (1968:21–22). This epistemology of coincidence suggests that there is no such thing as purely transcendent critique; all critique, like all knowledge, is in some way situated (Haraway 1988). It thus suggests that there is no such thing as pure comparison; all comparison, like all knowledge, is in some way situated. Finally, it suggests that there is no such thing as pure interdisciplinarity; all scholarship, like all knowledge, is in some way disciplined. Just as there is no way to speak without speaking some historically and culturally specific language — English, Italian, Zulu, Sudanese — so all scholarship is situated in communities of method.

My goal in this chapter is not to offer an exhaustive review or "eth-nocartographic" compendium of subjectivities and practices (Weston 1993). Instead, I point out a few patterns across the region with the hope of contributing to a comparative archive that can allow us to ask new kinds of questions about Southeast Asia and beyond. We can think of comparison as queer — as a transcendent form of critique, it "queers" established horizons of interchange — and of queerness as comparative, because "queer" is an antifoundational concept that seems to belong nowhere and thus invites linkages across time and space. With reference to Southeast Asia, I am thus aiming for a "critical regionality" that, in the words of Mark Johnson, Peter Jackson, and Gilbert Herdt, "is one way of reinvigorating the comparative project" (2000:372). A critical re-gionalities approach "enables us to think about the wider networks of material and symbolic relations within, and through which, gender and sexuality are made and experienced in particular locales" (361); by permitting "a shift away from speaking of regions to speaking of processes of regionalization and the making of world areas" (363), they "provide one means through which we can move beyond the essentialized field of the 'local' and the unspecified and unsituated field of the 'global' " (373).

Johnson, Jackson, and Herdt also note that "the act of comparison itself is a imaginative and strategic act which creates as it were a world area, a region of affinities, of connections and/or of dis-associations" (373). This emphasis on the imagination is crucial. A wealth of analyses demonstrate that nonnormative sexualities and genders are powerfully linked to a range of social forms from "local tradition" to "nation-state," but this is done in a negative sense; the analyses often appear as a kind of haunting, not unlike the way that warias "haunt" normative Indonesian masculinity (see chapter 2).

It is not possible to bring up haunting, comparison, and Southeast Asia without invoking Benedict Anderson's *The Spectre of Comparisons: Nationalism, Southeast Asia, and the World* (1998). In this book Anderson extends his analysis of nationalism (best known through *Imagined Communities* [1983]) by noting how it "lives by making comparisons" (229). While religions can imagine a world in which everyone is, say, Christian or Muslim, and kingdoms can imagine more subjects, "no nation imagines itself coterminous with mankind" (7). The comparative imagination of the nation-state assumes the existence of like entities worldwide; it can be considered a form of critical regionality. Drawing upon the work of the Indonesian novelist Pramoedya Ananta Toer, Pheng Cheah further explores how national consciousness is linked to comparison. Cheah recalls a moment in Toer's historical novel *Jejak Langkah* (Footsteps) when the main character, the "native" Minke, reflects on comparison as something brought to the Indies by colonialism: "Happy are those who know nothing. Knowledge, comparison, makes people aware of their own situation, and the situation of others, there is dissatisfied restlessness in the world of comparison [*gelisah dalam alam perbandingan*]" (2003:12).

This comparative impulse at the heart of nationalism is only strengthened by transnationalism. As Cheah notes: "The gradual defamiliarization of our daily lives by globalizing processes has made comparison an inevitable and even unconscious perspective" (2). The ground for the world of comparison can thus be construed as what Cheah terms an "anxious restlessness" (11); a sense of vertigo that Anderson describes as leading him to the notion of a "spectre of comparisons" in the first place

(1998:2). Since queerness can be understood in terms of haunting, how is the spectre of comparison a queer spectre, a spectre whose impulse to compare is "grounded" in marginalization from the normal, a marginalization from the heteronormativity that is so central to the modern nation-state? How might this sense of marginalization mark one as not really belonging to a place and thus free to move across boundaries, to haunt, to compare?

Anthropologists and others have long identified a tendency to associate men with a public sphere defined by movement and women with a domestic sphere defined by immobility (Rosaldo 1974). However, queer haunting is not solely a male province. In *The Apparitional Lesbian: Female Homosexuality and Modern Culture*, Terry Castle takes up queerness and haunting by noting how "the lesbian is never with us, it seems, but always somewhere else: in the shadows, in the margins, hidden from history" (1993:2). For Castle, the figure of the lesbian haunts the Western tradition as that which is denied yet present: "The ghost, in other words, is a paradox. Though nonexistent, it nonetheless *appears*" (46). To be an apparition is to move between two or more worlds, to haunt a world of comparison. Carla Freccero refers to this queer spectrality as "a suspension, a waiting . . . as the very force from the past that moves us into the future, like Benjamin's angel, blown backward by a storm" (2006:104). While this notion of queer spectrality remains within the temporal imaginary of straight time (see the introduction), I think this haunting can, in the sense of a queer spectre of comparison, work instead through a sense of coincidence, of queer timing. This queer spectrality is both a sense of selfhood and an analytical strategy that is increasingly familiar in the context of globalizing forces. By naming this "queer" I wish to place comparison at the empty center of queer studies and queerness at the anxious center of comparison.

Since 1896, when Franz Boas — key figure in the establishment of anthropology in the United States — delivered a paper entitled "The Limitations of the Comparative Method of Anthropology," anthropologists have tended to disavow comparison in favor of holistic frameworks in which elements of social life must first be compared with other elements within a culture (see Stocking 1974). Despite the fact that "comparative analysis was once anthropology's claim to distinction within the social sciences" (Strathern 1991:8), only in more quantitative or linguistic quarters of anthropology have comparative approaches been pursued in a sustained fashion (Burton, Moore, and Romney 1996; Greenberg 1990). Thus while the assumptions behind "area studies" support, say, an Indonesianist anthropologist drawing upon the work of Indonesianist historians and literary scholars, it remains less likely for an Indonesianist anthropologist to draw upon the work of anthropologists who work in the Philippines or Thailand. It is in this context that in the remainder of this chapter I examine Southeast Asia in a comparative vein, with the goal of inquiring about new ways to transnationalize queer studies as well as to queer the anthropological project.

SOUTHEAST ASIA: A SHORT QUEER HISTORY

The Space of Southeast Asia   Like "Latin America" or "Africa," "Southeast Asia" is part of a mode of organizing knowledge known as "area studies" or "regional studies." Since the 1980s, area studies approaches have sometimes been criticized for their historical linkages to colonialism and particularly to the geopolitics of the cold war. They have also been critiqued for their arbitrariness: for instance, where does the "Middle East" begin and end, and from whose perspective is it "Middle" and "East?" Southeast Asia has a particular history of analytical denigration: as Martin Lewis and Karen Wigen note, "Despite its centrality in the history of world trade and cultural interchange, Southeast Asia is cartographically relegated to the position of an insignificant backwater, a seemingly passive recipient of Chinese Indian, Muslim, and later European influences" (1997:133). Nonetheless, the notion of area remains crucial as a term of analysis and a social category. Areas provide a spatial scale quite different from the nation, a spatial scale useful for interrogating the theoretical lacuna so weakly papered over by the slash separating "local" from "global." The notion of area can be used "not as a 'truth' about the intrinsic and essential relationship between particular people, places, and cultures, but as both theoretically and politically useful and at times necessary 'fictions' or 'partial truths'" (Johnson, Jackson, and Herdt 2000:373; see also A. Wilson 2006).

Contemporary Southeast Asia is typically seen to be comprised of five "mainland" nation-states (Burma [now Myanmar], Cambodia, Laos, Thailand, and Vietnam) and six "island" nation-states (Brunei, Indonesia, Malaysia, the Philippines, Singapore, and East Timor [known also by its Portuguese name Timor Leste], though East Timor is sometimes

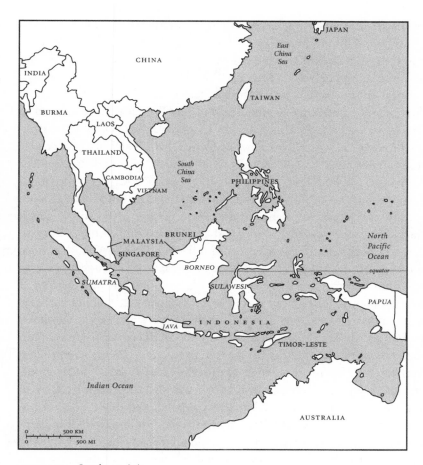

FIGURE 19 Southeast Asia.

grouped with Melanesia) (figure 19). Given the region's large population, it is remarkable that so little is known about the daily lives of
Southeast Asians—in the Western academy, work on Southeast Asia is
almost entirely limited to anthropology, history, literature, and the arts.
With regard to nonnormative sexualities and genders (and most other
topics as well) most of the available data is limited to the Philippines,
Thailand, and Indonesia — with surprisingly little on East Timor, Malaysia, Vietnam, and Singapore, and virtually nothing on Brunei, Cambodia, Laos, or Myanmar. While regional organizations exist (notably

ASEAN, the Association of Southeast Asian Nations), few inhabitants of this region think of themselves as Southeast Asians (Anderson 1998:3). It is understandable that some scholars question the relevance of Southeast Asia as an analytical category: "The concept of Southeast Asia as a political entity emerged almost by accident from World War II when, at the Quebec Conference in August 1943, the Western Allies decided to establish a separate South East Asia Command . . . This military expedient provided a cohesive framework for a region which had never previously been seen as a distinct geopolitical area. No single empire had dominated the whole region in pre-colonial times" (Tarling 1992:586).

While the term "Southeast Asia" dates to the early nineteenth century, its cold war consolidation means that, according to Lewis and Wigen, it "lacks the deeply rooted and widely shared religio-philosophical systems that give coherence to Europe, the 'Middle East,' South Asia, East Asia, and even 'Latin' America . . . many of Southeast Asia's connections with other parts of the world are, and will likely remain, as powerful as its internal bonds . . . In many ways, Southeast Asia is a residual and artificial category" (1997:173–76). As Lewis and Wigen note, Southeast Asia's queerness as a region is part and parcel of its emphasis on comparison, on "connections with other parts of the world." It is in this spirit that Anthony Reid has made a strong case for the existence of a "saucer model of Southeast Asian identity." In acknowledging that the region has never had a single ruling center and has always maintained strong connections to other parts of the world, Reid questions the assumption that inward-looking domination is necessary for regional identification: "Two inherently Southeast Asian factors determined that the region would be seen as one: (i) a positive view from what we now call Malaysia/Singapore, that it sits in the centre of a meaningful region called by a diversity of names. This self-conscious centrality is based, however, on communications, not on civilization or empire like the cores of many other historic regions . . . (ii) a negative decision by the peripheries of this region that they did not want to be appendages of their larger and more threatening neighbors, so that Southeast Asia became a kind of default option" (1999:7).

Reid's model of Southeast Asia as based upon "interaction around a communications hub" (1999:11) underscores how place making can involve coincidence as much as centralized power. Southeast Asia's long history of trade and interchange means that the region has presaged many aspects of what are now labeled globalizing processes: "Southeast

Asia borrows in order to create what defines it — a paradoxical formulation that one sees across nearly all human domains in the area" (Bowen 2003:12). As a rather queer place, Southeast Asia may prove useful for considering the "place" of nonnormative sexualities and genders.

Sexuality and Gender in Precolonial and Colonial Southeast Asia A consistent but contentious finding about the history of gender relations in Southeast Asia concerns women's relatively high status and a relative openness in sexual matters. As Reid states: "Relations between the sexes represented one aspect of the social system in which a distinctive Southeast Asian pattern was especially evident . . . [that is,] a common pattern of relatively high female autonomy and economic importance . . . In the sixteenth and seventeenth centuries the region probably represented one extreme of human experience on these issues" (1988:146).[1] Often the historically high status of women found cosmological sanction in regimes of gender complementarity where, for instance, the mythic origin of a group is located not in a husband and wife but in a brother and sister. While "man" and "woman" are often construed in oppositional terms, many Southeast Asian cultures historically downplayed gender difference: "All humans, after all, share a great deal of common anatomy: upright posture, stereoscopic vision, opposable thumbs. A culture, then, can conceptualize all human bodies and human 'persons' as very similar to each other" (Errington 1990:35; see also Garcia 1996; Peletz 1996:129; Proschan 2002; Yengoyan 1983:137–140).[2]

The historical analysis of nonnormative sexualities and genders in Southeast Asia has been dogged by the temptation to seek origins (not just antecedents) for these sexualities and genders in terms of "tradition" or "indigenous" culture, and thereby bracket both the colonial encounter and modernity. Across Southeast Asia, there have in various times and places existed individuals who blurred gender (for instance, a man dressing as a woman) in the context of religious rite, royal ritual, or community performance (see Peletz 2002b). In some cases these subject positions have included homosexual behavior as well, but to increase their power often individuals inhabiting the subject position in question were celibate, at least during the period of their lives that they occupied the subject position. Many of these practices have died out or are vanishing, but some persist to the present. Examples of these include *bissu*, *warok*, *bante*, and *basir* in Indonesia (Andaya 2000:39; Atkinson 1990;

Boellstorff 2005:38–41; Chabot 1996:1901–91; Fauzannafi 2005; Graham 2003a; Peletz 2002:240–44, 2006; Pelras 1996:166; Scharer 1963; van der Kroef 1992; Wieringa 1999b:216; Wilson 1999); *manang* in Malaysia (Sutlive 1992); and *asog, babaylan, bayoc,* and *labia* in the Philippines (Blanc-Szanton 1990:357; Brewer 1999; Garcia 1996:127, 135, 148; Johnson 1997:26–27; Murray 1992). For two primary reasons I term these "ethnolocalized homosexual and transvestite professional subject positions" or ETPs (Boellstorff 2005:41–46). First, while these subject positions are frequently misnamed as "third genders," they are not really genders at all but rather professions. Typically one must engage in some form of training to occupy them, or at least be seen to have a divine calling. In most cases one occupies these ETPs for only part of one's life course, part of the year, or even only during certain rituals or performances.

Much of what we know concerning "queer" Southeast Asians right up to the end of the colonial period in the mid-twentieth century focuses on courtly elites. It is in courtly texts like the *I La Galigo* narrative in southern Sulawesi that we find most of the available historical data on ETPs like bissus. Some courtly texts discuss sex between men (Anderson 1990b; Ricklefs 1998). In such texts we also find some of the only discussions prior to the twentieth century of sex between women (Blackwood and Wieringa 1999:41–42; Wieringa 1999:216): for instance, *len pheuan* or homosexual behavior between female concubines in the Thai court, which was punished (Loos 2005; Sinnott 2004:167). Because this literature focuses on an elite ruling class, it is difficult to know its implications for understanding the sexual practices and subjectivities of commoners. For example, there is relatively little discussion of transvestitism or transgenderism during this period, even after the rise of publicly visible male transvestite subject positions in the nineteenth century. This is probably because male transvestites were associated with markets and the lower classes rather than courtly elites.

By the eighteenth and nineteenth centuries, two major social shifts had altered the landscape of gender and sexuality relations in Southeast Asia — though not in a uniform manner, and by overlapping rather than displacing earlier cultural logics. The first shift was the arrival of Islam and Christianity. The general consensus is that these religions lowered women's status, though the effects were multivalent and contested. The second major shift — sometimes linked to the first, sometimes quite independent from it — was colonialism. The colonial history of Southeast Asia dates to the late 1400s and involved nearly every colonial power — Britain, France, Germany, Holland, Japan, Portugal, Spain, and the United States; in fact, "only the Italians and Belgians were missing" (Anderson 1998:4). There was also a vast range in the length of the colonial encounter (almost 350 years in parts of Indonesia) and in its intensity, with varying emphases on conversion (e.g., Spain in the Philippines) and resource extraction (e.g., Holland in Indonesia). Thailand was the only Southeast Asian country that was technically never colonized, but to remain nominally independent of France and Britain its rulers had to redefine the polity as a nation (Reynolds 1999:263; Winichakul 1994). Gender and sexuality became key sites for distinguishing colonist from colonized, thus acting to legitimate colonial rule through rhetorics of propriety and virtue (Stoler 2002). This included an obsession with strict gender roles and marriage. Colonial regimes found troubling the widespread pattern of gender complementarity in Southeast Asia — men and women using the same first names, dressing in a nearly identical manner, and so on — and they devoted great energy to spreading more restrictive and hierarchical gender norms. These historically quite recent regimes of gender have in many cases been reframed by postcolonial nation-states as "Asian Values" or "tradition" (Peletz 1996, 2002, 2006).

MALE TRANSVESTITES: PUBLIC BEAUTY

To most Westerners, the queerest aspect of Southeast Asia is the publicly acknowledged existence of men who dress and act in ways perceived as effeminate; who have sexual and romantic relationships with men seen as normal, yet typically do not try to pass as women. Although Westerners often wish to interpret these individuals as belonging to a third gender, across Southeast Asia it is more common for them to see themselves as men who have women's souls (or souls part male and female) and/or as male-bodied individuals who dress in a feminine manner (see Cannell 1999:214; Garcia 1996:59; Jackson 1999a:238; Johnson 1997:34, 89; Slamah 2005; Tan 2001:139; see also chapter 2 for additional discussion concerning the history of male transvestites in Southeast Asia). In no case to my knowledge have feminist organizations in Southeast Asia seen these individuals as falling within their purview as "women"; indeed, they are increasingly classed together with gay men in the category of MSM or "men who have sex with men" that HIV/AIDS discourse has promulgated throughout the region.

Following my practice in chapter 2, I heuristically refer to these individuals as "male transvestites." I believe this to be the least flawed English approximation, since across Southeast Asia such individuals' gendering is "not constructed on the model of a genuine femininity, but rather as a stereotype of unmasculinity" (Jackson 1997:175). These individuals are known by terms like *waria, banci, béncong, kedi,* and *wandu* in Indonesia; *kathoey* in Thailand, Cambodia, and Laos; *acault* in Myanmar; *bakla, bayot, bantut,* and *sward* in the Philippines; *bapok, darai, kedi, mak nyah,* and *pondan* in Malaysia; and *ah qua* and *bapok* (among other terms) in Singapore.[3]

In contrast to ETPs, it is not until the end of the nineteenth century that sustained discussions of male transvestites appear (for instance, the term *banci* does not appear in the early-nineteeth-century versions of the Javanese chronicle *Serat Tjentini* (Anderson 2001b:xiv; see Sinnott 2004:215). Early references suggest that these individuals were associated with urban mercantile environments like small-scale trading, sex work, and lower-class forms of drama, rather than with courts or rituals (Garcia 1996:65–66; Peacock 1968; Proschan 2002:445). Subject positions (socially extant categories of selfhood) do not necessarily exist in unbroken timelines, and it appears that male transvestites in Southeast Asia are not legacies of prior "traditions." Rather, the available evidence suggests that male transvestites emerged as "commodified transgender" subject positions only in the late nineteenth century or early twentieth: As Drucker notes, such "commodified transgender [sexualities] differed from any traditional transgendered sexuality in that [they were] largely urban, largely detached from rather than integrated into traditional kinship networks, more or less associated with prostitution for money rather than any kind of socially sanctioned marriage, and at odds with instead of sanctioned by the dominant religion" (1996:77).

Male transvestites usually identify themselves (and are identified by their families and neighbors) as such from childhood, often based on choosing to wear women's clothes, play with dolls, and the like (Doussantousse 2005; Johnson 1997:114–17; Winter, Sasot, and King 2006). As adults, male transvestites almost always desire sex and romance with "normal" men. Sex with women is typically assumed to happen only in the context of marriage; historically in some cases at least, marrying a woman helped male transvestites achieve social acceptance (Keeler 1990:149–50), but this situation is now quite rare and may be becoming rarer. Sex with another male transvestite or with a gay man is considered strange (Garcia 1996:97; Tan 2001:121).

Since approximately the 1960s, the visibility of male transvestites has increased and continues to grow across Southeast Asia (Heng 2001:81; Jackson 1999a:230; Johnson 1997:70). This shift appears linked to economic, social, and political factors including the rise of development discourse; it is probably not coincidental that this was the same time period that gay male subject positions appear to have formed, and that male transvestite organizations first arose (at least in Thailand, the Philippines, and Indonesia, the three nations where male transvestites appear to be most socially accepted; Garcia 1996:77). Since the 1970s it has become common for male transvestites to wear women's clothing or a mix of men's and women's clothing throughout the day, rather than only at night or on specific occasions (Tan 2001:122). From this time onward, it appears that male transvestites have also become more visible and common in rural contexts, though they remain most often associated with cities.

A linked shift is the growth in more permanent forms of body alteration like taking female hormones (often in the form of birth-control pills) and injecting silicone (Winter 2006a). Such shifts reinforce the sense of male transvestite subjectivity as a permanent aspect of one's selfhood rather than as something linked to particular times and places. In earlier periods, a male transvestite who rolled up socks or some other article of clothing to give the appearance of breasts could "remove" their breasts as well as their makeup and women's clothing, and thereby appear as a more-normative man. When a male transvestite has large breasts due to silicone injections or years of consuming hormones, such a shift is much more difficult and the male transvestite is likely to identify as such on an ongoing basis (and there is likely to be less social pressure to marry a woman). It is fairly common for male transvestites to be excused from the marriage imperative (Peletz 1996:124), both because of a long-standing belief that male transvestites have shriveled or non-functional genitals (Johnson 1997:94; Graham 2003a, Oetomo 1996a) and because of the hormone and silicone injection treatments that many male transvestites now undergo (Doussantousse 2005; Winter, Sasot, and King 2006).

There has typically been an increasing identification of male transvestites with beauty work (cutting and styling hair, applying makeup, including bridal makeup, and often tailoring and clothing design). The salon has become central to male transvestite subjectivity and community and a key site where male transvestites interface with public culture (Doussantousse 2005; Garcia 1996:73; Johnson 1997:177; Peletz 1996:124; Tan 2001:120–21; Winter 2006a). Male transvestites are now consistently associated with a notion of beauty as the product of conscious intervention, and thus as consisting of "good citizenship and a professional orientation" rather than natural attractiveness or a link to tradition (Johnson 1997:54; see Cannell 1995).

Besides beauty work, some male transvestites across Southeast Asia engage in sex work (Doussantousse 2005; Teh 2002; Winter 2006a). The association of male transvestites with sex work appears to go back to the emergence of their "commodified" subjectivities. Male transvestite sex workers have been hit particularly hard by the HIV/AIDS epidemic, with some of the highest infection rates in the region. While our knowledge of male transvestite sexual practices remains incomplete, it appears that the dominant expectation is that male transvestites take the penetrated role in anal sex (Johnson 1997:35, 90). However, at least in some parts of Southeast Asia male transvestites sometimes penetrate their male partners anally instead of the other way around. Another widespread pattern is that male transvestites in some cases pay "normal" men to have sex with them (Garcia 1996:95–96), a pattern that shades into male transvestites supporting their male partners on an ongoing basis.

Across Southeast Asia, it is typically assumed that the male partners of male transvestites are not themselves transvestite or even homosexual but "normal," and that it is the male transvestite who is the aggressor in the relationship (Cannell 1999:215; Garcia 1996:72; Johnson 1997:192). This tends to be the case even when the "normal" men in question fall in love with and/or cohabit with a male transvestite on an ongoing basis. The fact that the relationship is heterogenderal (Faderman 1992; see Garcia 1996:100–101), and thus that the male partner desires femininity, implies that his desires are in some sense "normal" (compare Kulick 1998).[4]

The "acceptance" of male transvestites in Southeast Asia is a complex question (Cannell 1995:240–41; Garcia 1996:125; Jackson 1999a; Tan 2001:122–23). Family reactions to a male transvestite child range widely, but in many cases across Southeast Asia the child is accepted to some extent (Winter 2006b). Compared to gay men and lesbian women, male transvestites are quite visible and are able to occupy public space. From singing in political rallies in Indonesia to kickboxing in Thailand, male transvestites are acknowledged as such, and in some cases they are quite visible in the mass media (Graham 2004). However, male transvestites are rarely celebrated as valuable members of society and are often excluded from formal, religious, or decision-making contexts. Some male transvestites would like to have sex-reassignment surgery (removal of the penis and surgical construction of a vagina; Winter 2002), but others say that they would not have such an operation even if they could afford it, either because of health risks or because they see themselves as male-bodied (Doussantousse 2005; ten Brummelhuis 1999).

Male transvestites in any one country are usually aware that their subjectivities are nationwide and not ethnic specific. Thus most kathoeys know that kathoeys are found across Thailand, most warias know that warias are found across Indonesia, and most bantuts know that bantuts are found across the Philippines (even if, as in the last two cases, the terms used may vary locally, so that *kawe-kawe* may be known in Indonesia as a Makassarese gloss of *waria*, and *bayot* may be known as a "Cebuano equivalent" for *bakla* [Garcia 1996:63]). Adding to the confusion is that male transvestites sometimes use a term derived from "gay" to refer to themselves; this has been the case in the Philippines since the 1970s, and since the 1990s it has occurred with some frequency in places like Thailand and Indonesia (Cannell 1995:241; Garcia 1996:79; Johnson 1997:104; Sinnott 2004:6). However, even when male transvestites use a reworked version of "gay," their subjectivities are usually quite distinct from those of gay men.

Male transvestites are less likely to know that there are male transvestites outside of their own country, though transnational imaginings are certainly part of their lives, particularly in the Philippines where economic migration is so prevalent (Cannell 1995, 1999; Johnson 1997). They may logically suspect that such individuals must exist, or they may have seen mass media that suggest as much. Relatively few male transvestites ever leave their nations of origin, though there are, for instance, male transvestites in the Philippines who travel to Malaysia or even the United States (Manalansan 2003); Muslim male transvestites from several Southeast Asian countries who travel to Saudi Arabia for the pilgrimage to Mecca and sometimes for employment; and Indonesian male transvestites who travel to Singapore for sex work (Johnson 1997:185–87). Nonetheless, across Southeast Asia male transvestites are important, if marginalized, elements of public culture, and their lives have important implications for understanding gender and belonging.

GAY MEN: SIMILITUDE, DIFFERENCE, AND HETERONORMATIVITY

In this chapter I use the phrase "gay men" to refer to Southeast Asian men who identify themselves using some transformed version of English "gay" (e.g., Indonesian *gay*, Filipino *gay*, Thai *gay*). In contrast to ETPs (many of which have existed for hundreds of years) and male transvestite subject positions (which are over a century old), gay subject positions appear to have taken form in Southeast Asia between the late 1960s and late 1970s, probably first in Thailand and the Philippines, and are linked to a series of socioeconomic and political changes, including a rise in popular mass media like television and women's magazines (Boellstorff 2005; Garcia 1996:71; Jackson 1999b:233; Sinnott 2004:2; Tan 2001:123).[5] In saying this, I do not mean to deny that men have probably always had sex with each other throughout the region.[6] My point is that the idea that one could organize oneself around a selfhood understood as "gay" is quite recent and linked to a range of factors.

From their beginnings, gay subject positions have been distinct both from ETPs and the male transvestite subject positions that preceded them, though blurring between the categories of "gay man" and "male transvestite" can occur (Boellstorff 2005:175–77; Garcia 1996; Jackson 1997; Johnson 1997). The prior existence of recognized male transvestites has had a profound impact upon gay subject positions, and it is a prime reason for some differences between gay and lesbian subject positions in Southeast Asia, since nowhere in Southeast Asia did there exist any female transgendered subject position with anything like the visibility of waria, kathoey, bakla, or other male transvestite subject positions.

The fact that gay male desire is a "desire for the same" rather than a heterogenderal desire arguably makes their subjectivities more transgressive than transvestite or transsexual subjectivities in Southeast Asia and beyond. As I have discussed elsewhere (Boellstorff 2005), questions of similitude and difference are central to any understanding of both homosexuality and globalization, and in fact the two have long been linked. While it is volume 1 of Foucault's *History of Sexuality* that holds a canonical place in queer studies (Foucault 1978; see Halperin 1995), a short discussion of the two volumes that follow it can be helpful in thinking through the relationship between sameness, difference, and sexuality.

In *The History of Sexuality, Volume 3: The Care of the Self* (1986), Foucault continued the examination of "modes of subjectivation" first taken up in *The History of Sexuality, Volume 2: The Use of Pleasure* (1985). As I read him, Foucault's ultimate goal in *The Care of the Self* was to chart the birth of heteronormativity in the first centuries AD of the Western tradition, though he did not use the term "heteronormativity" himself. Foucault's insight was that heteronormativity (which in the contemporary era has globalized in contingent yet powerful ways) was based on redeploying similitude and difference. Earlier Greek thought had understood sexuality to be fundamentally structured along lines of inequality: between husbands and wives, free men and slaves, older men and younger men. This overarching grid of difference made the question of whether sexual relations were between a male and female or male and male quite secondary, not to mention the question of sexual relations between women.

Foucault charted how, in the first centuries AD of the Western tradition, the care of the self came to be framed in terms of the monogamous conjugal relationship: "A natural privilege, at once ontological and ethical, is granted to this dual, heterosexual relationship at the expense of all others" (1986:163). The paradox, however, is that "this new erotics organizes itself around the symmetrical and reciprocal relationship of a man and a woman" (232). That is, heteronormativity, the presumption that desire should be the desire for difference, is made possible through what Foucault termed "symmetry," a sameness in desire itself.

Foucault deployed the notion of symmetry to emphasize how this claim of sameness (however unequal relations between husbands and wives might be in practice) made heteronormativity possible: "The traditional erotics laid strong emphasis on the polarity of the lover and the beloved and on the necessary dissymmetry between them. Here it is the double activity of loving, by the husband and the wife, that forms the essential element" (208–9). It is in this context that sex between an older and younger man, the model for "homosexuality" in the era under consideration, "lacks the double and symmetrical activity of loving, hence it lacks the internal regulation and the stability of the couple" (209).

This brief excursion into ancient Greek thought is important when considering gay men in Southeast Asia. This is because conceptions of sameness and difference are now central to understandings of both homosexuality and globalization: both are assumed to involve a desire for the same (see Boellstorff 2005, chapter 1). Since gay men appear more "similar" to Western models of sexual subjectivity than do the male transvestites discussed above, gay men are if anything more misunderstood; there has been a failure in queer studies (and to a lesser degree in anthropology) to set forth any theorization of the Southeast Asian gay subject that does not presume inauthenticity, complicity, or domination.

The three most common misperceptions about gay men concern their socioeconomic status, the form and intensity of their connections to Western gay men, and the degree to which they are accepted in their Southeast Asian societies. As is the case in the West, a stereotype persists that gay men in Southeast Asia come from the educated and wealthy classes.[7] Mass media coverage of gay men throughout Southeast Asia tends to reinforce this view, presenting gay men as closeted business executives or movie stars. In reality, gay men can come from any socioeconomic level, and since most Southeast Asians are not rich, it should not be surprising that few gay Southeast Asians are wealthy either (Boellstorff 2005; Garcia 1996).

A second misperception concerns the form and intensity of Southeast Asian gay men's connections to Western gay men. A frequent Western misunderstanding is that gay tourism or international gay organizations have played a significant role in the translocation of "gay" subjectivities to Southeast Asia, an assertion commonly made without a shred of supporting evidence. In reality such connections vary widely, with more gay men meeting Western gay men in nations with more intensive colonial legacies or more significant tourist industries (like the Philippines, Singapore, and Thailand [Heng 2001:82]), compared to nations like Indonesia or Laos. In general, Southeast Asian gay men have much less direct contact with Western gay men than is usually assumed to be the case. One reason for this assumption is that relatively few researchers are aware of the importance of everyday mass media in the formation and dissemination of Southeast Asian gay subject positions; in absence of this knowledge, scholars fall back on direct contact with Western gay men, transnational activism, or Western gay media as the only plausible explanations for the existence of gay subjectivities in Southeast Asia.

Third, there remains a misperception that gay men are accepted or at least tolerated in Southeast Asian societies. In most cases this misperception is rooted in a failure to distinguish between male transvestites and gay men; the relative visibility of male transvestites, the logic goes, must mean that gay men are accepted as well. What is more often the case is that it is the invisibility of gay men that allows them to find spaces of community free from direct oppression. However, this hardly qualifies as acceptance, and incidents of intolerance are by no means unknown. In fact, in many cases it appears that because it cannot be slotted into the heteronormative logic that desire is the desire of masculine for feminine and feminine for masculine, male homosexuality can be more stigmatized than male transvestism (or even female homosexuality, since men are often assumed to take the initiative in sex), and thus it is usually the prime target of state crackdowns (see chapter 5; Garcia 1996:57; Heng 2001:85–87, 91; Jackson 1999a:233–39; Keeler 1990:148–49; Peletz 2002:251–75; Sinnott 2004:121; Tan 1999:296; Yengoyan 1983:141).

Due to the fractured way to date by which most gay men in Southeast Asia have encountered Western notions of gay subjectivity, most are middle class or below, not directly linked to Western gay movements, and not accepted or even recognized by their societies. Most marry women, who may or may not know of their husbands' gay subjectivities, and many believe that Western gay men do not see heterosexual marriage as inconsistent with being gay. Gay men consistently speak of pressure from parents and siblings to marry, as well as more diffuse pressures to marry from religion and social norms, but many also speak of a desire to marry that is not just an external imposition (Boellstorff 1999; Maning 2000; Tan 2001:130). This is one reason why news of "gay marriage" in the West is often a topic of particular fascination to gay men in Southeast Asia.

Particularly in areas of Southeast Asia where English is not widely spoken, metaphors other than "coming out" may predominate, with consequences for understandings of gay subjectivity. For instance, for most gay Indonesians the notion of "opening oneself to the gay world" does not imply that it is necessary or inevitable to open oneself in all domains of one's life (such as one's family or workplace). The notion of "unfurling the cape" in the Philippines implies an ongoing change in subjectivity relative to the notion of "coming out" (Garcia 1996:117–18).

The sexual practices of Southeast Asian gay men appear to cover the same general range as those of men in other parts of the world defining themselves in terms of transformed versions of "gay." While the data is still woefully incomplete (and is compiled mainly by ethnographers and HIV prevention activists), it appears that compared to Western gay men, Southeast Asian men engage in anal-penile sex less often and interfemoral (penis-thighs) sex more often. Romance appears to be very important to gay men across Southeast Asia, and gay notions of romance typically draw heavily from broader views of love and choice that are in turn linked to national discourses.

Southeast Asian gay men tend to socialize in a "gay world" that is distinct from their "normal world." This is particularly the case if they are married to women, but even gay men not married to women may keep their "gay" and "normal" lives separate. Peter Jackson's observation that "there is comparatively little pressure for integrating one's public and private lives in Thailand" (1997:176) is quite accurate for Southeast Asia more generally.[8] Divisions across class and educational level are significant for gay men (Tan 2001:127–29), but they are mitigated by public or quasi-public venues like parks or discos, where gay men of varying socioeconomic levels can mingle to some extent. Gay men's social worlds revolve around parks and other public spaces (particularly for lower-class men), shopping malls and clubs (particularly for middle-class men), salons, and domestic spaces ranging from small apartments to private homes (Boellstorff 2005; Garcia 1996; Heng 2001; Howard 1996; Leong 1995).

Internet Web sites, e-mail, cell phones (particularly SMS messaging) and related technologies have swiftly become central to many gay Southeast Asians precisely because they can be easily harmonized with a selfhood organized around a separation between "gay" and "normal" worlds. Such technologies are much less significant to male transvestite communities, and this is not simply due to economic or educational issues, since many male transvestites use cell phones and Internet technologies. A more likely reason is that male transvestites do not use such technologies in the service of maintaining a sphere of sexual and gendered subjectivity separate from the public sphere.

Given such patterns of sociality, it should not be surprising that events like gay pride marches, which collapse the "gay" and "normal" worlds, are often less attractive to Southeast Asian gay men than are large indoor events from which the public is excluded. Nonetheless, gay pride events have taken place in Thailand and in the Philippines, and there is a long history of gay organizing in Southeast Asia. Gay organizing has rarely been oriented around political goals like changing antisodomy laws or establishing laws protecting gay men and other individuals with nonnormative sexual and gendered subjectivities from discrimination. Instead, gay organizing has historically focused on community-building events like drag shows.

While gay organizing in the West preceded the HIV/AIDS pandemic by many decades, from the beginnings of Southeast Asian gay men's organizing in the 1980s HIV/AIDS was a known entity seen as demanding a response, even if infection rates in much of the region were relatively low as well as further diminished by a lack of testing and reporting procedures. The rise of the HIV/AIDS pandemic in Southeast Asia has had significant effects upon gay men. In general, state and nongovernmental organizations have taken more interest in gay men than in lesbian women or male transvestites. Funding for HIV prevention and AIDS treatment from governmental and private sources, much of it originating in the West, has provided crucial support for many gay groups, allowing them to become organizations with offices and staff, though when such funding runs out the organizations are imperiled and may shut down. The rise of the MSM (men who have sex with men) category and its translocation to Southeast Asia has often led to the grouping together of gay men and male transvestites as a single "risk group" (Garcia 1996:189–93; Tan 2001:133–35).

TOMBOYS, FEMMES, AND LESBIANS: INTERSECTING SUBJECTIVITIES

Tomboys   A precise if provisional analytical vocabulary is necessary for discussing "lesbians." The vocabulary I set forth for this purpose reflects the most fundamental difference between "gay" and "lesbian" subject positions in Southeast Asia, which originates in the prior existence of visible male transvestite subject positions throughout the region. Across Southeast Asia, female transgender subject positions came into being more or less at the same time as did female homosexual subject positions, whereas many decades separate the emergence of male transvestite subject positions from gay subject positions. This does not mean that women in Southeast Asia never had sex with each other historically, but rather that socially recognized lesbian subject positions do not appear to have existed before the modern era. While male transvestites and gay men may be on friendly terms, in other cases they do not interact socially. Throughout Southeast Asia it is considered abnormal for male transvestites to have sex with each other or with a gay man: the very idea of such sexual pairings is often joked about as "lesbian" sex. Gay men normatively have sex with other gay men or with "normal" men, apart from any sex with women they may have; male transvestites normatively have sex with "normal" men, apart from any sex with women they may have.

In contrast, because the predominant female transgender and female homosexual subject positions in contemporary Southeast Asia came into being around the same time, they are far more intertwined, conceptually and practically, than are male transvestite and gay subject positions. I use "female *transgender*" (versus "male *transvestite*") to reflect this interlinkage. It is therefore not really possible to speak of "lesbian women" in Southeast Asia in the way that one can legitimately speak of "gay men"; what we find instead is a widespread tripartite distinction between what I will term "tomboys" (female transgenders seen in terms ranging from masculine woman to nonoperative female-to-male transsexual), "femmes" (normatively gendered women who inhabit a sexual subject position organized around romance and sex with tomboys), and "lesbians" (women who reject the tomboy/femme binarism and inhabit a sexual subject position organized around romance and sex with other lesbian women). A common pattern across Southeast Asia is to find debate and uncertainty as to whether these three subject positions are distinct or are part of one overarching "lesbian" subject position. And there is further debate as to whether "femme" is a distinct sexual subject position or a label for "normal" women who have romantic and sexual relationships with tomboys. The long-standing existence of male transvestites across the region means that such debates are far less common among male transvestites and gay men, though the rise of the "men who have sex with men" concept may blur male transvestite and gay male subject positions in the future.

"Tomboy" is a relatively novel subject position across Southeast Asia, having come into being in the 1970s in the context of socioeconomic changes in the region (Sinnott 2004:2, 63–64, 206–7). Individuals with subjectivities not unlike those of contemporary tomboys predate the emergence of tomboy subject positions. Oral history and ethnographic data indicate that such individuals could be found in urban and rural contexts in some parts of Southeast Asia in the early and mid-twentieth century, and in all likelihood earlier (Atkinson 1990:90; Boellstorff 2005:47–48; Sinnott 2004:53–56, 63). Because of the paucity of data concerning these individuals, the extent of these pre-1970s relationships and their causal relationship (if any) to contemporary tomboy subject positions remains unclear.

A range of terms exist in Southeast Asia for female-bodied individuals who act in a masculine manner and desire normatively gendered women (for instance, *hunter, cowok,* and *suntil* in parts of Indonesia; *binalaki* and *lakin-on* in the Philippines [Garcia 1996:86; Hart 1992:197]), but a common term transforms "tomboy" (*tomboi* in Indonesia, *tomboy* in Malaysia, *tom* in Thailand, *tomboy* in the Philippines, and so on).[9] Sometimes terms derived from the English word "lesbian" are used to refer to tomboys (Blackwood 1998). In line with my using the pronoun "she" when speaking of male transvestites (see chapter 2), I will use the pronoun "he" when speaking of tomboys, preferring this compromise to a neologism like "hir" or "s/he." The disadvantage of "he" is that unlike the ungendered third-person pronouns in many languages of Southeast Asia, particularly Austronesian languages like Indonesian and Tagalog, "he" is gender specific. The advantage of "he" is that neologisms like "hir" or "s/he" make it appear that tomboys are linguistically marked with unique indexicals, when in fact tomboys are referred to using existing gender terms and redeploy rather than transcend gender norms.

Unlike terms that rework "gay" or "lesbian," "tomboy" terms are not necessarily seen as transformations of English terms, because most national languages in Southeast Asia have since the 1970s had loanwords based on the English term "tomboy" — used, as in English, to refer to women (particularly girls) who engage in activities seen as the provenance of boys, like playing sports or climbing trees. A slippage between this more general definition and a specialized meaning of "tomboy" is typically significant to tomboy experience, thereby reflecting the range of views regarding the gender status of individuals identifying as tomboy: some see themselves as masculine women, others as men with women's bodies or women with men's souls.

Across the region it seems that one cannot be or become a tomboy if one is seen to have been born with a penis; tomboys usually see themselves (and are seen by others) as having been born a woman, not as men or a third gender (for instance, in South Sulawesi they receive the share of property accorded under Islamic norms to women, not men [Graham 2001; Wieringa 1999b:221]). Most tomboys begin acting in what is typically seen as a masculine manner as children — engaging in activities like climbing trees, riding bicycles, flying kites, and wearing boys' clothes (Webster 2004:27; see also Blackwood 1998, Graham 2001). They may be called "tomboys" by their families and playmates in the more general sense of the term. More serious teasing, including the use of derogatory words for male transvestites, can occur as well (see chapter 2; Sinnott 2004:58–59).

By the time they are adults, most tomboys seem to see themselves as women in some fashion (often as women with men's souls); they also see themselves as social men in some respects, and they may not like being described as "women who love women," "lesbians," or even "women" (Blackwood 1998; Sinnott 2004:173). Like male transvestites most tomboys do not have sex reassignment surgery; this is the case for a range of reasons including the cost and difficulty in obtaining the operation (Wieringa 1999:222), but also in many cases it is from a sense that they are ultimately a kind of woman. Like male transvestites, they do not necessarily identify in terms of a "third gender" (Sinnott 2004:6; Wieringa and Blackwood 1999:23–24).

It is important to most tomboys to have a man's haircut and to wear men's pants and shirts (Graham 2001; Wilson 2004:115). Many bind their breasts to make them less noticeable, but breasts sometimes serve as a useful reminder that they are physically women and few have them surgically removed (Sinnott 2004:54). A primary means of embodying tomboy subjectivity is to engage in stereotypically male behaviors like smoking, gambling, and driving a motorcycle (Blackwood 1999:188–89; Boellstorff 2005; Hart 1992:205–8; Sinnott 2004; Wieringa 1999b). At home, tomboys are less likely to engage in cooking than in activities like "general home and vehicle repair and maintenance" (Webster

2004:42). It is also expected that tomboys will support their femme partners financially; in practice this is often not the case, but for a femme to support her tomboy is "considered improper" (Sinnott 2004:153). That femmes sometimes end up financially supporting their tomboy partners reflects the discrimination that many tomboys face in gaining employment due to their visible deviance from feminine norms, though most manage to find some form of work (Wilson 2004).

A foundational element of tomboy subjectivity is that tomboys are supposed to pursue and engage in sexual and romantic relationships with normatively gendered women; the idea of two tomboys having sex with each other seems to be considered strange across the region (Sinnott 2004:86). In line with a common expectation of "normal" men and male transvestites, it is often assumed that tomboys are to be the initiators and pursuers of relationships (Boellstorff 2005; Graham 2003a; Hart 1992:207; Sinnott 2004:147). One reason for this is that it is often assumed that at least some of the femmes who partner with tomboys are actually "normal women" who would engage in romance and sex solely with men were it not for the efforts of their tomboy paramours. There is even less data available for the sexual practices of tomboys (and femmes and lesbians) than for gay men, but it appears that oral-vaginal and digital-vaginal contact are the most common and symbolically signifi-cant forms of sex (Boellstorff 2005; Idrus 2006; Sinnott 2004).

There is, however, one widespread way in which many tomboys across Southeast Asia diverge from stereotypical male roles: namely, tomboys usually see themselves as highly attentive to the emotional and sexual needs of femmes. This is often cited as a core aspect of occupying the tomboy subject position and a way in which tomboys are superior to men, who are said to be more self-centered. This attentiveness includes good listening skills and empathy along with prowess in pleasing femmes sexually, which typically is accompanied by "untouchability," or the refusal of the tomboy to be touched sexually or even remove his clothes (Sinnott 2004; Webster 2004:45; Wieringa 1999:218). As Sinnott notes for the case of Thailand, "The extreme irony of untouchability is that, rather than imitating sexual behaviors of men, it most fully demonstrates the femininity of [tomboy] identity" (Sinnott 2004:136, see also 90–92). Across Southeast Asia, prioritizing a partner's sexual pleasure and emo-tional needs is typically associated not with masculinity but with norms of modern femininity based on emotional management as a primary duty of the good wife (Jones 2004).

There appears to be significant variation as to whether or not tomboys in Southeast Asia marry men. It is striking that mass media and state scrutiny of tomboys and femmes has consistently focused on occasions when they seek official recognition for their relationships (Boellstorff 2005:47–48, 62–65; Hart 1992:208; Peletz 2002:253–58; Tan 1999). Some tomboys avoid marrying men all of their lives, but it is probably more common for them to marry and then divorce or separate to cohabit with femme partners (Blackwood 1998; Boellstorff 2005; Hart 1992:207). This reflects the fact that particularly in Islamic areas of Southeast Asia, marriage remains the norm despite the significant shift from arranged marriage to the predominance of chosen or "love" marriage (Baba 2001). In other cases, such as in Thailand, it appears that a lesser pressure for women to marry means that more tomboys are able to avoid marriage altogether (Sinnott 2004:72–73). Some tomboys (and a greater number of femmes) maintain coresidence with their husbands, carrying on sexual relations with or without their husband's knowledge. This is aided by the fact that across the region the greatest threat to women's virtue is not sex with other women but sex with men; sex between women is often not seen as sex at all (Sinnott 2004:14, 113, 220; Webster 2004:35).

Tomboys usually have greater difficulty in socializing and forming community in comparison to gay men or male transvestites. One reason for this is that because tomboys are still seen as women in some sense, it is difficult for them to spend time in places like parks and town squares, and the fact that femmes almost never enter such places (particularly at night or alone) removes a major incentive for going. Some tomboys do go out alone and at night, sometimes even being mistaken for men on the street (Blackwood 1998; Boellstorff 2005). Tomboys (and their femme partners) tend to hang out in more semipublic places like shopping malls (Boellstorff 2005; Wilson 2004), or at each others' homes, none of which are contexts that permit large groupings or open conversation. A common theme in tomboy narratives concerns the difficulty of forming and sustaining friendships with other tomboys due to concerns that their femme partner will be seduced by another tomboy. Class and status are significant factors throughout Southeast Asia, and like gay male communities, tomboy communities are strongly class marked. Even larger networks may not resolve into a single community, and there is little socializing or romance across class lines (Murray 1999, Sinnott 2004:121, 178–79; Webster 2004:31–32).

Femmes Paralleling everyday understandings of male transvestites, across Southeast Asia it is considered unusual for two tomboys to be in a romantic or sexual relationship. Instead, tomboys have sexual and romantic relationships with normatively gendered women, who in some cases see themselves (and are seen by tomboys and others) as having a distinct subjectivity, which I term "femme" subjectivity in this chapter. In some cases femme subjectivity has a distinct name (such as *dee* in Thailand, derived from the final syllable of English "lady"; or *kantil* and *cewek* ("girl") in Indonesia). In other cases, women partnered with tomboys simply term themselves "women" (or "normal women"), yet sometimes they have a distinct sense of sexual selfhood. While a few femmes speak of engaging in gender-atypical play as children, most do not. When they are able to cohabit with their tomboy partners, femmes typically engage in female-identified activities in line with the rhetoric of modern domesticity, like cooking, washing clothes, and cleaning the house; if they are working outside the home it is generally in professions like secretarial work (Graham 2001; Sinnott 2004:131; Webster 2004:42–43; Wieringa 1999:217).

Even for women identifying themselves as femmes in some fashion, since they are normatively gendered their femme subjectivities are as much sexual as gendered and are thus highly dependent on involvement with tomboys ("*dees* are only *dees* in their relation to a *tom*" [Sinnott 2004:30; see Nur and R. 1996:74]). Tomboys therefore usually fear not just that their femme will leave them for another tomboy, but that the femme will marry a man and reduce or end her involvement with tomboys altogether (Wieringa 1999:217).

Lesbians In Southeast Asia the pairing of tomboy and femme subject positions appears since the 1970s to have been the dominant form of female-embodied gender nonnormativity. In my own fieldwork I have encountered cases of femmes becoming tomboys (but not the reverse), but this appears to be rare across the region; most tomboys have gender-atypical childhoods, so it is unusual for adults to begin identifying as tomboy. Tomboys and femmes often reject the term "lesbian," not necessarily because it is Western derived (terms for tomboy and femme are also often loanwords) but because it is seen to imply an obsession with sex (Sinnott 2004:29). This appears to be the case because a primary way by which "lesbian" has become known in Southeast Asia is through heterosexual pornography that includes sex scenes between women, leading to the view that the term "lesbian" connotes bisexuality, promiscuity, and sex between two femmes rather than between a tomboy and a femme (Murray 1999:142; Sinnott 2004:205).

Despite these misgivings, many Southeast Asians now identify as lesbian (often using a loanword version of the English word "lesbian," like *lesbi* in Indonesia). Lesbians often say they are explicitly rejecting the tomboy/femme dichotomy, and they may speak of that dichotomy as restrictive, imitative, or oppressive. Lesbian subjectivities of this kind are typically associated with the wealthier and better-educated social classes as well as with being "modern"; tomboys and femmes are seen as more lower class (Blackwood 1999:196; Murray 1999). However, this is not absolute: there are lower-class women who identify as lesbian (Murray 1999:143, 151) and upper-class women who identify as tomboy or femme. Lesbians in Southeast Asia provide several reasons for preferring lesbian subjectivities to tomboy and femme subjectivities, though of course this is not always seen as a conscious choice and lesbians are not necessarily antagonistic toward tomboys and femmes. One source of dissatisfaction is the pattern of tomboy untouchability; in contrast, lesbians usually place value on both partners allowing themselves to be sexually touched (Sinnott 2004:149).

NINE QUEERLY COMPARATIVE THESES

My goal in this provisional discussion has been to illuminate some broad patterns with regard to nonnormative sexualities and genders in Southeast Asia. In this intentionally quasi-ethnocartographic survey of the region, my aim has been to set out a preliminary frame of discussion, and I end this chapter—and this book—by setting forth nine preliminary theses based on the material presented above. The phrase "in Southeast Asia" can be appended to each of these theses, since that is the primary spatial scale to which they are keyed; however, none of the patterns I discuss below can be found everywhere in Southeast Asia, and some of them are relevant beyond Southeast Asia and even worldwide. The purpose of the kind of queer comparison in which I engage here is not to distill underlying laws from the data, since I do not subscribe to a determinist view of the social (be it biological, environmental, cultural, or structural) that sees social life as produced by underlying laws in the way that (it is claimed) language is produced through grammar or life through genes. Queer comparison is not a form of law making but rather a form of critique and sensitivity to coincidence that complements ethnography; it does not set itself up as a transcendent critique that passes judgment on such work, but instead as an immanent critique that opens up new possibilities for scholarship and activism.

Thesis 1: There are three "layers" of nonnormative sexual and gendered subject positions. Across Southeast Asia we find three apparent "layers" of nonnormative sexual and gendered subject positions: ETPs (in some cases), which date back many hundreds of years; male transvestite subject positions, which date to the mid-nineteenth century; and gay, tomboy, femme, and lesbian subject positions, which date to the 1960s. This means that although tomboys may appear as the gendered complement to male transvestites, tomboy subject positions have a history more like that of gay, lesbian, and femme subject positions. There are variations in this chronology, of course, and nonnormative sexual and gendered subject positions with longer histories are usually not displaced by newer ones but coexist with them.

This thesis is a claim about the historicity of nonnormative sexual and gendered subject positions, and two aspects of this history seem particularly salient. One is the apparent fact of three "layers" rather than two or four or some other number. The first of these "layers" is somewhat of a misnomer, since ETPs are not really sexual subject positions but rather professions, and since they came into being over hundreds of years in a range of contexts (Boellstorff 2005, chapter 2). More significant is the clear existence of two subsequent "layers" or "waves" of nonnormative sexual and gendered subject formation, one in the nineteenth century and one in the latter part of the twentieth century. This demonstrates how subject positions of all kinds are the product of specific coincidences of history and power. It also suggests that new nonnormative sexual and gendered subject positions (and normative ones as well) will come into being at some point in the future, while older nonnormative sexual and gendered subject positions will variously persist — changing over time — or will die out.

A second striking aspect of the historicity of nonnormative sexual and gendered subject positions is their relationship to the normative gender subject positions "female" and "male" (see thesis 4). Both the first (and somewhat misnamed) "layer" of nonnormative sexual and gendered subject positions, ETPs, and the second "layer," male transvestites, have overwhelmingly been inhabited by individuals seen as male. In other words, only approximately in the 1960s and 1970s do there appear in Southeast Asia nonnormative sexual and gendered subject positions identified as properly inhabited by individuals seen as female — tomboys, femmes, and lesbians.

Thesis 2: The emergence of gay, tomboy, femme, and lesbian subject positions is historically linked to the rise of postcolonial societies and middle-class sensibilities. This is an extension of thesis 1. There is a long history of scholarship exploring the relationship between capitalism and queer sexualities (D'Emilio 1983; Hocquenghem 1978), though less often is it pointed out that many of these explorations assume that the economic exists as a self-evident category of experience (Maurer 2000; Mitchell 2002). Across Southeast Asia, the rise of a substantial middle class seems to have played an important role in the formation of gay, lesbian, tomboy, and femme subject positions. Even for those who are poor, a middle-class sensibility shaped by consumerism and advertising appears to have had a significant effect upon senses of sexual self-hood (Boellstorff 1999; Heng 2001:83–84; Sinnott 2004:64–65; Wilson 2004). The importance of these economic factors has been obscured by the focus of much queer research on uncovering "traditional" or "indigenous" homosexualities and transgenderisms. As Jackson emphasizes, "a dominant but unspoken question guiding [research by Western gay men and lesbians on homoeroticism in Asia] is: 'Is there someone else out there like me?' " (2001:9–10). What he terms this "Western quest for global self-affirmation" often takes the form of seeking out ostensible historical antecedents.

The role of economic factors differs for male transvestite subject positions, which as noted earlier first came into being in colonial-era market contexts. Contemporary male transvestites are of course powerfully shaped by economic forces, and subject positions themselves change through time like any aspect of culture; the difference is that this is a shaping of a previously existing subject position, rather than the shaping of an emergent subject position. The influence of contemporary economic changes on male transvestites seems most apparent in the rise of the salon as the prototypical site of male transvestite employment and sociality, the greater body modifications of contemporary male transvestites via hormones, silicone, and occasionally operations, and the tendency for male transvestites to be visible as such all day long rather than only in circumscribed contexts.

Thesis 3: Normative heterosexualities are just as historically and culturally embedded as nonnormative sexualities and genders. While it lies beyond the scope of this chapter to discuss this thesis in detail, it bears emphasizing that almost all of the scholarly sources cited thus far, including my own work, emphasize that contemporary notions of heterosexuality in Southeast Asia are just as constructed as nonnormative sexualities and genders (Ong and Peletz 1995); it is not coincidental that "normal" and "heterosexual" are as much loanwords in the region as "gay," "lesbian," or "tomboy." Denaturalizing these heterosexualities is an important project for queer critique in Southeast Asia, as elsewhere. As exemplified by the range of feminist literatures cited throughout this book, demonstrating the historical and cultural specificity of modern heterosexualities throughout Southeast Asia must be central to any queer project, since these heterosexualities form the dominant against which contemporary nonnormative sexualities and genders in the region are articulated.

Thesis 4: "Male" and "female" remain powerful structuring principles for nonnormative genders and sexualities, but in complex ways. As discussed earlier, regimes of gender complementarity are widespread across Southeast Asia, but gender difference certainly exists and has become more pronounced in the wake of colonialism, nationalism, and the rise of Islam and Christianity. Thus Megan Sinnott notes that "as females," tomboys and femmes in Thailand "face different family expectations from those that Thai males face, and thus any generalization about the Thai 'gay-lesbian' scene would need to account for these important differences between being male and being female in Thai society" (2004:70). In addition, gender segregation transcends the male-female binary in Southeast Asia, since there is often little socializing between male transvestites and gay men, or even between tomboys and femmes, on the one hand, and lesbians on the other. In addition to the family expectations that Sinnott emphasizes, differing access to public space, mobility, and financial independence distinguish the experiences of Southeast Asians with nonnormative genders and sexualities. Across Southeast Asia, gay activism is often linked to HIV/AIDS prevention and treatment networks, while tomboy, femme, and lesbian activism is more often linked to feminist networks (Murray 1999:144; Heng 2001:84; Webster 2004:32–33). As a result there is a good deal of independent organizing, and tomboy, femme, and lesbian groups may not feel that their concerns receive sufficient attention in organizations dominated by gay men or male transvestites (Marin 1996:49; Webster 2004:50). This is reflected in everyday socialization, where there is a great deal of separation between gay, male transvestite, and tomboy/femme/lesbian communities (reflecting the gender segregation that predominates, to varying degrees and in varying forms, throughout Southeast Asia; see Tan 2001).

Despite all of these important differences between Southeast Asians with nonnormative genders and sexualities, there has been far less research on possible commonalities between them, including actual social interaction. Forms of co-gendered or co-sexual community and activism may be under-reported by researchers whose methodological and theoretical frameworks predispose them to researching only one gender or sexuality at a time. Since most ethnographic research on nonnormative sexualities and genders in Southeast Asia has focused on only one gender or sexuality, we find a theoretical problem similar to the one I identify as "ethnolocality": for instance, discussions of gay men and lesbian women, like discussions of more than one locality, are assumed to take place in a comparative rather than ethnographic frame, thus limiting the range of critique. However, a number of researchers in the region have discussed multiple genders (gay men and lesbian women, gay men and male transvestites, male transvestites and tomboys, and so on), and such work on multiple genders and sexualities may represent a kind of multi-sited ethnography (Marcus 1995) pointing toward new possibilities for comparison. In the classic 1975 article that did so much to introduce the distinction between sex and gender, Gayle Rubin wrote: "Men and women are, of course, different. But they are not as different as day and night, earth and sky, yin and yang, life and death . . . The idea that men and women are more different from one another than either is from anything else must come from somewhere other than nature" (1975:179). This recalls my earlier point that notions of sameness and difference are crucial to understandings not just of gender and sexuality but globalization, so often assumed to homogenize the world's cultures. Part of our research agenda must be to investigate the notions of sameness and difference that shape "insider" and "outsider" understandings of non-normative sexualities and genders in Southeast Asia and beyond.

Thesis 5: Gender "transgressors" tend to be sexual "normatives" and vice versa. One way of cutting across the typical typologies used in gender analysis (male/female/transgender, homosexual/heterosexual/bisexual) is to distinguish "transgressors" (Blackwood 1998, 2005) and "normatives." It seems possible to group together tomboys and male transvestites as gender transgressors but sexual normatives. That is, they transgress their normative genders while retaining heterogenderal sexualities —namely, sexualities organized around a desire for difference. It also seems possible to group together gay men and lesbian women as gender normatives but sexual transgressors. That is, they do not transgress their normative genders, but do transgress normative (heterogenderal) sexualities, since their sexualities are organized around a desire for the same.

Like all heuristic categorizations, these statements oversimplify: gay men, for instance, are often effeminate, so to say they do not transgress gender is not quite right, and femmes as well as the male partners of transvestites appear to drop out of this framework altogether, since they do not appear to transgress sexuality (they are attracted to difference) or gender (they are effeminate women and masculine men). Yet linking male transvestites and tomboys on the one hand, and gay men and lesbian women on the other (rather than the more common analytic of grouping "gay men and male transvestites" versus "tomboys and lesbian women") might raise interesting new points of departure for ethnographic and comparative analysis. For instance, most Southeast Asian countries appear tolerant of nonnormative sexualities and genders compared to many other parts of the world, but such tolerance is not absolute and is often a tolerance of effeminate men or masculine women rather than of homosexuality (Jackson 1999a; Whitam and Mathy 1986).

Thesis 6: Mass media play a pivotal but contingent role in nonnormative sexualities and genders. It appears that print media, television, and movies have been crucial to the formation of gay and lesbian subject positions (and to a lesser degree, tomboy and femme subject positions) (Boellstorff 2005; Gayatri 1996:93–94; Jackson 1999b; Murtagh 2006; Sinnott 2004:127). This seems more consequential than either the historically rare consumption of Western gay and lesbian media or publications produced by Southeast Asians themselves (see chapter 1). It is thus in relation to print media, television, and movies that we must place the important role played since the mid-1990s by the Internet, cell phones, and other technologies (Heng 2001:92–93; Khoo 1993; Offord 2003). The Internet has become important to tomboy, femme, and lesbian experience for many Southeast Asians by helping to overcome the isolation caused by the difficulty these individuals face in accessing public space or time away from their families (Webster 2004:35). Internet access has become inexpensive and its use is no longer limited to educated elites; as a result, even lower-class lesbians, tomboys, and femmes make use of it to find partners, share experiences, and organize social events (Webster 2004:45). Gay men have also been using the Internet to meet each other and organize events, and chatting, instant messaging, and other Internet-related activities are important to the lives of many gay men. Only male transvestites seem to have made limited use of the Internet to date. This is largely due to their tendency to come from more impoverished economic and educational backgrounds, but also due to the fact that they are much more socially visible than gay men, tomboys, femmes, and lesbians, such that isolation per se tends to be less of a concern.

Thesis 7: Contemporary nonnormative sexualities and genders are linked more powerfully to both globalization and nationalism than to ethnicity or tradition. We live in an era where, it is assumed, "primordialism" takes the form of ethnic and religious attachments that are somehow socially (or even biologically) reproduced in a more lasting, visceral, and meaningful fashion than either national or global attachments. This view contributes to the assumption that gay men and lesbian women in Southeast Asia are incomplete members of their own societies. But how to understand the role of globalization in the constitution and dissemination of nonnormative sexualities and genders in the region remains unresolved (Altman 2001; Sinnott 2004:188). Some researchers claim that tomboy and femme individuals do not "engage in global imaginings" as gay men and perhaps lesbian women do (Sinnott 2004:205). This suggests that tomboy and femme subjectivities are in this respect more like those of male transvestites, who typically understand their subjectivities in national but not in global terms.[10] While many tomboys and femmes do not like the term "lesbian," it is clear that many Southeast Asian women do identify as lesbian and these subject positions may have trajectories quite distinct from those of tomboy and femme subject positions.

In no case to my knowledge are gay men in Southeast Asia unaware that there are men elsewhere who use terms derived from "gay," nor are tomboys, femmes, and lesbians unaware that there are women elsewhere who use terms derived from "tomboy" and "lesbian," even though their points of reference are typically Western rather than Southeast Asian (Sinnott 2004:29). Yet seeing Southeast Asian gay men as part of a global community elides the powerful and fundamental ways that national identity shapes gay subjectivities in Southeast Asia.[11]

This linkage between nonnormative sexualities and genders and national discourse is one of the starkest yet least researched aspects of these subject positions. Since national discourses in Southeast Asia both share common features and evince significant differences, it follows that this national discourse may represent one of the most fundamental, institutionally supported, and sustained ways by which ostensibly global notions of homosexual subjectivity become reterritorialized, and by which historically prior male transvestite subject positions are altered as well. Furthermore, despite the fact that homosexuality and transgenderism are generally less the focus of state, religious, or social opprobrium than has been the case historically in the West, the fact that heteronormativity has been so central in constituting notions of the postcolonial and modern citizen means that homosexuality and transgenderism may play a largely implicit role in the constitution of the nation itself (cf. Bunzl 2004a).

Relationships to this normativity are complex. In Southeast Asia, lesbians, tomboys, femmes, gay men, and male transvestites all tend to accept the dominant view that they are "abnormal"; do not see themselves as challenging dominant norms; and do not make public declarations calling for equal rights or recognition (Garcia 1996:4; Howard 1996; Jackson 1999a:240; Nur and R. 1996:75; Tan 2001; Sinnott 2004:141–42; Webster 2004:36). Theories of queer subjectivity based on oppositional consciousness or disidentification, theories that have had particular analytical purchase in Latin America and some racialized communities in North America (Muñoz 1999; Sandoval 1991), may thus have limited usefulness in Southeast Asian contexts.

Thesis 8: Despite rumors of the demise of the sexuality/gender binarism, it remains analytically useful and experientially real. The relationship between "sexuality" and "gender" has become a key point of somewhat muddled debate in queer studies. Often this debate takes as its point of departure the following passage from Gayle Rubin's essay

"Thinking Sex": "I want to challenge the assumption that feminism is or should be the privileged site of a theory of sexuality. Feminism is the theory of gender oppression. To automatically assume that this makes it the theory of sexual oppression is to fail to distinguish between gender, on the one hand, and erotic desire, on the other" (1984:307). In this passage, Rubin in effect took the conceptual distinction between sex and gender developed by herself and other feminist scholars (Rubin 1975) and extended it to a disciplinary realm. This move is sometimes seen as making possible the very idea of a queer studies that is distinct from feminist studies, however imbricated they might be in actual practice. Since the early 1990s, however, many scholars have challenged Rubin's separation between the study of sexuality and gender, though sometimes this challenge is a form of paranoid reading that sees Rubin as discrediting feminist inquiry (see the introduction). The distinction between gender and sexuality has also been challenged on an ethnographic level by scholars (many of whom work in Southeast Asia) who claim that there is no real concept of "sexuality" in Southeast Asia and that gender is the dominant way by which embodiment and desire is understood in the region (Jackson 1997; Johnson 1997; Graham 2003b; Valentine 2003).

However, collapsing sexuality into gender, and thereby erasing it as an analytical and experiential category, would impoverish our ability to make sense of "queer" Southeast Asians (and others). As I have noted elsewhere, the very fact that in Southeast Asia and beyond, terms based on "homosexual" and "heterosexual" are taken to refer to gender rather than race, ethnicity, religion, or any other social parameter, indicates the importance of a concept of sexuality (Boellstorff 2005:91–92). For instance, nowhere to my knowledge is a Christian's desire for another Christian termed "homosexual" while a Christian's desire for a Hindu is termed "heterosexual."

In the Southeast Asian literature, the claim for the supremacy of gender over sexuality is usually made with reference to gender transgressors —male transvestites and tomboys. This downplays the theoretical contribution to be gained by examining the lives of gay men and lesbian women who define themselves in terms of a desire for the same—that is, homosexuality—without emphasizing sexual role or nonnormative gendering. It is not coincidental that in their own national contexts, such individuals are more often vilified or denigrated as symptomatic of global cultural imperialism than are male transvestites or tomboys.

Many scholars of nonnormative sexualities and genders in Southeast Asia find that a distinction between sexuality and gender is necessary to an emically accurate understanding of the cultural context; for instance, the distinction between *silahis* and bakla hinges on a sexuality/gender distinction (Garcia 1996:17–19, 54, 110).

Far from it being the case that Western influence has introduced a spurious distinction between homosexuality and transgenderism, it may be their "fluid" conflation that is a Western import, a legacy of sexological discourses of inversion (Johnson 1997:33; Garcia 1996). What we find in Southeast Asia is not "fluidity" but multivalent deployments of gender and sexuality that always have some kind of cultural logic to them. This is a logic that the distinction between sexuality and gender — and at the same time, a recognition of the fundamental imbrication of sexuality and gender — can help illuminate. Like structure/agency, individual/society, and a host of other binarisms that seem to resist dismissal or supersession, the most effective approach seems not to be deconstruction (since the binarisms keep reappearing), but disontologization; that is, understanding the binarisms not as fundamental states of the universe but as frameworks of coincidence, immanent to the field of analysis and thus the field of critique as well.

Thesis 9: Comparison as well as ethnography can produce new coincidences between anthropology and queer studies. Throughout this book I have investigated possible collaborations between anthropology and queer studies through specific acts of analysis and critique, focused largely on "queer" Indonesians. In this chapter I hope to have indicated the possibility that comparison can be a queer methodology for producing new interdisciplinary coincidences as well. I am reminded here of the quotation from Roland Barthes that opens *Writing Culture*: "Interdisciplinary work, so much discussed these days, is not about confronting already constituted disciplines (none of which, in fact, is willing to let itself go). To do something interdisciplinary it's not enough to choose a 'subject' (a theme) and gather around it two or three sciences. Interdisciplinarity consists in creating a new object that belongs to no one" (Clifford 1986:1)

True interdisciplinarity requires theorizing disciplinarity in a nonparanoid manner. It makes me suspicious that in queer studies everyone seems to be in favor of interdisciplinarity; the lack of debate or critique makes me wonder if the apparent unanimity speaks to other concerns. It may be that the current valorization of interdisciplinarity in queer studies says as much about rhetorics of multiculturalism and diversity than any epistemological or methodological program: the projection of endlessly extendable "LGBT" thinking (now to include "I" for intersexed; one "Q" for "queer" and another for "questioning," and so on). Add disciplines along the trajectory of straight time like one adds identity categories, with the hope that at some point there will emerge a new formation, greater than the sum of its parts, pointing the way to a new critical intervention in academia and the social worlds in which we live. The promise of interdisciplinarity is real indeed, but its contribution may come into being not through the addition of identities or disciplines, but in a more coincidental, and thus radical, transformation of the politics and practices of knowledge itself. It may be a transformation that does not just add new foundations but questions the need for foundations; a transformation that seeks not just to add new knowledge but to reconfigure what counts as knowledge. Not a "writing culture" that inscribes the past or predicts the future, but a coincidence that remakes the present.

NOTES

INTRODUCTION

1. I consider disciplines like international studies and even anthropology or sociology to be sites of disciplinary identification, though in different ways.

2. Other social sciences can contribute an attention to sociality; in this book I emphasize the specific theoretical and methodological contributions of anthropology.

3. Malinowski did not take a tolerant stance toward homosexuality. In part this was due to his interest in countering the view that "natives" were sexually decadent, a common theme in colonialist thought (see Bleys 1995). Thus in *The Sexual Life of Savages* (prefaced by the sexologist and homosexual rights advocate Havelock Ellis), Malinowski claimed that "the natives achieve an almost complete freedom from perversion" (Malinowski 1987 [1929]: 453). He further notes: "Personally I find it misleading to use the term 'homosexuality' in the vague and almost intentionally all-embracing sense that is now fashionable under the influence of psychoanalysis and the apostles of 'Urning' love . . . The natives are well aware that venereal disease and homosexuality are among the benefits bestowed on them by Western culture" (472–73; see also Malinowski 1927: 90).

4. It lies beyond the scope of this chapter to review this literature in detail. It also lies beyond this chapter's scope to trace genealogies of queer studies (see, among others, Beemyn and Eliason 1996; Corber and Valocchi 2003; Jagose 1996; Sullivan 2003).

5. For general overviews of Indonesian history and contemporary Indonesia, including issues raised in this summary, see, among others, Cribb and Brown 1995; Dick 1990; Reid 1988, 1993; Ricklefs 1981; Schwarz 1994; and Vickers 2005.

6. See "Soviet Queers Fight Coup," *Advocate*, September 24, 1991, p. 50); "Gay Stanford Grad Fought Soviet Coup," *San Jose Mercury News*, December 2, 1991, p. 3B; "Famed Mac Ad Came True," *San Francisco Examiner*, September 30, 1991, p. C1.

7. I have conducted a total of about two years of fieldwork in Indonesia (in 1992, 1993, 1995, 1997–98, and 2000), with brief visits in 2001, 2002, 2004, and 2005.

8. Chapter 2 focuses almost exclusively on warias. Chapters 1 and 3 focus on *gay* men but include some material on *lesbi* women. Chapters 4 and 5 focus specifically on *gay* men. Chapter 6 draws upon the work of other scholars to balance as much as possible an analysis of gay men, lesbian women, and transgenders across Southeast Asia.

9. The original version appeared as "Zines and Zones of Desire: Mass Mediated Love, National Romance, and Sexual Citizenship in *Gay* Indonesia," *Journal of Asian Studies* 63(2):367–402, 2004.

10. The original version appeared as "Playing Back the Nation: Waria, Indonesian Transvestites," *Cultural Anthropology* 19(2):159–95. Copyright © 2004 by the American Anthropological Association.

11. The original version appeared as "*Gay* Language and Indonesia: Registering Belonging," *Journal of Linguistic Anthropology* 14(2):248–68. Copyright © 2004 by the American Anthropological Association.

12. The original version appeared as "Between Religion and Desire: Being Muslim and *Gay* in Indonesia," *American Anthropologist* 107(4):575–85. Copyright © 2005 by the American Anthropological Association.

13. The original version appeared as "The Emergence of Political Homophobia in Indonesia: Masculinity and National Belonging," *Ethnos* 69(4):465–86, 2004 (http://www.tandf.co.uk).

14. To protect my interlocutors and the communities in which they lived, I have changed the names of all Indonesians discussed in this book (except for Dédé Oetomo, who is a public figure). I have also changed the details of locations and interactions.

15. Throughout this book I use "anthropology" to refer to cultural anthropology rather than as an inclusive term encompassing the subfields commonly recognized in the U.S. tradition (cultural anthropology, biological anthropology, linguistic anthropology, and archaeology). In chapter 3 I touch upon possible articulations of queer studies and linguistic anthropology.

16. Although some emphasize the focus of queer studies on "sexual and gender practices such as sadomasochism, transvestism and hermaphroditism that cannot be reduced to the categories of either homosexuality or heterosexuality" (Corber and Valocchi 2003:1), I also understand queer studies to problematize the stability of homosexuality and heterosexuality from within those categories.

17. The *Oxford English Dictionary* online at http://www.oed.com.

18. The paranoia Sedgwick describes operates at a more general level in the university, which is often presented as in crisis (Clark and Royle 1995; Readings 1996; Spivak 2003).

19. *Social Text* 84–85, vol. 23, nos. 3–4, (fall–winter 2005), edited by David Eng, Judith Halberstam, and José Esteban Muñoz.

20. See Boellstorff 2007 for a discussion of how these notions of coincidental time might help us rethink debates over same-sex marriage.

1. Compare with Schneider 1980 for the American case.

2. See chapter 4 for further discussion of incommensurability.

3. A chapter specifically on *lesbi* zines would explore these issues in more depth and would include in its analysis books published on *lesbi* life (see Endah 2004; Herlinatiens 2003; Kartini 2003; Prawirakusumah and Ramadhan 1988; and Ratri 2000; as well as material on the Internet. The Internet was first mentioned in a *gay* zine in *GAYa Nusantara* (1996, no. 44). Since August 1999, a handful of zines have established Web sites (as have some individual *gay* and *lesbi* Indonesians). Since the impact of the Internet is different from that of zines, however, I do not discuss it in this chapter.

4. One letter to the editors of *Jaka* praised the zine because "the short stories happen to be almost exactly like my own experiences" (1986, 8:2). In a 1996 *GAYa Nusantara* readers' survey, true-experiences stories were the favorite genre.

5. On five occasions I have contributed articles to *GAYa Nusantara* (nos. 52, 53, 73, 77, and 78). I have also been interviewed by *GAYa Nusantara* on several occasions (nos. 23, 24, and 41).

6. Since 2000, *GAYa Nusantara* has started to carry a few advertisements.

7. *GAYa Nusantara*, the zine with the largest circulation, has had a print run of six hundred for most of its history (beginning in 1992 with no. 17), with a high of about eight hundred; by 2001 its circulation was down to about four hundred. *GAYa Nusantara* has also been the only zine that has carried advertising of any consequence (usually for salons or drag events), as well as the only zine to have had any kind of public distribution up through the early 2000s: beginning in the mid-1990s, *GAYa Nusantara* was sold at a few bookstores in Surabaya.

8. All information and quotations from zines are cited in the text by year, issue number, and page.

9. Many *gay* Indonesians are unaware that *gay* zines exist, even if they live in a city where such a zine is published. The primary relationship between *gay* zines and the regular mass media is that the occasional coverage of *gay* zines in these media (or even news on homosexuality more generally) can generate a flood of letters to the zines. The first such example was in May 1982, when the women's magazine *Sarinah* ran an article about *G*, the first *gay* zine; as a result, a number of *lesbi* women wrote to the zine seeking contacts and asking to become members of the organization associated with the zine (G 1983, 6:3).

10. Letters to the editor indicate cases of persons who — for fear of discovery of the fact that they live in an area where they do not know any *gay* and *lesbi* persons — obtain a single copy of a zine, then subscribe to it and do not share it with others. In such cases, the act of subscribing to the zine does not reduce social networks but rather simply fails to strengthen them or generate new ones.

11. In a twelfth-anniversary retrospective, the editors of *GAYa Nusantara* noted that the term *nusantara* "illustrates clearly that this group is national in scale [*berskala nasional*], meaning for the Indonesian *gay* people" (1999, 62:23).

12. Many letters to *gay* and *lesbi* zines express this sentiment. As one woman said with reference to the *lesbi* zine *MitraS*, "Through this bulletin I pour out my feelings" (*MitraS* 1998, 2:13); as a *gay* man from the troubled region of Aceh phrased it, "since I got to know *GN*, I've started to feel calm in my heart" (*GN* 2000, 76:11). One man from Surabaya wrote that "Since I've married, I've had to reduce my *gay* activities greatly, . . . but I can still observe my world through *GN*" (*GN* 2000, 76:8).

13. For example, Dédé Oetomo, who has played a major role in two of the most influential *gay* zines, *G: Gaya Hidup Ceria* and *GAYa Nusantara*, is a Ph.D. recipient from Cornell University. He was for many years a professor of anthropology and linguistics at Airlangga University, and he is well known to scholars of Indonesia (through academic publications, political work, and participation in language study programs) as well as to the Indonesian public (he is one of a handful of *gay* Indonesians willing to be identified in the general mass media as such).

14. In one case, such networks helped fund the zine *GAYa Celebes* in Makassar on the island of Sulawesi, which focuses on *gay* men, although *lesbi* women and especially warias are often addressed as well.

15. This relationship is, of course, not totally symmetrical, since it is typically men who choose women and not the other way around, but modern rhetorics of choice and love in Indonesia emphasize that just as women vote, consume, or even become president, they are also to be active participants in the act of choice.

16. Although homosexuality is increasingly a topic of discussion in mainstream Indonesian media, such coverage is overwhelmingly negative and the few textual or visual representations of homosexual desire are usually of Euro-Americans.

17. The only context in which sex consistently appears in *gay* zines is in articles on preventing HIV and other sexually transmitted infections. Such articles are fairly common in *gay* zines (but rare in *lesbi* zines) because many are funded directly or indirectly through HIV prevention programs, in most cases by international development agencies.

18. For other narratives of separation, see *NJJ* 1997, 2:17–21; *GN* 1998, 2:13–21; and *GN* 1997, 49:23–28.

19. English is the only language other than Indonesian that appears with any frequency in *gay* and *lesbi* zines. Short stories and personals sometimes contain English words or short phrases. *GAYa Nusantara* ran a one-page "Summary in English" in each issue from 1994 to 1997 (nos. 25–47), and *lesbi* zines have occasionally included entire articles in English (reflecting the high educational status of most of their producers). *GAYa Betawi* noted that some of the *lesbi* articles to be included within its pages would be in English so that it could conceivably reach readers at the international level [*tingkat internasional*] (*GB* 1993, 6:7).

20. To my knowledge, the only case to date of ethnicity entering the narrative in a *gay* zine

is in the "true experiences" story of Alfred, a student from Papua (the western half of the island of New Guinea). Alfred feels cursed because of his dark "Negroid" skin, and he believes that a Javanese student (in the city of Jayapura on the north coast) is staring at him, rejecting him for his ethnicity. In good national-culture form, however, it turns out that the Javanese student is desirous of Alfred, and they begin a sexual relationship (*GN* 1994, 25:22–23).

21. The first of these "customs of the archipelago" columns, examining male homosexuality in Aceh, appeared in *GN* (1989, 11:15–18). The only case where there is crossover between these sexualities and *gay* subjectivity in zines is in a true-experiences story where a *gemblak* (male understudy actor in East Java) begins to live as a *gay* man (*GN* 2000, 69:37–41).

22. My thanks to Leena Avonius for reminding me of this point.

23. With the critique of merography in mind, I do not interpret this interzone as a deep structure or organic whole; instead, I see it as a contingent but consequential effect of these zones of desire's copresence.

24. In other words, Har does not appear to believe that he can be *gay* and married to a woman at the same time; as noted above, such attitudes, while present among gay men for years, are still the minority view (see Boellstorff 1999).

25. In the following paragraph, where I attempt to evoke the affect produced by the intersection of the two zones of desire discussed in this chapter, I speak solely of *gay* men and *gay* zines. This is because English (unlike Indonesian) does not allow for gender-neutral pronouns, and as noted most of my data is based upon *gay* zines. However, this intersection is an area in which there seems to be considerable continuity between *gay* and *lesbi* zines: both typically express a desire for national belonging as well as homosexual desire.

TWO WARIAS, *NATIONAL TRANSVESTITES*

1. See Boellstorff 2005 and also chapter 6 for further discussion of the implications of collapsing gender into sexuality or sexuality into gender.

2. This scene took place in 1997; by 2002 the entrance fee was 3,000 rupiah. In terms of U.S. currency the fee has remained relatively steady at between 30 and 50 cents.

3. When asking if there are warias in the West, the word "transvestite" is the one that warias consistently choose. Since few warias speak English, I first assumed they encountered the term in a worn Indonesian-English dictionary and took it up because of ignorance concerning the more recent term "transgender." Later I came to realize that while warias may encounter "transvestite" in a dictionary, it provides an insightful gloss on the waria subject position.

4. Panky Kenthut, the former head of PERWAKOS (Persatuan Waria Kotamadya Surabaya or Surabaya Municipal Waria Union; see below), believed *banci* originates from the Javanese *bandule cilik* (or the Indonesian *bandul kecil*, "small testicles"). The suffix *-ong* is one of the most productive in Indonesian *gay* language and may predate

gay language itself (Oetomo 2001). In addition to *béncong*, there are several other *gay* language terms for warias — including *mak cik* ["youngest aunt"], *binan*, *bénces*, and *bés* — that are entering vernacular Indonesian to various degrees.

5. For instance, children use it to taunt boys perceived as effeminate, or parents employ it when a son plays with dolls (Oetomo 1996:261). Girls who act in a manner perceived as masculine — excelling in sports or climbing trees, for instance — are sometimes taunted with *banci* as well, and some *lesbi* women recall being called *banci*. Additionally, *banci* is occasionally used for gender-nonconforming (i.e., masculine) women or women in traditionally male professions, such as taxi drivers and athletes (Oetomo 1996:291).

6. The first nonderogatory term for banci appears to have been *wadam;* its appearance in the 1960s was linked to the greater social visibility and protection given to warias in Jakarta (Indonesia's capital) under the activist mayoral leadership of Adi Sadikin, the former major-general whom Sukarno appointed as mayor of Jakarta in 1966 and whose progressive policies throughout his eleven-year tenure transformed the metropolis. Wadam is usually explained to be a contraction of wanita (woman) and *Adam.* Another etymology by the early 1970s was *haWA-aDAM* or "eve-adam" ("Dua Dunia yang Belum Sudah," *Tempo*, October 6, 1973, 46). It speaks to the national character of the subject position that some individuals in Makassar in 2002 also used that etymology. By the mid-1970s some Muslim groups were expressing displeasure that the name of a prophet was incorporated into a term for male transvestites. To settle this problem, Alamsyah, who was the minister of religion at the time, coined the term *waria*, a decision apparently supported by President Soeharto and made official when published in the newspaper *Kompas* on June 7, 1978 (Budiman 1982:1). News of the decision appears to have spread quickly across the archipelago, as evidenced by the national ubiquity of the term *waria* today, and the decision is still remembered by some older warias.

7. A folk etymology among some of my Bugis-speaking interlocutors is that *calabai'* means "wrong penetration" [*salah tusuk* in Indonesian].

8. This may reflect the colonial regime's emphasis on dress as a status marker (Nordholt 1998). It is unclear to what extent the early identification of warias with performances and markets is simply a consequence of the fact that these are the places where travelers (the primary sources of these accounts) encountered them. I know of no autobiographical narratives from warias from any historical period right up to the present, with the exception of short interviews in *gay/lesbi* zines and in the mass media beginning in the 1990s and the biography of the waria Chenny Han (Soentoro 1996).

9. For instance, the Dutch lexicographer H. C. Klinkert mentions *kedi* as a Malay term in 1869 (Bleys 1995:179), whereas Vickers discusses *kedi* as emphatically Balinese, noting that they were punished in the Balinese version of purgatory in the *Kerta Gosa* law court paintings of Klungkung, East Bali (n.d.:14). Vickers cites Van der Tuuk

(1897–1912) as providing *bantut, bantjih* [banci], and *wandhu* as synonyms for *kedi:* in the contemporary period *bantut* is the term for a male transgender subject position in the southern Philippines (Johnson 1997), while *wandhu* is seen as a Javanese term (cognate to Madurese *bandhu*) that has now entered colloquial Indonesian and is, for instance, common in southern Sulawesi. This has been the case for some time; to my knowledge the earliest mention of *wandu* is by P. C. J. Van Brero in 1905 ("Young boys or *wandu*, whom [Van Brero] saw on the island of Java . . . showed [according to Van Brero] signs of physical effeminacy from early childhood" [Bleys 1995:180]). This is with reference to Java, but by the 1940s Kennedy could find that "as for the *bissu*, which is the name given them when they are state officials . . . the homosexual ones are called *wandu* or *tjalabai*" (Kennedy 1953:112). As C. Von de Wall, writing on "effeminate men" in Buginese communities living on the eastern coast of Borneo (Kalimantan) in the 1840s, claimed: "Known as *tjelebei* . . . they felt attracted to younger men, whom they showered with affection. A fairly high number among them were actual hermaphrodites and known among the Bugi[s] as *kedie*" (quoted in Bleys 1995:117). Hirschfeld noted that in the Moldenfliet neighborhood of Jakarta (then Batavia) Malay transvestites would gather "in good-sized crowds on and near a bridge where they go partly for purposes of prostitution, but chiefly to meet and disburden themselves to companions in sorrow" (Hirschfeld 1935:139). In Sulawesi, Kennedy recalled how an informant "went on and on about the scandalous behavior of the ordinary [non-*bissu*] homosexuals (*tjalabai*) [*calabai'*]. They dress and act like women and are found everywhere . . . they swish and flirt and stick rolled up handkerchiefs in their blouses to imitate breasts . . . many men are crazy about them and spend lots of time and money to have sex with them" (1953:213–14). In the late 1940s, Chabot provided observations on a waria [*kawe-kawe*] living in a village near Makassar who rarely worked in the rice fields but spent his time in the back part of the house with the women. "In his manner of sitting and speaking and in clothing he was scarcely distinguishable from them" (1996:190). In the city of Makassar he found that similar persons "now populate the marketplaces as male prostitutes" (1996:192).

10. Many of the ludruk dramas investigated by Peacock were performed in a "People's Amusement Park" that may well be the contemporary Taman Remaja. As in my experience, the performance was "placed in a back corner, next to the toilets" (1968:33). Moerthiko speaks in 1980 of the Taman Remaja waria show as having existed "for several years" (1980:82). While never using the term *banci* (perhaps because of its derogatory tone) it is clear that Peacock's performers were transvestite offstage. Peacock emphasizes that ludruk transvestite performers paid more attention to their appearance than necessary for performance (such as wearing perfume that the audience could not smell) and acted in an effeminate manner during their daily lives (1968:168, 170, 203–4). He further notes that these performers were effeminate from childhood and were teased by family and neighbors, worked in small business

environments identified with warias, and wore women's clothes "at home, sometimes in public" (1968:207). They also pasted "pictures of themselves — made-up as
women — on their mirrors" (207).

11. All such quotes come from my fieldwork interviews during the years 1995–2000.

12. Panky Kenthut has asserted that prior to the 1960s, entertainment genres such as
ludruk were the only context in which warias could dress as women.

13. This shift probably began in the cities of Jakarta and Medan (in Sumatra), spreading
throughout the archipelago by the late 1970s. Certainly some warias dressed as
women most of the time prior to the 1960s, as evidenced by oral history interlocutors
and also by Peacock's observation that in the early 1960s ludruk troupes felt it
necessary "in the name of 'progress' to clean up the transvestite's sexual image ... it is
considered *madju* [progress-oriented] for ludruk female impersonators to confine
their feminine role to the ludruk stage" (1968:206).

14. The preferred term *waria* is less well known.

15. Tessie, the "waria" appearing in the Bayer aspirin commercial, claimed in interviews
to be a man who dressed as a woman only for entertainment. In Makassar in 2000,
warias were unsure if Tessie was telling the truth, but they did not seem to mind, since
via Tessie the image of warias further entered society [*citra waria masuk*], and this
was seen to be good in itself. In 2003, a waria ran for mayor of the city of Malang in
East Java (Perlez 2003:4).

16. Everyone in Atmojo's sample of 194 warias in Jakarta started feeling like a waria
before twenty years of age (1986:34). Warias themselves say that besides becoming
waria because of being born that way or due to environmental influence, some people
become warias because a woman broke their heart [*putus asa dengan cewek*]; this
third etiology assumes the person to have been at least an adolescent.

17. This environment of gender play is shaped by a strong dichotomization of male and
female in contemporary Indonesia, despite the fact that historically many cultures
of the archipelago have downplayed gender difference and understood the male-
female binary in complementary rather than opposed terms (Errington 1990; Hoskins 1998:17). A naturalized gender dualism in Indonesia is the product not only of
"world religions" such as Christianity and Islam, but also of national discourse, as
in the case of most nation-states (Yuval-Davis 1997) and particularly postcolonial
nation-states (Chatterjee 1993). The clearly delineated male and female toilets at
Taman Remaja thus reflect not an eternal gendered binary but rhetorics of the modern
Indonesian nation-state (e.g., Anderson 1996; Sen 1998; Suryakusuma 1996). "Modern" clothing in Indonesia, for instance, is usually much more gender specific than
"traditional" forms of dress; such clear semiotic regimes provide the raw material that
warias rework and redeploy.

18. Here is a case where *banci* distinguishes a different class of persons than does *waria*.

19. See "Sebuah Masala buat Banci," *Tempo*, August 10, 1985, 59.

20. In 1988, H. Maya Rissa claimed to have made the hajj nine times and the lesser

pilgrimage [*umroh*] four times, all as a woman ("Bab Pakaian Ihram untuk Waria," *Tempo,* January 16, 1988, 83). In 1988, K. H. Hasan Basri, head of the Central Jakarta Ulama's Union, stipulated that warias should attend the hajj as men: "Warias are in truth [*pada hakikatnya*] men." Some of those in agreement with Basri quoted the *hadith* "I have applied the law in order with your birth [*Aku menerapkan hukum menurut lahiriahnya*]." Other religious leaders, however, said that warias could decide themselves if they wished to undertake the pilgrimage as men or women ("Bab Pakaian Ihram untuk Waria," *Tempo,* January 16, 1988, 82).

21. Thus one waria believed she was sinful "because there are only two kinds of people, men and women," yet concluded that "warias are born as a man with the temperament of a woman, and temperament is given by God [*sifat diberikan Tuhan*]. We are lying to ourselves if we do not live as warias. God has written the script, and we are just the artists." Another waria explained in an editorial that "in my opinion, Allah has not created two kinds of person [*insan*] but two feelings [*perasaan*], those of a man and of a woman. For if one says Allah created two kinds of person, man and woman, then what kind of creation am I? There's a third creation?" ("Waria: Mana Hukum yang Bisa Dipegang?" *Tempo,* February 6, 1988, 17.) Many non-warias do see warias as sinful; some Muslims link this to the Quranic concept of the in-between gender *khuntsa* [*huntsa*] (see Oetomo 1996:263; "Bab Pakaian Ihram untuk Waria," *Tempo,* January 16, 1988, 82, 83). For instance, when I asked Ita if her family's rejection of her in Lombok stemmed from religion or custom, she replied "It's because of Islam. They are anti-waria. So they're against men who have long hair or dress like women."

22. Blackwood (1998) argues that a similar precedence of desire over the body prevails for tomboys.

23. The waria Chenny Han claims to have consumed seven to eight birth control pills a day for six months, with side effects including a pounding heartbeat, lethargy, and an inability to have erections (Soentoro 1996:182).

24. This appears to have begun in the 1990s. In his discussion of plastic surgery among warias in Jakarta, Atmojo makes no mention of silicone injections (1986:39). Silicone injections are usually applied on the nose, chin, cheeks, and breasts; it appears that silicone is injected in the buttocks less frequently (cf. Kulick 1998).

25. The first case of such an operation to gain notoriety concerned Vivian Rubianty Iskandar (formerly Iwan Rubianto Iskandar), whose operation was performed in Singapore on January 8, 1973. On November 14, 1973, she applied to the Court of West and South Jakarta to change her gender and name (Moerthiko 1980:16); she was represented in court by the well-known lawyer Adnan Buyung Nasution when she had her gender legally changed, and she claimed that then-President Soeharto had invited her to a party on behalf of Tutut, one of his daughters ("Dua Dunia yang Belum Sudah," *Tempo,* October 6, 1973, 46). The case led to press coverage and even seminars on transgenderism that brought together doctors, lawyers, and religious

experts (see "Dua Dunia yang Belum Sudah," 46–50, and "Dorce di Surabaya, Sally di Mesir," *Tempo*, December 24, 1988, 78). Vivian's request was approved by the court, and in its wake there developed a general legal, political, and religious consensus permitting sex change operations in Indonesia. Nasution, Vivian/Iwan's lawyer during the proceedings, is reputed to have said that "laws are not to torture people, but to give them happiness and keep the legal system clear. If the judge refuses [Iwan's request], this means that we burden Iwan with misery and oppress her soul without end for as long as she lives, and this is clearly at odds with the philosophy and goals of the law" (Moerthiko 1980:17; see also "Dua Dunia yang Belum Sudah,"). I have no statistics on the current frequency of sex-change operations on warias, but it appears to be under 10 percent. In a 1997 interview, a prominent Surabaya waria knew of only about ten warias in Surabaya who had undergone the operation.

26.   The cost of these procedures had risen from 350,000–1,000,000 rupiah in the late 1970s to 4,000,000–6,000,000 rupiah in 1997 (US$500–$700). Warias sometimes travel to Singapore or other destinations outside of Indonesia for operations, but only warias with independent sources of wealth or a successful business, or who have saved carefully for many years, can afford this option.

27.   As one waria put it: "My friendships with warias have continued unabated after my operation, even though . . . my status is no longer waria" (quoted in Moerthiko 1980:59). Benedict Anderson gives the example of "Dorce, a transsexual who in the mid-1980s made a successful career as a TV talk-show hostess. Before her sex-change operation [but not after] he was known as a vehement spokesperson for the banci community" (1996:285). Dorce, whose original name was Dedi Yuliardi, had her sex change operation in Surabaya on May 3, 1988 ("Dorce di Surabaya, Sally di Mesir," *Tempo*, December 24, 1988, 79; "SK [Surat Keputusan] Menteri untuk Waria," *Tempo*, April 22, 1989, 82).

28.   While warias do have sex with each other on occasion, they tend to regard this as strange, and they joke good-naturedly that it is "like a woman sleeping with a woman." Warias usually assume that warias have sex with women only if heterosexually married. At least three warias who worked as sex workers at Makassar's Karebosi park in the 1990s worked during the day as male pedicab drivers [*tukang becak*] and had wives and children. According to friends of one of these warias, the wife knew of her husband's dressing as a woman at night and permitted it as long as the husband took care of the family. In other cases, warias dress as men at home and manage to hide their waria-ness from their wives. Such warias usually either came to waria subjectivity late in life without their family's knowledge, or the family may be complicit in hiding the waria's waria-ness from the wife. I have also encountered cases in Bali and Sulawesi (and I assume there are others elsewhere in Indonesia) where warias marry or carry on sexual relationships with tomboys, the waria finding attractive a masculine woman and the woman finding attractive a feminine man. It is said that tomboys have become pregnant from these unions.

29. Sex work can range from an occasional "date" supplementing wage labor to serving as a sole source of income. Beyond the financial benefits, warias say they enjoy sex work for its variable hours, thrill, camaraderie between waria sex workers, and the sex itself. However, sex work is not always a preferred occupation, and many of those involved have additional sources of income. Sex work is usually a low-paying job, ranging from fifty cents to as little as five cents per act. In many places local waria groups try to regulate sex work by requiring, for instance, that warias wishing to solicit in a certain area have an identity card provided by the organization. In the sex-work market, warias are in competition with female sex workers. Even though these women are often coerced into sex work, they are, in comparison to warias, better organized and more often officially registered. Many also work out of brothels with private rooms and other conveniences, thereby ensuring privacy for their clients. Warias also compete with male sex workers; in some cities (e.g., Makassar) these men sometimes also have small brothels. Being forced to solicit and engage in sex acts in public places such as parks and roadsides puts warias at risk not only of social opprobrium but physical violence at the hands of disgruntled or drunk clients, or even random passersby. Their most common clients are unmarried and unemployed men, often still in secondary school and as young as thirteen or fourteen years old. Older clients of warias are usually unemployed or in low-paying occupations, such as driving pedicabs, that put them in frequent contact with warias. Another unattractive aspect of sex work is the risk of sexually transmitted infections, including HIV. Waria sex workers who contract sexually transmitted infections find it difficult to obtain treatment, due to its cost and their unwillingness to be examined by a doctor who might make fun of them.

30. In 1949, one of Raymond Kennedy's male informants in rural South Sulawesi claimed that "many men go for [warias] . . . He said a man might get so infatuated that he would sell his rice fields and everything to give to a loved wandu. He personally was revolted by this idea" (1953:112). See also Peacock 1968:207.

31. "Dorce di Surabaya, Sally di Mesir," *Tempo,* December 24, 1988, 78–79.

32. One of the most famous cases is that of Chenny Han (see Soentoro 1996).

33. In July 1999, PERWAKOS appeared in national print media supporting the presidential candidacy of Megawati Soekarnoputri (the daughter of Indonesia's first president), who won the seat in 2001.

34. In 1949, Chabot found that in Makassar "the environment accepts a kawe-kawe [waria] as he is. People do not have the idea that it is his fault that he is the way he is" (1996:207).

35. This may refer to the Permesta rebellion of the 1950s (see Harvey 1977), during which the fundamentalist Muslim leaders of the rebellion tried to ban male transvestism (Lathief 2004).

36. One reason I find this image useful is that it allows me to present an example of warias "making up" someone without endangering the confidentiality of my Indonesian

interlocutors. As part of my ethical practice, I do not reproduce photographs show-ing the faces of Indonesians unless the image has already appeared in Indonesian mass media.

37. There is historical data that could be interpreted in this way, as when Chabot claimed in the 1950s that "The Makassarese divide people, as they say, into men, women, and kawe-kawe [warias]" (1996:189). Occasionally warias will be termed a "class of their own" [*kelas tersendiri*] or "special type" [*jenis khas*] ("Sebuah Masala buat Banci," *Tempo*, August 10, 1985, 59).

38. This exemplifies how "the same axes that divide and distinguish male from female (and indeed rank male over female) also cross-cut the gender categories, producing internal distinctions and gradations within them" (Ortner and Whitehead 1981:9).

39. The family principle holds that the nation is made up not of individuals but families, and that governance is to be modeled on the ostensibly benign rule of a father over the family rather than an emphasis on legal measures deemed to promote conflict. The principle is directly espoused by the state and also operationalized through family planning programs. See, for instance, Dwyer 2000; Robinson 1989; and Suryaku-suma 1996.

THREE GAY *LANGUAGE, REGISTERING BELONGING*

1. See Oetomo 2001 and Koeswinarno 1996, in which a word list from the "*waria* world" is almost entirely *bahasa gay.*

2. These include labor migration, letter writing, tourism, Internet linkages through e-mail and chat rooms (for a small but increasing number of people), and the word lists of *gay* language produced by the *gay* zine *GAYa Nusantara.* The zine formalizes these shifts but is probably not a major factor in their dissemination, given its lim-ited subscription (see chapter 1). The dissemination of the Philippine gay language "swardspeak" occurs both within the Philippines and between the Philippines and the United States (Manalansan 1995:206), but to my knowledge *bahasa gay* rarely leaves Indonesian shores, probably due to the relatively small number of Indonesians living permanently abroad.

3. Errington cites the estimate that 60 to 83 percent of Indonesians knew Indonesian in 1990, and he notes that some claim that all Indonesians will speak the language by 2010 (1998:282). Abas cites government claims that 100 percent of citizens will be competent in Indonesian by 2041 (1987:vii). Uncertainty as to what degree of profi-ciency qualifies one as a speaker makes these statistics speculative. See Boellstorff 2005, chapter 1.

4. Independent of my work, my colleague Dédé Oetomo (2001) has catalogued and analyzed nearly identical derivational processes for *bahasa gay,* helping to confirm its national character. The discussion in this section thus tracks Oetomo's own typology, except that I have given my own names to the various derivational processes and

reordered them in line with the frequency with which I have encountered them in my ethnographic work.

5. In standard Indonesian the infixing of *-em-, -el-,* and *-er-* existed historically, but all forms are now nonproductive and appear in such a limited number of words that the variant forms are usually listed separately in dictionaries and "the meaning of the infix is unpredictable" (Sneddon 1996:25). Examples include *tunjuk* [point] *telunjuk* [index finger]; *suling* [flute] *seruling* [flute]; *gigi* [tooth] *gerigi* [serration].

6. See Gaudio 1994 for perceptions of American gay men's pitch patterns.

7. The scene recalls the situation in some Western gay communities where historically phrases such as "Are you a friend of Dorothy?" could be used to determine someone's sexuality. Few *gay* Indonesians have MBAs: this story reflects the ideals of the perfect partner, not the typical socioeconomic status of *gay* Indonesians.

8. I thank Sharyn Graham for first bringing this article to my attention.

FOUR BETWEEN RELIGION AND DESIRE

1. Due to space limitations it is not possible to discuss *lesbi* Muslims in this chapter; "homosexuality" here refers to male homosexuality. From my own fieldwork (as well as several published sources — e.g., Prawirakusumah and Ramadhan 1988:122, 250, 427), it is clear that many *lesbi* women are Muslim and struggle with questions of faith and belonging. This is a crucial area for further research. See Boellstorff 2005 and references therein for discussions of *lesbi* Indonesians.

2. "Gays amongst Bandung's Students," *Republika*, June 4, 2005, http://www.republika.co.id/.

3. Bisexuality is rarely discussed in Indonesia as a category of sexuality, even though in a behavioral sense it is quite prevalent. See Boellstorff 1999, 2005.

4. There are also, of course, *gay* Indonesians who follow religions other than Islam, but due to space limitations I do not address them in this chapter, except for several references to *gay* Christians (Christianity is the next-largest religion in Indonesia after Islam). Additionally, I do not discuss the religious beliefs and practices of male transvestites in this chapter (see chapter 2).

5. It lies outside the scope of this chapter to discuss events like the "Jakarta Charter," an attempt to constitutionally require Muslims to follow Islamic law.

6. See, for instance, Ali 1990 [1936]:444–49; Esposito 1998:94; Idrus 2004; and Waines 1995:94.

7. All such quotes come from my fieldwork interviews during the years 1995–2000.

8. Howard (1996) claims that all of the *gay* men in his Jakarta sample, regardless of religion, saw becoming *gay* as the result of social relationships.

9. This five-fold division is termed *al-ahkam al-khamsah.* See Bowen 2003:14; Hallaq 1997:174–180; and Waines 1995:76.

1. The data presented here on the Kaliurang incident is complied from *PlanetOut.com*, November 13–14, 2000; *Detik.com*, November 13, 2000; *Kompas* November 12 and November 14, 2000, *GAYa Nusantara*, no. 77, and direct testimony from witnesses.

2. According to witnesses, some of the motorcycles driven by the attackers also had stickers from the Muslim United Development Party, or the Anti-Vice Movement (*Gerakan Anti Maksiat*, or GAM) (*Detik.com*, November 14, 2000). The *Ka'bah* is the holy shrine at the center of the Great Mosque of Mecca.

3. The statement was allegedly in Javanese (*lanang kok dandan wedok, banci metu;* in Indonesian it would be *laki-laki kok dandan perempuan, banci keluar*) (*Detik.com*, November 14, 2000).

4. *Detik.com*, November 13, 2000.

5. *GAYa Nusantara*, no. 77:16–17, 23.

6. While *lesbi* women groups and correspondents participate in this network, it is dominated by *gay* men.

7. Because of difficulties with attendance, this congress was renamed the National Working Meeting [*Rapat Kerja Nasional,* shortened to *Rakernas*], and scheduled for September 10–11 so as to coincide with "Joyous September" (*September Ceria*), a large *gay* event held annually near the city of Solo in Central Java.

8. Two of the groups' leaders, Hasan Mulachela and Boyamin, stated: "As citizens of Solo we cannot accept these practices a la Sodom and Gomorrah to take place in Solo. If the Lesbian and Gay National Meeting takes place in Solo that would publicize those practices" (*Kompas,* September 11, 1999). Mulachela also threatened to bring out "thousands of the Islamic community" to force the congress to be canceled (*Bernas,* September 11, 1999; Mulachela was also a member of the Pembaruan DPRD party fraction).

9. Many *gay* (also *lesbi* and waria) Indonesians who know of these two incidents see them as watershed moments, when for the first time nonnormative masculinity became the target of publicly articulated hatred and physical assault.

10. In a 1994 review article, Carole Nagengast noted that "until relatively recently, few anthropologists examined violence and conflict between groups and the state and among groups within states" (1994:110). Nagengast identified anthropology's focus on ostensibly self-contained communities at the expense of the nation as one reason for this lack of attention to violence outside domains of custom and tradition (112; see also Riches 1986). Also in 1994, John Pemberton presented anthropology with the image of Javanese peasants shoving each other aside over pieces of a cooked chicken in a *rebutan* or "struggle" (1994:18, 213). By counterpoising this vignette to Geertz's use of the tranquil *slametan* feast as master metaphor for Javanese culture (Geertz 1960; see chapter 4), Pemberton indexed the growing number of ethnographically informed studies of violence in Indonesian societies (e.g., George 1996; Robinson 1995; Siegel 1998; Tsing 1993). More recently, scholars of Indonesia have

responded to new and resurgent forms of violence following Soeharto's fall (e.g., Anderson 2001a; Barker 1998; Rafael 1999; Heryanto 2005; Stasch 2001; Wessel and Wimhöfer 2001). Some of this scholarship provides insights on everyday violence, including domestic violence and its linkages to state violence (Berman 2000; Butt 2001). The primary emphasis, however, has been on "political violence."

11. I am grateful to Joshua Barker for this turn of phrase, which originates in his insightful commentary on an earlier version of this chapter, given at the 2001 meetings of the American Anthropological Association.

12. See, among others, Aripurnami 1996; Blackwood 1995; Brenner 1998, 1999; Hatley 1997; Robinson 1989; Sen 1998; Tiwon 1996.

13. It is therefore not surprising that tomboys call themselves *hunter* in some regions of Indonesia, particularly South Sulawesi. They use this term because they "hunt" feminine women as potential partners; they consider the act of initiating contact to be a masculine one.

14. Ann Stoler notes her own "long-term and failed efforts" to find any significant discussion of homosexuality in the colonial Dutch East Indies (Stoler 1995:129).

15. See Oetomo 2001; "In Indonesia, Once Tolerant Islam Grows Rigid," *New York Times*, December 29, 2001.

16. See, for instance, the coverage of the incident in *Forum Keadilan* no. 3, May 25, 1995, 12–20. Since most *gay* men marry women, Ave's bachelor status at the age of fifty-one was noteworthy.

17. This new political homophobia in Indonesia is thus quite different from (though not entirely unrelated to) the arrest and conviction in Malaysia of Anwar Ibrahim, former deputy prime minister, on charges of sodomy and corruption. Antihomosexual groups like PASRAH (formed in October 1998) exist in Malaysia, but they have not been associated with physical violence (Peletz 2002:268).

18. Dédé Oetomo, personal communication.

19. For an example, see *Serambi Indonesia*, June 29, 1999. My thanks to Dédé Oetomo and Edward Aspinall for respectively bringing the Bali and Aceh incidents to my attention.

20. I thank Karl Heider for bringing this article to my attention. *Béncong* is a variant of *banci* [waria] (see chapter 3).

SIX *COMPARATIVELY QUEER IN SOUTHEAST ASIA*

1. In support of this thesis, Reid draws upon a range of factors, including the relative mobility of women, women's participation in trade (to the astonishment of early European visitors), and the fact that "throughout Southeast Asia wealth passed from the male to the female side in marriage — the reverse of European dowry" (1988:146). Reid also notes that "the relative autonomy enjoyed by women extended to sexual relations. Southeast Asian literature of the period leaves us in little doubt that women took a very active part in courtship and lovemaking, and demanded as much as they

gave by way of sexual and emotional gratification" (147). This included the insertion of metal balls or pins in the penis to enhance the sexual pleasure of women (149–51), a practice that continues to the present day in some parts of Southeast Asia (Hull and Budiharsana 2001). Women's relative autonomy meant that divorce was quite common and "virginity at marriage was not expected of either party . . . the majority Muslim population of Indonesia and Malaysia had divorce rates in excess of 50 percent as late as the 1960s" (Reid 1988:153).

2. For instance, many languages of the region do not mark gender in nouns or pronouns, emphasizing instead seniority in social relations. In Indonesian, for instance, one does not ask "How many brothers and sisters do you have?" but "How many older siblings [*kakak*] and younger siblings [*adik*] do you have?" (see Errington 1990:50). As a result, while "male" and "female" are typically used to mark opposites in the West, like a plug and socket, in Indonesia the phrase "male-female" [*laki bini*] was historically used to refer to things like a pair of shoes (Errington 1990:53).

3. In some cases (*banci* and *bakla,* for instance), these terms are sometimes used to refer to boys or adult men who act in effeminate ways (somewhat like the English word "sissy"), without implying homosexuality or transvestism (see chapter 2; Garcia 1996:52; Hart 1992:198).

4. To my knowledge *silahis* is the only widely known term in any Southeast Asian context for the male partners of male transvestites, and even here the term's meaning is more complex (Garcia 1996:110).

5. Jackson (1999a) dates the origins of gay subjectivity to 1969 in Thailand, and Garcia notes that a 1968 play written and produced in the Philippines that specified that the gay male protagonists not be effeminate in any way was "not very relevant to the situation of local homosexuals at this specific time" (1996:77).

6. I thus would question conclusions like "the Balinese do not (I think) generally engage in anal intercourse, for even between two men it was thought inconceivable by some that one could penetrate the other" (Duff-Cooper 1985:415).

7. See Tan 2001:123 for one discussion of this stereotype.

8. Concepts closely linked to "coming out" as typically understood in the West, however, exist in Southeast Asia and are not solely the provenance of elites (Garcia 1996:29).

9. Sometimes tomboy-like individuals are referred to with a term used for male transvestites (Atkinson 1990:88–91; Sinnott 2004:206). In some cases there exist ethnolocalized terms for such individuals, like *calalai'* in Buginese (Graham 2003a).

10. Of course, unlike male transvestites, tomboys across Southeast Asia (indeed, worldwide) predominantly use terms ultimately derived from the English "tomboy," suggesting a different relationship to globalization and spatial scale.

11. For male transvestites, using a term that reworks "gay" may happen precisely in moments of transnational imagining (Johnson 1997).

REFERENCES

Abeyasekere, Susan

1987   *Jakarta: A History*, revised edition. Singapore: Oxford University Press.

Abu-Lughod, Lila

1991   "Writing against Culture." Pp. 137–62 in *Recapturing Anthropology*, ed. Richard Fox. Santa Fe: School of American Research Press.

Aceto, Michael

1995   "Variation in a Secret Creole Language of Panama." *Language in Society* 24:537–60.

Adam, Ahmat

1995   *The Vernacular Press and the Emergence of Modern Indonesian Consciousness*. Ithaca, N.Y.: Cornell University Southeast Asia Program.

Adorno, Theodor W.

1967   "Cultural Criticism and Society." Pp. 19–34 in *Prisms*. Translated by Samuel and Shierry Weber. London: Neville Spearman.

Agha, Asif

1998   "Stereotypes and Registers of Honorific Language." *Language in Society* 27(2):151–93.

Alexander, M. Jacqui

1997   "Erotic Autonomy as a Politics of Decolonization: An Anatomy of Feminist and State Practice in the Bahamas Tourist Economy." Pp. 63–100 in *Feminist Genealogies, Colonial Legacies, Democratic Futures*, ed. M. Jacqui Alexander and Chandra Talpade Mohanty. New York: Routledge.

Ali, Maulana Muhammad

1990 [1936] *The Religion of Islam*. Columbus, Ohio: Ahmadiyya Anjuman Ishaat Islam.

Alisjahbana, Sutan Takdir
1966   *Indonesia: Social and Cultural Revolution.* Kuala Lumpur: Oxford University Press.

Al Marshal, Insap
2001   "Aku Bertemu 'Kucing' Brengsek di 'L.A.' " [I Met a Bad 'Cat' at 'L.A.']. *GAYa Nusantara* 82:43–48.

Al Qurthuby, Sumanto Adib, and M. Kholidul, et al., eds.
2004   "Indahnya Kawin Sesama Jenis" [The Beauty of Same-Sex Marriage]. *Justisia* 25:1.

Althusser, Louis
1971   "Ideology and Ideological State Apparatuses (Notes Towards an Investigation)." Pp. 121–73 in *Lenin and Philosophy and Other Essays*, translated by Ben Brewster. New York: Monthly Review Press.

Altman, Dennis
2001   *Global Sex.* Chicago: University of Chicago Press.

Andaya, Leonard
2000   "The Bissu: Study of a Third Gender in Indonesia." Pp. 27–46 in *Other Pasts: Women, Gender, and History in Early Modern Southeast Asia*, ed. Barbara W. Andaya. Honolulu: University of Hawai'i Press.

Anderson, Benedict
1966   "The Languages of Indonesian Politics." *Indonesia* 1:89–116.
1983   *Imagined Communities: Reflections on the Origins and Spread of Nationalism.* London: Verso.
1990a   "Sembah-Sumpah: The Politics of Language and Javanese Culture." Pp. 194–240 in *Language and Power: Exploring Political Cultures of Indonesia*. Ithaca, N.Y.: Cornell University Press.
1990b   "Professional Dreams: Reflections on Two Javanese Classics." Pp. 271–98 in *Language and Power: Exploring Political Cultures of Indonesia*. Ithaca, N.Y.: Cornell University Press.
1998   *The Spectre of Comparisons: Nationalism, Southeast Asia, and the World.* London: Verso.
2001   "Dari Tjentini Sampai GAYa Nusantara" [From Tjentini to GAYa Nusantara]. Pp. xi–xxvii in *Memberi Suara pada yang Bisu* [Giving Voice to the Voiceless], by Dédé Oetomo. Yogyakarta: Galang Press.

Anderson, Benedict, ed.
2001   *Violence and the State in Suharto's Indonesia.* Ithaca, N.Y.: Cornell University Southeast Asia Program.

Aripurnami, Sita

1996   "A Feminist Comment on the Sinetron Presentation of Indonesian Women."
Pp. 249–58 in *Fantasizing the Feminine in Indonesia*, ed. Laurie Sears.
Durham, N.C.: Duke University Press.

Asad, Talal

1986   "The Concept of Cultural Translation in British Social Anthropology." Pp.
141–64 in *Writing Culture: The Poetics and Politics of Ethnography*, ed. James
Clifford and George E. Marcus. Berkeley: University of California Press.

Asher, R. E.

1994   *The Encyclopedia of Language and Linguistics*. Oxford: Pergamon.

Asrori, Ma'ruf, and Anang Zamroni

1997   *Bimbingan Seks Islami* [Islamic Sexual Guidance]. Surabaya: Pustaka Anda.

Atkinson, Jane Monnig

1990   "How Gender Makes a Difference in Wana Society." Pp. 59–94 in *Power and
Difference: Gender in Island Southeast Asia*, ed. Shelly Errington and Jane
Monnig Atkinson. Stanford, Calif.: Stanford University Press.

Atmojo, Kemala

1986   *Kami Bukan Lelaki: Sebuah Sketsa Kehidupan Kaum Waria* [We are Not Men:
A Sketch of Warias' Lives]. Jakarta: Pustaka Utama Grafiti.

Austin, J. L.

1980   *How to Do Things with Words: The William James Lectures Delivered at
Harvard University in 1955*, ed. J. O. Urmson and Marina Sbisa. Oxford:
Oxford University Press.

Baba, Ismail

2001   "Gay and Lesbian Couples in Malaysia." *Journal of Homosexuality*
40(3/4):143–63.

Baker, Paul

2002   *Polari: The Lost Language of Gay Men*. London: Routledge.

Bakhtin, Mikhail Mikhailovich

1981   "Forms of Time and of the Chronotope in the Novel: Notes toward a Historical
Poetics." Pp. 84–258 in *The Dialogic Imagination: Four Essays*. Edited by
Michael Holquist; translated by Caryl Emerson and Michael Holquist. Austin:
University of Texas Press.

Barber, Stephen M., and David L. Clark

2002   "Queer Moments: The Performative Temporalities of Eve Kosofsky Sedgwick."
Pp. 1–53 in *Regarding Sedgwick: Essays on Queer Culture and Critical
Theory*, ed. Stephen M. Barber and David L. Clark. New York: Routledge.

Barker, Joshua

1998   "State of Fear: Controlling the Criminal Contagion in Suharto's New Order."
        Indonesia 66:7–44.

Barnard, Ian

1996   "Queerzines and the Fragmentation of Art, Community, Identity, and Politics."
        Socialist Review 26(1/2):69–96.

Barth, Fredrik

1993   *Balinese Worlds.* Chicago: University of Chicago Press.

Beatty, Andrew

1999   *Varieties of Javanese Religion: An Anthropological Account.* Cambridge:
        Cambridge University Press.

Beemyn, Brett, and Mickey Eliason, eds.

1996   *Queer Studies: A Lesbian, Gay, Bisexual, and Transgender Anthology.* New
        York: New York University Press.

Benjamin, Walter

1955   "Theses on the Philosophy of History." Pp. 253–64 in *Illuminations: Essays
        and Reflections.* Edited and with an Introduction by Hannah Arendt. New
        York: Schoken Books.

Berman, Laine

2000   "Surviving on the Streets of Java: Homeless Children's Narratives of Violence."
        Discourse and Society 11(2):149–74.

Biber, Douglas, and Edward Finegan

1994   "Introduction: Situating Register in Sociolinguistics." Pp. 3–12 in
        Sociolinguistic Perspectives on Register, ed. Douglas Biber and Edward
        Finegan. New York: Oxford University Press.

Blackwood, Evelyn

1995   "Senior Women, Model Mothers, and Dutiful Wives: Managing Gender
        Contradictions in a Minangkabau Village." Pp. 124–58 in *Bewitching Women,
        Pious Men: Gender and Body Politics in Southeast Asia,* ed. Aihwa Ong and
        Michael G. Peletz. Berkeley: University of California Press.

1998   "Tombois in West Sumatra: Constructing Masculinity and Erotic Desire."
        Cultural Anthropology 13(4):491–521.

2005   "Gender Transgression in Colonial and Postcolonial Indonesia." *Journal of
        Asian Studies* 64(4):849–80.

Blackwood, Evelyn, ed.

1986   *The Many Faces of Homosexuality: Anthropological Approaches to
        Homosexual Behavior.* New York: Harrington Park Press.

Blackwood, Evelyn, and Saskia E. Wieringa

1999   "Sapphic Shadows: Challenging the Silence in the Study of Sexuality." Pp. 39–
66 in *Female Desires: Same-Sex Relations and Transgender Practices across
Cultures*, ed. Evelyn Blackwood and Saskia E. Wieringa. New York: Columbia
University Press.

Blanc-Szanton, Cristina

1990   "Collision of Cultures: Historical Reformulations of Gender in the Lowland
Visayas, Philippines." Pp. 345–83 in *Power and Difference: Gender in Island
Southeast Asia*, ed. Shelly Errington and Jane Monnig Atkinson. Stanford,
Calif.: Stanford University Press.

Bleys, Rudi

1995   *The Geography of Perversion: Male-to-Male Sexual Behavior outside the West
and the Ethnographic Imagination, 1750–1918*. New York: New York
University Press.

Boellstorff, Tom

1999   "The Perfect Path: Gay Men, Marriage, Indonesia." *GLQ: A Journal of Gay
and Lesbian Studies* 5(4):475–510.

2002   "Ethnolocality." *Asia Pacific Journal of Anthropology* 3(1):24–48.

2004   " 'Authentic, of Course!' *Gay* Language in Indonesia and Cultures of
Belonging." Pp. 181–201 in *Speaking in Queer Tongues: Globalization and
Gay Language*, ed. William L. Leap and Tom Boellstorff. Urbana: University of
Illinois Press.

2005   *The Gay Archipelago: Sexuality and Nation in Indonesia*. Princeton, N.J.:
Princeton University Press.

2007   "When Marriage Falls: Queer Coincidences in Straight Time." *GLQ: A Journal
of Gay and Lesbian Studies* 13(2/3).

Bolton, Kingsley, and Christopher Hutton

1995   "Bad and Banned Language: Triad Secret Societies, the Censorship of the
Cantonese Vernacular, and Colonial Language Policy in Hong Kong."
Language in Society 24:159–86.

Bouhdiba, Abdelwahab

1998   *Sexuality in Islam*. Translated by Alan Sheridan. Los Angeles: Saqi Books.

Bourdieu, Pierre

1977   *Outline of a Theory of Practice*. Cambridge: Cambridge University Press.

Bowen, John R.

1993   *Muslims through Discourse: Religion and Ritual in Gayo Society*. Princeton,
N.J.: Princeton University Press.

2003   *Islam, Law, and Equality in Indonesia: An Anthropology of Public Reasoning.*
         Cambridge: Cambridge University Press.

Boy and Yasiano

1999   "Bahasa Hemong di Bandung" [*Gay* Language in Bandung]. *GAYa Nusantara*
         64:41–43.

Bravmann, Scott

1997   *Queer Fictions of the Past: History, Culture, and Difference.* Cambridge:
         Cambridge University Press.

Brenner, Suzanne April

1998   *The Domestication of Desire: Women, Wealth, and Modernity in Java.*
         Princeton, N.J.: Princeton University Press.
1999   "On the Public Intimacy of the New Order: Images of Women in the Popular
         Indonesian Print Media." *Indonesia* 67:13–37.

Brewer, Carolyn

1999   "Baylon, Asog, Transvestism, and Sodomy: Gender, Sexuality, and the Sacred
         in Early Colonial Philippines." *Intersections: Gender, History, and Culture in
         the Asian Context*, no. 1 (May), http://www.sshe.mureioch.edu.au/intersec
         tions/issue2/carolyn2.html.

Brodwin, Paul

2003   "Pentecostalism in Translation: Religion and the Production of Authority in the
         Haitian Diaspora." *American Ethnologist* 30(1):85–101.

Brown, Wendy

1995   *States of Injury: Power and Freedom in Late Modernity.* Princeton, N.J.:
         Princeton University Press.

Budiman, Amen

1979   *Lelaki Perindu Lelaki: Sebuah Tinjauan Sejarah dan Psikologi Tentang
         Homoseks dan Masyarakat Homoseks di Indonesia* [Men Who Yearn for Men:
         A Historical and Psychological Perspective on Homosexuality and Homosexual
         Culture in Indonesia]. Semarang: Tanjung Sari.
1982   *Wadam: Pengertian dan Masalahnya.* [Warias: Understanding Them and Their
         Problems]. Semarang: Tanjung Sari.

Bunzl, Matti

2002   "Time and the Other: Syntheses of a Critical Anthropology." Pp. ix–xxxiv in
         Time and the Other: How Anthropology Makes Its Object, by Johannes
         Fabian. New York: Columbia University Press.
2004a   *Symptoms of Modernity: Jews and Queers in Late-Twentieth-Century Vienna.*
         Berkeley: University of California Press.

2004b   "Boas, Foucault, and the 'Native Anthropologist': Notes toward a Neo-
         Boasian Anthropology." *American Anthropologist* 106(3):435–442.

Burton, Mike, C. C. Moore, and A. K. Romney
1996   "Regions Based on Social Structure." *Current Anthropology* 37(1): 87–123.

Bussmann, Hadumod
1996   *Routledge Dictionary of Language and Linguistics.* London: Routledge.

Butler, Judith
1990   *Gender Trouble.* New York: Routledge.
1997   "Against Proper Objects." Pp. 1–30 in *Feminism Meets Queer Theory*, ed.
         Elizabeth Weed and Naomi Schor. Bloomington: Indiana University Press.

Butt, Leslie
2001   "KB Kills: Political Violence, Birth Control, and the Baliem Valley Dani." *Asia
         Pacific Journal of Anthropology* 2(1):63–86.

Cannell, Fenella
1995   "The Power of Appearances: Beauty, Mimicry, and Transformation in Bicol."
         Pp. 223–58 in *Discrepant Histories: Translocal Essays on Filipino Cultures*, ed.
         Vincente L. Rafael. Philadelphia: Temple University Press.
1999   *Power and Intimacy in the Christian Philippines.* Cambridge: Cambridge
         University Press.

Castle, Terry
1993   *The Apparitional Lesbian: Female Homosexuality and Modern Culture.* New
         York: Columbia University Press.

Chabot, Hendrik Theodorus
1996 [1950] *Kinship, Status, and Gender in South Celebes.* Leiden: KITLV Press.

Chambert-Loir, Henri
1984   "Those Who Speak Prokem." *Indonesia* 37:105–17.

Chatterjee, Partha
1993   *The Nation and Its Fragments: Colonial and Postcolonial Histories.* Princeton:
         Princeton University Press.

Chauncey, George
1994   *Gay New York: Gender, Urban Culture, and the Making of the Gay Male
         World, 1890–1940.* New York: Basic Books.
2004   *Why Marriage? The History Shaping Today's Debate over Gay Equality.* New
         York: Basic Books.

Cheah, Pheng

2003 "Grounds of Comparison." Pp. 1–20 in *Grounds of Comparison: Around the Work of Benedict Anderson*, ed. Pheng Cheah and Jonathan Culler. New York: Routledge.

Clark, Timothy, and Nicholas Royle, eds.

1995 *The University in Ruins: Essays on the Crisis in the Concept of the Modern University*. Durham, UK: Oxford Literary Review.

Clifford, James

1986 "Introduction: Partial Truths." Pp. 1–26 in *Writing Culture: The Poetics and Politics of Ethnography*, ed. James Clifford and George E. Marcus. Berkeley: University of California Press.

Clifford, James, and George E. Marcus, eds.

1986 *Writing Culture: The Poetics and Politics of Ethnography*. Berkeley: University of California Press.

Cohen, Lawrence

1995 "The Pleasures of Castration: The Postoperative Status of Hijras, Jankhas, and Academics." Pp. 276–304 in *Sexual Nature/Sexual Culture*, ed. Paul R. Abramson and Steven D. Pinkerton. Chicago: University of Chicago Press.

Collier, Jane F., Michelle Z. Rosaldo, and Sylvia Yanagisako

1997 "Is There a Family? New Anthropological Views." Pp. 71–81 in *The Gender/Sexuality Reader: Culture, History, Political Economy*, ed. Roger N. Lancaster and Michaela di Leonardo. New York: Routledge.

Collins, Elizabeth Fuller, and Ernaldi Bahar

2000 "To Know Shame: Malu and Its Uses in Malay Societies." *Crossroads: An Interdisciplinary Journal of Southeast Asian Studies* 14(1):35–69.

Coontz, Stephanie

2005 *Marriage, a History: From Obedience to Intimacy, or How Love Conquered Marriage*. New York: Viking Press.

Corber, Robert J., and Stephen Valocchi

2003 "Introduction." Pp. 1–17 in *Queer Studies: An Interdisciplinary Reader*, ed. Robert J. Corber and Stephen Valocchi. Oxford: Blackwell.

Covarrubias, Miguel

1937 *Island of Bali*. New York: Knopf.

Cribb, Robert, and Colin Brown

1995 *Modern Indonesia: A History Since 1945*. London: Longman.

Cummings, William

2002   *Making Blood White: Historical Transformations in Early Modern Makassar.* Honolulu: University of Hawai'i Press.

Davis, D. L., and R. G. Whitten

1987   "The Cross-Cultural Study of Human Sexuality." *Annual Review of Anthropology* 16:69–98.

de Certeau, Michel

1984   *The Practice of Everyday Life.* Translated by Steven Rendall. Berkeley: University of California Press.

de Graaf, H. J.

1970   "South-East Asian Islam to the Eighteenth Century." Pp. 123–154 in *The Cambridge History of Islam, vol.* 2, ed. A. P. M. Holt, Ann K. S. Lambton, and Bernard Lewis. Cambridge: Cambridge University Press.

de Lauretis, Teresa

1991   "Queer Theory: Lesbian and Gay Sexualities. An Introduction." *Differences* 3(2):iii–xviii.

D'Emilio, John

1983   "Capitalism and Gay Identity." Pp. 100–13 in *Powers of Desire: The Politics of Sexuality*, ed. Ann Snitow, Christine Stansell, and Sharon Thompson. New York: Monthly Review Press.

Derrida, Jacques

1994   *Specters of Marx: The State of the Debt, the Work of Mourning, and the New International.* New York: Routledge.

de Saussure, Ferdinand

1959   *Course in General Linguistics.* New York: McGraw-Hill.

Dick, Howard W.

2002   *Surabaya, City of Work: A Socioeconomic History, 1900–2000.* Athens: Ohio University Press.

Dodd, Tim

2002   "Indonesia's New Lingo Is Talk of the Street." *Australian Financial Review*, January 12.

Doussantousse, Serge, et al.

2005   "Male Sexual Health: Kathoeys in the Lao PDR, South East Asia, Exploring a Gender Minority," July 28, http://web.hku.hk/sjwinter/TransgenderASIA/ paper _ doussantousse.htm.

Dreyfuss, Jeff

1983   "The Backwards Language of Jakarta Youth (JYBL), a Bird of Many Language Feathers." Pp. 52–56 in *Studies in Malay Dialects*, ed. James Collins. Jakarta: Badan Penyelenggara Seri NUSA, University of Atma Jaya.

1985   "A Coincidence of Metaphors: Notes on Two Modes of Text Building in the Indonesian Novel 'Surabaya.' " *Journal of Asian Studies* 44(4):755–763.

Drucker, Peter

1996   " 'In the Tropics There Is No Sin': Sexuality and Gay-Lesbian Movements in the Third World." *New Left Review* 218:75–101.

Duff-Cooper, A.

1985   "Notes about Some Balinese Ideas and Practices Connected with Sex from Western Lombok." *Anthropos* 80(4/6):403–419.

Duncombe, Stephen

1997   *Notes from Underground: Zines and the Politics of Alternative Culture.* London: Verso.

Durkheim, Emile

1963   *Incest: The Nature and Origin of the Taboo.* New York: Lyle Stuart.

1984   *The Division of Labor in Society*, translated by W. D. Halls. New York: Free Press.

Durkheim, Emile, and Marcel Mauss

1963   *Primitive Classification*, translated by Rodney Needham. London: Cohen and West.

Dwyer, Leslie K.

2000   "Spectacular Sexuality: Nationalism, Development and the Politics of Family Planning in Indonesia." Pp. 25–62 in *Gender Ironies of Nationalism: Sexing the Nation*, ed. Tamar Mayer. London: Routledge.

2004   "The Intimacy of Terror: Gender and the Violence of 1965–66 in Bali." *Intersections: Gender, History and Culture in the Asian Context*, no. 10 (August), http://wwwsshe.murdoch.edu.au/intersections/issue10/dwyer.html.

Edelman, Lee

2004   *No Future: Queer Theory and the Death Drive.* Durham, N.C.: Duke University Press.

Elliston, Deborah A.

1995   "Erotic Anthropology: 'Ritualized Homosexuality' in Melanesia and Beyond." *American Ethnologist* 22(4):848–67.

Emka, Moammar

2003   *Jakarta Undercover 2: Karnaval Malam.* Depok: Gagas Media.

Endah, Alberthiene
2004   *Jangan Beri Aku Narkoba*. Jakarta: Gramedia Pustaka Utama.

Eng, David L., Judith Halberstam, and José Esteban Muñoz.
2005   "Introduction: What's Queer about Queer Studies Now?" *Social Text* 23(3–4):1–17.

Engels, Frederick
1972 [1884] *The Origin of the Family, Private Property, and the State, in the Light of the Researches of Lewis Henry Morgan*. New York: International Publishers.

Errington, J. Joseph
1985   "On the Nature of the Sociolinguistic Sign: Describing the Javanese Speech Levels." Pp. 287–310 in *Semiotic Mediation: Sociocultural and Psychological Perspectives*, ed. Elizabeth Mertz and Richard J. Parmentier. Orlando: Academic Press.
1998   *Shifting Languages: Interaction and Identity in Javanese Indonesia*. Cambridge: Cambridge University Press.
2000   "Indonesian('s) Authority." Pp. 205–28 in *Regimes of Language: Ideologies, Polities and Identities*, ed. Paul V. Kroskrity. Santa Fe: School of American Research Press.

Errington, Shelly
1989   *Meaning and Power in a Southeast Asian Realm*. Princeton, N.J.: Princeton University Press.
1990   "Recasting Sex, Gender, and Power: A Theoretical and Regional Overview." Pp. 1–58 in *Power and Difference: Gender in Island Southeast Asia*, ed. Shelly Errington and Jane Monnig Atkinson. Stanford, Calif.: Stanford University Press.

Esposito, John L.
1998   *Islam: The Straight Path*. Third Edition. New York: Oxford University Press.

Evans-Pritchard, E. E.
1940   *The Nuer: A Description of the Modes of Livelihood and Political Institutions of a Nilotic People*. Oxford: Clarendon Press.

Fabian, Johannes
1983   *Time and the Other: How Anthropology Makes Its Object*. New York: Columbia University Press.

Faderman, Lillian
1992   "The Return of Butch and Femme: A Phenomenon in Lesbian Sexuality of the 1980s and 1990s." *Journal of the History of Sexuality* 2(4):578–98.

Fadhilah, Iman

2004   "Portret Homoseksual Dalam Wacana Fiqh Klasik" [A Portrait of
        Homosexuality in the Discourse of Classical Islamic Jurisprudence]. *Justisia*
        25:23–30.

Fauzannafi, Muhammad Zamzam

2005   *Reog Ponorogo: Menari di antara Dominasi dan Keragaman* [Reog in
        Ponorogo: Dancing between Domination and Diversity]. Yogyakarta: Kepel
        Press.

Ferguson, James

1999   *Expectations of Modernity: Myths and Meanings of Urban Life on the
        Zambian Copperbelt.* Berkeley: University of California Press.

Ferguson, Roderick A.

2003   *Aberrations in Black: Toward a Queer of Color Critique.* Minneapolis:
        University of Minnesota Press.

2005   "Of Our Normative Strivings: African American Studies and the Histories of
        Sexuality." *Social Text* 23(3/4):85–100.

Floyd, Kory

2000   "Affectionate Same-Sex Touch: The Influence of Homophobia on Observers'
        Perceptions." *Journal of Social Psychology* 140(6):774–88.

Ford, C. S., and A. B. Beach

1951   *Patterns of Sexual Behavior.* New York: Harper Brothers.

Foucault, Michel

1973   *The Birth of the Clinic: An Archaeology of Medical Perception.* New York:
        Vintage Books.

1978   *The History of Sexuality, Vol. 1: An Introduction.* Translated by Robert
        Hurley. New York: Vintage Books.

1985   *The History of Sexuality, Vol. 2: The Use of Pleasure.* Translated by Robert
        Hurley. New York: Vintage Books.

1986   *The History of Sexuality, Vol. 3: The Care of the Self.* Translated by Robert
        Hurley. New York: Vintage Books.

1991   "Governmentality." Pp. 87–104 in *The Foucault Effect: Studies in
        Governmentality,* ed. Graham Burchell, Colin Gordon, and Peter Miller.
        London: Harvester/Wheatsheaf.

Frazer, James George

1915   *The Golden Bough.* New York: Macmillan.

Freccero, Carla

2006   *Queer/Early/Modern.* Durham, N.C.: Duke University Press.

Frederick, William H.

1989   *Visions and Heat: The Making of the Indonesian Revolution.* Athens: Ohio
         University Press.

Freeman, Elizabeth

2000   "Packing History, Count(er)ing Generations." *New Literary History* 31:727–
         744.

Friedman, R. Seth

1997   *The Factsheet Five Zine Reader.* New York: Three Rivers Press.

Frykman, Jonas, and Orvar Löfgren

1987   *Culture Builders: A Historical Anthropology of Middle-Class Life.* New York:
         Rutgers University Press.

Gade, Anna M.

2004   *Perfection Makes Practice: Learning, Emotion, and the Recited Qur'an In
         Indonesia.* Honolulu: University of Hawai'i Press.

Gallagher, John, and Chris Bull

2001   *Perfect Enemies: The Battle between the Religious Right and the Gay
         Movement.* Lanham, Md.: Madison Books.

Garber, Marjorie

1992   *Vested Interests: Cross-Dressing and Cultural Anxiety.* New York: Routledge.

Garcia, J. Neil C.

1996   *Philippine Gay Culture, The Last Thirty Years: Binabai to Bakla, Silahis to
         MSM.* Diliman, Quezon City: University of the Philippines Press.

Gaudio, Rudolf P.

1994   "Sounding Gay: Pitch Properties in the Speech of Gay and Straight Men."
         American Speech 69(1):30–57.

Gayatri, B. J. D.

1996   "Indonesian Lesbians Writing Their Own Script: Issues of Feminism and
         Sexuality." Pp. 86–97 in *From Amazon to Zami: Towards a Global Lesbian
         Feminism*, ed. Monika Reinfelder. London: Cassell.

Geertz, Clifford

1960   *The Religion of Java.* Glencoe, Ill.: Free Press.

1973   "Person, Time, and Conduct in Bali." Pp. 360–411 in *The Interpretation of
         Cultures.* New York: Basic Books.

1980   *Negara: The Theatre State in Nineteenth-Century Bali.* Princeton, N.J.:
         Princeton University Press.

1983   "From the Native's Point of View: On the Nature of Anthropological Understanding." Pp. 55–72 in *Local Knowledge: Further Essays in Interpretive Anthropology*. New York: Basic Books.

Geertz, Hildred
1963   "Indonesian Cultures and Communities." Pp. 24–96 in *Indonesia*, ed. Ruth McVey. New Haven, Conn.: HRAF Press.

George, Kenneth M.
1996   *Showing Signs of Violence: The Cultural Politics of a Twentieth-Century Headhunting Ritual.* Berkeley: University of California Press.

Goyvaerts, Didier L.
1996   "Kibalele: Form and Function of a Secret Language in Bukavu (Zaire)." *Journal of Pragmatics* 25:123–43.

Graham, Sharyn
2001   "Negotiating Gender: Calalai' in Bugis Society." *Intersections: Gender, History, and Culture in the Asian Context*, no. 6 (August), http://wwwsshe .murdoch.edu.au/intersections/issue6/graham.html.
2003a   "Hunters, Wedding Mothers, and Transgendered Priests: Conceptualising Gender among Bugis in South Sulawesi, Indonesia." Ph.D. dissertation, University of Western Australia.
2003b   "While Diving, Drink Water: Bisexual and Transgender Intersections in South Sulawesi, Indonesia." *Journal of Bisexuality* 3(3/4):233–47.
2004   "AIDS Education from an Unexpected Corner: Government Officials and Waria in South Sulawesi." *Inside Indonesia* 75:17–19.

Greenberg, Joseph H.
1990   *On Language: Selected Writings of Joseph H. Greenberg*, ed. Keith Denning and Suzanne Kemmer. Stanford, Calif.: Stanford University Press.

Greenhouse, Carol J.
1996   *A Moment's Notice: Time Politics across Cultures.* Ithaca, N.Y.: Cornell University Press.

Grewal, Inderpal, and Caren Kaplan
2001   "Global Identities: Theorizing Transnational Studies of Sexuality." *GLQ: A Journal of Gay and Lesbian Studies* 7(4):663–79.

Groeneboer, Kees
1998   *Gateway to the West: The Dutch Language in Colonial Indonesia, 1600–1950. A History of Language Policy.* Amsterdam: Amsterdam University Press.

Grosz, Elizabeth

2004   *The Nick of Time: Politics, Evolution, and the Untimely.* Durham, N.C.: Duke
        University Press.

Gupta, Akhil

1995   "Blurred Boundaries: The Discourse of Corruption, the Culture of Politics, and
        the Imagined State." *American Ethnologist* 22(2):375–402.

Gupta, Akhil, and James Ferguson

1997   "Discipline and Practice: 'The Field' As Site, Method, and Location in
        Anthropology." Pp. 1–46 in *Anthropological Locations: Boundaries and
        Grounds of a Field Science*, ed. Akhil Gupta and James Ferguson. Berkeley:
        University of California Press.

Hacking, Ian

1992   "Making Up People." Pp. 69–88 in *Forms of Desire: Sexual Orientation and
        the Social Constructionist Controversy*, ed. Edward Stein. New York:
        Routledge.

Halberstam, Judith

1998   *Female Masculinity.* Durham, N.C.: Duke University Press.
2000   "Foreword: The Butch Anthropologist Out in the Field." Pp. ix–xvii in
        Margaret Mead Made Me Gay: Personal Essays, Public Ideas, by Esther
        Newton. Durham, N.C.: Duke University Press.
2005   *In a Queer Time and Place: Transgender Bodies, Subcultural Lives.* New York:
        New York University Press.

Hallaq, Wael B.

1997   *A History of Islamic Legal Theories: An Introduction to Sunni usul al-fiqh.*
        Cambridge: Cambridge University Press.

Halley, Janet

2004   "Take a Break from Feminism?" Pp. 57–81 in *Gender and Human Rights*, ed.
        Karen Knop. Oxford: Oxford University Press.

Halliday, Michael A. K.

1976   "Anti-Languages." *American Anthropologist* 78:570–84.

Halperin, David M.

1995   *Saint Foucault: Towards a Gay Hagiography.* New York: Oxford University
        Press.

Hansen, Thomas Blom

1996   "Recuperating Masculinity: Hindu Nationalism, Violence and the Exorcism of
        the Muslim 'Other.'" *Critique of Anthropology* 16(2):137–72.

Haraway, Donna

1988   "Situated Knowledge: The Science Question in Feminism as a Site of Discourse on the Privilege of Partial Perspective." *Feminist Studies* 14(3):575–99.

1991   *Simians, Cyborgs, and Women: The Reinvention of Nature.* London: Routledge.

Hart, Donn V.

1992   "The Cebuano Bayot and Lakin-on." Pp. 193–230 in *Oceanic Homosexualities,* ed. Stephen O. Murray. New York: Garland Publishing.

Harvey, Barbara S.

1977   *Permesta: Half a Rebellion.* Ithaca: Cornell Modern Indonesia Project.

Harvey, David

2000   *Spaces of Hope.* Berkeley: University of California Press.

Hatley, Barbara

1971   "Wayang and Ludruk: Polarities in Java." *The Drama Review: TDR* 15(2):88–101.

1997   "Nation, 'Tradition,' and Constructions of the Feminine in Modern Indonesian Literature." Pp. 90–120 in *Imagining Indonesia: Cultural Politics and Political Culture,* ed. Jim Schiller and Barbara Martin-Schiller. Athens: Ohio University Press.

Hefner, Robert W.

1985   *Hindu Javanese: Tengger Tradition and Islam.* Princeton, N.J.: Princeton University Press.

2000   *Civil Islam: Muslims and Democratization in Indonesia.* Princeton, N.J.: Princeton University Press.

Helmreich, Stefan

Forthcoming. *Alien Ocean: An Anthropology of Marine Microbiology and the Limits of Life.* Berkeley: University of California Press.

Heng Hiang Khng, Russell

2001   "Tiptoe Out of the Closet: The Before and After of the Increasingly Visible Gay Community in Singapore." *Journal of Homosexuality* 40(3/4):81–97.

Herlinatiens

2003   *Garis Tepi Seorang Lesbian* [A Lesbian on the Margins]. Introduction by Saskia E. Wieringa. Yogyakarta: Galang Press.

Hervey, Sándor

1992   "Registering Registers." *Lingua* 86(2/3):189–206.

Heryanto, Ariel

2005   *State Terrorism and Political Identity in Indonesia: Fatally Belonging.* New York: Routledge.

Hirschfeld, Magnus

1935   *Women East and West: Impressions of a Sex Expert.* London: William Heinemann (Medical Books) Ltd.

Hocquenghem, Guy

1978   *Homosexual Desire.* London: Allison and Busby.

Hoskins, Janet

1993   *The Play of Time: Kodi Perspectives on Calendars, History, and Exchange.* Berkeley: University of California Press.

1998   *Biographical Objects: How Things Tell the Stories of People's Lives.* New York: Routledge.

Howard, Richard Stephen

1996   "Falling Into the Gay World: Manhood, Marriage, and Family in Indonesia." Ph.D. dissertation, University of Illinois, Urbana-Champaign.

Hull, Terence H., and Meiwita Budiharsana

2001   "Male Circumcision and Penis Enhancement in Southeast Asia: Matters of Pain and Pleasure." *Reproductive Health Matters* 9(18):60–67.

Ibhoed, Budi

1999   "Bahasa Gay Menjadi Bahasa Gaul" [*Gay* Language Becomes a Slang]. *GAYa Nusantara* 60:29–30.

Idrus, Nurul Ilmi

2001   "Marriage, Sex, and Violence." Pp. 43–56 in *Love, Sex, and Power: Women in Southeast Asia*, ed. Susan Blackburn. Clayton, Australia: Monash Asia Institute.

2004   "Behind the Notion of Siala: Marriage, Adat and Islam among the Bugis in South Sulawesi." *Intersections: Gender, History and Culture in the Asian Context*, no. 10 (August), http://wwwsshe.murdoch.edu.au/intersections/issue10/idrus.html#t23.

2006   " 'Hunter and Lines': Gender, Sex and Sexuality among Same-Sex Relations in Globalised South Sulawesi, Indonesia." Unpublished manuscript.

Ingleson, John

1975   *Perhimpunan Indonesia and the Indonesian Nationalist Movement.* Clayton, Australia: Monash Papers on Southeast Asia.

Irvine, Judith T., and Susan Gal

2000   "Language Ideology and Linguistic Differentiation." Pp. 35–84 in *Regimes of Language: Ideologies, Polities and Identities*, ed. Paul V. Kroskrity. Santa Fe: School of American Research Press.

Iwasaki, Shoichi, and Preeya Ingkaphirom Horie

2000   "Creating Speech Register in Thai Conversation." *Language in Society* 29(4):519–54.

Jackson, Peter A.

1997   "*Kathoey*><Gay><Man: The Historical Emergence of Gay Male Identity in Thailand." Pp. 166–90 in *Sites of Desire, Economies of Pleasure: Sexualities in Asia and the Pacific*, ed. Lenore Manderson and Margaret Jolly. Chicago: University of Chicago Press.

1999a   "Tolerant but Unaccepting: The Myth of a Thai 'Gay Paradise.'" Pp. 226–42 in *Genders and Sexualities in Modern Thailand*, ed. Peter A. Jackson and Nerida M. Cook. Chiang Mai: Silkworm Books.

1999b   "An American Death in Bangkok: The Murder of Darrell Berrigan and the Hybrid Origins of Gay Identity in 1960s Thailand." *GLQ: A Journal of Gay and Lesbian Studies* 5(3):361–411.

2001   "Pre-Gay, Post-Queer: Thai Perspectives on Proliferating Gender/Sex Diversity in Asia." *Journal of Homosexuality* 40(3/4):1–25.

Jagose, Annamarie

1996   *Queer Theory: An Introduction.* New York: New York University Press.

Jawa Pos

2000   "Dari Talk Show Dentisty's Sex di Hotel Simpang" [From Dentisty's Sex Talk Show at the Hotel Simpang], http://www.jawapos.com.

Johnson, Mark

1997   *Beauty and Power: Transgendering and Cultural Transformation in the Southern Philippines.* Oxford: Berg.

Johnson, Mark, Peter Jackson, and Gilbert Herdt

2000   "Critical Regionalities and the Study of Gender and Sexual Diversity in South East and East Asia." *Culture, Health, and Sexuality* 2(4):361–75.

Jones, Carla

2004   "Whose Stress? Emotion Work in Middle-Class Javanese Homes." *Ethnos* 69(4):509–28.

Jones, Gavin W.

1994   *Marriage and Divorce in Islamic South-East Asia.* Kuala Lumpur: Oxford University Press.

Jurriëns, Edwin

2004   *Cultural Travel and Migrancy: The Artistic Representation of Globalization in the Electronic Media of West Java.* Leiden: KITLV Press.

Kartini, Putri

2003   *Suara Perih Perempuan: Lesbian dan Kawin Bule* [The Pained Voice of a Woman: Lesbian and Married to a White Man]. Yogyakarta: Galang Press.

Keane, Webb

1997   *Signs of Recognition: Powers and Hazards of Representation in an Indonesian Society.* Berkeley: University of California Press.

Keeler, Ward

1983   "Shame and Stage Fright in Java." *Ethos* 11(3):152–65.

1990   "Speaking of Gender in Java." Pp. 127–52 in *Power and Difference: Gender in Island Southeast Asia*, ed. Shelly Errington and Jane Monnig Atkinson. Stanford, Calif.: Stanford University Press.

Kennedy, Raymond

1953   *Field Notes on Indonesia: South Celebes, 1949–50.* New Haven: HRAF Press.

Khoo, Olivia

2003   "Sexing the City: Malaysia's New 'Cyberlaws' and Cyberjaya's Queer Success." Pp. 222–44 in *Mobile Cultures: Mass Media and Queer Asia*, ed. Audrey Yue, Fran Martin, and Chris Berry. Durham, N.C.: Duke University Press.

Koeswinarno

1996   *Waria dan Penyakit Menular Seksual: Kasus Dua Kota di Jawa* [Warias and Sexually Transmitted Diseases: The Cases of Two Cities in Java]. Yogyakarta: Pusat Penelitian Kependudukan, Universitas Gajah Mada.

Kroskrity, Paul V.

2000   "Regimenting Languages: Linguistic Ideological Perspectives." Pp.1–34 in *Regimes of Language: Ideologies, Polities and Identities*, ed. Paul V. Kroskrity. Santa Fe: School of American Research Press.

Kulick, Don

1998   *Travesti: Sex, Gender, and Culture among Brazilian Transgendered Prostitutes.* Chicago: University of Chicago Press.

2003   "No." *Language and Communication* 23:139–51.

Lacan, Jacques

1977   "The Agency of the Letter in the Unconscious, or Reason since Freud." Pp. 146–78 in *Écrits: A Selection.* New York: Norton.

1985   "A Love Letter." Pp. 149–61 in *Feminine Sexuality: Jacques Lacan and the École Freudienne*, ed. Juliet Mitchell and Jacqueline Rose. New York: Norton.

Laffan, Michael Francis

2003   *Islamic Nationhood and Colonial Indonesia: The* Umma *Below the Winds.* London: Routledge/Curzon.

Lathief, Halilintar

2004   *Bissu: Pergulatan dan Peranannya di Masyarakat Bugis* [Bissu: Their Struggle and Role in Bugis Society]. Depok, Indonesia: Desantara.

Lawrence, Bruce B.

1998   *Shattering the Myth: Islam Beyond Violence.* Princeton, N.J.: Princeton University Press.

Leach, Edmund

1961   "Two Essays Concerning the Symbolic Representation of Time." Pp. 124–36 in *Rethinking Anthropology.* London: Althone.

Leckie-Tarry, Helen

1995   *Language and Context: A Functional Linguistic Theory of Register*, ed. David Birch. London: Pinter.

Leong, Lawrence

1995   "Space and Place in Gay Singapore: Implications for AIDS Prevention and Control." *Act* 12:4–5.

Lewis, Martin W., and Karen E. Wigen

1997   *The Myth of Continents: A Critique of Metageography.* Berkeley: University of California Press.

Liddle, William

1988   *Politics and Culture in Indonesia.* Ann Arbor: University of Michigan Press.

Loos, Tamara

2005   "Sex in the Inner City: The Fidelity between Sex and Politics in Siam." *Journal of Asian Studies* 64(4):881–910.

Lucas, Ian

1997   "The Color of His Eyes: Polari and the Sisters of Perpetual Indulgence." Pp. 85–94 in *Queerly Phrased: Language, Gender, and Sexuality*, ed. Anna Livia and Kira Hall. New York: Oxford University Press.

Lyons, Andrew, and Harriet D. Lyons

2004   *Irregular Connections: A History of Anthropology and Sexuality.* Lincoln: University of Nebraska Press.

Mahmood, Saba

2004   *Politics of Piety: The Islamic Revival and the Feminist Subject.* Princeton, N.J.: Princeton University Press.

Maier, H. M. J.

1993 "From Heteroglossia to Polyglossia: The Creation of Malay and Dutch in the Indies." *Indonesia* 56:37–65.

Malinowski, Bronislaw

1922 *Argonauts of the Western Pacific.* New York: E. P. Dutton and Co.

1927 *Sex and Repression in Savage Society.* London: Routledge and Kegan Paul.

1945 *The New Tasks of a Modern Anthropology.* Westport, Conn.: Greenwood Press.

1987 [1929] *The Sexual Life of Savages.* Boston: Beacon Press.

Manalansan, Martin F.

1995 "Speaking of AIDS: Language and the Filipino 'Gay' Experience in America." Pp. 193–220 in *Discrepant Histories: Translocal Essays on Filipino Cultures,* ed. Vicente L. Rafael. Philadelphia: Temple University Press.

2003 *Global Divas: Filipino Gay Men in the Diaspora.* Durham, N.C.: Duke University Press.

Maning, Joanna Therese

2000 *Identitas, Pernikahan, Pengakuan: Cerita, Kekuatiran dan Harap Hati Kaum Gay Generasi Sekarang di Yogyakarta* [Identity, Marriage, Confession: Narratives, Fears, and Hopes of the Present Gay Generation in Yogyakarta.] Malang: FISIP Universitas Muhammadiyah.

Marcus, George

1995 "Ethnography in/of the World System: The Emergence of Multi-Sited Ethnography." *Annual Review of Anthropology* 24:95–117.

Marcus, George, and Michael M. J. Fischer

1986 *Anthropology as Cultural Critique: An Experimental Moment in the Human Sciences.* Chicago: University of Chicago Press.

Marin, Malu

1996 "Stolen Strands: The In and Out Lives of Lesbians in the Philippines." Pp. 30–55 in *From Amazon to Zami: Towards a Global Lesbian Feminism,* ed. Monika Reinfelder. London: Cassell.

Massad, Joseph

2002 "Re-Orienting Desire: The Gay International and the Arab World." *Public Culture* 14(2):361–85.

Maurer, Bill

2000 "Sexualities and Separate Spheres: Gender, Sexual Identity, and Work in Dominica and Beyond." Pp. 90–115 in *Gender Matters: Rereading Michelle Z. Rosaldo,* ed. Alejandro Lugo and Bill Maurer. Ann Arbor: University of Michigan Press.

2005   *Mutual Life, Limited: Islamic Banking, Alternative Currencies, Lateral Reason.* Princeton, N.J.: Princeton University Press.

Mead, Margaret
1949   *Male and Female: A Study of the Sexes in a Changing World.* New York: Morrow.

Merleau-Ponty, Maurice
1968   *The Visible and the Invisible.* Evanston, Ill.: Northwestern University Press.

Milone, Pauline Dublin
1967   "Queen City of the East: The Metamorphosis of a Colonial Capital." Ph.D. dissertation, University of California, Berkeley.

Mitchell, Timothy
2002   *Rule of Experts: Egypt, Techno-Politics, Modernity.* Berkeley: University of California Press.

Miyazaki, Hirokazu
2004   *The Method of Hope: Anthropology, Philosophy, and Fijian Knowledge.* Stanford, Calif.: Stanford University Press.

Moerthiko
1980   *Kehidupan Transexual dan Waria* [The Lives of Transsexuals and Warias]. Solo: Surya Murthi Publishing.

Morgan, Louis Henry
1870   *Systems of Consanguinity and Affinity of the Human Family.* Washington, D.C.: Smithsonian Institution Press.

Morgan, Marcyliena
1993   "The Africanness of Counterlanguage among Afro-Americans." Pp. 423–35 in *Africanisms in Afro-American Language Varieties*, ed. Salikoko S. Mufwene. Athens: University of Georgia Press.

Morris, Rosalind C.
1997   "Educating Desire: Thailand, Transnationalism, and Transgression." *Social Text* 15(3/4):53–79.
2000   *In the Place of Origins: Modernity and Its Mediums in Northern Thailand.* Durham, N.C.: Duke University Press.

Mosse, George L.
1985   *Nationalism and Sexuality: Respectability and Abnormal Sexuality in Modern Europe.* New York: Howard Fertig.

Munn, Nancy D.

1992   "The Cultural Anthropology of Time: A Critical Essay." *Annual Review of Anthropology* 21:93–123.

Muñoz, José Esteban

1999   *Disidentifications: Queers of Color and the Performance of Politics.* Minneapolis: University of Minnesota Press.

Murray, Alison

1999   "Let Them Take Ecstasy: Class and Jakarta Lesbians." Pp. 139–56 in *Female Desires: Same-Sex Relations and Transgender Practices across Cultures,* ed. Evelyn Blackwood and Saskia E. Wieringa. New York: Columbia University Press.

Murray, Stephen O.

1992   "Early Reports of Cebuano, Tinguian, and Sambal 'Berdache.' " Pp. 185–92 in *Oceanic Homosexualities,* ed. Stephen O. Murray. New York: Garland Publishing.

1997   "Male Actresses in Islamic Parts of Indonesia and the Southern Philippines." Pp. 256–61 in *Islamic Homosexualities: Culture, History, and Literature,* ed. Stephen O. Murray and Will Roscoe. New York: New York University Press.

Murray, Stephen O., and Will Roscoe

1997   "Conclusion." Pp. 302–19 in *Islamic Homosexualities: Culture, History, and Literature,* ed. Stephen O. Murray and Will Roscoe. New York: New York University Press.

Murtagh, Ben

2006   "*Istana Kecantikan*: The First Indonesian *Gay* Movie." *Southeast Asia Research* 14(2):211–30.

Nagengast, Carole

1994   "Violence, Terror, and the Crisis of the State." *Annual Review of Anthropology* 23:109–36.

Nanda, Serena

1990   *Neither Man nor Woman: The Hijras of India.* Belmont, Calif.: Wadsworth Publishing.

Newton, Esther

1972   *Mother Camp: Female Impersonators in America.* Chicago: University of Chicago Press.

Nordholt, Henk Schulte, ed.

1998   *Outward Appearances: Dressing State and Society in Indonesia.* Leiden: KITLV Press.

Nur, Rais, and A. R.

1996   "Queering the State: Towards a Lesbian Movement in Malaysia." Pp. 70–85 in *From Amazon to Zami: Towards a Global Lesbian Feminism*, ed. Monika Reinfelder. London: Cassell.

Oetomo, Dédé

1996a   "Gender and Sexual Orientation in Indonesia." Pp. 259–69 in *Fantasizing the Feminine in Indonesia*, Laurie Sears, ed. Durham, N.C.: Duke University Press.

1996b   "Bahasa Indonesia dan Kelas Menengah Indonesia" [Indonesian and the Indonesian Middle Class]. Pp. 195–212 in *Bahasa dan Kekuasaan* [Language and Power], ed. Yudi Latif and Idi Subandy Ibrahim. Bandung: Mizan.

1999   Introduction to "Dictionary of Bahasa Gay." *GAYA Nusantara* 62:28.

2001   *Memberi Suara pada yang Bisu*. Yogyakarta: Galang Press.

Offord, Baden

2003   "Singaporean Queering of the Internet: Toward a New Form of Cultural Transmission of Rights Discourse." Pp. 133–57 in *Mobile Cultures: Mass Media and Queer Asia*, ed. Audrey Yue, Fran Martin, and Chris Berry. Durham, N.C.: Duke University Press.

Ong, Aihwa, and Michael G. Peletz

1995   "Introduction." Pp. 1–18 in *Bewitching Women, Pious Men: Gender and Body Politics in Southeast Asia*, ed. Aihwa Ong and Michael G. Peletz. Berkeley: University of California Press.

Ortner, Sherry, and Harriet Whitehead

1981   "Introduction: Accounting for Sexual Meanings." Pp. 1–28 in *Sexual Meanings: the Cultural Construction of Gender and Sexuality*, ed. Sherry Ortner and Harriet Whitehead. Cambridge: Cambridge University Press.

Paolillo, John C.

2000   "Formalizing Formality: An Analysis of Register Variation in Sinhala." *Journal of Linguistics* 36(2):215–59.

Peacock, James L.

1968   *Rites of Modernization: Symbolic and Social Aspects of Indonesian Proletarian Drama*. Chicago: University of Chicago Press.

Peletz, Michael G.

1996   *Reason and Passion: Representations of Gender in a Malay Society*. Berkeley: University of California Press.

2002   *Islamic Modern: Religious Courts and Cultural Politics in Malaysia*. Princeton, N.J.: Princeton University Press.

2006   "Transgenderism and Gender Pluralism in Southeast Asia Since Early Modern Times." *Current Anthropology* 47(2):309–40.

Pelras, Christian
1996   *The Bugis.* Oxford: Blackwell.

Pemberton, John
1994   *On the Subject of "Java."* Ithaca, N.Y.: Cornell University Press.

Perlez, Jane
2003   "For These Transvestites, Still More Role Changes." *New York Times,* July 24, p. A4.

Picard, Michel
1996   *Bali: Cultural Tourism and Touristic Culture.* Singapore: Archipelago Press.

Plummer, David, and Doug Porter
1997   "The Use and Misuse of Epidemiological Categories." Pp. 41–49 in *No Place for Borders: The HIV/AIDS Epidemic and Development in Asia and the Pacific,* ed. Godfrey Linge and Doug Porter. St. Leonards, New South Wales: Allen and Unwin.

Povinelli, Elizabeth A.
2001   "Radical Worlds: The Anthropology of Incommensurability and Inconceivability." *Annual Review of Anthropology* 30:319–34.

Pratt, Mary Louise
1987   "Linguistic Utopias." Pp. 48–66 in *The Linguistics of Writing: Arguments between Language and Literature,* ed. Nigel Fabb, Derek Attridge, Alan Durant, and Colin MacCabe. New York: Methuen.

Prawirakusumah, R. Prie, and Ramadhan K. H.
1988   *Menguak Duniaku: Kisah Sejati Kelainan Seksual* [Revealing My World: A True Story of Sexual Deviance]. Jakarta: Pustaka Utama Grafiti.

Proschan, Frank
2002   "Eunuch Mandarins, *Soldats Mamzelles,* Effeminate Boys, and Graceless Women: French Colonial Constructions of Vietnamese Genders." *GLQ: A Journal of Gay and Lesbian Studies* 8(4):435–67.

Rafael, Vincente L., ed.
1999   *Figures of Criminality in Indonesia, the Philippines, and Colonial Vietnam.* Ithaca, N.Y.: Cornell Southeast Asia Program.

Rahardja, Prathama, and Henri Chambert-Loir
1990   *Kamus Bahasa Prokem* [Dictionary of Prokem]. Jakarta: Pustaka Utama Grafiti.

Ratri M, ed.

2000   *Lines: Kumpulan Cerita Perempuan di Garis Pinggir* [Lesbians: Collected Stories of Women at the Margins]. Jakarta: Millennium.

Readings, Bill

1996   *The University in Ruins.* Cambridge, Mass.: Harvard University Press.

Reddy, Gayatri

2005   *With Respect to Sex: Negotiating Hijra Identity in South India.* Chicago: University of Chicago Press.

Reid, Anthony

1988   *Southeast Asia in the Age of Commerce 1450–1680, Volume 1: The Lands below the Winds.* New Haven, Conn.: Yale University Press.

1999   "A Saucer Model of Southeast Asian Identity." *Southeast Asian Journal of Social Science* 27(1):7–23.

Reynolds, Craig J.

1999   "On the Gendering of Nationalist and Postnationalist Selves in Twentieth-Century Thailand." Pp. 261–74 in *Genders and Sexualities in Modern Thailand*, ed. Peter A. Jackson and Nerida M. Cook. Chiang Mai: Silkworm Books.

Riantiarno, Nano

2004   *Cermin Merah: Lakon yang Tak Pernah Selesai* [Red Mirror: An Unending Drama]. Jakarta: Gramedia Widiasarana Indonesia.

Riches, David

1986   "The Phenomenon of Violence." Pp. 1–27 in *The Anthropology of Violence*, ed. David Riches. Oxford: Basil Blackwell.

Ricklefs, Merle C.

1981   *A History of Modern Indonesia.* Bloomington: Indiana University Press.

Robinson, Geoffrey

1995   *The Dark Side of Paradise: Political Violence in Bali.* Ithaca: Cornell University Press.

Robinson, Kathryn

1989   "Choosing Contraception: Cultural Change and the Indonesian Family Planning Programme." Pp. 21–38 in *Creating Indonesian Cultures*, ed. Paul Alexander. Sydney: Oceania Publications.

Rodgers, Susan

1995   *Telling Lives, Telling History: Autobiography and Historical Imagination in Modern Indonesia.* Berkeley: University of California Press.

Rofel, Lisa

1999   *Other Modernities: Gendered Yearnings in China after Socialism.* Berkeley: University of California Press.

Roof, Judith

1996   *Come as You Are: Sexuality and Narrative.* New York: Columbia University Press.

Rosaldo, Michelle Zimbalist

1974   "Women, Culture, and Society: a Theoretical Overview." Pp. 17–42 in *Women, Culture, and Society*, ed. Michelle Zimbalist Rosaldo and Louise Lamphere. Stanford, Calif.: Stanford University Press.

Rubin, Gayle

1975   "The Traffic in Women: Notes on the 'Political Economy' of Sex." Pp. 157–210 in *Toward an Anthropology of Women*, ed. Rayna R. Reiter. New York: Monthly Review Press.

1984   "Thinking Sex: Notes for a Radical Theory of the Politics of Sexuality." Pp. 267–319 in *Pleasure and Danger*, ed. Carole S. Vance. London: Routledge and Kegan Paul.

2002   "Studying Sexual Subcultures: Excavating the Ethnography of Gay Communities in Urban North America." Pp. 17–68 in *Out in Theory: The Emergence of Lesbian and Gay Anthropology*, ed. Ellen Lewin and William L. Leap. Urbana: University of Illinois Press.

Sahertian, Debby

1999   *Kamus Bahasa Gaul* [Dictionary of Bahasa Gaul]. Jakarta: Pustaka Sinar Harapan.

Said, Edward W.

1978   *Orientalism.* New York: Pantheon.

Saleh, Budiman

1988   "Prokemkah 'Argot' Itu?" [Is Prokem an Argot?] Pp. 11–18 in *Nuansa-Nuansa Pelangi Budaya* [Nuances of the Cultural Rainbow], ed. Kusman Mahmud, Kusnaka Adimihardja, and Wiwi Martalogawa. Bandung: Pustaka Karsa Sunda.

Sandoval, Chela

1991   "U.S. Third World Feminism: The Theory and Method of Oppositional Consciousness in the Postmodern World." *Genders* 10:1–24.

Sapir, Edward

1921   *Language.* New York: Harcourt, Brace, and World.

Scharer, H.

1963   *Ngaju Religion: The Conception of God among a South Borneo People,*
translated by R. Needham. The Hague: Martinus Nijhoff.

Schlecker, Markus, and Eric Hirsch

2001   "Incomplete Knowledge: Ethnography and the Crisis of Context in Studies of
Media, Science and Technology." *History of the Human Sciences* 14(1):69–87.

Schneider, David M.

1980   *American Kinship: A Cultural Account.* Second Edition. Chicago: University of
Chicago Press.

Sedgwick, Eve Kosofsky

1991   *Epistemology of the Closet.* London: Harvester/Wheatsheaf.

1993   "How to Bring Your Kids Up Gay: The War on Effeminate Boys." In
Tendencies, pp. 154–64. Durham, N.C.: Duke University Press.

2003   "Paranoid Reading and Reparative Reading; Or, You're So Paranoid, You
Probably Think This Essay Is about You." Pp. 123–53 in *Touching Feeling:
Affect, Pedagogy, Performativity.* Durham, N.C.: Duke University Press.

Sen, Krishna

1998   "Indonesian Women at Work: Reframing the Subject." Pp. 35–62 in *Gender
and Power in Affluent Asia*, ed. Krishna Sen and Maila Stivens. London:
Routledge.

Siapno, Jacqueline Aquino

2002   *Gender, Islam, Nationalism, and the State in Aceh: The Paradox of Power,
Co-Optation, and Resistance.* London: Routledge/Curzon.

Siegel, James T.

1969   *The Rope of God.* Berkeley: University of California Press.

1997   *Fetish, Recognition, Revolution.* Princeton, N.J.: Princeton University Press.

1998   *A New Criminal Type in Jakarta: Counter-Revolution Today.* Durham, N.C.:
Duke University Press.

Silverstein, Michael

1979   "Language Structure and Linguistic Ideology." Pp.193–247 in *The Elements:
A Parasession on Linguistic Units and Levels*, ed. Paul R. Clyne, William F.
Hanks, and Carol L. Hofbauer. Chicago: Chicago Linguistic Society.

1992   "Metapragmatic Discourse and Metapragmatic Function." Pp. 33–58 in
Reflexive Language: Reported Speech and Metapragmatics, ed. John A. Lucy.
Cambridge: Cambridge University Press.

1998   "The Uses and Utility of Ideology: a Commentary." Pp. 123–45 in *Language
Ideologies: Practice and Theory*, ed. Bambi B. Schieffelin, Kathryn A. Woolard,
and Paul V. Kroskrity. New York: Oxford University Press.

Silverstein, Michael, and Greg Urban

1996   "The Natural History of Discourse." Pp. 1–20 in *Natural Histories of Discourse*, ed. Michael Silverstein and Greg Urban. Chicago: University of Chicago Press.

Sinnott, Megan J.

2004   *Toms and Dees: Transgender Identity and Female Same-Sex Relationships in Thailand.* Honolulu: University of Hawai'i Press.

Slamah, Khartini

2005   "The Struggle to be Ourselves, neither Men nor Women: Mak Nyahs in Malaysia." Pp. 98–112 in *Sexuality, Gender, and Rights: Exploring Theory and Practice in South and Southeast Asia*, ed. Geetanjali Misra and Radhika Chandiramani. New Delhi: Sage Publications.

Sneddon, James N.

1996   *Indonesian: A Comprehensive Grammar.* London: Routledge.

2003   *The Indonesian Language: Its History and Role in Modern Society.* Sydney: University of New South Wales Press.

Soentoro, Isye

1996   *Anak Kehidupan* [Child of Life]. Jakarta: Cipta Cinta.

Spencer, Herbert

1864   *Illustrations of Universal Progress: A Series of Discussions.* New York: D. Appleton.

Spivak, Gayatri Chakravorty

2003   *Death of a Discipline.* New York: Columbia University Press.

Stasch, Rupert

2001   "Giving Up Homicide: Korowai Experience of Witches and Police (West Papua)." *Oceania* 72:33–52.

Steedly, Mary Margaret

1999   "The State of Culture Theory in the Anthropology of Southeast Asia." *Annual Review of Anthropology* 28:431–54.

Steenbrink, Karel

1993   *Dutch Colonialism and Indonesian Islam: Contacts and Conflicts, 1596–1950.* Amsterdam: Rodopi.

Stocking, George W. Jr.

1974   "The Basic Assumptions of Boasian Anthropology." Pp. 1–20 in *A Franz Boas Reader*, ed. George W. Stocking Jr. Chicago: University of Chicago Press.

Stoler, Ann Laura

1995   *Race and the Education of Desire: Foucault's History of Sexuality and the Colonial Order of Things.* Durham, N.C.: Duke University Press.

2002   *Carnal Knowledge and Imperial Power: Race and the Intimate in Colonial Rule.* Berkeley: University of California Press.

Strathern, Marilyn

1987   "An Awkward Relationship: The Case of Feminism and Anthropology." *Signs: Journal of Women in Culture and Society* 12(2):276–300.

1991   *Partial Connections.* Savage, Md.: Rowman and Littlefield Publishers, Inc.

1992a   *Reproducing the Future: Anthropology, Kinship, and the New Reproductive Technologies.* New York: Routledge.

1992b   *After Nature: English Kinship in the Late Twentieth Century.* Cambridge: Cambridge University Press.

2004   *Commons and Borderlands: Working Papers on Interdisciplinarity, Accountability, and the Flow of Knowledge.* Watage, U.K.: Sean Kingston Publishing.

Sulistyo, Hermawan

2002   *Ke Mana Indonesiaku? Kumpulan Wawanara Imajiner* [To Where, My Indonesia? Collected Imaginary Interviews]. Jakarta: Pensil-324.

Sullivan, Nikki

2003   *A Critical Introduction to Queer Theory.* New York: New York University Press.

Suryakusuma, Julia I.

1996   "The State and Sexuality in New Order Indonesia." Pp. 92–119 in *Fantasizing the Feminine in Indonesia*, ed. Laurie Sears. Durham, N.C.: Duke University Press.

Sutlive, Vinson H. Jr.

1992   "The Iban Manang in the Sibu District of the Third Division of Sarawak: An Alternate Route to Normality." Pp. 273–84 in *Oceanic Homosexualities*, ed. Stephen O. Murray. New York: Garland Publishing.

Sutton, Laurel A.

1996   "All Media Are Created Equal: Do-It-Yourself Identity in Alternative Publishing." Pp. 163–180 in *Reinventing Identities: The Gendered Self in Discourse*, ed. Mary Bucholtz, A. C. Liang, and Laurel A. Sutton. Oxford: Oxford University Press.

Szymanski, Dawn M., Y Barry Chung, and Kimberly F. Balsam

2001   "Psychosocial Correlates of Internalized Homophobia in Lesbians." *Measurement and Evaluation in Counseling and Development* 34(1):27–38.

Tambiah, Stanley Jeyaraja

1990   *Magic, Science, Religion, and the Scope of Rationality.* Cambridge: Cambridge University Press.

Tan, Beng Hui

1999   "Women's Sexuality and the Discourse on Asian Values: Cross-Dressing in Malaysia." Pp. 281–307 in *Female Desires: Same-Sex Relations and Transgender Practices across Cultures*, ed. Evelyn Blackwood and Saskia E. Wieringa. New York: Columbia University Press.

Tan, Michael L.

2001   "Survival through Pluralism: Emerging Gay Communities in the Philippines." *Journal of Homosexuality* 40(3/4):117–42.

Tarling, Nicholas, ed.

1992   *The Cambridge History of Southeast Asia, Vol. 2: The Nineteenth and Twentieth Centuries.* Cambridge: Cambridge University Press.

Teh, Yik Koon

2002   *The Mak Nyahs: Malaysian Male to Female Transsexuals.* Singapore: Eastern Universities Press.

ten Brummelhuis, Han

1999   "Transformations of Transgender: The Case of the Thai *Kathoey.*" Pp. 121–40 in *Lady Boys, Tom Boys, Rent Boys: Male and Female Homosexualities in Contemporary Thailand*, ed. Gerard Sullivan and Peter Jackson. New York: Harrington Park Press.

Tiwon, Sylvia

1996   "Models and Maniacs: Articulating the Female in Indonesia." Pp. 47–70 in *Fantasizing the Feminine in Indonesia*, ed. Laurie Sears. Durham, N.C.: Duke University Press.

Towle, Evan B., and Lynn Marie Morgan

2002   "Romancing the Transgender Native: Rethinking the Use of the 'Third Gender' Concept." *GLQ: A Journal of Gay and Lesbian Studies* 8(4):469–497.

Tsing, Anna Lowenhaupt

1993   *In the Realm of the Diamond Queen: Marginality in an Out-of-the-Way Place.* Princeton, N.J.: Princeton University Press.

Tylor, Edward Burnett

1958 [1871] *Primitive Culture, Vol. 1: The Origins of Culture.* New York: Harper and Row.

Valentine, David

2003   " 'I Went to Bed with My Own Kind Once': The Erasure of Desire in the Name of Identity." *Language and Communication* 23:123–38.

van der Kroef, Justus M.

1992 [1954] "Transvestitism and the Religious Hermaphrodite in Indonesia." Pp. 89–97 in *Asian Homosexuality*, ed. Wayne R. Dynes and Stephen Donaldson. New York: Garland.

Vance, Carole S.

1989   "Social Construction Theory: Problems in the History of Sexuality." Pp. 13–34 in *Homosexuality, Which Homosexuality?*, ed. Dennis Altman et al. London: Gay Men's Press.

Vickers, Adrian

1989   *Bali: A Paradise Created*. Hong Kong: Periplus Editions.
2005   *A History of Modern Indonesia*. Cambridge: Cambridge University Press.

Visweswaran, Kamala

1997   "Histories of Feminist Ethnography." *Annual Review of Anthropology* 26:591–621.

Wagner, Roy

2001   *An Anthropology of the Subject: Holographic Worldview in New Guinea and Its Meaning and Significance for the World of Anthropology*. Berkeley: University of California Press.

Wahid, Abdurrahman

1999   *Tuhan Tidak Perlu Dibela* [God Does Not Need to Be Defended]. Yogyakarta: LKiS Yogyakarta.

Waines, David

1995   *An Introduction to Islam*. Cambridge: Cambridge University Press.

Watson, C. W.

2000   *Of Self and Nation: Autobiography and the Representation of Modern Indonesia*. Honolulu: University of Hawai'i Press.

Webster, Tracy L. Wright

2004   *Beyond "The Closet": The Voices of Lesbian Women in Yogyakarta*. Yogyakarta: Pusat Studi Wanita, Institut Agama Islam Negeri Sunan Kalijaga.

Weed, Elizabeth, and Naomi Schor, eds.

1997   *Feminism Meets Queer Theory*. Bloomington: Indiana University Press.

Wessel, Ingrid, and Georgia Wimhöfer, eds.

2001   *Violence in Indonesia*. Hamburg: Abera.

Weston, Kath

1993   "Lesbian/Gay Studies in the House of Anthropology." *Annual Review of Anthropology* 22:339–67.

2002   *Gender in Real Time: Power and Transience in a Visual Age.* New York: Routledge.

Whitam, Frederick L., and Robin M. Mathy

1986   *Male Homosexuality in Four Societies: Brazil, Guatemala, the Philippines, and the United States.* New York: Praeger.

Wickberg, Daniel

2000   "Homophobia: On the Cultural History of an Idea." *Critical Inquiry* 27:42–57.

Wiegman, Robyn

2002   "Difference and Disciplinarity." Pp. 135–56 in *Aesthetics in a Multicultural Age*, ed. Emory Elliott, Louis Freitas Caton, and Jeffrey Rhyne. Oxford: Oxford University Press.

2004a   "On Being in Time with Feminism." *Modern Language Quarterly* 65(1):161–77.
2004b   "Dear Ian." *Duke Journal of Gender Law and Policy* 11:93–120.

Wieringa, Saskia E.

1999a   "Sexual Metaphors in the Change from Sukarno's Old Order to Suharto's New Order in Indonesia." *Review of Indonesian and Malaysian Affairs* 32:143–78.

1999b   "Desiring Bodies or Defiant Cultures: Butch-Femme Lesbians in Jakarta and Lima." Pp. 206–29 in *Female Desires: Same-Sex Relations and Transgender Practices across Cultures*, ed. Evelyn Blackwood and Saskia E. Wieringa. New York: Columbia University Press.

2002   *Sexual Politics in Indonesia. New York:* Palgrave Macmillan.

Wieringa, Saskia E., and Evelyn Blackwood

1999   "Introduction." Pp. 1–38 in *Female Desires: Same-Sex Relations and Transgender Practices across Cultures*, ed. Evelyn Blackwood and Saskia E. Wieringa. New York: Columbia University Press.

Wilson, Ara

2004   *The Intimate Economies of Bangkok: Tomboys, Tycoons, and Avon Ladies in the Global City.* Berkeley: University of California Press.

2006   "Queering Asia." *Intersections: Gender, History, and Culture in the Asian Context* 14 (November).

Wilson, Ian Douglas

1999   "Reog Ponorogo: Spirituality, Sexuality, and Power in a Javanese Performance Tradition." *Intersections: Gender, History, and Culture in the Asian Context*, no. 2 (May).

Winichakul, Thongchai

1994   *Siam Mapped: A History of the Geo-Body of a Nation.* Honolulu: University of
        Hawai'i Press.

Winter, Sam

2002   "Thirteen general propositions about TG in Asia" (February 5), http://
        web.hku.hk/sjwinter/TransgenderASIA/thirteen_general_statements.htm
2006a   "Thai Transgenders in Focus: Demographics, Transitions and Identities."
        International Journal of Transgenderism 9(1):15–27.
2006b   "Thai Transgenders in Focus: Their Beliefs About Attitudes Towards and
        Origins of Transgender." *International Journal of Transgenderism* 9(2):47–62.

Winter, Sam, Sass R. Sasot, and Mark King

2006   "Transgender in the Philippines." Unpublished manuscript.

Wright, L., H. Adams, and J. Bernat

1999   "Development and Validation of the Homophobia Scale." *Journal of
        Psychopathology and Behavioral Assessment* 21(4):337–47.

Yanagisako, Sylvia, and Carol Delaney

1995   "Introduction." Pp. 1–19 in *Naturalizing Power: Essays in Feminist Cultural
        Analysis*, ed. Sylvia Yanagisako and Carol Delaney. New York: Routledge.

Yengoyan, Aram

1983   "Transvestitism and the Ideology of Gender: Southeast Asia and Beyond."
        Pp. 135–48 in *Feminist Revisions: What Has Been and Might Be*, ed. Vivian
        Patraka and Louise A. Tilly. Ann Arbor: Women's Studies Program, University
        of Michigan.

Yuval-Davis, Nira

1977   *Gender and Nation.* London: Sage Publications.

Anthropology (*continued*)
197; and situational knowledge, 18; and
temporality, 24, 28. *See also* Ethnogra-
phies/ethnographic method;
Ethnolocality
Anthropology and Homosexual Behavior
(Blackwood), 5
Anti-Vice Movement, 232 n.2
Apparitional Lesbian, The (Castle), 185
Archipelago concept (wawasan nusan-
tara), 44, 47
"Archipelago Lesbian and Gay Network,"
56
Asad, Talal, 139
Asher, R. E., 116
Asia. *See* Southeast Asia
Asli (authenticity), 90, 97–98, 112
Asrori, Zamroni, 148
Atkinson, Jane Monnig, 189, 203, 234 n.9
Atmojo, Kemala, 226 n.16, 227 n.24
Austin, J. L., 140
Australian Financial Review, 137
Authenticity (asli), 90, 97–98, 112
Ave, Joop, 174, 233 n.16
Avonius, Leena, 223 n.22
Azas kekeluargaan (family principle), 38,
111, 144, 146, 166, 230 n.39

"Bab Pakaian Ihram untuk Waria"
(Tempo), 226–27 n.20, 227 n.21
Bahar, Ernaldi, 172
Bahasa *gay* (*gay* language): and acronyms,
128, 134–35; and bahasa banci, 114–
15; and bahasa béncong, 115; and
bahasa gaul (national vernacular), 136–
38; and bahasa waria, 115; as community language, 16, 129, 132–36, 138;
and connection/inclusion in *gay* world
(dunia *gay*), 134, 138; and creation of
gay terms from the Indonesian language,
123, 230–31 n.4; defined, 114, 122; derivation of, 123–28; and desire for same

(sama), 188; and *gay* men, 138; and *gay*
subjectivities, 138; and globalization,
16; and hemóng language, 137; and heteronormativity, 138; history of, 118–19;
and homosexuality, 138; and humor,
123; and infixing, 127, 231 n.5; and
intonation, 128–29; and Java, 119, 132;
linguistic analysis of, 16; and local
vocabularies, 119; and Makassar, 119–
220, 132–34; and mass media, 137; and
national belonging, 138; and national
discourse, 122, 138; and nationalism,
16; and national media, 123; and neologism, 125, 131; and *normal* world
(dunia *normal*), 136–38; and Polari language, 123; and popular culture, 114,
116, 138; and power systems, 114, 117;
and pragmatics of use in daily interactions, 129; and prokem (street language), 118–19, 123, 128, 134; and
public appropriation, 138; regional and
local distinctions of, 115; and registers,
116, 132, 134, 138; and secret language
(bahasa rahasia) hypothesis, 129–31,
137; and semantic links with Indonesian
language, 123–25; and semantic shift,
125; and sense of *gay* men in Indonesia,
138; and -se' suffixing, 128; and sexuality, 16; and si-prefixing, 126–27; and
stereotyped personality types, 116–17,
138; and suffixation and vowel shift,
125–26, 135; and swardspeak, 123,
129; and syllabic substitution, 123–25;
and warias, 138; and zines, 230 n.3. *See
also* Languages
Baker, Paul, 123
Bakhtin, Mikhail, 27, 28
Bali, 6, 11, 29, 86, 234 n.6
Bancis: and bahasa banci (banci language),
114–15; as day-to-day term for warias,
83, 85, 100, 223–24 n.4; as derogatory
term, 80, 145, 234 n.3; as different class

of person from warias, 89, 226 n.18; as
joking term, 115; and *lesbi* woman term,
224 n.5; origin of term, 223–24 n.4; and
women who act masculine, 224 n.5. *See
also* Male transvestites; Warias
Bantji Batavia (Batavian Transvestite)
dances, 85
Barber, Stephen, 22
Barker, Joshua, 232–33 n.10, 233 n.11
Barnas (periodical), 232 n.8
Barth, Fredrik, 146, 152
Barthes, Roland, 217
Basri, K. H. Hasan, 226–27 n.20
Batam island, 44
Batavian Transvestite (Bantji Batavia)
dances, 85
Beach, A. B., 4
Beatty, Andrew, 145
Beauty pageants, 105
Belonging, geography of. *See* Geography
of belonging
Belonging, national. *See* National
belonging
Béncong: and bahasa béncong (béncong
language), 115; as day-to-day term for
warias, 80, 83, 223–24 n.4; as deroga-
tory term, 80, 145, 180, 233 n.20. *See
also* Male transvestites; Warias
Benjamin, Walter, 28
Berskala nasional (national scale), 222
n.11
Biber, Douglas, 116
Bimbingan Seks Islami (Islamic Sexual
Guidance), 148
Bin Laden, Osama, 180
Birth control pills, 94, 193, 227 n.23
Bisexuality, 231 n.3
Blackwood, Evelyn: *Anthropology and
Homosexual Behavior*, 5; and femmes
subject position in Southeast Asia, 208;
and homosex between women, 190; and
sexual or gender transgressors, 213; and

third person singular pronouns, 83; and
tomboys, 203, 204, 206, 208, 227 n.22
Bleys, Rudi, 85, 100, 224–25 n.9
Boas, Franz, 185
Boellstorff, Tom: and anthropology of similitude, 121, 197; and archipelago concept (wawasan nusantara), 118; and
bahasa *gay* (*gay* language), 115; and
boundary between *gay* subject position
and male transvestites, 196; and
customs of the archipelago articles, 64;
and desire (nafsu) of *gay* men, 93; and
dubbing culture, 97, 140, 158; and ethnolocality, 120–21, 143, 165; and ETPs,
84, 190, 209; and fieldwork, 10; *Gay
Archipelago, The,* 10; and *gay* men's heterosexual marriages, 49, 147, 199; and
gay subjectivities in Southeast Asia, 196;
and geography of belonging, 60; and
Indonesian language, 230 n.3; and mass
media, 213; and meeting places for gay
men, 200; and national selfhood, 45;
nonnormative sexualities and genders
origins in adat (traditional customs),
167, 190; and pronoun terminology, 83;
and sama (desire for same), 188; and
sexuality, 216; and social classes, 198,
210; and terms for warias linked to eth-
nolocalities, 83; and tomboys, 203, 204,
205, 206
Bolton, Kingsley, 130
Bouhdiba, Abdelwahab, 141, 145
Bourdieu, Pierre, 29
Bowen, John R., 142, 143, 144, 145, 148,
189
Boyamin, 232 n.8
Bravmann, Scott, 31
Brazil travesti, 101
Brenner, Neil, 101, 151
Brewer, Carolyn, 190
British Polari language, 123
Brodwin, Paul, 159

Brown, Wendy, 10
Budiharsana, Meiwita, 6, 233–34 n.1
Budiman, Amen, 129, 133, 224 n.6
Bugis culture, 104
Bull, Chris, 142
Bunzl, Matti, 20, 24, 121, 215
Bush, George W., 180
Bussmann, Hadumod, 116
Butler, Judith, 23, 79, 92, 111

Cannell, Fenella, 92, 191, 192, 194, 195
Capitalism, 22–23, 117, 210
Castle, Terry, 185
Cerita pendek or cerpen (short stories), 39, 57, 59–61, 224 n.4
Ceweks, 80
Cewoks, 93
Chabot, Hendrik Theodorus, 51, 108, 190, 224–25 n.9
Chambert-Loir, Henri, 118, 125, 126, 128, 134
Chatterjee, Partha, 226 n.17
Chauncey, George, 51, 145
Cheah, Pheng, 184
China/Chinese people, 139, 170
Chosen/love relationships, 51–52, 154, 166–67, 222 n.15
Christ, and messianic time, 28
Christianity, 140, 141, 156–57, 190, 231 n.4
Cinta (love). See Love (cinta)
Citizenship, sexual. See Sexual citizenship
Civil Islam: Muslims and Democratization in Indonesia (Hefner), 142
Clark, David, 22
Classes. See Social classes
Clifford, James, 13, 217
Cohen, Lawrence, 95
Coincidence: and closure, 181; and Jane F. Collier, 4; and comparisons, 182; and kebenaran (coincidence/truth), 30; between producers, consumers, and

national discourse, 37, 50; and queer studies, 2–5, 17–21, 24–25, 31–34, 81, 219 n.4;
Collins, Elizabeth, 172
Colonialism: and courtly texts, 190; and Dutch East Indies period, 6, 169, 233 n.14; effects of, on sexuality and gender relations, 190; and ethnolocality of culture, 121–22; and homosex, 190; in Indonesia, 5–6; and postcolonial period in Indonesia, 6–8; and precolonial era sexuality and gender history, 189–90; and Southeast Asian sexuality and gender history, 190–91
"Coming out," 49–50, 199–200, 234 n.8
Commitment relationships (pacarans), 1, 100–102, 229 n.29
Communal feast (slametan), 156, 159–60, 232–33 n.10
Community-building: and bahasa gay (gay language), 16, 129, 132–36, 138; and co-gendered/co-sexual communities in Southeast Asia, 212; and ethnolocality, 143; and gay men in Southeast Asia, 201; and public events, 201; and tomboys, 206
Comparative approach, 182–86
Coontz, Stephanie, 51
Corber, Robert J., 19
Covarrubias, Miguel, 85–86
Cowok, 80. See also Tomboys
Critical regionalities approach, 183–84
Critical theory, 17–18
"Cronus and Chronos" (Leach), 25
Crying Game, The, 103
Cultural anthropology. See Anthropology
Culture: and adat (traditional customs), 141, 143, 167, 189–90, 192; and anthropology, 31; area/space as representing partial truths in Southeast Asian, 186; and bahasa gay (gay language), 114, 116, 138; Bugis, 104; dubbing, 97,

140, 158; and incommensurable limits, 16, 139–40; popular, in Indonesia,, 114, 116, 138; warias' intersection with Indonesian national, 102–7, 229 n.34. *See also* Ethnolocality

Cummings, William, 11

Customs (adat), traditional, 141, 143, 167, 189–90, 192

Davis, D. L., 4

De Certeau, Michel, 15, 132

De Graaf, H. J., 143

Delaney, Carol, 36, 78

De Laurentis, Teresa, 21

D'Emilio, John, 210

Déndong (putting on makeup), 93–94, 106, 111, 229–30 n.36

Derrida, Jacques, 16, 28, 111

Desire (nafsu): and divine origins of homosexuality, 151–52; and faith, 144; and *gay* men, 93, 223 n.25; and *lesbi* women, 223 n.25; and love (cinta), 59; for national belonging, 37, 223 n.25; and sama (desire for same), 188, 196–97, 198; and similitude, 196–97; and social relations, 36; and zines, 47, 222 n.12. *See also* Zones of desire

Detik.com (web publication), 232 n.2

Dick, Howard W., 11

Dion, Celine, 97

Disciplinarity, 31–34, 181

Discovery/recognition stories, 59–62

Discrimination. *See* Acceptance/recognition

Dodd, Tim, 138

"Dorce di Surabaya, Sally di Mesir" *(Tempo)*, 227–28 n.25, 228 n.27

Doussantousse, Serge, 192, 194, 195

Dreyfuss, Jeff, 29, 30, 118

"Dua Dunia yang Belum Sudah" *(Tempo)*, 227–28 n.25

Dubbing culture, 97, 140, 158

Duff-Cooper, A., 234 n.6

Duncombe, Stephen, 39

Dunia *gay* (*gay* world): in Indonesia, 49, 117, 118, 134, 138; in Southeast Asia, 199–201, 210

Dunia *normal* (*normal* world), 102, 117, 136–38

Durkheim, Émile, 3–4, 42

Dutch East Indies, 6, 169, 233 n.14. *See also* Colonialism

Dwyer, Leslie K., 144, 154, 165, 230 n.39

Edelman, Lee, 22

Elliston, Deborah A., 116

Emka, Moammar, 99, 137

Emotions: amok reactions, 166, 168, 173–74, 177; as divine politics, 166, 171; and intersection with violence, 165, 177–78; lek (stage fright), 171; malu (shame/embarrassment), 168, 170–74; and masculine sexuality, 174–77; and *normal* men encounters with nonnormative men in public, 175–76; by *normal* men seduced by *normal* men, 172–73

Eng, David L., 23

Engels, Frederick, 4

Eroticism, and zines, 52–55, 57

Errington, J. Joseph, 38, 122, 132, 177, 189, 226 n.17, 230 n.3, 234 n.2

Ethnographies: and anticipation, 12–13; and comparative approach, 182–86; defined, 24, 45, 182; and ethnic groups, 214; and globalization as universal process, 138; and "halfie" researchers, 12; and participant observation, 11–13, 15; compared with queer studies in Southeast Asia, 217–18; and reverse ethnographic experience, 70; and situational knowledge, 13, 18; and transgenderism, 81; and zines, 47. *See also* Anthropology

ing out," 200, 234 n.8; and comparative approach, 182; and *gay* subjectivities in Southeast Asia, 196; and gender differences, 189; and homosexuality vs. transgenderism, 217; and male transvestites, 191, 194, 234 n.4; and meeting places for gay men, 200; and MSM classification in Southeast Asia, 201; and nationwide subjectivities of male transvestites, 195; and nonnormative sexualities and genders origins in adat (traditional customs), 190; and occupations of male transvestites, 192, 194; and political homophobia, 199; and sexuality/gender binarism, 217; and sexual practices of male transvestites, 193, 194; and social classes, 198; and terms for male transvestites, 195, 234 n.3; and tomboys, 203

GAYa Batam, 44

GAYa Betawi (GB), 44; and acceptance/recognition by nation-state, 66; and bahasa *gay* (*gay* language), 134–35; and "coming out" terminology, 50; and discovery/recognition stories, 60; and eroticism, 54; and language, 222 n.19; and love (cinta), 59

GAYa Celebes, 44, 222 n.14

GAYa Intim, 44

GAYa LEStari (GL), 44, 53, 56, 57, 62, 67

GAYa Nusantara (GN), 44; and acceptance/recognition, 65–66, 67; and activism, 66; advertisements, 43; and bahasa *gay* (*gay* language), 230 n.3; "Bahasa *Gay* Menjadi Bahasa Gaul" ("Bahasa *Gay* Becomes Bahasa Gaul"), 136; circulation, 43; and "coming out" terminology, 50; and context for understanding desires, 47, 222 n.12; and costs for production, 43; and discovery/recognition stories, 59, 62; and English language, 222 n.19; and eroticism, 55, 57; and ethnolocality, 63, 222–

23 n.20, 223 n.21; and Euro-American gay men, 55, 64; history of, 41, 44, 222 n.11; and the Internet, 221 n.3; and love (cinta), 57, 72–76; and Oetomo, 222 n.13; and prestasi (acts/performance of deeds), 68–69, 72–76, 74; and separation experience, 61, 62; and social status, 50; and visibility/invisibility of women, 56, 57

GAYa Pandanaran (GP) (formerly *K-79* zine), 39, 44–45, 54, 59, 66, 68

Gay Archipelago, The (Boellstorff), 10–11

GAYa Siak, 44

GAYa Tepian Samarinda, 44

Gayatri, B. J. D., 213

Gay language (bahasa *gay*). *See* Bahasa *gay* (*gay* language)

Gay men in Indonesia: and acceptance/recognition, 66–67; and authenticity (asli), 112; author's access to, 13, 14; and berskala nasional (national scale), 222 n.11; and "coming out" terminology, 49–50; and commitment relationships (pacarans), 1; concepts of, 8; and discovery/recognition stories, 59–61, 62; and family principle (azas kekeluargaan), 38; and feelings of isolation, 60; and *gay* world (dunia *gay*), 49, 117; and gender vs. sexuality, 51; and geography of belonging, 60; and heterosexual marriages, 75, 144–45, 147, 155, 174, 223 n.24; and history of gay identification, 145; and desire (nafsu), 93, 223 n.25; and Indonesian language, 122; and interpretations of Islam, 148–56; and Islam, 144–45, 148–56, 155; and meeting places, 118, 125, 175; as *modern*, 167; and national belonging, 51, 71–77, 223 n.25; and national networks, 162, 232 n.6; and opening oneself (membuka diri), 49; and Pancasila (national principles), 67; and prestasi (acts/perfor-

egories, 109, 230 n.38; and national belonging, 144; normatives, 213; and playback (lip-synching), 79; and queer studies, 220 n.16; and sexuality binarism, 19–20, 51, 78–79, 212, 215–17; and third gender concept, 16, 81–82, 90, 108, 226 n.17, 230 n.37; and toilets for public use, 82, 108–9, 226 n.17; transgressors, 213; and warias, 88, 111–12, 226 n.17. *See also* Transgenderism

Geography of belonging: and *gay* men, 60; and male transvestites, 193; and spatial scales, 143–46, 160, 234 n.10; and warias, 104; and zines, 39, 41–42

George, Kenneth M., 232–33 n.10

Gerakan Pemuda Ka'bah (Ka'bah Youth Movement), 161, 232 n.2

G:Gaya Hidup Ceria (G), 67, 76, 221 n.9, 222 n.13

Globalization (globalisasi), 16, 138, 197, 214–15, 234 n.10

Goyvaerts, Didier L., 130

Graham, Sharyn, 190, 193, 195, 204, 207, 216, 231 n.8, 234 n.9

Greece, 26, 31

Greenhouse, Carol, 25

Grewal, Inderpal, 18

Grosz, Elizabeth, 23

Gupta, Akhil, 47–48, 121

Hacking, Ian, 111

Halberstam, Judith, 3, 22, 23, 32, 108

"Halfie" researchers, 12

Hallaq, Wael B., 155

Halley, Janet E., 32, 33

Halliday, Michael, 122, 130

Han, Chenny, 98, 106, 224 n.8, 227 n.23, 229 n.32

Hansen, Thomas Blom, 171

Haraway, Donna, 13, 32, 183

Hart, Donn V., 203, 204, 206, 234 n.3

Harvey, David, 34, 229 n.35

Hatley, Barbara, 51, 104

Haunting, queer, 111, 184–85

Hefner, Robert W., 142, 145, 160, 170

Heider, Karl G., 233 n.20

Helmreich, Stefan, 13

Hemóng language, 137

Heng Hiang Khng, Russell, 193, 198, 199, 200, 210, 212, 214

Herdt, Gilbert, 183–84, 186

Hervey, Sándor, 116–17, 138

Heryanto, Ariel, 232–33 n.10

Heteronormativity: and families, 52; and family principle (azas kekeluargaan), 166; and gender, 78; heteronormative theory, 3–4; and homophobic violence, 16; and national belonging, 52, 146, 167; and queer studies, 19, 20, 23, 220 n.16; and similitude, 197–98, 212–13; and Southeast Asia, 211; and tomboys' desire for women, 227 n.22; and warias' desire for men, 91; and zines, 37. See also *Normal* men; *Normal* women

Heterosexism, 168–69, 170, 177

Heterosexuality. *See* Heteronormativity

Heterosexual marriages: and arranged marriages, 51, 167; and chosen/love relationships, 51–52, 154, 166–67, 222 n.15; of *gay* men to *normal* women, 75, 144–45, 147, 155, 174, 199, 223 n.24, 233 n.16; and *gay* subjectivities, 49, 50; and homosexuality, 75, 153–54, 223 n.24; and illicit sexual relations of spouses, 101; and Islam, 141, 144–48, 155, 157, 206; and ludruk theater stories, 51; and male transvestites, 193–94; and national belonging, 169; and tomboys' marriages to *normal* men, 206; and warias, 100, 228 n.28; and women's acts of choice, 167, 222 n.15

Heterosexual nuclear families, 38, 111, 144, 146, 166, 230 n.39. *See also* Family principle (azas kekeluargaan)

vestites, 191; and warias' intersection with national culture, 102–7, 229 n.34. *See also* New Order of Soeharto

Interdisciplinarity, 16, 18, 46, 183, 217–18

International Gay and Lesbian Human Rights Commission (IGLHRC), 9

Internet, 200, 214, 221 n.3

Intersectionality, and temporality, 30

Invisibility/visibility. *See* Visibility/invisibility

Irvine, Judith, 116

Iskandar, Vivian Rubianty (Iwan Rubianto), 227–28 n.25

Islam: and adat (traditional customs), 143; and anal sex between men (liwath), 147; and *Bimbingan Seks Islami* (Islamic Sexual Guidance), 148; and categories of human actions, 154–55, 231 n.9; and community (umma), 156, 158; and David story, 149; and ethnolocality, 143; and faith, 16, 144, 146; and fundamentalism, 16, 170–71; and heterosexual men, 140–41; and history of Indonesia, 143, 145; and homophobic violence by Islamic youth groups, 161–62, 163–66, 169, 170, 232 nn.2, 3, 9; and homosex between men, 146; and homosexuality, 16, 139, 141–42, 145, 147, 148, 155–56; and *lesbi* women, 231 n.1; and Lot (Nabi Luth) story, 147, 149; and marriages, 141, 144–48, 155, 157, 206; and multiculturalism, 16; and Muslim Cleric's Council, 163; and Muslim United Development Party, 232 n.2; and national belonging, 144; and national networks of Muslim organizations, 163–64; and *normal* world, 156–58; and Pancasila (Five Principles), 155; and personal beliefs, 140; and pilgrimage to Mecca (hajj), 89–90, 95, 196, 226–27 n.20; and political homophobia, 170–

71, 179; and prayer, 140; and reconciliation of sexuality with religious devotion, 16; and sexuality, 146; and slametan (communal feast), 156, 159–60; and Sodom, 149; and spatial scales for *gay* men, 143–46, 160; and tensions between doctrine and lived exegesis, 16, 145, 146–54; and visibility of *gay* men, 142–43, 147; and warias, 89–90, 95, 226–27 n.20, 227 n.21, 229 n.35; and zina (adultery), 141, 147–48

Island of Bali (Covarrubias), 86

Iwasaki, Shoichi, 116

Jackson, Peter, A.: and activism of nonnormative sexualities and genders in Southeast Asia, 215; and area as partial truth about cultures in Southeast Asia, 186; and critical regionalities approach in Southeast Asia, 183–84; and delinking homophobia and heterosexism, 169; and gay subject position in Southeast Asia, 196, 234 n.5; and gay world in Southeast Asia, 200, 210; and homosexuality in Southeast Asia, 176–77; and male transvestites, 191, 192, 193, 195; and mass media's effects in Southeast Asia, 213; and political homophobia in Southeast Asia, 199; and positionality of researcher in Southeast Asia, 182; and selfhood of gay men in Southeast Asia, 210; and sexuality/gender binarism in Southeast Asia, 216

Jaka (zine), 43, 53, 57, 59, 64, 70, 71–72

Jaka-Jaka (JJ), 48–50, 66, 68

Jakarta-Jakarta (magazine), 54

Jaringan *Lesbi* dan *Gay* Indonesia (JLGI) (*Lesbi* and *Gay* Network), 162

Javanese culture: and bahasa *gay* (*gay* language), 119, 132; and courtly texts, 190, 192; and dances of Bantji Batavia (Batavian Transvestite), 85; and gemblak

Javanese culture (*continued*)
(male understudy actor in East Java), 84, 223 n.21; and Javanese language, 132; and ludrug/ludruk theater, 51, 85, 86, 225–26 n.10, 226 nn.12, 13; and *Serat Tjentini* (Javanese chronicle), 192; and shadow puppet theater (wayang), 84–85

Jawa Pos (newspaper), 137

Jejak Langkah (Footsteps) (Toer), 184

Johnson, Mark: and area as representing partial truths, 186; and boundary between *gay* subject position and male transvestites, 196; and critical region-alities approach, 183–84; and hetero-sexual marriages of male transvestites, 193; and homosexuality vs. transgender-ism, 217; and male transvestites, 191; nonnormative sexualities and genders and adat (traditional customs), 190; and *normal* men's relations with male trans-vestites, 194; and pronoun terminology for male transvestites, 83; and salon work of male transvestites, 192, 194; and sexuality/gender binarism, 216; and sexual practices of male transvestites, 194; and terms for male transvestites in Southeast Asia, 195, 224–25 n.9; and transformative warias, 92; and transna-tional imaginings by male transvestites, 195, 234 n.11; and travel from nation of origin by male transvestites, 196

Jones, Carla, 38, 206

Ka'bah Youth Movement (Gerakan Pemuda Ka'bah), 161, 232 n.2

Kalimantan (Indonesian Borneo), 44

Kaliurang incident, 161–62, 170, 232 n.2,3

Kamus Bahasa Gaul (Dictionary of Bahasa Gaul), 137

Kamus Indonesia Inggris (Echols and Shadily), 97

Kaplan, Caren, 18

Keane, Webb, 116

Kebenaran (coincidence/truth), 30

Keeler, Suzanne J., 193, 199

Keeler, Ward, 171–72

Kennedy, Raymond, 224–25 n.9, 229 n.29

Kenthut, Panky, 223–24 n.4, 226 n.12

Khoo, Olivia, 214

King, Mark, 192, 193, 194

Kinship, 4

KISS (television program), 136

Klinkert, H. C., 224–25 n.9

Kompas (periodical), 232 n.8

Kroskrity, Paul V., 116

K-79/GAYa Pandanaran (GP), 39, 44–45, 54, 59, 66, 68

KTP (Kartu Tanda Pendukuk) (identity card), 80, 104, 109, 144

Kulick, Don, 97, 99, 101, 108, 194, 227 n.24

Lacan, Jacques, 16, 108

Laffan, Michael, 122, 140, 141, 144, 145, 165

Language: banci, 114–15; béncong, 115; bahasa gaul (national vernacular), 136–38; and dubbing culture, 97, 158; English, in zines, 222 n.19; and *gay* world (dunia *gay*) in Indonesia, 117; hemóng, 137; Javanese, 132; Malay/Melayu, 121, 122; and national belong-ing, 63, 222 n.19; national, of Indonesia (bahasa Indonesia), 114, 122, 230 n.3; and *normal* world (dunia *normal*), 117; plesetan (non-*gay* urban language), 125; Polari, 123; prokem (street language), 118–19, 128, 134; regional, 121; and religious beliefs, 140; and social dif-ferentiation, 114; theory, 140; and tom-boys, 203–4; and zines, 63, 222 n.19. *See also* Bahasa *gay* (*gay* language)

Lathief, Halilintar, 229 n.35
Latin America, 169
Lawrence, Bruce B., 171
Leach, Edmund R., 25–28, 30–33
Leckie-Tarry, Helen, 116
Lek (stage fright), 171
Lenong Rumpi (Wicked Folk Theater) (television program), 137
Leong, Lawrence, 200
Lesbi and *Gay* Network (Jaringan *Lesbi* dan *Gay* Indonesia [JLGI]), 162
Lesbian Internalized Homophobia Scale, 168
Lesbians in Southeast Asia, 64, 185, 205, 207–8, 212, 214
Lesbi women in Indonesia: author's access to, 13, 14; and bancis term, 224 n.5; concepts of, 8; defined, 202; and desire (nafsu), 223 n.25; and discovery/recognition stories, 59; and eroticism, 53; and homophobic violence, 65; and Islam, 231 n.1; and national belonging, 223 n.25; and national networks, 162, 212, 232 n.6; and separation experience, 62; and subject position, 201–2, 207–8; and view of homosexual life in Euro-America, 38, 64–65; and warias, 94. *See also* Tomboys
Lesbi zines: circulation of, 44; and discovery/recognition stories, 59, 60, 62; and Euro-American homosexual life, 38, 64–65; and family principle (azas kekeluargaan), 38; and globalization, 48, 64; history of, 38, 41, 221 n.3; and HIV/AIDS prevention activities, 48, 222 nn.14, 17; and homophobic violence, 65; and images, 39; and inclusiveness, 42–43; and language, 222 n.19; and love (cinta), 55, 59, 60; as prestasis (acts/performance of deeds), 69; and sex, 222 n.17; and view of Indonesia, 38; and visibility/invisibility of *normal*

women, 38, 55, 56, 57; and women's mobility and privacy, 38. *See also* Zines
Lewis, Martin, 186, 188
Liddle, R. William, 122
"Limitations of the Comparative Method of Anthropology, The" (Boas), 185
"Linguistic Utopias" (Pratt), 114
Lip-synching (playback), 79, 95–98
Liwath (anal sex between men), 147, 151, 200
Local culture. *See* Ethnolocality
Löfgren, Orvar, 30
Loos, Tamara, 190
Love (cinta): and chosen relationships, 51–52, 154, 166–67, 222 n.15; and desire (nafsu), 59; and heterosexual marriages, 51–52; and homosexuality, 76; and interzone of love (cinta), 51, 71–77, 223 n.23; and national belonging, 37, 76; and prestasis (acts/performance of deeds), 37, 71–76; romantic, 200; and sexual citizenship intersection, 51, 71–77, 223 n.23; and short stories (cerita pendek or cerpen), 57, 59–61; and zines, 37, 50, 55, 57–61, 72–76
Love sick (sakit cinta), 50–51
Lucas, Ian, 123
Ludrug/ludruk theater of Java, 51, 85, 86, 225–26 n.10, 226 nn.12, 13
Lyons, Andrew, 3
Lyons, Harriet D., 3

Magic (ilmu) skills, 153
Mahmood, Saba, 147
Maier, H. M. J., 121
Makassar, 11, 39, 40, 119–20, 132–34
Makeup (déndong), putting on, 93–94, 106, 111, 229–30 n.36
Malaysia, 121, 122, 190, 191, 203
Male-male sexuality, 52–55, 174–75
Male-to-female transgenders (hijras) in India, 96

Male transvestites in Southeast Asia: about, 191–96; and acceptance/recognition, 193, 195; and adat (traditional customs), 192; and bodily modifications, 193; and boundary with gay men, 196; and boundary with *gay* subject position, 196; and clothes/dress of women, 192, 193; defined, 191; and femininity, 191–92; and geography of belonging, 193; and heterosexual marriages, 193–94; and HIV/AIDS epidemic, 194; and MSM (men who have sex with men) classification, 192; and nationwide subjectivities, 195; and *normal* men, 193, 194, 234 n.4; and occupations, 192; and salon work, 194; and selfhood, 192, 193; and sex-reassignment surgeries, 195; and sexual practices, 192–93, 194; and sex work, 194, 196; and social classes, 190, 210–11; subject positions of, 192; terms for, 191, 195, 234 n.3; and third gender concept, 191; and transnational imaginings, 195, 234 n.11; and travel from nation of origin, 195–96; visibility of, 193, 211. *See also* Bancis; Nonnormative men; Warias

Malinowski, Bronislaw, 4, 84, 140, 219 n.3

Malu (shame/embarrassment), 168, 170–74

Manalansan, Martin F., 33, 123, 129, 195–96

Maning, Joanna Therese, 199

Marcus, George, 13, 18, 212

Marin, Malu, 212

Marriages. *See* Heterosexual marriages; Same-sex marriages

Masculinity: and banci as term for women who act masculine, 224 n.5; and emotions, 174–77; and family principle (azas kekeluargaan), 166; and malu

(shame/embarrassment), 173; and national belonging, 165–68, 170, 177, 180; and U.S. actions toward Bin Laden, 180; and warias haunting normal masculinity, 111, 184

Massad, Joseph, 138

Mass media: and bahasa *gay* (*gay* language), 137; and crisis of context, 45–46; and *gay* subject position, 145, 162, 222 n.16; and *gay* terminology, 145; and Southeast Asia, 198–99, 213–14; and tomboys, 206; and views of homosexuality, 162, 222 n.16

Mathy, Robin M., 213

Maurer, Bill, 28, 210

Mauss, Marcel, 4

Mead, Margaret, 86

Meeting places, 1, 118, 125, 200

Merleau-Ponty, Maurice, 183

Merography, 16, 46, 47, 223 n.23

Messianic time, 28

Method of Hope, The (Miyazaki), 33–34

Milone, Pauline, 85

MitraS, 48, 65, 66–67, 69, 222 n.12

Miyazaki, Hirokazu, 33–34

Moerthiko (author), 96, 227–28 n.25, 228 n.27

Moment's Notice, A (Greenhouse), 25

Morgan, Henry Louis, 4

Morgan, Lynn Marie, 81

Morgan, Marcyliena, 122

Morris, Rosalind C., 139

Mosse, George L., 144

Mother Camp (Newton), 5

MSM (men who have sex with men) classification, 192, 201

Mulachela, Hasan, 232 n.8

Multiculturalism, 16, 218

Munn, Nancy D., 25

Muñoz, José Esteban, 23, 117, 215

Murray, Alison, 86, 190, 207, 208, 212

Murray, Stephen O., 147

Murtagh, Ben, 213
Muslim Cleric's Council, 163
Muslim United Development Party, 232 n.2

Nafsu (desire). *See* Desire (nafsu)
Nagengast, Carole, 232–33 n.10
Nanda, Serena, 95
Nasib (fate) of being homosexual, 152–53
Nasution, Adnan Buyung, 227–28 n.25
National belonging: and desire (nafsu), 37, 223 n.25; and ethnolocality, 63–64; and Euro-America lifestyle deemphasis in zines, 63, 64; and Euro-America lifestyle in zines, 63, 64; and family principle (azas kekeluargaan), 144; and *gay* men, 51, 71–77, 223 n.25; and gender, 144; and heteronormativity, 52, 146, 167; and heterosexual marriages, 169; and homosexuality, 71–77; and "Indo*G*sian people" (bangsa Indo*G*sia) term, 65; and Islam, 144; and language, 63, 222 n.19; and *lesbi* women, 223 n.25; and love (cinta), 37, 76; and masculinity, 165–68, 170, 177, 180; and nonnormative men's claims, 162–66, 169, 170, 173–74, 178–79, 232 n.7,9; and selfhood, 155; and sexual citizenship, 71–77; and warias, 81, 107, 112–13; and zines, 16, 37, 38, 51
National discourse: and bahasa *gay* (*gay* language), 122, 138; and *gay* subject position, 36, 49; and selfhood, 8, 36, 45; and zines, 37, 45, 49, 50
National Gay and Lesbian Congress(es), 162–64, 232 n.7
Nationalism: and comparative analysis, 184; and nonnormative sexualities and genders, 214–15; vs. patriotism, 8; and sexuality, 41; and Southeast Asia, 214–15; and warias, 16
National networks, 162–64, 212, 232 nn.6, 7

Nation-state: and acceptance/recognition, 65–67; and comparative imagination, 184; and homosexuality, 167; and political homophobia, 166, 176–77, 199; and power systems, 114, 117; and tomboys, 206. *See also* New Order of Soeharto
Networks, national, 162–64, 212, 232 nn.6, 7
New Jaka-Jaka (NJJ), 39, 48, 62, 68, 69, 70
New Order of Soeharto: family planning, 154; family principle (azas kekeluargaan), 38, 111, 144, 146, 166, 230 n.39; and *gay* subject position, 167; history of, 7; and Indonesian language, 122; and interior/exterior presentations, 177; and prestasis (acts/performance of deeds), 68; and Seven Charms program, 68; and success (sukses), 67–68; and zines, 42
Newton, Esther, 5
No Future: Queer Theory and the Death Drive (Edelman), 22
Nonnormative men: and amok reactions, 166, 168, 173–74, 177; and Euro-American homophobic violence, 164; and homophobic violence, 164–66, 169, 170, 173–74, 175, 232 n.9; and national belonging claims, 162–66, 169, 170, 173–74, 178–79, 232 n.7,9. *See also Gay* men in Indonesia; Gay men in Southeast Asia; Male transvestites; Warias
Nonnormative sexualities and genders: and colonial period, 190–91; and differences/similarities in gender and sexualities in Southeast Asia, 212–13; and globalization, 214–15; and haunting, 111, 184–85; historicity of, 209–10; and mass media in Southeast Asia, 213–14; and modern technologies, 200, 214; origins in adat (traditional customs), 167, 189–90; and precolonial era, 189–90; and selfhood, 215; and social

Paolillo, John C., 116

Paranoia, 21–22, 32–33, 34, 220 n.18

"Paranoid Reading and Reparative Reading" (Sedgwick), 21

Participant observation, 11–13, 15

Patrio, Eko, 136

Patriotism, 8

Peacock, James, 104, 174, 192, 225–26 n.10, 226 n.13, 229 n.30

Peletz, Michael G.: and gender differences/similarities, 189; and heteronormative constructs in Southeast Asia, 211; and male transvestites, 192, 193; and nonnormative sexualities and genders origins in adat (traditional customs), 190; and political homophobia, 199; and salon work of male transvestites, 192, 194; and sexuality and gender roles in Southeast Asia, 191; and tomboys, 206

Pelras, Christian, 190

Pembaruan DPRD party fraction, 232 n.8

Pemberton, John, 68, 106, 232–33 n.10

Penal-anal sex between men (liwath), 147, 151, 200

People's Democratic Party (Partai Rakyat Demokratik or PRD), 162, 164

Performance of deeds (prestasis). See Prestasis (acts/performance of deeds)

Performativity, 79, 92, 97, 104, 111

Perlez, Jane, 189, 226 n.15

Permesta rebellion of 1950, 229 n.35

"Person, Time, and Conduct in Bali" (Geertz), 28–29

Philippines: and acceptance of male transvestites, 193; and gay pride events, 201; and gay subjectivity, 234 n.6; and gay subject position, 234 n.5; and nation-wide subjectivities of male transvestites, 195; nonnormative sexualities and genders origins in adat (traditional customs), 190; and swardspeak, 123, 129;

and terms for male transvestites, 191, 195, 224–25 n.9; and tomboys, 203; and transnational imaginings by male transvestites, 195

Picard, Michel, 11

Pierce, Charles, 13

Playback (lip-synching), 79, 95–98

Plesetan (non-gay urban language), 125

Plummer, David, 80, 81

Polari language, British, 123

Political homophobia: and amok reactions, 166, 168, 173–74, 177; and Civil Code, 169; defined, 165; and emotion as divine politics, 166, 171; and family planning, 154; and gay men's access to public space, 147; and interior/exterior presentations, 177; and Islam, 170–71, 179; and Kaliurang incident, 161–62, 170, 232 n.2,3; and malu (shame/embarrassment), 166; and nation-state, 166, 176–77, 199

Political issues: and emotions as divine politics, 166, 171; and Islam, 144, 231 n.5; and public events, 201; and violence, 165, 232–33 n.10; and warias' political positions, 103–4, 226 n.15, 229 n.33; and zines, 39. See also New Order of Soeharto

Porter, Doug, 80, 81

Portret (Portrait) (television show), 136

Postcolonial period, 6–8, 210

Povinelli, Elizabeth A., 139, 159

Power systems, 114, 117

Pratt, Mary Louise, 114

Prawirakusumah, R. Prie, 231 n.1

Precolonial era, and nonnormative sexualities and genders, 189–90

Prestasis (acts/performance of deeds): and authenticity (asli), 112; defined, 67, 70–71; and gay men, 112; and love (cinta), 37, 71–76; and reverse ethnographic experience of author, 70; and sexual cit-

Sarinah (magazine), 221 n.9
Sasot, Sass R., 192, 193, 194
Saussure, Ferdinand de, 108
Scharer, H., 190
Schlecker, Markus, 46, 47
Schor, Naomi, 32
"Sebuah Masala buat Banci" *(Tempo)*, 230 n.37
Sedgwick, Eve Kosofsky, 20, 21, 31, 90
Selfhood: and discovery/recognition stories, 59–62; and ethnolocality, 143; and *gay* men, 155, 196, 210; and identity, 36, 145, 166, 188; and "Indo*G*sian people" (bangsa Indo*G*sia) term, 65; and national belonging, 155; and national discourse, 8, 36, 45; and power systems, 117; and tomboys, 204, 207
Semarang zines, 39, 40
Sen, Krishna, 38, 226 n.17
Separation experience stories, 37, 61–63, 73
Serat Tjentini (Javanese chronicle), 192
Sex and Repression in Savage Society (Malinowski), 4
Sex-change/sex-reassignment operations, 94–95, 99, 195, 204, 227–28 n.25, 228 nn.26, 27
Sexual citizenship, 51, 63–65, 71–77, 72–76, 144, 223 n.23
Sexuality: and bisexuality, 231 n.3; and contexts and practices of male and female subjects, 13–14; and gender binarism, 19–20, 51, 78–79, 212, 215–17; and malu (shame/embarrassment), 172; and nationalism, 41; and normatives, 213; and race in context of social relations, 36, 46; and transgressors, 213; and warias, 98–102, 228 n.28
Sexuality in Islam (Bouhdiba), 141
Sexual Life of Savages, The (Malinowski), 219 n.3
Sexual practices: and gay men, 147, 151,

200, 234 n.6; and queer studies, 220 n.16; and warias, 98–102
Sex work, 85, 87, 98–100, 194
Shadow puppet theater (wayang), 84–85
Shame/embarrassment (malu), 168, 170–74
Short stories (cerita pendek or cerpen), 39, 57, 59–61, 224 n.4
Siapno, Jacqueline Aquino, 145
"Sick person" (orang sakit), 50–51
Siegel, James T., 47, 97, 98, 145, 151, 154, 232–33 n.10
Silicone injections, 94, 193, 227 n.24
Silverstein, Michael, 47, 116
Similitude, theory of, 121, 196–98, 212–13
Sinnott, Megan J.: and activism of nonnormative sexualities and genders, 215; and femmes subject position in Southeast Asia, 207; and *gay* subjectivities in Southeast Asia, 196; and homosex between women, 190, 206; and lesbians, 208; and male/female binarism in Thailand, 211–12; and mass media, 213; and political homophobia, 199; and social classes, 210; and terms for male transvestites, 195; and tomboys, 203, 204, 205, 206, 234 n.9; and untouchability, 208
"SK (Surat Keputuasan) Menteri untuk Waria" *(Tempo)*, 228 n.27
Slamah, Khartini, 191
Slametan (communal feast), 156, 159–60, 232–33 n.10
Sneddon, James N., 8, 122, 231 n.5
Social classes: and femmes in Southeast Asia, 208; and *gay* men, 167, 198, 199, 200; and lesbians, 208; and male transvestites, 190, 210–11; nonnormative sexualities and genders, 190, 210–11; and tomboys, 206–7, 208
Sociality patterns, 200–201, 206

Soeharto, New Order of. *See* New Order of Soeharto

Soentoro, Isye, 98, 101, 106, 224 n.8, 227 n.23, 229 n.32

Southeast Asia: and activism, 215; area of, 186–89; and co-gendered/co-sexual communities, 212; colonial period sexuality and gender subjectivities, 190–91; and "coming out," 199–200, 234 n.8; and comparative approach, 182–86; and cultural antipathy toward homosexuality, 169; and ethnography compared with queer studies, 217–18; and ETPs, 209–10; and Euro-American influences on gay subject position, 217; and gay men's transnational connections, 198–99; and gay subjectivities, 196–201; and gay subject position, 196; and gender differences/similarities, 189, 197–98, 212–13, 234 n.2; and gender normatives, 213; and gender transgressors, 213; and globalization, 188–89, 214–15; and heteronormative constructs, 211; and heterosexual marriages, 206; and identity, 188; and layers of nonnormative sexual and gendered subject positions, 209–10; and lesbians, 207–8, 214; and male/female binarism, 211–13; and male transvestites, 191–96; and mass media, 213–14; and nonnormative sexualities and genders, 208–9; and normative heterosexualities, 211; and postcolonial period, 210; and precolonial sexuality and gender subjectivities, 189–90; and selfhood for nonnormative sexualities and genders, 215; and sexuality/gender binarism, 215–17; and sexual normatives, 213; and social classes, 210–11; and socioeconomic status of gay men, 198; and terms for male transvestites, 191; and warias, 85

Spatial scales, 143–46, 160, 234 n.10; and

geography of belonging, 143–46, 160, 234 n.10

Spectre of Comparisons, The (Anderson), 184

Spencer, Herbert, 4

Stage fright (lek), 171

Stasch, Rupert, 232–33 n.10

Steedly, Mary Margaret, 164

Steenbrink, Karel, 143

Stoler, Ann Laura, 42, 191, 233 n.14

Straight time, and queer time, 23–25, 27–28, 30–31, 36

Strathern, Marilyn, 12, 13, 19, 32, 46

Street language (prokem), 118–19, 128, 134

Subjectivities: and identity cards (KTP or *Kartu Tanda Pendukuk*), 80, 104, 109, 144; and power systems, 117; and warias, 16, 96, 103, 111; and zines, 16. *See also under specific subjectivities*

Subject positions. *See under specific subject positions*

Sulawesi zines, 44

Sulistyo, Hermawan, 49

Sullivan, Nikki, 21

Surabaya, 11, 39, 40, 222 n.12

Suryakusuma, Julia I., 38, 146, 166, 226 n.17, 230 n.39

Sutlive, Vinson H., Jr., 190

Swara Srikandi (Swara) (zine), 48, 69, 70

Swardspeak, and Philippines, 123, 129

Systems of Consanguinity and Affinity of the Human Family (Morgan), 4

Szymanski, Dawn, 168

Taman Remaja, and warias showcases, 79–80

Tambiah, Stanley Jeyaraja, 139

Tan, Michael L.: and acceptance/recognition of male transvestites, 195; and activism of nonnormative sexualities and genders, 215; and clothing/dress of male transvestites, 193; and femmes subject position, 206; and gay subject position, 196; and heterosexual marriages of gay men, 199; and male/female binarism, 212; and male transvestites, 191; and MSM (men who have sex with men) classification, 201; and political homophobia, 199; and social classes, 200; and tomboys, 206

Tarling, Nicholas, 188

Technologies, modern, 200, 214

Teena, Brandon, 22–23

Teh, Yik Koon, 194

Tempo (periodical), 226–27 n.20, 227 n.21, 227–28 n.25, 228 n.27, 230 n.37

Temporality: and anthropology, 24, 28; and disciplinarity, 31–34, 181; and femininity, 32; and intersectionality, 30; and messianic time, 28; and oscillation sequences, 26–27, 28, 34; permutational time, 28–30; and phallus trickster, 26, 27; and queer chronologies, 26–28; and queer chronotopes, 27, 28; and queer time, 22–28, 30–31, 36, 210; and time/timing, 25, 31; and Western concepts of time, 25–27; zines, and continuity of chronology and geography, 39, 41–42

Terrorists, 165, 180

Thailand: and acceptance of male transvestites, 193; and femmes subject position, 207; and gay pride events, 201; and *gay* subjectivity, 234 n.6; and gay world (dunia gay), 200; and heterosexual marriages, 206; history of, 191; and homosex, 190; and male/female binarism, 211; and nationwide subjectivities of male transvestites, 195; and spirit possession paradox, 139; and terms for male transvestites, 191, 195

Theatrical performances, and Javanese culture, 51, 84–86, 223 n.21, 225–26 n.10, 226 n.12,13

"Thinking Sex" (Rubin), 4–5, 212, 215–16

Third gender concept: and ETPs, 190; and male transvestites, 191; and tomboys, 204; and warias, 16, 81–82, 90, 108, 226 n.17, 230 n.37

Time. *See* Queer time; Temporality

Time and the Other: How Anthropology Makes Its Objects (Fabian), 24

Toer, Pramoedya Ananta, 184

Tomboys: and acceptance/recognition, 206; and attentive behavior to women, 205–6; and bahasa *gay*, 129–30; and community-building, 206; defined, 80, 202, 203–4; as female transgenders, 202; and femininity, 206; and femmes subject position, 202, 207, 208, 212, 214; and *gay* men, 94; and globalization, 214, 234 n.10; and heterosexual desire for women, 227 n.22; and heterosexual relations, 228 n.28; as hunters, 205, 233 n.13; and the Internet, 214; and language, 203–4; and marriages to *normal* men, 206; and national networks, 212; and occupations, 205; and pregnancies, 228 n.28; and pronoun terminology, 83, 203; and selfhood, 204, 207; and sexual practices, 205; and social classes, 206–7, 208; and sociality patterns, 206; and subject position, 201–2, 203–7; terms for, 203, 207–8, 234 n.9; and third gender, 204; and untouchability, 205, 208; and visibility, 80

Towle, Evan B., 81

Traditional customs (adat), 64, 141, 143, 167, 189–90, 192

Transgenderism: and colonial period, 190; and ethnographies/ethnographic method, 81; and female transgenders, 202; vs. homosexuality, 217; Indian male-to-female transgenders (hijras), 96;

Zines (*continued*)

(adat Nusantara) articles, 64, 223 n.21; and data sources, 39; defined, 36, 39, 42–43; and discovery/recognition stories, 59–61; and educational status, 48, 222 n.19; and English language, 222 n.19; and eroticism, 52–55, 57; and ethnographies/ethnographic method, 47; and ethnolocality, 63, 222–23 n.20, 223 n.21; and Euro-American homosexual life, 38, 42, 55, 63, 64–65; and fieldwork, 37–38, 39, 221 n.5; and GAYa names, 44, 63; and Gay Seven Charm Program (Sapta Pesona Gay), 68; and *gay* subject position, 47, 49; and gender vs. sexuality of *gay* men, 51; and globalization, 16; and heteronormativity, 37; history of, 15, 36, 38–39, 41–42; and HIV/AIDS prevention and treatment networks, 48, 222 nn.14, 17; and homosexual desire, 37; and images, 39; and imaginary interview (wawancara imaginer), 48–50; and inclusiveness, 42–43; and intentionality, 16; and the Internet, 221 n.3; in Jakarta, 39, 40, 44; and language, 63, 222 n.19; and love (cinta), 37, 50, 55, 57–61, 72–76; and mass media, 221 n.9; and merography, 16; and national belonging, 16, 37, 38, 51; and national discourse, 37, 45, 49; and New Order of Soeharto, 42; and non–Euro-American homosexual life, 64; and open (terbuka) *gay* men, 47, 48; and politics, 39, 48–50; and positive discussions of homosexuality, 52; and prestasis (acts/performance of deeds), 37, 67–71, 74; producers of, 37, 43, 48–50, 222 n.13, 19; publication data, 43–44; and relationship to sexual subjectivities, 37; in Semarang, 39; and separation experience, 37, 61–63, 73; and sex, 222 n.17; and short stories (cerita pendek or cerpen), 39, 57, 59–61, 224 n.4; and social networks, 44, 221 n.10; and social status, 48, 50, 222 n.13; as sociocultural data, 47–48; in Sulawesi, 44; in Surabaya, 39, 40; and text distinguished from context, 47; and transnationalism, 48, 64; and true experience narratives (pengalaman sejati), 37, 39, 50, 62, 224 n.4; and warias, 51, 224 n.8; in Yogyakarta, 39, 40. *See also Lesbi* zines; *and under specific zines*

Zones of desire: and acceptance/recognition, 65–67; and homosex, 52–55; and interzone of love (cinta), 51, 71–77, 223 n.23; and sexual citizenship, 51, 63–65, 71–77, 223 n.23; as spatial metaphor, 47, 60–61. *See also* Desire (nafsu)

TOM BOELLSTORFF is an associate professor of Anthropology

at the University of California, Irvine.

LIBRARY OF CONGRESS CATALOGING-IN-PUBLICATION DATA

Boellstorff, Tom, 1969–

A coincidence of desires : anthropology, queer studies,

Indonesia / Tom Boellstorff.

p. cm.

Includes bibliographical references and index.

ISBN-13: 978–0-8223–3974–8 (cloth : alk. paper)

ISBN-13: 978–0-8223–3991–5 (pbk. : alk. paper)

1. Homosexuality, Male — Indonesia. 2. Ethnology — Indonesia.

3. Gay men — Indonesia — Social conditions. 4. Indonesia — Social conditions.

I. Title. GN635.165B654 2007

306.76′6209598 — dc22

2006034548